CHELMSFORD

- 3 MAR 2016

Bere̶ ̶sion

Alice Addison

chipmunkapublishing
the mental health publisher

Essex County Council

3013021035877 5

All rights reserved, no part of this publication may be reproduced by any means, electronic, mechanical photocopying, documentary, film or in any other format without prior written permission of the publisher.

Published by
    Chipmunkapublishing

http://www.chipmunkapublishing.com

Copyright © Alice Addison 2013

Edited by Melissa Latchford

ISBN   978-1-84991-995-1

Chipmunkapublishing gratefully acknowledge the support of Arts Council England.

For Maisie

Why is memory fractionated? Somewhere it splits and the meaning is dispersed. All components are there but not all are accessible, only parts are revealed: the unending jigsaw puzzle. Is that why I write? Does putting pen to paper make it any less distorted? Does writing bring clarity of further the disparity?

It dampens the confusion.

But, perhaps it is futile: any attempt to explain things that affect us the most are wasted efforts. Words cannot do justice in illustrating my overwrought self. Simplicity ensures events aren't insulted.

Who am I?

The worthless warrior
Relentlessly fighting
The unabating blackness
No one else can see.

August 2007

ALICE

When Mum was dying, I tried to think of all the empty spaces there would be when she was gone but this I didn't dwell on. I had five months to prepare for Mum's death and yet, this was no time at all. Our lives were so dominated by the present, by the hideous nature of the disease, that precious little time was left for anything else and preparation was meaningless. Nothing can even approach the devastating loneliness that consumes me now.

Others want to help: they offer me their own experiences of loss, but my mother's death was not a topic I wished to discuss – for no-one knew what it was like for me, everyone else felt like a bystander, an observer through distorted glass. Horrifically ill people cannot be described. No-one will ever comprehend those last indistinguishable days and nights.

Even Dad and my brother Ethan don't understand how I gave Mum myself. I devoted my very being to her. We became, quite literally, inseparable. Her physical dependence on me was obvious but, mentally, we became one. I could finish her sentences or answer for her when she was unable and I always knew that what I was saying was right. When questions were asked, we answered, half a sentence each, following on as if one voice. When lethargy or fear consumed her, Mum deferred to me. I became her communicator as what I said was what Mum wished to convey.

My mother has always been my best friend, my most treasured person. At a young age, what superseded any rebelliousness on my behalf was respect. Mum reciprocated this by putting her trust in me. She told me everything, in detail, without hesitation.

My mother is the most honest person I know. She was incapable of lying which is why she had such a vast network of friends: with an incredibly open nature, it was impossible not to warm to her. This honesty policy was the reason she would never understand why I wanted to shield her, not from the disease itself (we did not use metaphors or euphemisms) but from other people. I would open the door to visitors and let in a draught of uneasiness. They would hesitate, searching eyes on me as if I would tell them what they should say or what they should do.

There is not one right way of being with the dying but I was there to flatly reject any reference to "fighting". Why is this always insisted upon with cancer? No other disease is described as "conquering a battle". My mother wasn't defeatist, she was realistic. She knew the inevitability of death. How can you win the duel when the outcome has already been decided?

Friends were also desperate to do something practical. This must be in our human nature: a physical job relieves some of the helplessness. While such offers were meaningful, it increased the burden on me. I would rifle through the trivial tasks which were either not important or I could have done myself in half the time and without expending thinking effort.

The hardest part was protecting Mum from Dad and Ethan. I hate to say this but it was true. Many are under the misapprehension that, when a family member is told they are dying, all previous arguments are instantly dismissed and an aura of peace descends. This is emphatically false. There was an improvement, I don't wish to deny Dad and Ethan of their efforts, but still the old disruptions held true. Many times I shielded Mum from their raised voices and cross words. This was not how Mum envisaged her last months. I didn't exactly lie but edited the truth. I could not bear to see them cause Mum more agony, the physical pain was enough without adding to her mental anguish.

Even with morphine from the first week of diagnosis, Mum's body was racked with pain, undulating in its intensity but always present. I tried in utter desperation to latch on to a fraction of this ordeal. I needed to feel it, experience it. I wished to empathise, if only partly, to Mum's crippling illness. I could not comprehend how excruciating the disease or how overwhelming the anxiety could be. Mum and I became one but our bodies remained separate; I fought to join us but suffered defeat. A well person cannot consume the living death.

Despite such intensity, I can no longer form Mum's image in my mind. I can't see her living. I am denied this picture. What does materialise, is her dead form. I see her withered body, stiff in bed, sickly grey-yellow skin taut, skull disturbingly prominent, paper-thin lips stuck to plastic teeth, eyelids not quite closed. A discarded doll, disfigured. She doesn't look real. When life has gone, the body somehow doesn't appear genuine. Mum has been replaced by a grotesque copy.

Once Mum died, Dad ushered us out of the room. I sat on the stairs, huddled knees, and watched Mum, the door frame enclosing my picture of her – a painting of death. The door shut but the image was fixed on my mind. This is now all I have left. Does that room exist anywhere except in my head? Death, in all its ghastly glory, had swallowed up my Mum.

There is no sanctuary against impounding thoughts. I tell myself to sleep…forget…don't run away any more, don't hide any more, just sleep. But even with sedatives, my slumber is weak and unsatisfying. My days stretch ahead in a haze of partial reality. I have developed a flimsy sheen of a bubble, protecting me from ongoing life but shielding me from any means of participation. I am a floating person in a world I no longer know, inhabiting a life I no longer desire.

Dreams seem to be ingraining themselves into my waking self and the same recurring sequence toys with me. I don't know where I am, perhaps the location changes, but the family are all participants. We are talking. Everyone knows Mum is dead. I know Mum is dead. But then she is there. I see her. I talk to Mum. It is effortless and the comfort envelops me. The others tell me to stop it. Stop talking Ali. They think I am mad but I'm not going to stop. My Maisie is there.

I start to get sad. Mum hugs me and that so familiar embrace is a delight. Our bodies sink together. We are the jigsaw of perfect fit. I cry. My tears turn into heaving sobs and to Mum I say, "I want to die. I want to die with you together. Don't leave me Maisie. I love you so much", and the words are repeated and haunting me because I never let Mum know of my longing for death.

As if I already know the ending, Mum begins disintegrating. Her performance of the most distressing vanishing conundrum concludes. I am left standing, nothing in my arms, a distraught mess in front of scorning family. I then awake, crying and with such a longing that it manifests itself as a physical ache.

* * *

It was only a few weeks after Mum died. Dad had bought tickets for them both for the opera at Glyndebourne. He had taken Mum as a special treat for her fiftieth birthday and Mum had had an exquisite time. She still spoke about it at length, months later. She had found the whole day fantastic. Dad even mentioned this at Mum's funeral. He talked about her love of music, the fabulous day they had spent together at Glyndebourne.

Dad had bought two tickets again, way in advance owing to such popular demand, before Mum had been diagnosed. By the time the date was looming, it was absolutely certain Mum would not be going: alive or not, she was far too poorly.

After the funeral, Dad said he was going alone. I thought this sad and appropriate. He could go and remember that marvellous time he and Mum had shared four years ago. Dad likes doing things by himself; he enjoys his own company.

It was my half sister who first noticed. Holly said, "Why isn't he taking you, Ali?". I hadn't even thought about this. Dad and I have never done anything together, just us, but then Ethan also wondered why Dad wasn't asking me to go with him. I explained that Dad probably needed time, it was a special occasion, and perhaps he needed space to remember Mum in his own way. I didn't want to be an intrusion.

Less than a week before the concert and we discovered Dad had changed his mind; he was now going with Mary. Ethan and I don't know this woman. We think Dad used to work with her, although she has never been mentioned before. When Mum was ill, Ethan caught (I don't like how this word sounds but I suppose that is the reality) Dad in town one day. He was sitting, having a leisurely lunch with, whom we now know to be, Mary. Mum was terrifically poorly at home; Ethan came back to me, relating what he saw. I felt so sad. I knew Dad wished to continue working, that was accepted, but if you had a couple of hours available for a relaxed meal out, wouldn't he want to come home and spend that time with his dying wife? That is what devastated me the most: Dad's seeming lack of care or compassion.

Dad and Mary went to Glyndebourne and spent the whole weekend there. He didn't return until Sunday afternoon. I couldn't bring myself to ask him if he had a nice time. I didn't want to know the answer. I didn't care.

That week, I was in the car with Dad: only a short trip but it served my purposes. When I try and talk to Dad about anything important or upsetting or anyway emotional, he either walks off or begins shouting and gets very angry: trapped in a car, he was unable to do either. I try and explain to him how it was devastating for Ethan and me to see him spending time with another woman at a concert in which he should have been with Mum. Not only that, they spent the entire weekend together. Mum has only been dead four weeks: it was so insulting towards her. Dad refused to acknowledge my side, he kept repeating that he does not understand why I am offended and tells me off for talking to him about it. It was his money, his decision. He got cross; I felt like crying. We arrived home and didn't talk.

I miss Mum terribly. I can't remember her funeral with great clarity, brief moments keep presenting themselves, but then, at home, upset with Dad, I recalled some of what he said. I don't wish to sound boastful or self-congratulatory but, if Mum was asked what she was most proud of, she would have said her children. I think this is a mother's prerogative and it was true. Ethan and I were her greatest achievement. I believe most mothers would say the same. Having your own child must be an amazing thing but, at the funeral, Dad only mentioned us once as an aside. He spoke more about Holly and Jack, Dad's children from his first marriage. I'm beginning to sound like such a spoilt child but, even though Mum loved Holly and Jack dearly, they weren't her children, they were her step-children, so of course she felt Ethan and I were more special. We came from her.

I'm not jealous of Holly and Jack, I have been blessed with two extra siblings with whom I get on with so well; it is Dad who upsets me. Even at the funeral of our mother, he couldn't bring himself to praise us.

September 2007

I don't want to go back to medical school. I don't want to be a doctor. No-one understands why. In a bid to actively avoid anything medical, I seem to have encountered more than necessary. I wish that, in deciding to give up my degree, I could forget all that I have learnt. Go back to the beginning. I am asking the impossible. Too much knowledge - I didn't think there was such a thing.

Since Mum died, I feel I have been thwarted by other people's medical problems. Do I cause these bad things to happen? Why am I always around? I want to help but feel I am fighting a losing battle. If I caused them in the first place, then anything I do after the event is negligible to allowing them to occur initially. All this I seem to forget at the time and fully engage myself, whatever the situation. Dr. Alice knows what to do in crisis time: she is calm, confident and, more importantly, competent. It is always afterwards that the nightmares begin but, herein lies the fundamental problem, I still have the knowledge accumulated over four years' work and everyone still knows the course that I have followed, so they defer to me. How to escape?

I honestly doubt whether I could inject anyone ever again and, compared to my peers, I'm probably good at it – Mum's veins were dreadful. The thought of treating patients fills me with the fear and anxiety that leapt upon me during the night times when Mum was alive. Apart from anything else, this wouldn't be fair on the poor, unsuspecting patients. Who wants a nervous wreck at their bedside? Patients should feel calm; doctors need to instil confidence and trust. Aside from the all-too-true clichés, I wouldn't feel happy "helping" patients if I was adding to their unease. Would I be able to hide my own angst? Or would I crumble into an unsightly mess?

People say, am I disillusioned with the NHS after Mum's care? was it truly dreadful? was Mum not treated as well as expected? No! Even if I had to go through that all again, I would not change a thing. I would also have spent four years at medical school just to look after Mum and enable her to stay at home. If someone had told me before I started that I was doing all the training for the sole reason of looking after Mum and then, once Mum had gone, that was it, a different career, I would have said yes. More than that, I would have jumped at the chance, it being such an absolute honour to do that for my darling mother.

I could care for Mum to the best of my ability because I had such compassion, such love, such drive to look after her. I used to have that towards patients, obviously not to the same extent as

Mum, but it was always there. Every day in hospitals filled me with an excitement that was unmatched to anything I have known. What if that desire has vanished? What if there is nothing? I couldn't be a good doctor if all it was to me was a job. I wouldn't be doing my best. It wouldn't be fair on my patients. I can't do that to other people. It would be selfish of me to continue with something that directly influences others if my passion has disappeared.

Is this the naivety of youth or obtained wisdom? Whichever, I need to decide if I have lost all of this. What if it is still there, just obscured by too much hurt? The conflicting and confusing thoughts pain my head. What do I do? I can't focus my mind sufficiently for sensible thought. My concentration, which was always rather lacking, has now diminished to pitiful levels. I can't be a doctor, I can't even manage measly tasks at home without tremendous effort and then they invariably go wrong.

I feel I am competing against everyone who says I shouldn't give up medicine. I feel I need to justify my rationale. I don't want to fight against them because my reasons sometimes don't make logical sense to me, so explaining to others is near impossible.

Then there are the ones who show insight, which makes me feel ever so sad because, even with their understanding, they still believe I should be a doctor. I spoke to Uncle Peter at length; he knows I have more understanding about his situation than most. Aunty Maggie has cancer, terminal, has been fabulous still going on holidays and making the best of each day, but now she has become more poorly. Uncle Peter says that it is so hard when Aunty Maggie is ill. He doesn't know what to do: call an ambulance? give her more painkillers? take her to hospital? He says he feels helpless. But then he demonstrated remarkable and unselfish empathy towards me. He said it is one thing to feel helpless but it is quite worse to feel completely helpless when you should know what you are doing. He said he admired me for that. Everyone expected me to know what to do; I expected myself to know. The pressure, at times, almost felt unbearable. I did all I could. I did my absolute best. It was petrifying. I'm so scared to go near that again.

And then there was Mum. My darling mother who always had exceptional confidence in my abilities, all of which she had taught me. She fostered the caring nature that she had instilled. That is why I knew I was the best person to look after her, not because I was especially wonderful, but because she had shown me how to care for her in the best possible way.

21st September 2007 – Aunty Maggie poorly – her chemo stopped as it was no longer having effect. She quickly deteriorated and was admitted to hospital last night. I drove to Reading today to see her. Horrific. I could keep it together when seeing Mum but everything with Aunty Maggie seemed too intense, as if my senses had been heightened. Aunty Maggie was jaundiced, had ascites and was being sick. She was on a syringe driver, all the same drugs as Mum: the memories of injections leaping back to haunt me. It was all too real, everything was too big, it rushed at me and I felt claustrophobic. I stayed in the hospital. I talked. Aunty Maggie's speech had that morphine quality.

Driving home I cried lots and felt sick. I drove down a road the wrong way and nearly caused an accident. Aunty Maggie died on the Sunday morning: 23rd September.

* * *

I have to go up to Newcastle to see someone about my medical course. Typically, the medical school is in the main hospital. I walk round the outside of the building but then can't go in. I get scared. I rush away.

Later in the day I decide I'm being ridiculous, I must be. I have to prove I can do it. I don't know why. I still have my swipe card. 3am in the morning I run, I sprint down the corridors of the hospital. No-one is around. Hospitals are eerie places at night. I do it. I go through the entire building. I have been in.

* * *

Dad had a table for a charity event, something to do with work, so it was mainly his colleagues going. It was being held at some nice venue with a lavish three course meal. Dad asked Ethan and me to go. We found this decidedly odd. Dad has never asked us to attend anything like this with him. Perhaps this will be a new bonding time between father and children.

We then discovered who is going and Dad's hidden agenda. Mary was going to be there; Dad wanted us to meet her. I didn't think I wanted to go. It would be bad enough on a table of twelve, middle-aged professionals but now, with Mary there too, I don't think I would cope. I would either get hideously drunk or extremely upset: Ethan's reaction, to declare that he is certainly going and will tell Mary just how awful Dad is, no illusions, and to steer clear of him.

Ethan's friend, Grace, replaced me and Ethan drank half a bottle of wine before he even left the house. Dad had done the seating plan and put Ethan next to Mary. Ethan phoned me at several intervals throughout the evening: outside, crying, angry, upset, and drunk. He said Mary had been hideously nice to him, so lovely it was far too over the top. Ethan was also worried that she was ill and Dad hadn't told us – stick thin and barely eating.

By 10.30pm, Grace phoned me and said to pick them up. Ethan was wasted and staggering, fell into the car and could not co-ordinate seatbelt wearing. I strapped him in. Grace was a darling and had been taking care of him but, dessert hadn't yet appeared, Grace made the executive decision it was time to leave. Ethan was becoming rowdy and then emotional when they escaped to the toilets or outside to have a cigarette.

Once home, Ethan developed verbal diarrhoea and repeated and reiterated and analysed the evening's events. I listened and talked but Ethan was in a drunken spiel and could not comprehend. It took Grace and me two hours to finally coax him into bed, clothes still on, red wine stains down his white shirt. I gave Grace a lift home.

In the morning, I spoke to Dad. I said it may have been slightly inappropriate to sit Ethan and Mary next to one another. Dad took offence and started to get angry and shouted. He walked off and, this time, I followed. I said how distraught Ethan was. Dad denied this and said I was making it up. It transpires Dad didn't even notice Ethan was drunk or had been crying. He is the least observant person I know, or he deliberately ignores these things. Grace reassured me that everyone else could tell: Ethan's eyes were puffy, his cheeks red and drunkenness apparent. An argument developed and I ended up in tears. Dad said such hateful things.

All I can think about are the bad times when Dad was terrible towards Mum. She was so ill. How could Dad do that? Ethan comforts me and we sit talking. He and I. We now only had each other.

We discovered later that Mary has anorexia. She used to be quite overweight but is now only seven stones. No wonder she looked ill.

October 2007

I always knew I would reach that point where life becomes unbearable. What I didn't envisage was how I got there. I'm not there yet, but I'm on the path. On this path you can only head in one direction. There is no choice, nor ability to reverse. Inevitably, death is the end point, the only way to complete the journey. No rest is allowed along the way.

I must have assumed that, for life to escalate to intolerable proportions, I would lose my grip, be unable to function, break down under the sheer strain. Those around me would see my weaknesses, my lack of the ability to live, notice my decline. However, it is not so. It is the cruellest of ways. Superficially, I am the ultimate coper. It acts like a shield, no-one able to penetrate beneath; my insides fester in the gloom. The darker I become, the less is shown.

My life is not being taken by one episode of released madness, I am slowly ebbing away. I am being taken, piece by piece, until there won't be anything left. The last to go are other people's memories of me. They will be siphoned off and taken in the breeze: no dramatics, nothing superfluous. My life is a gradual disintegration, so subtle it goes unnoticed.

No one knows the exquisite pain I feel because I am trapped inside my own body. It is a petrifying place to be. When death becomes her, the release is relief.

> Death's door is an intriguing place;
> I'm knocking it at an unknown pace.

* * *

12th October – I took an overdose. I had kept all Mum's diamorphine. It made me feel safe knowing it was there, but as I snapped the vial and mixed the liquid, not just my hands, but my whole body was shaking: the needle filled me with anxiety, all those times injecting Mum. I couldn't do it. I used to be able to inject myself but not this time.

I felt cheated by myself and frustrated. In retaliation, I took Mum's remaining tablets in the bag. I can't remember anything more. I spent three days in hospital and only vaguely remember coming round on the Sunday. I had to speak to a psychiatric nurse but, after that, they let me go. I walked home. No-one cared.

Lily, the GP who lives down our road and was a great friend of Mum's, talks with me and refers me to a psychiatrist. I see Dr. Floyd who, in turn, says I have to see the ISS – a team of psychiatric nurses – everyday. I see them at the hospital as refuse to have them come to the house. How is that helpful in any way?! I'd feel far more on edge at home! Especially now Ethan is back this week.

I don't really want to speak to ISS as I feel it is all so depressing talking over the same things again and I can't always be completely honest. I can't say, "Yes I am suicidal, I do wish to die and think about it much of the time" because then they were implying me going into hospital. Well, that is the last place I want to be! It won't help either. I keep telling them I'm not ill, it is a reaction to Mum dying as she meant everything to me. I don't think they understand. I could have told them all of this would happen even before Mum died.

Psychiatrist, Dr. Floyd, has now put me on two types of anti-depressants. I'm highly sceptical and feel sure the drugs will do absolutely nothing. Perhaps I should take them for a few weeks just to prove a point and then they will stop them once they realise drugs aren't going to help me. I still want temazepam though – I am sleeping so much better. It was Mum's favourite drug…and mine too! It does make me sleepy and when I wake in the middle of the night I'm still drowsy so I can fall back to sleep again. They can keep giving me this!

November 2007

10th November – I took another overdose. Ethan had been back all week and I do get on well with him, without external problems, we are actually very close but then he went out on Thursday night. At 4am I heard him come home. I had only got to bed at 2am and, with all the medication I'm taking, I awoke feeling rather confused and dazed. Maybe I'm making up excuses.

I could hear him running riot around the house. He had a load of mates with him and there was a drunken tirade of screaming swear words. They stamped around the house, slamming doors, followed by ominous crashing sounds. I suddenly felt fearful. Before, I have always gone down, would have at least attempted to talk to Ethan, stop him or calm him down. I would have also been protective over Mum, I couldn't have left her alone.

That night, I was paralysed with dread. I couldn't move. I drew my knees up to my chest and sat shaking, either out of cold or anxiety. It finally quietened down and I ventured downstairs. The house had been wrecked, every room trashed: smashed glass all over the floors and carpets; alcohol spread over floors and walls, thick, darkly staining; front door wide open; cigarettes littering the place. Mum's house, devastated, destroyed. Mum's house.

Mum and Dad's room and the spare room were locked. I banged and banged on the doors, worst-case scenarios playing through my mind. I expected to find Ethan throwing up…passed out…dead. Severity increasing with each outcome. I didn't get a response and so fumbled through our collection of Edwardian keys and managed to jiggle one into the locks. Ethan wasn't there. I phoned him on his mobile again and again: no response. I sat in the squalor and cried and cried.

Wendy, from next door, came round late morning, checking to see if I was OK. She had obviously heard everything and wanted to know I was safe. She was lovely. She saw the state of the house and said she was phoning the police. I begged her not to. It is never helpful.

Still no contact with Ethan so I decided to occupy myself and clean the house. People said not to, that it was not my responsibility, but what choice? You can't live in a house full of broken glass. You can't leave port and wine and whisky to stain even more.

Ethan finally came home at 3pm. He looked rough: goodness knows what drugs he had taken the night before. He then got really aggressive, shouting and swearing and blaming me. He said it was my fault. He said I should have stopped him. He said I know what he's like when he's wasted. It's all true. I should have done something and, in the event, I did nothing. Why? Why did I just stay in my room? He then started saying he couldn't care what the house looked like so he wasn't going to tidy a scrap. His Mum had just died so he was basically allowed to do anything he wanted. That was what he told me.

I talk to Mum. I tell her I need her, I want her back, I can't do this without her. Mummy, I need you so much. Please come back.

Later, the house was almost back to normal: Ethan had gone back to London. Dad arrived home. He came in and started getting cross. He complained that the floors were sticky, the house was dirty. He blamed me. I grabbed a bag full of my tablets and ran. I walked for a few hours, I should imagine. Thinking and walking. All depressing. I took all the tablets, shovelling them into my mouth, swallowing handfuls. I felt them squeezing down. I don't know what happened next.

I woke up in a ward and panicked. The clinicalness of the hospital, everything about it, filled me with such an anxiety. I had to get out of there. I hurriedly stood up and immediately fell back into the bed. I then saw a cannula in my arm and yanked it out, blood spilling over my gown. I phoned Lily, Mum's ever reliable GP friend. She arrived and, with all her usual charm, took charge. She spoke to the consultant, whom she knew, told me to get dressed, calmed me down and said we'd be leaving soon. She carefully took out my other cannula and plastered me up. With her there, I did settle. I was feeling rather ropey, dizzy and distinctly sick. Lily put her arm around my waist and I leant against her, exhaustion creeping upon me. The doctor arrived, had a quick chat, then Lily led me to her car, telling me to warn her if I was going to faint! She took me back to her house and we drank tea. I then came home and crawled into bed, sleeping away meaningless hours of life.

Still having to see psychiatric support team. They do come to the house now. I've said it must be when Dad is at work. They are nice but I don't think any of it is helping. They all ask what am I going to do today or next week. Everyone says it might be good to talk about what happened with Mum, but no-one asks me those questions. The doctors appear to listen, I explain why I'm not depressed: they nod, then give me a load of anti-depressants! Although, "load" is a slight exaggeration: they will only give me three days worth now as apparently I can't be trusted! I suppose I do agree with them when they say I have acted impulsively recently...I got a tattoo just because I walked past the tattoo shop!

A few weeks later, Dad came home one evening and launched into his ongoing nag. Why am I not getting a job? Why don't I care? Why am I not moving out? He threatens to throw me out of the house and then declares he is going to sell it. I try to explain. He tells me I need to move on. I get upset. I tell him I have taken two overdoses since Mum has died, a fact I had concealed from him. Lily thinks it is best not to have secrets. He reacts exactly as I knew he would. He gets cross, then tells me it is hard for everyone and I just need to pull myself together, then tells me I'm selfish and that I need to cope because he's coping and he's gone back to work.

I walk out of the house once he's finished talking. I don't want to be in the same place as him. I walk to the bridge and stand there, feeling such control. The temptation to jump is so great but, in my indecision, I remember what Mum said. My lack of decisive action hinders me. Mum wished she could jump off the roof when she was in hospital having chemotherapy. She fantasised about killing herself but then Mum said that how could she do that because some poor person would, quite literally, have to pick up the pieces. I watch the cars and decide that I couldn't jump onto some unsuspecting driver below. Oh, but the longing to have the courage to do so. I wanted to die so much. Being fixated on death makes living practically unbearable.

I finally venture home, shivering uncontrollably. It is almost midnight. Dad pretends he hasn't, but I realise he has waited up for me. He says he is going to bed while I am in the kitchen filling a glass of water. He comes up behind me and wraps his arms around me tight. He holds the embrace and I tilt my head against his. I say thank you in a whisper and silent tears roll down my face. He says goodnight and goes upstairs. For Dad to do that, it means everything to me. I can disregard all his earlier negativity. In that moment, nothing else mattered.

* * *

Maybe I'm in the middle of something that I don't really understand, but the place beyond belief is truly terrifying. I don't want to be taken there. To evade the nightmare, you must engage. It is all in the game and the way you play it, and you've got to play the game. I know I can surrender my king: it is the timing that must be right, and I can feel it coming. The fall is soon; the sense is mounting. I used to look down and it was a long way to fall but now that expanse has diminished; the distance is small.

You see, in the game of life, each person is in charge of their players, you hold your own hand, but I wanted to give my players away. I saw others in need and willingly submitted my players to them. I expected no payment in return. But now all my players are gone; I was undeserving. Was this right? For me, yes, although I wouldn't advise it to others. I'd tell them to keep a few players back, keep them close, and reserve them for themselves. This way, the fall can be avoided. This is how I appear strong when really I am the weakest. I did my best but now my stores are exhausted, my strength diminished.

Ironically, I have accumulated extra players in this vicious game: however, they are rogues. They roam amongst my dearly beloved, causing havoc. Orders which I have not given. They are my players. I am at fault, and yet they are not under my control. A demon has broken in. My defences are weak. These players can do bad things. Some are all too obvious but, of others, I am unaware. I have to chase these unleashed players and attempt to reel them in but they do not listen to my call. Instead, I am chasing, making amends, not altogether successful. They are mine but they are not from me. A conundrum I try to solve but I will never do so. The boundaries of the game have been flung widely open. I cannot keep track.

There is only one solution: I have to end my game. This is the only thing left over which I have complete control. They know this and that is how they taunt me. The unrelenting intimidation only gets stronger. I don't know if they are daring me, as my resolve weakens daily, or if this is what they want me to do. Without me, there is no them.

* * *

I agree with Beryl Bainbridge. She found her writing was inspired by challenging circumstances. When adversity comes, I am provoked to write. It is hovering on the brink of my control but maybe I fool myself. Pages of my ramblings are produced. I have to put pen to paper. If I was willing, could I stop myself? Prevent the tirade of words? I don't know. I have never tried. For words dance in my head, uncoordinated spiralling, materialising into lengthy, unpunctuated sentences. My challenge: to decipher. Sometimes the ability is granted and partial streams of thought are conveyed to paper, a physical recollection is produced, haphazard in its nature, but snippets nonetheless.

22nd December 2006

I cried in front of Mum. After forcing myself not to do so, it happened innocently enough. I was trying to help but, in helping, had burnt the food. Mum was not so much cross, as frustrated. She was tired with too much to do and too little time. Her patience had been used up on others.

The tears came, silently but streaming, joining at the bottom of my chin and dripping onto my t-shirt. I couldn't speak. I knew to do so would just encourage the emotion that had been released. I thought Maisie saw me as self-dramatising, a pathetically trivial incident to cry over. I was over tired partly from caring for Dr. Lawson, Mum's friend Julia's elderly father, but Mum wasn't to know the other reasons. She didn't know that, inside my head, there was a ravaging hurricane of memories, voices and emotions that I didn't know how to control.

I needed to leave, to be away from her in case that wrong thinking happened again. I wanted to protect her from myself. I ran, but, half way up the stairs, Maisie called me back. I came down. She hugged me and said she didn't want to argue. I sobbed, still trying to restrain myself but I knew I was losing. There is a subtle difference between hugs - you can hug someone or they can hug you. We stood there, a mother's all-empowering embrace overwhelming me and I gave up the fight and sank into her arms. I felt so safe. I wanted to tell her everything but, through my tears, I could say nothing.

We parted: the magic stopped and everything returned. I went to my room and curled up in a ball on the floor. Hugging my knees, I cried and cried, unable to catch my breath. I loathed myself. I couldn't bear the person I was. I didn't know whether I felt bad because I almost told her and should not have done so or, whether I almost told her and did not do so. The constant battle of my thoughts still occupying my mind.

27th December 2006

Mum and I relished our last day together before I returned to university. I cannot remember how our conversation led us to this point but, as we walked to the front door, Maisie said, "He is very proud of you, you do know that?" Mum was referring to Dad. I'm unsure as to whether it was a rhetorical question or not. Either way, my eyes welled up with tears and I couldn't answer for fear of being unable to stop myself crying.

Do I think my father is truly proud of me? Is pride an expression of care and love? I do know he cares, from what he does for me. Always practical, always organising and eager to give me what I need. He wants to spend money on me and willingly gives his time to help me arrange practical things. He gives me all this unselfishly and expecting nothing in return but is that what I want? what I need? I know Dad loves me but I want to hear that he does; he has never told me. He doesn't cuddle or put his arm around me. He doesn't use endearments. Is this what I am yearning for? I crave his love and so I do find it but, perhaps just once, I would like him to show me his love so I don't have to go looking. Maybe I'm pining after such an obvious sign of affection, so that it doesn't have to be interpreted, so that I don't have to think. I want all this because I really do love him too.

1st January

2007

New Year's Resolution:

Stop running, Alice. You need to learn to be still.

2008

New Year. Someone said to me that they bet I was glad 2007 was over. No. At this time a year ago, I still had my mother.

2nd January

2007

First day back on the wards – I love patients! Surely they are the best people in hospitals: they feel ill, they're stuck in a bed or chair, and yet they positively light up when you talk to them and are delighted to chat. How fantastic is that?!

I'd be a terrible patient. I can't bear being unwell, especially if you are confined. I marvel at their temperament and even the ones who seem bitter, aren't really, like Mr B who has dysphagia but can still yell, "Fuck Off!" and be clearly heard. He's not just a grumpy old man, he's an old man who can't move and has had a stroke: all he can hear is doctors discussing him in medical jargon, punctuated by a good deal of notes rustling to find the blood results that the consultant is after. But, when you approach Mr B on the right side of his bed, just you, not a whole army of medics, his eyes widen, his head fractionally turns towards you and he smiles, revealing a mouth full of broken, wonky, yellowed teeth. I love him already. It's only then that you find out that he has left sided inattention and the explanation for all of this. That may be important from a clinical point of view but, at this moment, I don't think I am particularly in need of an answer to his behaviour. All you need to know is to go to the right side of Mr B, instead of standing where he can't see you, and then he's happy.

3rd January

2007

MUM

A fairly anxious day, wondering whether GP would telephone with the results of the blood tests. Slept well last night and indigestion not bad today (hardly any back pain) but nauseous. I am so frightened and have convinced myself that it is cancer and terminal. Really wanted to get the house in order – in anticipation of hospitalisation! – but, apart from the spare room and some half-hearted taking down of the Christmas decorations, achieved little.

ALICE

Passed my exams, effectively my written finals, and was awarded a merit. Odd feeling when I got the results: I thought I would fail. I certainly deserved to fail. Despite doing more work for these exams than I have for any others, the amount of revision I managed was far from desirable. My inability to sit still and learn was marked. I fidgeted from my desk to my bed to the floor, and then the whole house became my study: kitchen, living room, even in the bath. I needed constant distraction from my surroundings in order to focus my attentions on the work. If all my senses were bombarded at once and occupied externally, my mind internally could then concentrate because it no longer had to compete.

Unfortunately, exam conditions always specify silence. Two exams, three hours each: I lasted no longer than an hour and a half in either of them. It was pathetic; I just couldn't stay. Words lost their meaning and instead, scuttled across the page like insects. An indecipherable word soup. I had let it slip. My attention was lost, not to return.

But the space that is left is never empty for long, always replaced by what I try so hard to suppress. It brings the restlessness, the agitation, the feeling of enclosure. I have to run, escape. Being outside is always safer; confinement is harder to achieve in the open. I deserved to fail because my mind was elsewhere. I wasn't satisfied with what I knew; it wasn't enough. Passing the exams, and passing well, made me angry. I felt uncomfortable, a disturbing feeling that it wasn't quite right. But how to resolve my unrest? Every practical aspect of my course I loved. I relished the prospect of seeing patients. I wanted to be a doctor. I should be pleased, so why this nagging feeling of doubt? It's almost like the sensation you get after cheating and subsequently passing. Except, I didn't cheat.

4th January

2008

ALICE

I took an overdose. I swallowed everything I could find in the house: citalopram, mirtazepine, temazepam, co-codamol, paracetamol. Someone found me outside and so I ended up in Casualty. They cut my clothes off and revealed multiple bruises and scratches. My heart went slightly awry so I was hooked up to a monitor.

I came round the following afternoon. I was still rather dazed and couldn't remember anything that had happened. I had to talk to the psych nurses and social worker and a doctor from ISS but I'm not sure what was said.

They let me out in the evening and I automatically walked home. All these memories are still scattered and vague but I reached my sister Holly's house (empty as Holly was in Barbados) exhausted, and collapsed on the sofa. The ISS nurse came to see me; Lily popped in. I spoke to Sarah (my dear friend Mog's mum) on the phone but, the next day, I was unaware of any visitors.

5th January

2007

MUM

Still no telephone call from surgery re. bloods. Was going to pursue it but, since I started to feel better from about yesterday evening, decided not to. Now that I'm feeling quite cheerful – stopped choosing funeral music etc! – seemed silly to risk conversation with a secretary who wouldn't be able to give me the results and might make me more anxious in the process. Want to avoid spending the entire weekend worrying just because she said, "You'll have to make an appointment with the doctor", or something like! Monday it is then.

Celebrated lack of indigestion and nausea with visit to the supermarket. Bought trout and broccoli for supper. Very healthy! Trout label was boasting omega 3 so I thought of Ethan, on some ridiculous omega 3 diet which seems to involve a lot of special yoghurts and vitamin tablets! Hence purchase of fresh fish – in defence of well-balanced meal!

6th January

2008

Having to see ISS nurses twice a day. They come and talk and I barely move from the sofa for several days as my body feels it has taken a beating and my tummy is unsettled and causes me to be sick. There is talk of me going into hospital. They don't think I am safe and feel I am liable to actually kill myself next time. The dreaded hospital. I want to run away but have to comply with visits as otherwise they will call the police. I dream up my escape route, a life on the run. Fantasy.

They say I am a high risk because I have taken three overdoses in as many months and this behaviour is alarming, especially as I have not done this before. This is not strictly true and I only remember it now. I took an overdose when I was 11 years old. Well, I use the term "overdose" broadly as feel this recollection doesn't even begin to fit into the category.

I cannot remember the specifics but there had been the usual arguments at home between Ethan, Dad and Mum. Lots of shouting: Mum in tears. Once they had been separated and, in the rebound silence full of thick, treacly, atmospheric tension, I reached up to the medicine box, kept on a cupboard shelf in the kitchen. The usual bottles of Piriton and cough mixture jingled, but I plucked out the box of paracetamol. I knew I wasn't supposed to have more than two but there were six left. I filled a glass of water, carefully but quickly, popped the tablets out and swallowed them one by one. It made me feel defiant, as if I was making a point, standing up to the pain inside.

I did not tell anyone. It was my secret, my power. I suffered no ill effects and had almost erased the event from my files of memories, until now.

8th January

2008

I feel I need to be relieved of the mounting pressure. I book a ticket to Barbados (only £150 – Christmas money can just about stretch!), flight leaving day after tomorrow. They can't get me in hospital if I'm out there!

It is a crazy, sporadic impulse. I have no summer clothes, I don't know how I'll cope for a week out there but I need to escape. There is no time to think or get anxious. I have no idea if I'm even going to find Holly… Barbados isn't that big, is it? I guess I should have been excited but I couldn't get myself to react. I felt very still and empty: a china doll.

10th January

2007

MUM

Not the best of nights, indigestion-wise. Otherwise, continuing to feel better in general. Phoned for results on Monday. Blood tests fine but liver function only just within the range of normality. On asking for advice on how to improve this, Dr. Pearce said normal diet, not too many fatty foods and no alcohol! Fine! Don't eat fatty foods much anyway and haven't had a drink since New Year's Day. Got to see doctor again in two weeks time when she'll review whether or not a gastroscopy is advisable.

Email from Maggie today. Cancers in liver enlarged and increased in number and spread to bones either side of base of spine – responsible for back pain and limping. More radiotherapy and, on January 26th, eight month course of chemotherapy starts. What a truly amazing, brave and courageous person Maggie is. She puts me to absolute shame.

Wasted most of the day. Can't seem to get moving. TATT! (tired all the time!)

ALICE

Unsure as to what I did wrong today. Started well, lovely chats with patients. I was fully engaged with the part of myself which loves what I do. My mind was completely occupied, void of any of the bad thoughts. It wasn't an effort to ignore the badness because I wasn't even aware any of it was there.

I'd been on PICU and seen tiny babies, gorgeous-looking despite their appearance marred by tubes and monitors. Walking away, along the expanse of corridors, everything turned into my head. I couldn't focus or concentrate on anything around me. I walked into the disabled toilet almost automatically and then there was nothing in my head, a blank canvas, complete emptiness. The nothingness was all-consuming. I think I liked it because I wanted it to last. I felt it would give me rest.

I must have fainted because I was on the floor and aware of all my thoughts seeping back, slowly at first but then they all crashed in, disordered, fighting for attention.

11th January

2007

ALICE

Took blood today – ahhh! Haven't done so since Third Year so was on such a high after I managed it! Did take me two attempts, however. I must really take this opportunity to take lots of bloods so my confidence will increase and then I'll be able to be more gentle with patients if my technique improves. Well, that's the theory anyway.

The patient today had a friend with her whom, at the mention of blood, leaped up, ran over to me and explained how she *loved* this stuff and had always wanted to train as a nurse and I did I think she was too old? But, she just *loved* hospitals and all that goes on and could she watch me taking blood? She wanted to learn.

I missed the vein first time and told her that I probably wasn't the best person to observe! The patient's friend said that always happens and just have another go at a different angle and…etc. The roles had been reversed. Shouldn't I have been the one calming the patient, talking in a soothing but confident voice? And yet she was the one reassuring me. I learnt from her learning from me. I like it when that happens.

Second time, easy: straight in and three bottles of blood are dropped into their coloured envelopes.

12th January

2007

MUM

Not a very good night. Awake from about 3-5am with abdominal pain, which three trips to the loo didn't shift! More loose motions [!] this morning and recurrent, niggling back pain – at least, not necessarily back, could be side ribs for example. Feel the pain is in my bones. It's a dull ache but comes in sort of spasms which sounds like a contradiction in itself. Trouble is, can barely distinguish between genuine ailment and death-wish, fuelled by anxiety!

ALICE

First day of forensic psychiatry placement. Friends ask if it is scary and I can honestly answer that it is not, but it is my first time in prison. Swiped ID cards, air-lock doors, compulsory personal alarms: none of the rigmarole of security to get onto the wards seemed to phase me. The patients weren't frightening in a threatening way. Most were rather subdued (probably medication induced) and spoke calmly, which I found more disturbing given the content of what they were saying.

The crimes they had committed varied but the diagnoses were invariably the same: schizophrenia with borderline/antisocial personality disorder; the odd bipolar affective disorder thrown in. The most upsetting aspect was listening to the patients' upbringings. Not a single person had had a "normal" childhood. All were punctuated with influential figures having their own problems: alcoholism, violence, abuse, drug-addiction. The knock-on detrimental effect to children seems an unrelenting, irreversible, hideous circle. The patients I met had had their own children removed from their care, only being allowed occasional supervised visits, but much of this intervention was, I suspect, too late. The damage had already been done.

The index offences seemed to get increasingly worse as the day progressed or was it just the cumulative effect all these patients were having on me? I still don't know. Can you really compare the atrocities of the severely mentally ill? It feels decidedly gruesome.

Case 1 – Paranoid schizophrenic living alone in a flat. Believes his neighbours are spies. Endless conspiratorial thoughts threaten him: he is being tracked, others are listening to him through the walls, people are watching him from the floor and ceiling, his phone is tapped, people can see him through his mirrors. He takes what seems to him to be the only course of action: douses his flat in petrol and sets the whole place alight. Except, he lives in a block of flats so manages to damage much of the building as well.

Case 2 – Manic episode with drug-induced psychosis; violent rampage through town with several armed robberies.

Case 3 – Psychotic patient who strangled a doctor.

Case 4 – Depressive with psychosis jumps off a bridge in suicide attempt. Lives but has a massive head trauma. Now suffering from frontal lobe syndrome. In lectures you are always taught about Phineas Gage. How different that is from actually meeting a patient.

Writing these down, I definitely feel uncomfortable about myself. Is knowing intricate details of patients' crimes beneficial to the patient or helpful to me? I fear neither. I wonder if it is a deadly, addictive curiosity rather than anything tangible. Almost a morbid fascination with despicable acts, amplified by conversing with the individuals responsible.

13th January

2007

MUM

Feeling thin – even my arms look thinner – and hope I'm not losing more weight. I mean, it's nice to be thin but I don't want to be ill. A lot better than I was but don't exactly feel 'right'.

14th January

2007

MUM

John and I went for a walk in the morning, followed by pub lunch. Determined that Sunday walks become a regular feature. Needless to say, fell asleep in a chair in the afternoon! Why am I so tired all the time?

15th January

2007

MUM

Quite a bit of indigestion and backache today. Don't know whether my extreme anxiety is giving me psychosomatic symptoms or whether I really do have something terrible like cancer of the stomach and it's spread to my bones and vital organs! So tired as well.

As it was, I practised the Brahms Requiem, in readiness for tonight's rehearsal. It's embarrassing to own up to singing it before and then struggling with the notes. And it paid off! Enjoyed the rehearsal (despite gnawing pains) – a really good sing.

ALICE

I heard about it in the local news. Newcastle United were playing at St. James' Park on Saturday. Somebody had run onto the pitch, been wrestled to the ground and then escorted off. I learnt today that it was one of our patients on day leave. I should have guessed! Amusing anecdotal tales still punctuating the unrelenting sombre insights into the actions of the mentally ill.

16th January

2007

MUM

Bad night – sleepless, anxiety-ridden dreams and backache. Phone call first thing to see if I would go and do teaching supply work. Protested, in view of stomach problems, but was persuaded to do Wednesday to Friday. Got it into my head that my symptoms were being exacerbated by anxiety so maybe I should transfer my stress to the classroom! Needless to say, was soon regretting the decision. Very painful indigestion after lunch, persisting as I write this. I know there is something wrong.

Supermarket in the morning – trying to buy extra healthy foods. Not that anything makes a difference.

Spoke at length to Alice in the evening. She is a dear. Wants to come home the weekend after next to help out at the post-concert party. I am very lucky to have such a daughter.

Do hope I manage to sleep tonight. Feeling fairly grim at present.

ALICE

There is always the issue of public safety. Integrating these patients back into society is a delicate and complex procedure. I strongly feel patients deserve a chance but, at the same time, I do wonder whether some of them will ever be able to function in the community. They have been institutionalised for so long that the ability to cope on their own eludes them.

Allowing patients out of a secure hospital is a gradual process. Leave is first accompanied, then length of time off site is extended, and finally they are allowed out alone. However, things do go wrong. Maybe the outside world is full of temptation, the seduction too strong.

One patient, an alcoholic before admission, saw the opportunity and couldn't stop. He managed to consume three litres of vodka and a bottle of cough syrup. For the following three days he was shaking continuously. I saw him today and think I was shocked by the visible effects of alcohol ravaging his body.

Another patient came back to the ward, his shirt covered in blood. He couldn't explain and had no memory of his time away. Two women had been stabbed in the stomach: one was pregnant and lost the baby. No-one was ever charged for the stabbings but this patient was always suspected. As this is now on record, his rehabilitation is being handled with a significantly increased degree of caution, as would be expected. But, what if he didn't do it? What if it was all just circumstantial? Is that a miscarriage of justice? Is he being mistreated? Or is it necessary to restrict him unfairly for the greater good, to protect the public? Is that a priority that should be respected over one man's freedom?

The stabbings had taken place sixteen years ago. The patient had been in secure hospitals ever since. Of course, this might have been the case regardless of the suspected crime. He might have been too ill to leave. I do not envy those who have to make these choices. I would struggle; I'm afflicted with the ability to see all points of view, which makes it almost impossible to try to reason and choose a side.

2008

I return home from Barbados without mishap and, within half an hour, psych nurse Carrie is there, checking on me. This makes me feel safe. I like talking to Carrie. ISS concern for my welfare startles me. I've never had that before, as no-one ever knew about my demons within but now, with this intense support, I am unable to know how to respond. In many ways it is daunting, but also reassuring. Conflicting feelings induce confusion. I don't know how to think or what to say to anyone.

Coming home is always emotionally trying and I am liable to descend into the depths of my own mind, physical reality slipping from my awareness. Probably compounded by tiredness due to the overnight flight, I embark on a hazy walk across the fields, through the tree arches of muddy paths, in a dream-like state, my mind detached from my body. The two part. They sometimes cannot keep as one: a separation which I struggle to control, desperately clinging, a gripping hand on each side. But the effort is exhausting and my hands can only stretch so far.

> I felt a cleaving in my mind
> As if my brain had split
> I tried to match it – seam by seam
> But could not make them fit
>
> Emily Dickinson

Perhaps hours later, I follow my footsteps which are leading me home. ISS have been trying to get hold of me – I'd left my phone at home. They are seeing me in the evenings as well. Joanne, a nurse I get on really well with, has already been to the house to find it empty. I feel quite bad about this. She does come and see me, however. It is odd, despite my reluctance to see the ISS before Christmas, I now find it comforting. I don't dread the visits. It is a support. By seeing them every day, it gives me a focus, a routine and knowledge that I am responsible to someone.

I didn't like the host of different faces, asking similar questions. They knew me but I didn't know them. I found that unnerving. But now, I mostly see Carrie and Joanne whom are both lovely. I want to tell them everything. I realise I trust them. Trust is such an importance to me. I am unable to speak if I have even niggling doubts. They induce a calmness within me, can understand what I am attempting to explain, can decipher my body language when I am uncomfortable with the direction of conversation and know when I'm not quite elaborating on the truth. They are good at saying the right things to encourage me to talk. I feel blessed to have them.

17th January

2007

MUM

After misgivings first thing, a surprisingly successful day. Didn't notice or think about any pain during teaching lessons. The distraction I needed after all?

Today was tough: my mind bubbling, filling with unruly thoughts. I told Mum about the patients, their stories, antics on the ward. I told her how ill they are, how sorry I feel for them and, ultimately, how little I feel they can be helped. For some, there is no cure for mental illness, just suppression.

19th January

2007

MUM

Teaching has been therapeutic. Nonetheless, stomach area tender when pressed and I'm beginning to think that a gastroscopy might be a good idea. Chinese takeaway in the evening with John but I struggled and didn't finish mine. I get full so quickly and can't manage very big meals anymore.

20th January

2008

It is Mum's choir concert next Saturday. The choir girls had asked me if I wanted to go; Dad hadn't. I didn't want to be there and watch, see the place, in the front row, where Mum used to stand.

This was Mum's final concert. Last year, she had been feeling ill and was so anxious that she wouldn't be able to sing, let alone have everyone back to our house afterwards for her famous party. For several years now, she would invite over a hundred people back, post-concert, and cook chilli and make little chocolate truffles and provide wine and beer for everyone. I would usually help except, since being in Newcastle, it became more tricky. Mum was so ill however, I took the Monday off and drove home for a long weekend. Mum was fantastic: she sang and enjoyed herself at her party, although she didn't drink at all, convinced alcohol triggered symptoms. We served the food together and laughed lots.

The final stragglers left at 3am and Mum said to me at the time that she felt she was saying goodbye to everyone. Only later did we realise she was. Being too poorly after that for any excursions (bar hospital), only a few friends came to visit as Mum just could not manage any more.

This concert was especially important for me. Dad wanted to go. He still likes doing things and it is nice that he is able to. I wish I could do more. Then, a week before, there was a phone call from a woman whose husband is in the choir. I answered. She wanted to confirm that Dad was coming for dinner after the concert. I asked Dad. In his jolly, exceedingly irritating, voice he said, "Oh yes, Mary and I". I walked off without speaking. I wanted to be outraged but all I felt was sadness. Dad is going to Mum's concert with Mary (who didn't know Mum or any of the choir group) and then taking her to dinner at Mum's friend's house. It is absurd. Dad knows how upsetting the whole opera at Glyndebourne was for me; how can he be doing this again? I tried and talked to him but didn't get anywhere. Dad dismissed me with a grunt; I felt on the verge of tears.

People misunderstand my devastation. They think I am upset because Dad is, seemingly, with another woman. I am not sad about this. Mum said he would probably re-marry and I do not pretend they had a wonderful, loving marriage – this was far from true. Dad can see whom he pleases. Ethan and I are old enough to not view a different woman as a mother figure. We have already grown up. She would just be Dad's partner.

What I find terrifically hard to deal with is Dad's neglect for our feelings. If he wants to see Mary, why can't he take her to things that have no link to Mum? Why does he have to invite her to occasions which were so special to Mum, which Mum loved and enjoyed and hold so many fond memories? I did try and explain this to Dad but he won't acknowledge me; his anger lashed out.

21st January

2007

MUM

Alice is 23! My baby! Telephoned her in the morning. Seemed to be celebrating her birthday doing the usual – work with her learning disabled kids, church, church disability group! Perhaps we can do something nice next week when she is home.

ALICE

Holly has never forgotten the date of my birthday but she rang today, and twice left messages. She spoke quickly, words tumbling out, lengthy explanations deciding whether my birthday was this weekend or next. There wasn't anything peculiar or particularly worrying in what she said, it was the manner in which she spoke. And also, she has always remembered before. Are these signs of an impending slide into mania? Possibly. Am I being an over-analysing sister, seeing warnings in innocent circumstances? Probably. But is this OK? Surely I'm allowed to be over-protective. She is my sister. But there is that nagging feeling that I'm never going to speak to Holly again without that tug of doubt, a wariness that she may be getting unwell, her bipolar disorder roaring into view. Will I ever just see her as Holly again?

2008

My birthday. Been a really tough weekend: I was in suspended animation. I didn't have the energy to kill myself but I had no will to live. This indifference is terrible. You have to be passionate about living or dying. Not being able to do either is a half life. Nothing about me is real. I am a pretence in the world. I have no understanding of me; I don't know when I got lost. Where have I gone?

I was dreading today. All so sad. Saw Joanne from ISS over the weekend but I was very low and really struggling to concentrate. I couldn't stay with what she was saying. Didn't see Dad this morning. He left me a card though. I couldn't face opening any cards or presents. It was all meaningless. Carrie came round with an ISS doctor. I wasn't very good. They know I don't like my birthday anyway. We did talk, although I was rather monosyllabic. I didn't have the mental energy to explain. They said they wanted me to go into hospital. I obviously didn't want this, but then there was no choice – either go in voluntarily as an informal patient or be sectioned. They took me in.

A nurse reeled through my admission process and I complied in a daze: height, weight, medication, blood glucose, blood pressure, pulse, oxygen sats. A doctor saw me and I had to explain the same things I had told ISS. I know this is necessary but I cannot bear the repetitive nature. In a stand of contempt, I asked to see my notes: maybe I would understand more. They said no.

I am here for my physical safety but I have little regard for that. It is my mind that petrifies me. Once it is evening and dark outside, my head is bombarded with thoughts and memories and fears. Being confined in my room only compounds the torrent of emotions. There is no escape here. I cannot go outside and walk away some of the consuming anxiety. I sit huddled, shaking, full of fear. What is happening? What am I doing here? The loneliness mocks me, the dreaded external silence which makes the noise in my head much louder and easier to hear.

Where do I go from here? I no longer believe in me. I am not my own. When I was younger, if there had been shouting or violence or dreadful arguments, I would stick them out. I would hate it but I stayed, desperate to get them to stop and make amends, protect my Mum. However, once the argument dissipated, I would retreat to my bedroom. Here, I could see another life, another me. I would gaze through my mirror and look at all the angles of my room reversed. It was the room I dreamt I would escape to. I would pretend I could sit there, because, in the reflected room, all was tranquil. It was fundamental that the room was reflected. It meant that everything there was the opposite to the side of the mirror on which I had to stay. I imagined that I climbed through the mirror and hid in my delightful second bedroom. It was a secret. No-one knew about my special room.

I would be careful, when looking through the mirror, never to actually touch it. For, I knew that if I felt the solid glass, my illusions would be shattered. I could not actually climb through but, if I didn't touch, the possibility was there. I could still think that my fantasy room was open to me. It welcomed me; it liked a visit.

Sometimes, I would longingly stare for too long. My mirror would become all misty from my breath being so close. I would move my position but soon an opaque circle of condensation would obscure my view. My secret place would disappear, access denied until the next time I was allowed to dream. For, my mirror wasn't always special. It would only sporadically offer me that divine hope. Most of the time, my mirror was just an ordinary mirror.

10pm – Lily comes. I dissolve into sobs, uncontrollable emotion. 24 years old: why is that a celebration? I also talk to rational, calming Sarah on the phone. I'm afraid and anxious. Sarah is always wonderfully able to calm me and help me see sense but tonight, all that is lost. Her soothing words are meaningless to me.

A different nurse comes and talks with me. I find this terribly tiring. Gone midnight, I finally collapse, completely drained, into bed.

22nd January

2007

MUM

Appointment with GP Dr. Pearce in the morning. I am to continue taking omeprazole for a further two weeks. If the soreness (stomach) hasn't cleared up by then, it's a gastroscopy. Actually, I am feeling a lot better.

Kind phone calls from friends and family – everyone enquiring about my health.

2008

One of the ISS nurses escorted me home in the morning. They wouldn't let me go alone but I needed clothes and a towel etc. I spent five minutes running round, gathering belongings and then we had to go back.

I picked up my birthday cards and opened them in the confinement of my room – so depressing. Sweet sentiments are lost on me. At least I now have a newspaper to read.

By the afternoon, I'm hideously claustrophobic. I wander down the corridor just for something to do. I observe the other patients and feel I really will go mad if I stay here for any length of time.

I watch Ann. She is a lady who looks pushing sixty. She has short grey hair that probably hasn't seen a comb in a while but this "ruffled" look suits her. Ann is wearing several woollen jumpers, including roll necks, and black leggings, although, the leggings end just below her knees so there is a glimpse of bare leg before they disappear into huge Ugg boot effects. Light brown boots with the fluffy lining overflowing at the top, a colour which should have been white but isn't quite clean enough. She sits, legs crossed, and has a wicked cackling laugh revealing uneven teeth. I never do discover what she is finding funny.

Later, I'm struggling. This is so hard. Lily comes in the evening and I relish our embrace. I dreadfully miss my hugs with Mum. We play the GP card and the nurses allow me to go out for a walk with Lily. It is muddy and dark but Lily has brought torches. I find it incredible how quickly you can become institutionalised. I haven't even been here two days but outside, in the open, there is quite an overwhelming feeling of freedom.

I've barely eaten anything in here so Lily takes me to the supermarket to get fruit and biscuits and chocolate. She is so wonderful to me. Why do I wish to die? I have amazing family and friends. I'm far more privileged than most and yet I am unable to live. Guilt is consuming.

23rd January

2007

MUM

Indigestion and painful stomach today. I don't know what to think. If the medication really is working, why isn't there gradual improvement? Seems to be much better – then a bad day again.

Alice phoned, very excited – her elective placement has been confirmed as Uganda. Hope she keeps safe. No doubt I shall worry! Snowing in Newcastle too. Not here – despite promises in weather map!

2008

I meet Rob, sweet guy with bipolar but he's stabilised so is going home today. He tells me there are four types of people on this ward: the shufflers, who, when they do get up from their seat, shuffle along painfully slowly; the pacers, who just stride up and down the corridors; the kick-offs, who are rather volatile and end up particularly animated, swearing and the like; and the relatively normal. He says we fit in the last category!

I meet Phyllis. She is a shuffler but a very amicable woman in her forties. Everything she does is prolonged. I decide to talk to her. She speaks slowly, lengthening her vowels and her speech is disjointed by overly long pauses. She doesn't like the staff (everyone here seems to have "issues" with those helping: as far as I can see they are wholly unfair) but she will talk to me. She says, "What is wrong with you? You don't seem to have any problems". Quite.

It is a very unique relationship between fellow patients, something I keenly observed as a medical student, and also with the learning disabled groups I worked with. However well staff relate to patients, they cannot achieve that bond in unity. Perhaps this stint in hospital will help me to become a better doctor. Talking to Phyllis, I suddenly remember why I loved being a medical student. It wasn't the procedures, it was simply talking to people, gaining their trust, and then, hopefully, trying to help them.

Afterwards, this scares me. I am confused. I adored medicine but now, when a glimpse of that excitement returns, I feel fearful. I can cope being with people for a short period but it exhausts me. I need time afterwards to recuperate. Tiredness prevents me from spending a whole day with other people. I glaze over eventually and delve into a state where people talk but I cannot hear, things are happening but I cannot relate to them, questions are asked but I am unable to speak. I am in the world but not part of it. I am here, alive, but my mind wonders elsewhere. Half living. Half flying.

Isobel, a close friend of Mum's, visits and brings me a radio. This certainly changes my whole perception of being in hospital. When Mum was ill, she couldn't bear silence so radio or television was on continuously and now, I have to do the same. My mind is distracted by the noise and, despite not especially listening (I wouldn't be able to tell you what programme was just on) it occupies my head sufficiently, preventing painful thoughts from completely consuming me. My background is always Radio 4. The dial remains unchanged from Mum's days, this little chink of light, making life just ever so slightly more bearable.

I see Dr. Floyd, my consultant. She is very good and I feel she understands. She agrees with me (finally, after all my protestations to various doctors/nurses!) that it doesn't appear to be a simple depression. She thinks my mood is quite unstable and I'm acting on impulse (overdoses, tattoo, Barbados etc.). She suggests starting me on a mood stabiliser, lithium or sodium valproate, and I flatly refuse. I am certain neither will help. I feel the citalopram has not affected me in the slightest but I remain on the anti-depressant. Dr. Floyd suggests quetiapine instead and I relent. Compromises must be made and I have to be compliant. She says it will help me to sleep better and she will gradually reduce my temazepam as I've been on it for nearly two months continuously and will end up addicted. It should also calm the muddle in my head. She says I'm not going home: I'm not safe and they want to monitor me. I'll be staying here for a few more days.

Dr. Floyd is concerned that I haven't told Dad I'm in hospital. She asks, won't he be worried about me? I tell her that, no, he won't notice. It is Wednesday evening, I haven't seen Dad for four days; it has been my birthday and he hasn't even rung. She says I should tell him. I have a review with her tomorrow and it would be helpful if he was there. I think it will be distinctly unhelpful but feel my resolve dissipating.

I talk to Lily. She says she will phone Dad for me. I don't want to explain to him. It transpires that Dad tells Lily he hasn't seen me for a few days and that he has a meeting but should be able to fit my review in! Don't bother interrupting your work for me Dad.

Not knowing how to tell anyone else in my family, I realise I must, even though I will hurt them when I explain, however briefly, what I have done. How can I be such a despicable, unfeeling person? I hate myself for being so cruel towards them. I would be distraught if it was the other way round. I phone Aunty Beth, Mum's sister. She is wonderful but understandably upset. She is all for driving down immediately but I reassure her I am OK and, as am in here, safe. She says she will definitely come at the weekend. I love her so much.

Gone midnight. Dad hasn't even phoned me. I sort of thought he would want to come and see me tonight. Dad has never been able or willing to acknowledge pain. Illness should not invite lavish attention from others. Illness is a chance to prove what you are made of, to be strong. For Dad, this is to ignore it for the majority.

I remember, what was most likely the first time I hurt myself when only Dad was around and not Mum. I was eight years old. I ran out of the house in my sandals and tripped, knee landing smack on the metal grate outside. I sat, stunned on the ground, and saw a gaping hole in my knee, blood smeared and trickling down to my ankle. I didn't cry, I gulped back that immediate urge, and, back door still open, I called out for Dad. He came and got me to walk over to the wooden picnic bench. He then left me to fetch some tissues. I fainted. I can't have lost consciousness for long because I became aware that my face was on the ground, a gravelly taste in my teeth, and, on realisation, I quickly scrambled up and sat down on the bench. I knew fainting was a bad thing to do. I didn't think Dad would approve. He would think of it as a weakness. He would think me pathetic.

I obediently waited for him. He took a while as had trouble locating the first aid box, an alien tool to him. He wiped my knee with tissues then stuck on a plaster. He asked if I was OK and I said yes. I was not going to look weak in front of my father. Dad carried on with whatever I had interrupted him from but the plaster wasn't sufficient. In minutes, it had filled with blood and peeled off under the weight. I sat in the bathroom and held tissues on my knee and watched as the white paper absorbed and turned bright red. I then put a bigger plaster on my knee, hoping that would hold.

In the evening, Mum returned from her choir rehearsal. She was so sorry that she wasn't at home and hugged and stroked me. I had changed the plaster several times by then and Mum said it looked quite deep. She got some antiseptic, the trusty bottle of TCP, as Mum told me it would otherwise get infected. She thought I may need stitches so took me to Lily who steri stripped the gash and put a proper dressing on my knee; Mum held my hand. She doted on me and cared because she knew the inadequacies of Dad in an accident situation. Mum did so wish she had been at home.

I never did tell her that I fainted, however. Dad hadn't even noticed and so I doubted myself. When you try and pretend something hasn't happened, part of you begins to believe it.

24th January

2007

MUM

Practised music for concert – less enjoyable than usual because deep breaths cause discomfort in stomach.

Saw Maggie and Peter for dinner. Good food and restaurant full. A very pleasant evening. Maggie still looking good, although movement of neck restricted and can't walk very far/fast apparently.

2008

I have my review with Dr. Floyd. Dad comes at 2pm so at least I feel protected by seeing him first with the staff. Dr. Floyd briefly explains why I am here. She asks Dad how I've changed. He says, before, I was always on the go, busy, vivacious, active. He is right. My whole philosophy of life was to be up and doing every moment. So many things used to bring me so much pleasure. He hates to see me, usually effervescent energy, listless and can't acknowledge that I am ill. Illness offends him. Dad is never at ease with people who are sick. He seems unable to put it into perspective so chooses, always, to dismiss it. Ignore and then he will not have to confront.

After the review, I spend time with Dad alone. He is reasonable and kind but can't seem to comprehend. He says he doesn't think I should be taking any medication and he doesn't like the idea of me being referred to a psychologist. Dad is against talking! He does, however, open up to me slightly. This is the main problem with Dad, communication. He, albeit briefly, talks about his feelings and how Mum dying has affected him but he tells me how he has coped by working and keeping busy. He thinks I should just pull myself together and get on with it. I realise he is unaware of the great lethargy that consumes me, or the concentration required to be with and talk to people, or the absolute desperate longing for death. How to live when I want no life? He said that he had never felt he wanted to die. He called it giving up. He is right of course: I am giving up on life, but, put in those words, it makes me feel pathetic, as if I am choosing these feelings. Dad thinks I should snap out of it.

Dr. Floyd had said, when it is discovered that a family member is going to die, loved ones usually begin grieving before the death actually occurs. She tells me that I never had that due to the nature of care I was giving. Afterwards, Dad picks up on this. He says he found he did begin grieving in March and April and even found those months harder than subsequent ones. Dad was prepared, as much as one can be, for the dire outcome whereas I was thrown into a state of shock, as if I had lost a limb. I was flailing with no mother to catch me.

In our lengthy conversation, Dad says it might be nice to have Mary round for dinner: I could cook. This is almost unbelievable except I expect it from Dad. Sitting there, in a psychiatric unit, unable to leave, I now have the enticing evening to look forward to of a threesome of Dad, Mary and I when I will be cooking for an anorexic, attempting to make polite conversation and having to put up with sickly sweet sentiments from Mary, whom I'm sure is a lovely woman: I don't want to! Only Dad would be saying things like this the first time he sees me in hospital, on a ward which I am confined to. What is he thinking?

At 9pm the lovely Joanne from ISS comes to see me to check that I am getting on reasonably. She has been so fantastic towards me. She appears and I immediately hug her in a rush of emotion. I know and trust Joanne. She suddenly makes me feel safe in my unfamiliar hospital room, all with pale wooden furniture and cream walls. We talk and it does not require that great effort I so often need; I am not sapped of what little energy is left in my resources. I feel calm and willing to talk and expressing myself is helpful. I purge my mind of some pent-up anxieties. I am so grateful towards Joanne.

We are then, however, interrupted by the penetrating wailing of the fire alarm (bells are always going off for various reasons!) so just stay chatting but, no, someone has actually started a fire in the dining room! A horrible burnt-plastic smell disperses down the corridor and smoke curls out of the windows. The fire is out but it certainly injects some excitement into the evening. I am appreciative of anything that cuts into my boredom which is compounded by tiredness.

Joanne leaves. She has spent a long day at work and, instead of going home, she has come to see me! She is a dear. She asks if I need anything. Can she bring me magazines, sweets etc? The loveliness of the nurses I have met is immense! Such special people.

25th January

2008

Worst day in hospital. Utterly exhausted. Spent much of the day crying or sitting on the floor hugging my knees. Felt dreadful. Wanted to die but no energy or thought to even contemplate how to kill myself.

In the evening, Lily arrives and is confronted by me in a state. She takes me outside for a walk. I, rather dazed with swollen, bleary eyes from crying, stumble along, hugging Lily's arm for support. It is fresh and cold and the chilling wind catches my face and neck. I like the infinity of the sky. It offers escape. It can hold all my rogue thoughts, unlike my mind which buckles under the intensity.

Once Lily leaves, I sit outside on the bench, star gazing. It induces a fake calmness, masking my internal unrest. I am suspended in a shadow world that no-one else inhabits. The raised voices of two other patients seep into my ears and I am roused into consciousness. An argument is developing and I enter into this unknown exchange. One disputer grasps a green plastic garden chair by the arms and wields it above her head, brandishing it towards the other patient. I leap up, swipe the chair and return it to the ground then begin talking away in a ridiculously happy voice, emitting such trollop as, "Now, let's not argue", "Violence won't help matters", "Best not go to bed on an argument"... "Anyone want a drink?"!! I escort one of them inside as feel a bit of distance is required; she is still ranting away.

Patients can always be relied upon to provide a slither of entertainment during the days which are a continuous struggle. Endlessly long hours but they seem to pass: one bleeding into another, light to darkness, the days are consumed.

26th January

2008

Awake at 5am. I am too tired to even sleep. Feel very restless all morning, partly because I am anticipating Aunty Beth arriving. I fret from my room to the lounge to outside...help, am I becoming a pacer?!

Sammy is, as always, skipping around. She is in her thirties but looks much younger. She appears to favour wearing much of her wardrobe at once: jeans, tucked into big knitted slipper socks which have bobbles dangling from them; long floaty skirt, hippyish but odd over bulky jeans; several tops and jumpers. The whole ensemble is finished off with a tartan dressing gown! Sammy is lovely. She roams the ward, talking or singing continuously, and always materialises to hold open a door for you or say hello. She is quite jolly this morning, arms swinging.

I then see Rote, who speaks to people I cannot see. He does find them amusing, however. He wears the same clothes every day: ripped denim dungarees, torn t-shirts over ragged tops, sleeveless jacket and usually fingerless gloves revealing hands bedecked in big chunky rings. He reminds me of Fagin in Oliver Twist. He has black, curly ringlet long hair, fighting to escape from many rubber bands he has used in an effort to tame unruly locks.

Aunty Beth arrives at midday and I fill with warmth as I fold into her arms. We have a lovely time together, walking through the fields, arms linked, chatting all the while. My dear aunty, so willing to care for me. We then venture to the supermarket and this feels too much. Aunty Beth says I look odd, very pale, and I think I'm about to faint - the lights, the hustle of shoppers, the noise, all too intense. I grip onto the trolley and try to fix my gaze on the cereal box in front of me. Once out, I sink into the car seat, relieved to be away.

Dad cooks dinner, very good for him! But I feel bad as can only manage a morsel. Feeling distinctly nauseous, although nothing to do with the food. Aunty Beth and I then retreat to the front room, bottle of wine in tow. I curl up beside her on the sofa and, lying against her, I feel protected. We watch some daft singing talent show on television and I am enveloped in a sleepy warmth. All too soon, I have to leave. Dad, punctual as always, says he's driving me back. I hate to go. I want to stay.

Eventful evening. After night-time medication, commotion ensues, all surrounding Maureen. Maureen is an exuberant woman with white flowing hair, never tied back. She has a penchant for woollen roll-necks (they seem to be popular in here!) and always has, clamped to her side, an oversized, silver handbag. She is most certainly a kick-off and marches everywhere. She is commonly found ranting in a raised voice to staff, frequently refusing her medication, clashing with other patients and talking over everyone. Anyway, tonight she descends into the lounge, declaring that someone punched her and dramatically collapses into a chair. I have no idea if she was actually hit but there is the resulting ruckus. The staff show concern and take charge of the situation. Maureen relishes in all the attention. The guy who was accused of hitting her is spoken to. Everyone has a cup of tea. Calm is restored.

Late to bed but I sleep well after a busy day.

27th January

2008

Aunty Beth picks me up and we go for a walk around the lake. I get tired and we sit, huddled on a bench against the biting wind. Talking about me and all the help I am getting, I almost tell her. Aunty Beth knows there were things before Mum was ill and I nearly break my staunch silence. She looks at me, almost like she is waiting, an unspoken secret between us. I could have told her everything but it is the aftermath I am afraid of, the repercussions, the debt I shall have to repay.

We carry on walking and I manage to get us lost!

Aunty Beth and I make lunch for Dad and Holly (well, cheese, biscuits and salad!) and I feel OK amongst the chatter. Lindsey, Holly's Mum (Dad's first wife), then arrives in her whirlwind fashion. No-one else can get a word into her excitably loud monologue, except Holly who joins in and is equally as bad! Lindsey says it's her bipolar (a self diagnosis which I am inclined to agree with) and she's on such a high at the moment, so much better than when she was depressed a few weeks ago.

Aunty Beth has heard about Lindsey from Mum and I and has met her once before, although years ago when all of us children were little. Even so, Aunty Beth wasn't quite prepared for such a bombardment! No wonder I don't want to tell Holly and Lindsey that I am in hospital – I think should be unable to cope with such erratic behaviour.

Aunty Beth and I then walk to Lindsey's to see all her plants for sale in her front garden. People have donated more and more and currently, she has raised over a thousand pounds for Cancer Research. It is fantastic.

Late afternoon and Aunty Beth must go home. She drops me off at the hospital. It is a sad departure and she hugs me tight. I feel quite despondent returning to my room.

Feel quite sick all evening: uneasy tummy. I am blaming the quetiapine. It has made me feel pretty dreadful ever since I started taking it. Think I am going to make the executive decision to stop.

Later, Sasha, a fellow medic with me in Newcastle, phones and she really helps as I know I am struggling. I explain everything and Sasha is wonderful. She is very gifted with words and knows what to say, even in these difficult circumstances. I value this tremendously.

It is very trying being with people who avoid a subject because it makes them feel uncomfortable. What amazing friends I have. I appreciate them putting up with me and remaining in contact, as I am liable not to phone anyone. Sometimes I don't know what to say. My mind needs encouragement, a stimulus from those who recognise and care.

28th January

2007

MUM

Successful post-concert party yesterday, I think – the house packed with people. Many complements. Lovely having Alice here helping and being delightful. The concert went well, on the whole, but a few glaring mistakes! John got up at the crack of dawn, after very little sleep and did all the washing up and general tidying. I felt very tired and threatened to nod off at various points of the day.

Watched DVD with Alice in the evening, which I've seen already but we enjoyed. Quite a few thank you cards and phone calls for the party.

2008

Same distractions as usual – newspaper, books, crossword, phone calls. Ethan phoned this evening and I felt I must tell him about my current predicament. He was lovely and caring and said he was coming home straight away. I persuaded him to sort himself out and come tomorrow. I don't think he's coping that well; I'm not sure how much he actually talks to his friends and now I've placed this burden on him. I really hate myself. I feel incredibly protective over Ethan and want to be so strong for him and I've let him down, deserted him at the moment he needs me most. I am pathetic.

However, it will be lovely to see Ethan. He is incredibly easy to talk to, something he really has learnt from our wonderful mother, but then I'm filled with dread. Dad will get cross that Ethan is home and they will resume their arguing as if they has seen each other only yesterday.

Fighting and animosity and it will all be my fault. I have forced this situation. I always attempt to keep the peace, usually in vain, and now I'm causing the problem. What am I thinking? Alice, you are becoming increasingly selfish and self-centred. Sort yourself out or kill yourself properly. Either or, Alice: no in-between.

29th January

2007

MUM

Lovely, relaxed morning chatting to Alice before she set off for Newcastle at lunch time. Got into bed with me. I'm so lucky to have a daughter – and such a daughter!

2008

Saw Ethan in the afternoon. When things matter, he really is smashing. He, understandably, had lots of questions to ask me but the ease with which we can talk is quite calming. He'd bought some nice bread and ham and cheese so we had lunch together.

Ethan came back in the evening so I asked the staff if I could go out. Ethan was my responsible adult! We went to the pub – fantastic! Spoke about normal things and had a really nice evening. Grace joined us. She has been such a support to Ethan and a caring friend for me.

I had two large glasses of wine and was feeling the effects, having no dinner and not having drunk for a while. Dad gave me a lift back to the hospital. I felt slightly unsteady and managed to lock myself out of my room…twice! Oh well, in here, no one bats an eyelid. I think if I drank everyday I'd fit in much better.

Once all had settled on the ward, I had a chat with Adam. He is very nice and helpful and takes time to listen and understand what I'm saying but then it was 1am and my tablets, compounded by alcohol, pretty much knocked me out. As I was getting into my pyjamas, I heard Edward next door. His Chinese take-away had just arrived! He seems to eat them for every meal. Yesterday, he offered me a spicy rib. I declined! He says he phones them up (they know him by name, given his frequency of orders) and tells them he's working on night shift at the hospital as doesn't want to admit to being a patient!

30th January

2007

MUM

Dreadful diarrhoea first thing – felt tired and ill. Had to lie down and then nodded off. Feeble attempt to do some chores.

Tired out again and nodded off watching TV in the evening. What *is* wrong with me?

2008

Nurse Katy came banging on my door at 9am saying to get up for meds. I was fast asleep, oblivious to the morning noises, and opened my sleep filled eyes and said, "I'm awake, can you bring them to me?!" Katy laughed and said I was so lazy! I replied I may have drunk a few glasses of wine last night and it certainly worked as a sleeping draught.

I saw Andrew in the morning. He is a talkative fellow, rather short with a little pot belly. He insists on wearing various Liverpool shirts and loves talking about football. He has been here four weeks now, on a detox programme. Been an alcoholic for years apparently. He looks fifty odd but I guess he is in his forties, lifestyle aging his face. He came up to me beaming, explaining that his wife was visiting today. He said he had asked the staff if he could spend half an hour in his room with "the wife" and accompanied this with an over-exaggerated wink. I tentatively asked if his request was granted. Do I really want to know?! He said they said no. He did appeal though, telling them that he would be quick! He carried on his excitable chatter: he can't wait to get home, the wife will be in for a treat etc. At this juncture, I wheedled my way out of the conversation. I have heard quite enough! I do not wish to be discussing someone else's sex life.

Ethan took me out for dinner. Really lovely evening. We went to an Italian place on the high street – delicious king prawns. I certainly ate better than in here.

Returned to the ward slightly worse for wear again after managing to consume half a bottle of wine with the meal. Result: staff not impressed! Sanctions imposed: I'm no longer allowed out late in the evenings. If I go out, it has to be during the day with someone. Of course, I could always drink then but it holds less appeal and I don't want all outings to be vetoed.

31st January

2007

MUM
Took a long time to get to sleep last night. May have dozed a bit beforehand, but looked at the clock at 2am. My back hurting a lot – in the end took paracetamol – and full of anxiety about the children. Convinced myself that a) Alice would be raped and murdered in Uganda and b) Ethan hadn't been in touch because his essays hadn't passed. Who would have imagined, when embarking on parenthood, that a life-time's anxiety was in store? Must get a grip!

12.30am Decided to telephone Ethan but he was in bed and too half asleep to talk. Anyway, his essays did pass.

2008

Disturbed night, trouble getting off to sleep and then, from 4am onwards, Ann was kicking off. Shouting, swearing, banging doors so I never got back to sleep. I prayed for her instead, and all the poor staff whose patience and composure was really tested.

Otherwise, bit of a boring day. I had my review with Dr. Floyd. I was honest with her: my sleep has improved slightly – 5 or 6 hours without waking (aside from this morning!) but still don't have a desire to live. I am indifferent to life. I'm not actively planning on killing myself but, concurrently, each day is a challenge to get through.

The days have past and now it's a week and a half later but do I feel any different? At times I feel that, if I'm stuck in here any longer, I will start planning my suicide properly, instead of my half-hearted, ill thought through, impulsive reactions. They say suicide is a very decisive action, no going back, but perhaps that is what I need. At the moment, I am dangling in existence, not dead, but not part of life either. I am a spectator in a horrific dream, unable to intervene.

Dr. Floyd said she was going to stop the temazepam and increase the quetiapine. I agreed. This was where I was dishonest. I didn't disclose that, actually, I haven't been taking the quetiapine at all. Instead, I flick the tablets under my tongue, swig some water and then I am signed off. I am getting quite good at this. Not wanting to cause suspicion, I can now even talk with tablets nestled in my mouth, before retreating to my room to spit them into a tissue. Alice, you are rather cunning. This is, perhaps, not a good thing.

Dr. Floyd wasn't happy to send me home yet. She said I could have overnight leave on Saturday and then she will see me again on Monday. If everything is OK, I should be discharged next week sometime. I'm not even sure that going home still holds appeal. In the three hours I'm allowed off, I feel that I don't really want to be at home either. I don't want to be anywhere. I no longer fit in the world. The fleeting moments that I'm at ease are when I am walking, no purpose, alone aside from nature.

All the world is a stage. Our physical bodies are purely puppets, obedient to us, the puppet masters. But my puppet master is dusted with a little darkness. This infiltration adjusting the boundaries. The puppeteer speculates between the real and the unreal, although the unreal, nevertheless, appears to be real. With real real and apparent real (which is real in disguise) the puppet is thrown into chaos. Havoc runs amok in the world which no longer defines the real. Once you have entered the unreal that deceives you as real, there is no return to ordered way of living. You cannot go back to the innocence of a world of rules. I am trapped, unable to escape for, what I think is real, may be unreal in a mask. I can no longer distinguish the true realities from the false. I am in a maze with only dead ends. How do I become myself again? I cannot fathom the difference between the truth and the lies.

Dad didn't come to my review. He had a meeting. I didn't want him there but I felt he should want to be there. His daughter is in hospital and he puts work first. I don't expect anything different though; this was exactly what he did with Mum.

I'm not sure why I am writing in here. Partly, writing may have contributed to me being ill in the first place. I got quite obsessive committing pen to paper when looking after Mum. I couldn't stop. I had to record what happened. I thought otherwise it would be lost. No-one saw what I saw. I felt that, in the midst of time, even my memories would fade. I had to preserve them somehow.

It was several weeks after Mum died that I read her diary of those poorly months. It surprised and comforted me that we wrote about similar things in a similar way. Maisie and I became one. Inseparable yes, but it went deeper than that. I became her voice. I wove my way inside her head and knew by instinct, care, love, devotion, what was required. Our diary was completed and I could write no more. I felt I had abandoned my pen forever but now, it has begun again, my furious scribble, too slow for the rapidity of my thoughts but, perhaps, just tangible to begin to make sense of them. And also, my experience in here and the other patients, have produced highlights which I found sad to lose to the annuls of time.

1ˢᵗ February

2008

Didn't really manage much today. I could have gone for a walk but was too spaced out and distanced from everything. Spent the day writing lots, crazy stuff.

Day was also peppered with seeing various people. Firstly I saw Francis, my social worker whom I like very much. I'm glad about that. Then I had to have an ECG. I also had an OT assessment. The OT asked if I wanted to join in with any of the groups here as I haven't appeared to have participated. Must say, I'm not keen on "current affairs" (reading newspapers), "art therapy" (drawing), "interactive group" (playing board games and cards), "get creative" (more drawing?!). All these I would prefer to do on my own. Lastly, "creative writing", well this perhaps makes me even worse. Compulsion to record things has trapped me again but this is a private activity; I like to be solitary. I show interest in the "walking group" with no intention of going!

At 6pm, Julia, one of Mum's closest friends, comes to pick me up. I did say I could meet her elsewhere. Her daughter has been in this psychiatric unit and I can't imagine this place holds the fondest memories for Julia but, she does come, and drives us both to the gallery where Prue, another dear friend of Mum's, has an art exhibition. Before we go in, I suddenly feel a pang of anxiety. I'm apprehensive about being able to cope, especially with so many strangers. Julia reassures me and says we can leave whenever I want. Prue is delighted that we have come and is her usual buoyant self, enthusiastically explaining her art work. She has done a series of prints, on paper she made herself from beech leaves. She has experimented with various home-made paper. I remember Mum dutifully saving onion skins for another of Prue's projects!

I last about an hour: with lots of new people to meet, it requires such extreme concentration. The effort physically weakens me and I feel my legs transforming into pathetically weak and shaky appendages. I pretend to study a picture but really my mind is flying. My surroundings dissolve into that unfamiliar blur which has become so familiar to me. There is noise, but I can't decipher it. The physical space I am inhabiting suffocates me, the walls close in, thick and dense and I am swallowed into the half life. Present but not inhabiting. The trap of solitude: unable to get out, no-one else allowed in.

Julia drops me home and I walk back to the hospital alone. I need the repetitive nature of walking and the chilling wind to bring me back into the real world, re-inhabit my senses. I hide in my room with cup of tea, shaking and breathing shallowly from the cold but I can feel: I am real.

About 10pm Carrie, my ISS key worker, comes to visit. She says she hasn't forgotten me! It is wonderful to see her. I feel safe. I know her. I trust her. She says I'll be back with the ISS, probably next week, but they will have to be convinced that I am safer. Honestly, am I safer? I don't feel any different. I tell Carrie that I constantly vacillate between contrasting states. I feel bored and lonely but then I need space and no company. I feel claustrophobic contained here but then, let out, I become almost agoraphobic in the outside world, abuzz with people. Occasionally I am overcome with emotion, weeping unrelentingly, but mostly I feel nothing, an empty case. There is no pattern that I can fathom; nothing appears to induce any behaviours. Carrie says I'm a tough cookie. Well, quite! What *is* wrong with me? I promise I'm not just trying to be awkward.

2nd February

2008

I wake before 6am, so drowsy I can't move at first and lie stationary, heavy eyelids closed. I cannot return to my slumber and, now awake, I become irritable from the stillness. I get up and drift in a transient state. A shower doesn't stimulate my weary body, getting dressed is an effort, eating breakfast is slow. The morning is uninspiring as I exchange bed for chair and read various bits of newspapers and magazines, unable to focus sufficiently. At lunch time I am allowed home for 24 hours. I walk, seeking refreshment, but arrive home exhausted.

The length of the day increases my somnolence and I am wrapped in a blanket of depression. I am unable to do anything as my weighted mind runs rampant, draining my resources. My mind is a parasite on my body. It sucks out any goodness and leaves me in a pool of badness, swimming without a hope. I enter the shadow world. The desire to die so forceful. I want to surrender now. I think of hanging but do not have sufficient awareness to think it properly through. Knots which will hold. But my mind doesn't work and I cannot find a single knot.

Too low to die. I think there is such a thing. Dying requires effort and concentration, the two skills I lack when absorbed in the ghastly shadow land. I feel worse at home than I did in hospital. What does that mean? Home induces all my deathly desires. Hospital is only a pause, a time to reflect on my life, which will soon be no more.

3am – gloaming light of the near full moon. I look at myself. I go the wrong way. My image is reversed. How do I exist outside of the mirror? Outside. I walk outside and spy the star of melancholy. I tiptoe the streets of the shadow land. I will vanish in the morning light; I was only an invention of darkness. I do not possess myself. I am a haunted house absolved into a mysterious solitude. I am impenetrable. Sleeping and waking and walking and writing. I am the one person in no-man's land, hovering between life and death, achieving neither. The living features of death upon my mind; the deathly features of living upon my face.

3rd February

2008

Sleep seduces me until 9.30am when Dad appears, telling me he is going out. The morning is spent occupying my body with banal activity: making breakfast, washing up, cleaning and packing clothes, sorting old newspapers to take back with me, having a lingering shower, walking around the garden. This saddens me - our neglected plants missing Mum's tender care.

She was not an avid gardener but restored and maintained its beauty. Now, all is dead. Naked brown twigs and branches prickling the borders, retreating to the soil. No illumination of colour. A ghostly silhouette of my mother's decay.

On closer observation, tiny green shoots emerging from clumpy, rough soil. Earth swallows death and brings forth life. Renewable source. Life does sprout again. But I do not. I remain suspended. When Mum died, I did too. Despairingly, a thread of me got tangled in the trap, coiled to a life which is no longer mine. I am dangling above death's consuming pit.

I walk back to hospital and Katy greets me. She says I am agitated and distanced. We talk. I struggled at home. I was waiting, almost willing the time to move, so I could come back. However, I don't want to be here. I don't want to be at home. There is no place that holds my desires. I do not wish to be anywhere. So, what is the choice? And it's there, weaving its way back. Death. That is the answer. By dying, there is no living left to do.

Dad comes in the evening but has little to say. I don't either and I struggle with the effort of forcing conversation and seeking subjects on which to talk. Words become our enemy.

Dad only stays twenty minutes. He says he is leaving and gives me a perfunctory kiss on the cheek, full of the awkwardness that hinders any of his physical gestures. Contrary to popular opinion, death and illness do not change people. We all remain the same, embedded within our personality. Nothing alters.

In the evening, I say hello to Sophie. She only arrived on Friday and, as I haven't been here, I only caught a glimpse of her.

The first thing Ethan said, when I told him I was in the psychiatric hospital, was, "Yeah, I think a mate of mine is in there". Only Ethan would respond with such a reaction! I thought this young girl may be her. She is a pretty thing, clothes reflecting her age as well as her features. She is wearing tight jeans, long-sleeved detailed top and a checked short jacket. Her hair is long, falling over her shoulders, dyed blonde and obviously straightened. Across her cheek is a deep gash, red contrasting against eyes decorated with make-up. Her neck holds long, thick, white scars, remnants of horrors in the past.

I explain to her that I am Ethan's sister. She attempts a smile but I know that is not what is meant. She looks at me, eye-contact present, but I see through and she is not really there. She does talk but it is almost a neglected speech on her part.

4th February

2008

I saw Greta this morning. I don't think she has been physically very well as has remained in her room the last few days. I know this because she always sits in the same armchair in the lounge, morning till night. Greta is a shuffler, so slow that often I think she has stopped. She has long, dark hair, reaching her waist, but it is straggly and greasy and an unflattering fringe. Her face has a gnarled quality, her mouth puckering. Greta rarely talks. The first few days I was in here I thought she was electively mute. She only emits words (very few) when she is scrounging for a cigarette. She doesn't ask, but demands and then hovers, piercing you with her stare. She stands one step from the door, takes a couple of drags and then throws down an almost untouched cigarette! Perhaps she is trying to give up.

Anyhow, Greta was back, restoring the aesthetics of the lounge. She is always sucking the straw to a carton of build up drink, again so slowly it is almost imperceptible. She is very thin, which isn't concealed by her thick cotton trousers and jumpers. I don't recall ever having seen her actually eat.

This is the pattern: no-one is a normal size. They are either too skinny, probably caused by little nutrition, constant ambling and no sleep, or overweight, resulting from medication, little exercise, two cooked dinners a day and numerous cups of tea with milk and sugar. I suspect, staying here, I will transform into a fat, wobbling lump, exhaustion preventing activity, tablets increasing my bulk.

I have been doing better at eating sensibly these last few months. When Mum died I was less than eight stone and, despite my round face, adopted a gaunt appearance. They weighed me when I came in here – eight and a half stone. People were saying I looked better. But I don't want to gain weight just from medication, renew my erratic eating patterns and result in developing an eating disorder. I think I have quite enough problems to occupy me for the moment.

The lovely Grace surprises me and arrives at the hospital in the evening. She is so sweet and caring. It is very easy to talk to her. We find Sophie (Grace went to the same school) and all chat. Sophie seems less agitated today and willingly participates in the conversation, telling us humorous stories of her various stints in psychiatric units. She has been in and out of hospital pretty much since she left school. Poor thing.

As I write this, Audrey has decided to camp outside my room. She is lying full length in the middle of the corridor, hoodie up, tapping her hands. I say hello. She seems content.

Later, Mum's friend Isobel comes and we sit in the, all too familiar, hospital side room, deceptively-looking comfy chairs which are actually rather hard. We talk, having not seen her for over a week I have to offer a brief summary of events including, of course, the odd anecdote about fellow patients.

Isobel has brought me apples and ginger cake that she made in the morning. The kindness! And she is a terribly good baker. When she leaves, I share the cake with Sophie and we eat and drink tea in the lounge. I then see Phyllis, who looks pretty low. I sit and talk with her. She gouged her face today with a pencil. I give her my last piece of ginger cake as a friendship offering.

The day concludes and, for reasons unknown to me, I feel definitely cheerful. I begin to suspect Aunty Beth is right. I appear to be responding to routine which, in here, is enforced. Institutionalisation can be beneficial but how to transfer that to lonely home life? Leaving here, I fear I will relapse. No-one is around to guide and encourage me. Will I be able to do it myself? Here, I take my tablets at the same times each day, meal times are non-negotiable, people are always around so one is naturally forced to socialise or at least acknowledge their presence. All these basic functions are particularly hit and miss with me when left to my own devices. And then I smile. I remember that, once home, I am in control of me. I can hurt myself whenever I want. I feel positively jolly at the thought.

5th February

2008

Disturbed night, waking frequently for no discernable reason. I see Ann, pacing the corridors, fully clothed. Does she ever sleep? At 4am I go to the staff room, feigning boredom. I am not specifically bored, just unsure as to what to do with myself. I wander back to my room and try and channel my concentrations into a book. I'm reading "Saturday" by Ian McEwan and the medical terminology is frequent and specific. I understand these words. Learning medicine is, initially, grasping a foreign language. Medics have a host of intriguing and complicated long words which have layman's translations.

It makes me feel strange hearing the words again. I was part of a medical world whose conversations were hidden without translation. The safety of the doctors' jargon. But now I have become the patient, instead of unknowing, informed. I am caught between the two sides. Are they compatible? Mental health is a particularly delicate area. Do I know that what I am saying and thinking is right? Or, perhaps more importantly, do my doctors and nurses? The unresolved dilemma.

On this ward, there is a special section for mother and baby which is occupied at the moment. There have been a couple of rare occasions when I've seen them. The baby is a delightful, beautiful creature, wrapped in loose-knit sky-blue blankets. I saw it being pushed passed, cocooned in the pram. The mother, whose name I don't know, is a reserved little thing. She too is pretty and has fair, unblemished skin with a face which I'm sure makes her appear younger than she is. I haven't seen her talk to anyone bar staff. She seems low, withdrawn into herself. I can't imagine being here with a demanding, clinging, tiny person, someone you are responsible for. I feel sad for her.

Dad comes to visit after work and it is nice to see him. We can actually talk: it isn't forced, it isn't punctuated by uncomfortable silences. I feel pleased that he has come. When we say goodbye, he doesn't give me the standard kiss on my cheek but, instead, hugs me. It is full of his stiffness, a telling sign of someone who so rarely engages in physical affection but this means so much more. Dad is really trying.

When Dad leaves we encounter uproar outside. Jess, a young girl on the other ward, has managed to get out of the front door. She throws herself into the car park and runs blindly forward. Nurses launch themselves and she is quickly surrounded. She manages to put up a token struggle but the escapade is over. She is marched back inside, a male nurse flanking either side.

Later, Sophie and I are outside in the walled square of grass. Jess comes and joins us. She knows Sophie from previous multiple admissions. She explains she caught the door as someone was leaving and then just ran for it. She shrugs: "Might as well have a try". Jess has her review on Thursday so decides she needs to behave tomorrow in an attempt to lesson the blow.

Weary evening. This place has a soporific effect on me. Even writing was unusually slow tonight. 9.30pm and I needed space, I needed fresh air, I needed to stretch my aching legs. I found Katy. She was reasonable and I felt probably trusts me to an extent. I said I only wanted to walk around the lake which borders the hospital car park. She allowed me, but no longer than half an hour. I was in my flip flops and, once outside the locked doors, I took them off and padded through the damp long grass. Walking serves a purpose, the repetitive nature helps organise my mind to a degree. It also prevents the restless rocking in my room.

I considered my precarious situation but it was not quite sound. I was watching myself, as you do in a safe dream, but when I delved into its depths, it unravelled into one of those ghastly dreams where you are hunted, trapped inside, unable to get out. Except, this wasn't a dream. My wet, sticky feet brought a sensual experience, physical: this was real. There, the essence of sanity: to know the difference between being in a dream world and being in the waking reality. I struggle when these boundaries bleed into one another. With no clear defining point, I am thrown into a maze of multiplying possibilities and reality is the victim. It gets lost along the way.

6th February

2007

MUM
Terrible night. Awake with back pain and then over-tired. Saw GP in the afternoon. I am to have gastroscopy.

2008

Each day, without fail, I am greeted with my morning text from Aunty Beth, always before breakfast. Her words arrive textspeak and they hold that symbolic power which wills me out of bed to face the daunting day. Aunty Beth offers heart felt sincerities which I grasp to propel me through the hours. My unfailing aunty, a rock in times of distress. How I love her dearly.

Same morning meds routine. I leave it until the last possible moment but they come and get me. I don't want to take the tablets. It is pointless. Nothing has changed; it makes no difference. I feel like refusing but reluctantly agree. I don't want to end up with a needle in my bum! And also, reason gets the better of me. If I take the morning meds, which have absolutely no impact, they will be less likely to suspect my nightly spitting out of other drugs. I'm still almost waiting to be caught. At the moment, I am too devious to be found out.

Isobel picks me up at 1pm and we go to her house and make a birthday cake for Dad. Isobel has all the ingredients laid out ready. She is wonderful. It is successful probably because I have baking guru Isobel to hand! We fill the cake, once cooled, with cream and fresh strawberries.

I carry Dad's, now finished, cake up the road to our house where I'm going to leave it on the kitchen table with a card. I encounter several road maintenance trucks, complete with young men in reflective jackets, wolf whistling at me. They are filling some pot holes with tar and the street is blocked to cars. As I walk through the designated taped off path, I realise one guy is having a pee! His vehicle side-door is open and he has his back half towards me but I am inches away! I hear the loud, splashing of piss hitting the newly surfaced road and can see the fountain pooling on the ground. He turns his face towards me and flashes me a cheeky grin: young boy being caught in the act but actually rather proud of it. I hurry past to get my cake to safety.

In the evening, Kelly from church phones. She is concerned as hasn't seen me for a while. I briefly explain present circumstances. She asks if it is OK to come and see me now. Her Mum has the kids so she is free. What a superb friend. She is so incredible.

Ten minutes later, I find myself enwrapped in Kelly's delightful embrace. I spend over an hour with her, talking about me, talking about her and her children, talking about God. She prays over me and I am literally filled with a seeping warmth. Perhaps it is my so diagnosed "impulsivity" but, Kelly arriving, with only a few minutes' notice, has a calming effect. She makes me smile; she calms my restless energy which manifests as agitated rocking or fist clenching. With no warning, I do not have time to become anxious about her visiting. I do not worry about what I am going to say: it just happens. With less thought, I seem to function more normally, speech is emitted naturally, nothing is forced. I am more like how I used to be. From now on I have decided: no preparation. Everything has to be done immediately. Planning is dangerous territory. Structure is a parasite, feeding off my mind.

Unsure as to what happened tonight. It is tricky to explain. It is very late now. I started getting the sense that I am losing control of my thoughts, I am only a bystander, while they are bustling past. I am frightened. Everything in my head gets worse. I have to do things to make it all OK otherwise someone may get hurt. The bad things might catch someone else. I hit myself, a punishment for all the thoughts I have, irrational, horrible thoughts but what if they are right? I cannot take the risk by asserting logic. They don't play by the laws of science. Bad, dark musings that I don't own but they are there and I shall never, ever understand why. I am despicable. Sleep is not allowed tonight. I must be alert, ready to stand against impending terrors of the dark. Everywhere is a trap. No safe places, Alice: don't get complacent.

There is no rest for the wicked. Who said that? God gives us peace. Was this said in reference to the bible? Was the person a Christian? Or were they like I was before, suspended in ignorance, feeling the truth but not understanding? I understand now but there is still no rest for me. Wickedness is part of my very being. If there is no wickedness, there is no me.

7th February

2007

ALICE

I need to be relieved of the monotony of student past-times. My poor concentration and distractible mind requiring constant input from various sources. Too much of the same and I am bored. They say only boring people get bored. I must be the most boring person in the world. The mental occupation I desire cannot be met all the time, not even for a day. Maybe that's why I love patients. Talking to and asking questions of others, I always find fascinating. Very rarely are you bored when conversing with another human being. No wonder solitude is torture.

Worried about Mum. She is still really quite poorly. I know I told her that pancreatic cancer was the worst possible outcome from her symptoms but that was because Mum likes to be informed. She did brilliantly at her party but that was only one night.

2008

I did actually sleep last night, eventually. They gave me temazepam to calm me down. I awake to the tell tale signs of the night before: biro on my fingers, from furious scribbling's; red, raised grazes, from angry scratching's. I have a shower to rid today of yesterday's demons.

I meet Neil, talkative guy from the other ward. He was brought in on Tuesday night by police, high off amphetamines and cocaine. He's had several suicide attempts, various methods, and currently has a raging drug and alcohol problem. He's on a host of medications, including diazepam to reduce his withdrawal symptoms and calm him. He says he is much less anxious but has an unrelenting energy, so talks at length and hasn't yet slept. He is young, in his twenties, and a skinny bloke. He was brought up in Newcastle. It is so nice to be able to talk to a fellow patient normally.

Last night he caused a bit of a scene – unscrewed a light bulb in his room, smashed it, and had a go at his wrist with the shards. A nurse doing obs found him cutting away. He hadn't gone too deep so was bandaged up and is now on ten minute checks.

There is a new guy in solitary: quite a muscly chap with a fiery spirit by the sounds of it. He was brought in by four armed police officers who restrained him while he was drugged and has been locked up ever since. They will surely be moving him soon; this place isn't really equipped for outrageous types. Everyone here has some element of control, whether they choose to excise that is an area of debate.

Have my review with Dr. Floyd. The time changed so, 10am, knock on the door, I'm still in my pyjamas. I hurriedly pull on a jumper, tugging the sleeves down over the backs of my hands which are red and raw and bleed if I clench my fists. Not a good start, I don't feel I'm giving the best impression!

Dr. Floyd is still unsure as to discharging me. I'm being too honest again and admitting to suicidal ideation. She thinks lithium will help with this but I do not want to take it. She says my mood is lower now, compared with when I came in. Her explanation is that, because I am less anxious (true), the depression is now more pronounced. Before, she feels I was covering up much of my state of mind by buoyant, even manic, chatter, not necessarily purposely but because I didn't know how else to react. My defence mechanism was falsely adopting a cheery persona. Now, my defences lowered, it is more difficult to keep up that front. Dr. Floyd is uncannily accurate. How does she know this when I can't recall actually telling her? She must be very astute.

She changes meds (again!) – increases citalopram, maintains quetiapine and adds a sleeping tablet (name forgotten!) which is an anti-histamine. Hopefully she will find something that will put me to sleep that doesn't involve temazepam – my favourite drug, her least favourite! I am to go on home on Saturday night for two nights' leave, returning Monday for reassessment. I did tell her that I found last weekend tough. Not quite sure that I went into such detail as to say I was desperate to kill myself. Felt I shouldn't elaborate quite that much: I'll be here for ever!

I realise today I have been particularly sociable and spent the majority of my time with people. Chatting to Jess (who hopes to join this ward soon which will be good) and Sophie. The doctors want us all on lithium! They are both funny, in a ranting way, making sarcastic comments about some of the staff and, although I don't agree, they make me laugh. They also relate their past escapades when, at times, they were definitely kick-offs! You have to be amusing when talking of self harm. If not, you result in a self pitying mess which isn't helpful to anyone.

Adam back working today. I talk to him and then have a bit of a whine over the whole lithium thing. He asks me why I am so against it and I forget most of the reasons. I'll have to have blood tests and if they start lithium, I'll be on it for months. I also think it is going to have a limited effect on me. I ask Adam what his opinion is. He is tactical. I can't decide whether he thinks it is a good thing and I should be on lithium or whether he doesn't think I should be on it but is disinclined to contradict Dr. Floyd.

People say writing helps, it is an outlet for expressing emotions, it can induce more order. So, while I am in a relatively stable frame of mind, I will try, no doubt inarticulately, to describe my moments of madness. It starts with unexpected, involuntary trances, moments of disconnection. It progresses. My thoughts have a questionable quality. I can't hold an idea long enough to obtain any sense from it, ideas are too fast, too many to contain. Overwhelming confusion replaces clarity, a profound spinning of every thought imaginable. My mind floats away, despite my efforts to tether it. Control is taken by an unknown entity. It is a petrifying place to be.

Bad things happen. Being prepared to die makes living safe. Without me, life would be more secure. Not being, I could cause no more harm because, this is not me, but I do not know how to become myself again. The only option is death. Then all the badness will cease to be.

On the ward, I saw George in a side room. George is almost like an apparition. He always stays in his room and I only ever pass him on the odd occasion when he is getting meds or some food. He is young, perhaps my age, has a cute face and floppy longish hair. He wears (usually two) shirts with jeans or cords that hang so low I am surprised they do not fall to his ankles. This also means I have seen a good deal of his boxers. He can appear unaware of his surroundings but I have heard him speak and his voice has a high pitched quality, complementing his boyish looks.

Tonight he was with a visitor: by her manner, I assumed she was his mother. She was preparing to leave and wrapped her arms fully round him, encompassing his body with hers, complete protection. She rocked him gently form side to side, offering all-consuming love.

I had paused too long; I was suddenly aware I was staring. I ran to my room, a physical tightening in my stomach. How I dreadfully miss my darling mother. To have her incredible warmth seep through me, to touch her once again, hold her hand in mine, slip into her arms. My ultimate comforter. My life is a desert of despair without her; I desperately long for her.

I closed my eyes, tried to imagine, resurrect her in my mind. I wanted to feel her stroke my forehead, feel her arms across my back as she cuddled me, feel our hands holding but I was unable. The result: I saw Mum in my mind, dead, her body in death, that haunting image still infiltrating my thoughts. I tried to banish that form but it lingered, on the tip of my brain, hovering until it is called upon again. It obscured any other pictures of my mother that may be there; they remained hidden: access denied. I must rid the bad but to do that, you suffocate the source. I am the source, therefore I must die.

Golly, rather lengthy ramblings tonight. Is that wise? The nurses advise that perhaps writing to such extent could be unhelpful for me. Writing is my new devotion but will they stop me; can they? Sent to seclusion, not for uncontrollable rages, but for uncontrollable pen usage! Alice, you are becoming paranoid.

At night time meds I had an attack of conscience. Stopping quetiapine was perhaps not my best idea. I take it.

8th February

2008

Disturbing night. I awoke thinking Mum was alive. The new sleeping tablet gave me a lengthy rest but I endured distressing dreams. I was with Mum. I could see her; I could touch her. We were both crying. She asked why I was in hospital. I said I wanted to die. She told me it was OK, she was here now and stroked my hair with such loving tenderness. She clasped my hands and I told her not to worry about me. I said everything would be alright now because she will make me better. Mum was her wonderful self. She was going to take me home, no more hospital, and look after me. Her astounding care was the best medicine. I felt at one with myself, with life.

The illusion was shattered. The nurses didn't believe me. They said Mum was dead but she wasn't, she was here, with me. I wanted to show them my fabulous mother, parade her in front of all, but they didn't understand, they couldn't see. Mum was only mine.

All morning I clung to the knowledge that I had been with Mum. However illogical, however non-sensical, when I go home at the weekend, Mum is going to be there, waiting eagerly for my return. She delights in me coming back when I have been away. I want tomorrow to come today. I wish to see my darling mother now. Alice, patience is a virtue, bide your time.

Katy came to talk to me. She listened and let me explain but it was a replica of last night, just like they told me, she knows my Mum is dead. I don't mind, I can keep my incredible secret to myself. No-one else could possibly share my exquisite joy.

Alice in Wonderland, that is what they call me. This place is a wonderland; it is real but it is a fake way of living. Here is a bubble, an anomaly in time, secluded from the real world but maintaining nebulous links with what happens on the outside. We are all cocooned in a pretend life, united by the terrors we all harbour.

I speak to Mog on the phone late afternoon. We talk for ages. She knows what to say and helps me think properly. I sent her a crazy text on Wednesday night when consumed with badness. She tells me it won't always be like this and she truly believes, with the right help, I will get better. She asks, do I believe this too? I'm unsure. I am unable to see how improvements will occur and, fundamentally, I don't seem to mind being like this. Granted, it isn't pleasant, but I don't possess any motivation to actually live my life. I am indifferent to pleasure and indifferent to pain. These are contradictory emotions, but not quite, and it's the degree of overlap that they possess which I need to comprehend.

I have no anger. There is nothing there. How easy it is to forgive, but always with one exception: malice towards myself doesn't cease, it harbours inside. Mog tells me I do not need to hurt myself; hang in there. I must concentrate on calming down, stilling the thoughts, praying for rest.

She asks me about my writing. She thinks lengthy prose on the badness will be detrimental – it might encourage me to dwell upon it all. Instead, limit myself to only one page, no more; impose restrictions, take control Alice, it will benefit you. I don't think I'm strong enough to give this up yet; it is my thread of sanity, once on paper, it becomes more real. Mog asks me to incorporate some positives and write down my ideas (which must be brief – one page limit!) on the following: firstly, I must think of a time when I felt really full of life and enjoyed being alive; secondly, what did that feel like?

I promise to reflect on what she has said, and I shall, the challenge is to transfer that to paper. Words are abundant in times of distress but positive writing is on a different spectrum. I tell Mog I don't solely write bad stuff; I describe other patients here too. Mog is dubious that any of this is helping me to move forward. She is right. Putting together a group of suicidal, self-harming, mentally ill, emotionally deranged patients probably worsens the matter. Amongst patients, we exchange stories of drastic measures taken and we can sympathise but all that happens is another dimension is added to our ever-circulating ideas. It encourages more thought on suicide, adds a different perspective, viewed from another angle, for the possibilities are infinite.

Compulsive behaviours and obsessions are intensified under claustrophobic routine. Some write and draw but does this dampen my resolve or provoke me to write more? I can talk to other patients, rationally, reasonably, sensibly, ask them questions, support their struggle, gently probe into their head, show understanding of their demons, have some insight, encourage when they are having a good day, perhaps discuss future plans, I know all about the drugs. The question I ponder, is this real? Do I transform into a fake person, functioning as I know how but not feeling engaged. For, behind this façade, this robust exterior is a smouldering furnace of rampaging badness, desperately contained by my fighting but weary body. I never know when the darkness will consume me, the mask taken away. It happens sometimes, but I must always be alone, protect others from my plight.

In some respects, this ward has similarities with a prison. Fair enough, a particularly nice prison, with comfortable beds and chairs, but our restriction is the same. Mostly confined to our individual rooms, dinning room open for the half hour allocated to each meal, square of grass our fresh air quota, lights out at 11pm, set times for everything. Patients become your comrades.

Put a group of drug dealers in prison and they form more connections, better resources. Cigarettes become currency. They are exchanged for everything. Confiscated razors, pens, lighters, phone chargers can be obtained because, thrust together, it automatically becomes fight against the authority. Us versus them. I have been offered ecstasy, cocaine, cannabis. No drugs screening for me here, no searching of visitors. When the ease is apparent, it is harder to resist but, perhaps it is the simplicity that thwarts us: we demand more of a challenge, it injects the dull, dreary, depressing days with a fraction of excitement.

I curl into bed, enduring the night sweats, hideous dreams, the wild lurching's of my mind but satisfied in the knowledge that Mum will appear tomorrow, scoop me in her arms and rescue me from the sleeping and waking nightmares.

9th February

2008

This morning, Ann is sporting her leggings (as always) but this time with fluffy pink bed socks and running trainers. She has on a hideous, round-neck, black jumper with ghastly gold detail. She's looking cross. Phyllis is having a bad day, slowly approaching staff, then standing in front of them, shifting her weight from one foot to the other and saying, in her drawn out way, "I want to hit you!". The staff remain cheerful and respond with such phrases as, "You say the nicest things, Phyllis".

I gather together my few belongings, haphazardly shove them in my rucksack and collect my meds, ensuring they have given me promethazine – my new sleeping tablet which is successfully committing me to hours of sleep. I walk home without a coat, sunshine warming my face, rucksack bouncing along behind me.

Writing has lost its appeal now at home. I have leave until Monday, if I look after myself and don't do anything too drastic, I will be discharged on Thursday.

I got home and Mum wasn't there. Had to keep occupied so I didn't get too anxious waiting. I made an elaborate salad, but then had little appetite. I washed all my clothes. I went for a walk in the park. I had a hot shower and washed and dried my hair. I put fresh clothes on. I phoned Granny as hadn't spoken to her whilst being in hospital. Aunty Beth phoned me. It got dark. Mummy, where are you? I have Boggle ready and a bottle of wine.

It got late and, overtaken by my drooping eyelids, I transferred from chair to bed and fell into a drunken, medicine filled sleep.

10th February

2007

MUM

Awoke in the night after only a short sleep, and then again, feeling dreadfully sick. Diarrhoea too. Really did feel terribly ill. Spent the entire day in bed, with constant trips to the bathroom and the odd sip of water. Simply dreadful.

2008

I get up groggy, but satisfied in the knowledge that I had six and a half hours sleep, without waking once. Lucy, my old school friend, is home for the day and she suggests walking her grandmother's dogs. Lucy picks me up, I have no idea if I should be driving or not but, as Lucy offered, perhaps that is the wisest decision. We walk through the woods. I don't think anyone realises how hard I find being in company because I talk without ceasing. I keep up a front of inconsequential chatter; it quietens my inner monologue. I jump off tree stumps, I throw sticks for the dogs, I rub their thick hair and encourage their playful nature: hectic activity to cover up my fear: my duel with death.

Lucy is patient with me and listens, asking the right questions, allowing me to witter on, but it is different, our hyperactive natures were intensified by being with each other, the games we made up were exciting and always reduced us to fits of giggles but I no longer find anything funny. I can omit a pretend laugh, show a fake smile, but none of it is real, it is just a learned response.

I get home and Holly arrives, ready to go out for Sunday lunch, in honour of Dad's birthday. We walk along the sea front; it is a glorious day. The sky is without a cloud and the sun sprinkles the sea with rays of light which the water returns, glittering silver, undulating with the gentle waves.

Dad chooses to eat in the fish restaurant, basic wooden tables and chairs, crammed in as much as possible, a lingering smell of freshly caught fish, staff in air-tex t-shirts, and always busy. We have to queue for almost half an hour but the food is so delicious it is definitely worth the wait. Standing queuing, the conversation between the three of us is disjointed, broken by letting other people pass, waiters handing us menus and obtaining drinks. I begin to feel claustrophobic and the fellow customers seem to get bigger and closer, the noise blurring into indistinguishable sounds. Holly and Dad talk but I am not listening: a murky, mental narrative breaks in. I am unsurprised by this. Confronted with what is now a frequent occurrence, I have become adept at covering my tracks, continuing to nod and force my clamped lips into a smile, until the moment passes and I am dispatched, once again, into the real world.

A table is pointed out to us and we squeeze round, navigating a push chair. Dad has his favourite, mussels, and Holly and I delve into the seafood platter, a treasure trove, all washed down with crusty white bread and butter. The food is plentiful and, despite best attempts, we are defeated so they very kindly wrap the left overs (a common occurrence as they also do fish to take away). I have another tasty treat for tomorrow.

Once home, I relish the quiet and sip a cup of coffee and I notice the birthday cake I baked for Dad, sitting on the side board. It contains fresh cream and should be in the fridge. Opening the cake tin, I find the inevitable culprit: the beginnings of green grey mould, spattered on exposed sides where several slices have already been removed. I salvage what I can of the sponge, crumble it in my fingers and take it into the garden. I sprinkle the low walls, next to the little tin ornament which Mum fills with water as a drink for the birds: they now have dinner too.

Throwing the remains on the grass, I feel my mouldy cake somehow symbolises my relationship with Dad, although I can't quite identify the comparison exactly: the metaphor eludes me. I dismiss the thought. Fruits of my labour not completely wasted, we have many satisfied birds, greedily pecking away.

In the evening, the house turns on me, it interchanges at various intervals: Jekyl and Hyde. It is a place of refuge, safety, beauty, an indulgence of Mum's personality, but then the evil twin takes charge, the house becomes a venomous emanation of all the dark badness that surrounds me. Dad seems unaware of the dynamics that this house possesses: he is content with his tea and chocolate biscuits, engrossed in rugby on the television.

At night, I do what Mog says, I keep the routine: pyjamas on, take tablets, clean teeth, in bed with a novel, all before midnight, but I am unsettled and anxious. I open the door of Dad's bedroom a fraction to see if Mum is there. Her side of the bed is vacant; Dad is fast asleep, lying, as always, on his back.

I am unprotected – I'm not secure without Mum - and this is where the waking nightmare begins. I see Mum in her bed: dead, naked, rigid. I must touch her, my outstretched hand, but my arm recoils in alarm as I hear Mum calling for me, "Ali, Ali". I race downstairs and burst into the front room but all is dark and empty. I scamper into the kitchen: nothing. The back room: nothing. I go into the garden, frost freezing my feet: I am real, I can feel, but nothing. Perhaps she was upstairs: I misheard. And so I search, the entire house, each room twice. Mummy, where are you? You were calling me, you needed me. I'm here. Please Mummy, don't leave me now. I peer around Dad's bedroom door that I left ajar. Dad's position remains unaltered. Dead Mum has gone.

11th February

2007

MUM

A largely sleepless night. Such short snatches. A lot of back pain. This morning the nausea has just about gone but I feel very tired and thin and washed out and convinced I have cancer which has already spread to my bones.

2008

I make everything take twice as long this morning. I linger in the shower, appreciating the pounding jet of water dousing my back, I turn the water as hot and as fast as I can bear, then slip out. I am too warm now so I remain naked, padding throughout the house, enjoying the sensation of my feet skimming the carpets.

My dripping hair eventually shivers me so I wave the hair dryer all over my body, then half heartedly get dressed, reaching for the nearest clean clothes. Downstairs, I make a breakfast of muesli, fresh fruit and yoghurt. I make a cafétiere of fresh coffee, fully intending to drink the whole pot. I switch on the radio, sprawl the newspapers across the table and relax, savouring each mouthful, reading the day's news.

All too soon, my freedom is up. I am back in hospital but not in the same room. Last night, Phyllis became, by the sounds of it, extremely frustrated. She started kicking off which resulted in her smashing the sink in her room. She was transferred to the room I was in as it is near the nurses' office. Bar clothes, all her belongings have been confiscated. This means I am now in Phyllis's old room. Despite the defunct sink, I much prefer it. I have two windows, a desk and it is far quieter because it is at the end of the corridor. I am quite happy in my new digs.

Another warm day so I join Sophie and Jess sitting outside. They update me on the weekend's events which doesn't take long. "What have you been up to today?" isn't a question that is asked around here because the answer is always, "Nothing much". There is a new guy who they say is really creepy. I had met him briefly; he was trying to get fags off me. He has an extremely penetrating stare and latches on, following you. He also has an unfortunate resemblance to Snape from Harry Potter: slicked back greasy hair and a particularly hooked nose. He was another patient who thought I was staff.

In some ways I think I am the most dangerous person in here. To the observer, I am perfectly normal, I have an impenetrable mask that descends as soon as I am with company. I can exchange pleasantries, am even sometimes likable, but nothing is real. Automated response. My only means of defence. It is also what will eventually kill me as no-one can get in. This is their most controlling power over me, their ability to hide within. If they were exposed, then perhaps change could be initiated but they remain concealed, destroying me from the inside. I wonder if I am going to go mad, or whether even this escape is denied me.

Sophie has a line of criss cross stitches on the side of her throat, now bandage free. Her whole neck is a patchwork of scars, white jagged skin from clavicles to jaw bones. I bet she doesn't even feel the incision anymore. Neil has been hacking at his wrists, five stitches and an afternoon in A+E: well, change of scenery at least, as has dear Jess.

Later, Miriam joins us. When she was admitted a week ago, she was on Level 3 obs. This means a member of staff with you 24 hours a day, even watching you sleep. I think this alone would send me crazy! I was on Level 2 obs (six checks an hour) when I first came in and that was bad enough. Miriam is on incredible quantities of medication taken throughout the day. Talking to her, you wouldn't know. Her anxiety manifests in leg shaking: a knee bounces up and down when she is sitting but she is good to chat to. Tomorrow she is having her first ECT treatment – ten sessions, twice a week - so she is resigned to the fact that she will be here for at least another five weeks. I would be nervous.

The afternoon brings another patient onto the ward, restrained by police officers, under a 136 section, and put in seclusion. Apparently she jumped out of a car on the A12. She isn't here long and is transferred to another unit shortly afterwards.

With all the patients here, I do ponder what their lives are like on the outside, what I would see if I encountered them on the street, how they interact with husbands, wives, children, how everything is different from this regimental way of living. It is hard to visualise.

Coming back here, I should be devastated. I haven't seen Mum at home but, strangely, I don't feel this. Here is a place where Mum doesn't belong. It is too far removed from our conjoined relationship. Mum does not feature in my hospital wonderland. She is dead to me in here. She can't know anything. She can't feel anything. I can't feel anything either, but I'm not dead.

12th February

2007

MUM

A miserable day, pouring with rain. Prue coming to take me to the hospital for my gastroscopy appointment at 4pm. Feeling totally washed out, again after a night of very little sleep owing to back pain.

Not too much waiting around after all. A lovely nurse, who had had the procedure herself, gave really helpful advice – and gave me confidence to try without sedation. I did just as she said – kept my eyes shut and concentrated on my breathing. In the event, although not a pleasant experience, not too bad, all things considered. At least I didn't panic and start pulling out the tube! The doctor couldn't see anything amiss but biopsies taken to look for bacterial infection. Back to square one then?

I came back and looked up the symptoms in my doctor's book and decided it was cancer of the pancreas! Just as Alice had said at Christmas. Spent most of the evening on the phone – kind enquiries from Alice and Beth.

Human frailty and mortality: how do we ever get through life in possession of knowledge of the inevitable?

2008

This morning, waiting for meds, I pass Toby masturbating in the corridor. Grim! Hand down trousers, oblivious to all else. I've never spoken to Toby. He talks a lot, more of a mutter, but to people only he can see. I think he experiences vivid hallucinations.

Although, on second thoughts, perhaps some of the other patients can see his conversation buddies: I certainly can't. He is unable to sit still, always jiggling his legs, balls of his feet on the floor, knees knocking side to side, up and down. I hate to think what lurks beneath his clothes now!

Ethan phones me while he's on the bus – he's coming home! Got a reading week and isn't very well so decided to return. He sounds very guttural on the phone and is generally feeling sorry for himself, excesses from the weekend not helping matters. It will be great to see him. I must remember to help him with his latest essays which, he keeps reiterating, he is starting early, although no work has materialised yet. I'm trying to avoid the trauma of his last deadline – him fretting, with hours to go and making himself ill from the ordeal! Last minute with Ethan means exactly that!

In my allocated two hours leave, I walk home fast so my legs burn. Ethan arrives after me and there is time for a brief exchange. His stomach is sore (as well as his cold symptoms) which is an ongoing, remitting problem, diagnosed by Ethan as irritable bowel syndrome. He could be right. He sees the backs of my hands: now a collection of raised, ugly, brown scabs. I have no desire to lie, so I tell him the truth. If he didn't think I was mad before, he certainly will now. Exchange injury for injury. Ethan shows me his head. On Saturday night, intoxicated with drugs and alcohol (his recollection is a little hazy), he ended up in a fight and someone smashed his head against a wall. The skin must have been broken because the morning revealed matted hair and t-shirt blood-stained. He asks me, Dr. Alice, to take a look. Amongst his hair, I find the cut, knitting together, and palpate a sizable lump. I reassure him it's fine – well, if he had an extradural haematoma surely he would have collapsed by now?! Cognitively, he is normal and most probably better than me. Who am I to be offering reassurance?

We depart, Ethan to crash on the sofa in front of TV, me hurriedly walking as I shall now be late back. I'm glad he's home; I'll see him properly tomorrow. Journeying back to the hospital is a feat. I am gradually aware of a nagging pain spreading horizontally across my lower back. It intensifies, as if a vice is slowly tightening. Each hip swing causes a painful click, which isn't audible but radiates throughout my body so I almost believe I can hear it. Up the hill, destination in sight, my legs develop pins and needles, running down towards my feet in bursts of electrical energy.

I reach the sanctuary of my room and carefully lie down. I am clammy and my skin is red, heart heaving, but goose bumps grow and I cannot fathom whether I am hot or cold. My back has that quality which can't quite be described as pain, rather a prolonging ache which worsens on movement. My legs shiver uncontrollably, not exaggerated movements but more akin to repeated fasciculations. I stare at the dirty ceiling, body jiggling away, and am swept into a half-conscious state, too exhausted for thought but not sufficiently sedated for sleep.

My mind eventually seeps back, awareness of the room apparent. Legs are stationary now but I am too weary to lift my head. Utter exhaustion and I cannot pin point the trigger. I have walked most days, hospital life is mostly tedious, punctuated with eventful handfuls, but at a linear rate. My physical form has given up, demanded a break, forced a pause. There is no choice; I am overridden. A stark reminder of how little control I possess, even blinking requires effort.

I compose myself and tentatively sit up, closing my eyes while the dizziness fades. Perhaps fresh air will rejuvenate some power of mine, recapture that possession. I edge along the corridor, but my legs are overcome with what is accurately described as "jelly", I can place my feet, one in front of the other, but my legs have their own, additional, rippling amplitude. I change my mind: walking is not beneficial. I lie in silence, back flat on the bed, no pillow, and ease my heels towards my bottom, knees bent.

Hours later, time for night time meds. I make it to the meds room, just, clinging to the rail as I feel I am in that pre-fainting stage, abandoning myself to a wave of dissociation. Nadia checks my blood pressure (it's normal) and gives me ibuprofen. I sway into my room and clumsily slide into bed, lacking any ability to read.

I haven't seen Sophie today, I ponder if she has run away, but feel sleep quickly, gently, swallow me up whole.

13th February

2007

MUM

Appointment with Dr. Pearce in the morning. Apparently the letter from the hospital says I have gastritis – which isn't saying anything very much! Agreed that a blood test for pancreas might be a good idea – and entered it on screen as "Cancer Referral Form". Help! Results tomorrow.

2008

Although I slept well, I wake with horrific recollections of disturbing nightmares. My entire body is damp, pyjamas sticking to me but chilly from the moist sweat. Mum was desperately poorly; I was tending to her at home but then she went missing. She had wondered off, out of the house and I was fraught with fear. Family were telling me not to worry, she'll come back but I couldn't convey to them how ill she was; they thought it was histrionics on my part. I ran into the darkness and launched myself on strangers, mistaking them for Mum. They were all wearing long black clothes, with their backs to me. None of them were Mum, just mute woman with faces contorted into querying looks. I ran and ran, desperation increasing to ever higher levels, escalating beyond all proportion. I was made acutely aware that I was sprinting through a wood; I was naked and the brambles were cutting me, like fingers with sharpened nails, clawing through my skin. It was cold and dark and raining and I was becoming hysterical – shouting, screaming for Mum through loud, unhindered sobs: mounting distress.

Then I was transported, as happens in dreams, back home. No-one believed me. They dismissed my claims. I was told off for such behaviour. Mum was dead, Alice. I ran away again, still desperately searching for my darling Mum. I felt confused and lonely and utterly bereft. No-one believed me but my Mum would. She would hug me and all would be restored.

I go to breakfast, with no desire to eat, and make myself strong, black coffee. The stuff they give you here is all decaf but my mouth demands the rich, bitter flavour. I sit next to Dawn. She is a tiny woman with girlish features and a cute button nose. Her forehead is littered with scars and, above her right eyebrow, is a thick, white bandage concealing her latest cut. She has only been here a few days and I haven't spoken to her yet.

In the afternoons and evenings, Dawn sits in the lounge, feet dangling as her legs are too short for the large arm chairs. She is wrapped in her duvet with a padded tray resting on her lap. She has an array of arts and crafts materials neatly arranged beside her and she produces, in painstaking detail, cards for a variety of occasions. I ask her about these and her face becomes animated as she eagerly explains to me all her artistic skills.

In my room, gathering towel and toiletries for a shower, I hear an ominous crashing sound. I venture outside to investigate. Audrey has smashed a window. She is such an unassuming woman, gentle, polite with a softening grin; it is hard to imagine her being so forceful. However, she does enjoy dismantling items and yesterday, did believe she was the Terminator! Audrey was admitted because she dragged all her furniture outside into the yard and told people to help themselves as she no longer wanted it – psych team got anxious so pulled her in here!

The debris is quickly swept away and the window taped up as, for any one of us, a large shard of glass is too great a temptation.

I catch up with Sophie. She regales me with yesterday's adventures. She was on a few hours leave (I say was, don't think she will be anymore!) and had gone back to her flat where she smoked and drank the day away. The police finally picked her up during the night and kept her in a cell until she was sufficiently sober to be brought back here. She remained in bed most of the morning, nursing a hangover, then emerged in a jumper and a pair of rather slinky, too short, black acrylic trousers. When she came back to the ward, she was wearing a mini skirt so these trousers were produced for her! Of course, I teased her.

Sophie's feet and ankles became cold so she borrowed a pair of thick, cream socks and pulled them up high. As we concluded, no-one (including ourselves) really minds about your clothing. I have lived in similar outfits everyday. Who cares if they are dirty?! They just become inanimate articles to be tugged on in the morning and peeled off at night.

Outside I talk with Mirium and Amy. Mirium's ECT went OK, aside from mild headaches post-procedure, so she is calmer about her weekly impending ordeal. Amy is probably in her early thirties and has beautifully soft skin. She is voluptuous with large, round breasts which are emphasised by spaghetti strapped vest tops. Her hair is voluminous: wavy curls dyed a soft auburn similar to Mum's henna days. Although, Amy assures me, she is most likely to get bored as, in the last several years, her hair has changed from black to pink to blonde to red. Amy is lovely. She was admitted last week in a heightened state and was a kick-off, although not aggressively so, more the cross toddler type leading into grumpy teenager mode. She is bipolar and fine once stabilised on meds but then she decides she no longer requires the tablets so stops taking them, has a relapse and ends up back in here. Vicious circle.

Went home for an hour or so this afternoon. Ethan sprawled on the sofa, heaving himself up to go to the toilet every fifteen minutes: jippy tummy. I plied him with Lucozade and yoghurt, then settled in the arm chair and we talked about his latest endeavours in London, his plans to move into a new flat, get a job, spend his summer abroad. He never mentions my predicament and I am exceedingly grateful. I do not wish to discuss my suicidal tendencies.

I don't want to leave, I love our aimless chatter, and I want to look after him, mother him, fetch him drinks, tempt him with morsels to eat, fill a hot water bottle, but I am resigned to the fact that I must return, I don't wish to scupper my chances tomorrow at my review. Hopefully I shall be home for good.

The evening ticks by at an even, mediocre pace. Joanne passes onto the ward, going to the staff office. She stops and says hello. I smile and ask how her weekend was, say I'll hopefully be back with ISS tomorrow (although, will they be pleased? I feel I am a particularly awkward patient!), small talk but I like it and Joanne is ever so endearing. Then I feel the piercing stares of patients sitting in the lounge. I am being jovial with the other side, fraternizing with the enemy. Their looks of evil intent deter me and I make my excuses and leave.

I feel I am split between the two opposing sides. I am a patient, they are my peers, but I am also staff: I have worked with professionals like these before. Torn priorities I cannot remedy for I wish to be pleasant to all. Sophie, I'm sure for her own reasons, demonstrates a particularly stark contrast. She is happy to chat away, retelling stories, laugh about daft anecdotes, get angry with certain things, ask questions when she is with us, her friends in this compact bubble, but, with staff, she is monosyllabic, offering only grunts, or ignores them outright and walks away. I wonder if they will ever know what she is really like, really feeling. I fear they will never discover her hidden secrets.

Starfish

Does knowledge mean help? Everyone tells me to talk but I have yet to be honest, lay my life down, and display it fully to anyone. Perhaps I will discover the answer when I do. But will this yield results? Why? I wonder if anyone in the world ever knows why. It seems to me that people pretend to know why when really they don't know themselves.

Outside descends a think fog, bringing with it a sharp bite of cold. The hospital chimney stacks are still stretching to the sky but their outline is blurred and dusty. Jess and I sit on the bench alone in the garden. I tell her about Mum. I am not sure why but Jess has an open, unsearching nature and does not pry, only listens when I want to talk. She talks to me too. Her Dad died eleven years ago when she was fifteen. I say I still believe that my Mum is going to come back, just appear, waltz in and rescue me from this mess. Jess says she has the same conviction with her Dad – he will arrive and everything will be OK. We are either mad together or grieving together, either way in union. A bond is formed and that is a comfort. Jess really has been my saving grace in here.

I am glad because Jess has been moved over to our ward tonight. We discuss our nightmares, not looking for understanding but more as an outlet, a sounding post for each other. Jess has collections of art materials in messy piles that occupy her bed and desk and floor. She has photographs and a soft toy. I make the stark comparison to my bedroom: the floors are bare, the cupboards empty. A couple of plastic bags are wrapped up on the window sill. My desk balances five small notebooks of my scribbling's and yesterday's newspaper. That is all.

The day I arrived, I was determined that I was only staying a few days, feeling outraged that it could be any longer. I had the bare minimum of belongings which would require thirty seconds to gather up. I kept that hope alive through being minimalistic. I was drowning in an expanse of magnolia (choice paintwork for this place). I could not include any offerings from my life, for here I did not belong. It had to be kept separate. Another time, another world, another me. Each has their coping mechanisms, mine is total detachment.

Tonight, just before I was bed bound, Jess said to me, "I know it would be great if you are let out tomorrow an' all but I kinda hope you stay. You are the one who is keeping me sane in here". Jess is such a sweetie and I am truly touched and almost sad to be leaving her behind. Perhaps I will miss the atmosphere this place induces. And Jess is a friend I want to keep. I wish I could bundle her up and take her with me.

Much later, ward in minimum lighting, me devouring my novel as feeling wide awake, Jess sneaks into my room. We draw the curtain across the door window and sit cross legged on my bed, talking in muted tones. You aren't allowed in each other's rooms. Earlier in the day, she had overheard a staff member telling another one the key code to upstairs. The first floor holds the doctors' offices and all our, no doubt lengthy, notes and care plans and goodness knows what else. We think we have the last three digits – 553 – so all it needs is trying each number, 0-9, as a prefix. We decided night time was the best for this. The door is down a short corridor, opposite the pay phone, so I stand watch while Jess enters the numbers. Several attempts later, access granted! 7553. We don't open the door but leg it, the staff shall be doing checks soon, don't want to arouse suspicion.

Slightly breathless and back in my room (Jess in her's), I feel giddy: giggling, naughty school girl. We have no desire to peruse the guarded paperwork of upstairs, it is the excitement of the chase. Breaking rules can be, if fleetingly, exhilarating. It proves we can still experience heightened feelings, we aren't a flatline of emotions. Confidential files, restricted areas all hold that window. For now, we shall bide our time, savour the moment and wait until an adventure upstairs is required.

14th February

2007

MUM

Tired as usual. Slept better last night – back pain at least reduced with paracetamol and codeine – but still woke several times and didn't get many hours sleep. Half-hearted attempt to do some ironing in the morning – ended up watching day-time TV!

I telephoned the surgery for results. Normal! Relieved not to have cancer of the pancreas [!]. On the other hand, nothing resolved and beginning to think I am a headcase!

Watched a DVD in the evening. Was a complete load of rubbish! Can't wait to get well, find some energy and get my life back on track.

2008

Starfish

Up early, distracting myself before my review. I sit outside with Jess. I tidy my room, bare belongings fit into my rucksack: a condensed existence. My review is 10.30am, no Dr. Floyd, her registrar instead. Very brief, not much is discussed, he doesn't ask about my suicidal thoughts. I say that I was fine at home last time and he grants me weekend leave. I barter and ask to go home today; he agrees. Four days leave, not required to return until Monday.

I have to wait for a couple of hours for the pharmacy to dispense my meds. I read a magazine full of celebrity gossip which doesn't capture my attention and bores me. I find Jess, exchange our phone numbers and promise to bring her some goodies back with me. Room empty, signed out, I walk home.

Ethan is still poorly, heavily coughing, GP diagnosed chest infection so he is now on a course of antibiotics. He is supine on the sofa. I make us both tea and sit beside him, soft chatter between us has a calming effect and I relax slightly, allowing myself to sink into the armchair.

Tea finished, Ethan drifting into a doze, lulled by television, I go upstairs to my bedroom. Here, I am busy. In a fairly organised manner, I tidy. I produce a bag of washing, bag of rubbish, pile of waste paper for recycling, dirty cups. My carpet is almost clear from clutter, bar the ordered stack of various paperwork I have yet to turn my attentions to. My room still feels over-crowded, areas where, all too easily, phantoms can hide. Systematically, I empty my wardrobe and chest of draws. Ruthlessly, I discard the clothes which no longer have a place. A bin liner is filled, charity shop awaits. I kept some of Mum's garments, convincing myself I would wear them, but most I haven't touched. They must go as well.

My room is purged, the washing machine is on, the cups are drying on the draining board, my rubbish is in the bin. A clean, orderly atmosphere.

I speak to Aunty Beth in the evening as usual. I voice my apprehensions about the family get together in Lincolnshire on Saturday. I would have to be OK for the entire weekend, no slips allowed, no lapses in control over the darkness within, nothing could escape. My guard would need to stay strong throughout, is it up to the challenge? Aunty Beth is wonderful and I feel the tug, a duel between the safety of my aunty, a welcoming presence, and the knowledge of the fight I would have to endure if I go.

Aunty Beth asks me how I am to be home. I say nice. More lies. When I hang up, I ponder what my actual feelings are. It is an uneasy sensation, a floating of my body throughout the rooms, I am unsure as to what to do with myself, what I should be doing, and flitter. Writing anchors my mind and body, they are united, if briefly, the enormous mental energy becomes partly real, physical once produced in written form.

The evening brings a ghastly aura which suffocates my entire being. I am sucked into a treacherous place. I fling myself into the darkness and walk with quick, short steps, almost running but not quite, willing the vast expanse of air to dilute my horrific, foggy surroundings of the badness I exude. I wish the wind to suck some away, dispel the burden. My own mortality is again questioned and, in order to experience safety, I need the knowledge that I can commit myself to the grave.

I go home and spread the tablets across my bed, methodically arranging them in pairs: citalopram, zopiclone, temazepam, quetiapine. All even numbers. Even with the packet of paracetamol and some ibuprofen downstairs, this is not enough. I question whether I would even lose consciousness, necessary if I were to conceal myself in the comforting darkness of the woods and curl into the fallen leaves, waiting for hypothermia to soak me up.

I hear Ethan. I know I cannot do anything too drastic when he is here. It wouldn't be fair. Ignorance, even in part, is blissful. I make him a Lemsip, engage in non-committal chatter, then say goodnight. I maintain my routine, all too aware that insomnia encourages the terrors. I read my latest novel, my mind succumbing to a false sense of security. I hear Dad come home: the recognisable engine, slowly up the incline, reversing into the drive, the car door shuts, the click of the automatic lock, key turning in the front door, shoes wiped on the mat. He knows I am home and he surely knows I am still awake, my bedroom light is on which is visible from the street and, once upstairs where slithers of illumination strike across the darkened landing, through the slits between door frame and door – an imperfect fit, Edwardian structure, not quite flush surfaces.

Dad doesn't come up to see me, welcome me back. I hear him go to the bathroom and then to bed. I realise he is tired, it is late for him, and I am perhaps unfairly comparing him to Mum who would always make such an effort when I came home, especially if I had been in hospital.

I rebuke myself. I am also at fault. I wasn't waiting for his return, eager, downstairs, listening out for his car. He went out for a drink with colleagues instead of coming to see me. I try and dispel this unhelpful notion, prop myself against my enormous cushion (made from the material of curtains I have had since I was a child) and become absorbed into the fantasy world that books invite you to indulge in.

They are here tonight. I have too much insight. Knowledge can become the enemy. I can hear them; I can see them. Never clearly enough for certainty. Little shapes dance like hands playing shadows on the wall. They twist, merge, form larger images. There are the voices but they are never concise. Not logical sentences but snatches of phrases that I must piece together, unravel the puzzle. Does that make it real because I know what they are doing or does that make it unreal because I can't see? I can analyse myself almost too well, but to what means? Knowledge isn't power. They gained control long ago. Knowledge is fear.

The more I delve into the shadow world, the more scared I become, but, I must not be afraid. I feel no pain. That sensation fled long ago. No, the destructive force of fear. Courage, Alice, be courageous. But this dissolves when in confrontation with them. For courageous or cowardess, all is meaningless. Reduced to nothing, neither is beneficial.

15th February

2008

I have to see ISS in the morning. Nice guy, called Bernard, who stays for ages, encouraging me to talk. He wants me to explain, elaborate how I am feeling, describe it in detail, don't let it fester within, but he asks how I am feeling now, this moment. The honest answer is nothing. Mostly, I feel nothing. I am an empty shell. There is nothing there so I have no capacity to experience emotion.

I go out for a walk and when I arrive home Ethan has been anxious over my whereabouts. His eyes are red and blotchy and I see he has been crying. I give him a hug, tightening my arms around his muscly body, he reciprocates and I am so safe within his strong arms. I tell him I'm so sorry. I did not mean to worry him. I don't want to cause him such anxiety, a very selfish thing for me to do.

Ethan, I'm sorry, but I feel the tension in the atmosphere, detected by my senses like the smell of cooking, wafting from the kitchen. This is not a pleasant odour. This is full of years of disturbing hate and violent disruption to family dynamics. An argument has been developing and Dad, feigning oblivion, says hello in that false, cheery way when he is covering up, patching over anything even vaguely resembling emotions. This riles Ethan. He can't bear the pretence. Ethan gets upset and I talk to him, away from Dad. Ethan angrily says how Dad doesn't give a fuck about me and he is selfish and arrogant and doesn't fucking care. Ethan was really concerned about me. He had tried to talk to Dad who got cross with him. I feel guilty. I was the argumentative factor.

Ethan phoned Aunty Beth who was gentle and calm and talked to him. I feel so pleased he spoke to Aunty Beth. He has her. I would hate to leave him in such a position where loneliness and abandonment were all too prominent. I tell Ethan I am sorry, it was my fault. He accepts the apology so gracefully and isn't cross with me, he just became worked up with worry. I reassure him that Dad's complete distance and lack of care is nothing new. I know Dad doesn't care, he can't, an inability which I have difficulty in seeing changing.

My brother and I, in this together. I am thankful for such an intuitive, mutual relationship. Both being brought up by our mother, we have our fundamental similarities and morals. She taught us a great deal.

Ethan and I go to Holly's house, perhaps we are in need of an injection of normality, unhindered conversation, topics which aren't so meaningful. I drive as Ethan is still unwell, coughing chestily and feeling lethargic.

I bring Ethan home and he crawls upstairs to bed. I make myself a cup of tea and stand in the kitchen, warming my fingers on the mug, staring out of the window. Tiredness evades me but I go through the motions, my pre-sleep order of tasks, and lie on my back in bed, gazing at the ceiling. Through the muffled house noises of the clinks and clicks of plumbing, I hear it distinctly, cutting through me like a blade, tearing at my mind. "Ali, Ali", Mum is calling me, she is in distress. I leap up, afraid I have left her alone, and bolt down the stairs, grabbing the banister as, in my haste, I trip and stumble.

Thrusting my feet into trainers, pulling a fleece jacket over my pyjamas, I throw myself into the night and sprint. Running and running, I can hear her, Mum I'm coming, don't worry darling, I'm here ducky, I'm coming, I'm coming. I scrape through the brambles. I'm here Mum, I promised you wouldn't be alone, I stayed by your side, I held your hand, I stroked your forehead, I never would leave you. Help me. Mummy where are you? Frantic, horrendous distress in the knowledge that I've lost you. Frantic searching.

I do not know how I came home, perhaps it was the frost biting at my feet or the bursting, breathless pain in my chest, or my flushed body, skin red, attempting to resist the cold. Walking up our street, I realise where I am, what I had been doing. I can no longer sense Mum or hear her anguished cry. The luminous, green digital clock indicated I had been gone over three hours. There is no rest for the wicked.

16th February

2007

MUM

Feeling so ill as I write this. Can't go on much longer. Poor night last night and didn't get up until 1pm, sleeping fitfully throughout the morning. Spent the afternoon lying on the sofa watching rubbish on TV. The nausea and back pain are unbearable. I just don't know what to do

2008

I am definitely not going to Lincolnshire – Dad's reaction, to leave early! I speak to Aunty Beth. She is going to tell Granny and Granddad et al. the truth. Perhaps won't elaborate too much, but will say I'm in hospital. In some ways it is a relief, not to be drowning in lies. They can see me for who I really am – messed up and confused. I am tired of pretending. Because Ethan is unwell, he doesn't go either which is nice because we now have the weekend to spend together.

Lily pops in early evening – tanned from two weeks sailing abroad – and it is a delight to see her. She gives me lots of hugs and we talk. Probably hospital this week but, next week, Lily is keen for me to come to the GP surgery with her and observe as a medical student, just for a few hours, and stay by Lily's side continuously. I don't trust myself alone with a patient yet. Lily will help me to conquer my fears and perhaps reignite that sparkle I once held.

I write into the night, words dancing around me like a swarm of flies. The pain is there, in the written word, but I am a bystander, a conduit, transmitting the message but without compassion. There is no feeling. I lash out, slashing my hip where the bone protrudes. This time, I feel the sting, I see the blood, bobbling, dripping. Blood means life.

After composing myself, I blindly negotiate the stairs, lights are off, the house is black, and softly pad to the kitchen. I pour myself a large glass of red wine, blood red, a sacrifice. I drink, too quickly but absorbing its enviable powers of numbing the physical pain and slowing the turntable of thoughts and ideas in my mind. I allow the alcohol to wash through me; I enter into a distended drowsiness, leaning on the side board to steady my gentle sway.

Blood is
The liquid of life:
God's ink

But it hides
Within me
So I cannot see.

Reality is
Deceptively false:
A contradiction

But I am led
Into an illusion
Of fear.

Existence is
Questionable:
Until proven otherwise

But I need
The authenticity
Of life.

God's ink
Earnestly provides
The unequivocal truth.

17th February

2008

Joanne from ISS comes to see me in the morning. I am still in my pyjamas after a lazy start. I feel more comfortable talking to her and she is such a dear. I try and explain more about the badness inside me but I do become afraid, I don't want to hurt her. I know it is illogical, I know I'm not about to hit her, but the fear remains. What if, by knowing, somehow I caused some terrible knock-on effect. I really do want to die and banish the evil forever, for death will destroy them.

I have learned that you can bury the past but the past always scratches itself to the surface. You see, I was bad all along, though I didn't always know it. Now, it takes an almost physical effort to stop the onslaught. But I daren't remember properly, I daren't let them into my head incase because remembering is the darkening and I am getting blacker. Even if you can't banish the darkness, it is better than no light at all. Illumination I strive towards but the conflicting sources are strong, their grip too tight, how long before I succumb to the inevitable? My past of unatoned sins.

If everything were to stop, how beautiful that would be. All nothingness. No one would come. I long for sleep and never to wake, for I despise myself utterly and hate what I have become. So much badness within. I function = their strength. No reality. All the world is scary, no safe places. They are inside me, an unstoppable current. What destruction will happen if I live? I am scared of myself. I must die to prevent the relentless terror, sever the connection, obliterate my evil ways.

18th February

2007

MUM

Spent yesterday in bed and on the sofa, watching TV. Usual symptoms – nausea, stomach ache, backache, exhaustion. Beside myself. In the evening, John went out to dinner party at our friends' house on his own and, on his return, I begged him to call the emergency doctor. John reluctant and, frankly, rather unpleasant. Bedside manner: nil. Eventually he did but the doctor only told me to take more pain killers because my own doctor was carrying out all the right investigations, which is true but it's been going on for so long and I'm so worn out and, at times, feel so ill.

In no pain today but no energy either. Dozed in bed in the morning and in front of the TV in the afternoon. John nicer – getting drinks and made soup for supper: practical tasks that he's much more comfortable with.

2008

Ethan leaving today which is a shame, although he says he shall be back on Friday to see Aunty Beth, Uncle Angus and cousin Zac so I am pleased in the knowledge of seeing him so soon. Holly's Mum Lindsey pops in this morning – needing the phone number of Ethan's mate who has a steady market in cannabis distribution. She had mislaid it and, now no longer growing her own, is in need of a dealer. Rightly, she was relieved Dad wasn't in as didn't especially want to explain her reasons for coming round! Business over, I give Ethan a lift to the station. He gives me a hug and says he will be ringing to check how I am.

I drive home, now alone. With Ethan gone, the desire to die returns. I would never do anything drastic with Ethan around. It wouldn't be right. I park the car and go into the garage. I want to bring the car in, leave the engine running, slip into a deathly poison of carbon monoxide fumes but our garage does not accommodate cars. It is a collection of tools and tables and bicycles and the old fridge. I would need to manoeuvre too much, including a moped which I am not strong enough to move by myself (we don't have the keys so it would have to be pushed or lifted). I resign myself to the inevitable: my sudden plan has no substance.

I phone Joanne from ISS, I have a growing sense of unease gnawing at my throat. I'm frightened for her; I need assurance that she is OK. We talk, Joanne says she is fine, there is no need to worry about her. But I am scared of going back to hospital. I am less safe there, being confined, I can't do the things I need to do to make everything alright. Joanne gently talks me towards sense. She says I know the police will be called if I do not return. They will come and find me and drag me back, most likely under a section. In my voice, she can hear my nervousness, she knows I am on edge. Joanne tells me to come to the entrance of the psych unit and she will come and see me first.

I fill my rucksack – radio, pyjamas, paper and pens. Nothing more is required. I walk to the hospital; it is cold and I do not have a coat. Joanne meets me and ushers me into a side room. She calms me. She takes time form her work to talk to me, such an altruistic quality. I accept her offerings of reassurance in my logical persona. My other beastly side is hushed. Joanne leads me onto the ward and hands me over to the nurses. And so, to the psych ward I return.

I have a different room, smaller, but size is irrelevant, as long as there is a place to be alone, partitioned from external influences, somewhere that is solely mine. There is an unsightly print (lacking artistic ability) in a wooden picture frame, no glass allowed here. Previous occupants have scrawled a number of phrases across the bland landscape, almost a competition to condense the most swear words into one sentence.

I venture out of my room, hoping the kitchen will be open to get a hot drink, and encounter Phyllis, with no top on. Phyllis told me she doesn't wear bras, even though now I can see she is well-endowed, as is naked from the waist up. Jess tells me Phyllis has been doing this flashing routine throughout the weekend. Water then flows down the corridor, soft and wet and cold. Sammy, who has been screaming since I got back, blocked a sink and toilet with paper, then turned the taps as fast as they would go.

On the ward Jess and I go from my room (they come and evict Jess), to Jess's room (they evict me!), to the activity room where we sift through the questions of a board game. The evening is slow, the activity room is shut, we go our separate ways.

The normal meds dispensing at 10pm. Sophie takes hers, then runs back into her room and keeps going until she hits the window. The window brakes and she is taken out. So, Sophie and I were sitting outside before the door was locked for the night and Jess joins us looking alarming, eyes bulging and face red. She has tried to hang herself but the rope wasn't tight enough and, from the bed post, there wasn't enough weight. Staff found her and checked her over but Jess is distinctly nauseous and says she feels as if her head is about to explode, the pressure so extreme.

We go inside. I want to stay with Jess, look after her, make sure she is OK. I don't like to think of her on her own, in her room. I suggest she talks to one of the nurses, they will, at least, be company. We find Adelle, a nurse whom Jess likes, and I leave.

Sophie is moved rooms, due to the window incident, and I hide in mine. A wave of nausea engulfs me and I run to the bathroom and vomit. I didn't eat any dinner so not much comes up but my tablets do – blue and yellow ones – so no drugs coursing through my veins now. I can feel the badness seeping out, it needs to be contained. I absorb myself in writing, willing words to paper to force the concentration into a pen, stem the flow, but the darkness is brewing and I feel it bubbling inside. The rocking commences, I need to get out, walk it through, somehow prevent the badness within. I then get frightened. I hear the threats in my head. I know I can't do all these things but the badness says I can.

I get scared for Joanne; I get scared as to what will happen in here. My room is a trap, the walls condense, there is nowhere for the evil to be expelled. My writing becomes a mess, illegible, sentences do not form. Frustration and fear well up. I crash the pen down on the table and crush it beneath my palm. The dagger of plastic, splintered biro glints at me. I grasp it in clenched fist and thrust it into my wrist. The blood spurts and is plentiful. I hadn't hit an artery, my intentions weren't death, but a superficial vein, and I watch the thick, red liquid escaping, trickling through my fingers. Its path is unhindered, the soft drip to the floor, food for the demons, feast on me, let not your anger be repaid on others. I have to do this, I have to try, if I don't, terrible stuff will happen. I can't risk it.

I pull the plastic shard out, a feeling of being cleansed, and wait patiently, constantly focusing on the blood, until the clots form, the bleeding stops and the sacrifice is over. I rinse my arms and hands in the sink; I mop the floor with tissues. My wrist still has a hole, reduced to a pathetic trickle of blood.

I go to the staff room apologetic. I feel guilty for them; they should not have to sort me out, I should do it myself. I ask for a plaster but Adelle whisks me into the meds room. She is nice. I say I'm sorry, I don't want to cause a problem for her. She tells me it is myself I have hurt, no-one else. She disinfects my cut and the damage is clearer. I haven't slashed myself, the incision is small, the depth is greater. Adelle considers stitches but I do not fancy a trip to A+E, 1am in the morning. She manipulates the skin, edges together, then steri strips me up, then gauze, then bandage. She asks why I did it. I tell her bad things in my head.

I am shaky and have difficulty putting my jumper back on. Adelle says she will come and check on me in a little while but, please try to find her first to talk, before cutting myself. I tell her I shall. The badness is waning now, the calming of the storm. I change into my pyjamas with difficulty, limbs jiggling away, then go to the toilet, clean my teeth, close the curtains and slip into bed, my body finally allowing exhaustion to set in. Adelle comes with temazepam and extra blankets, a freezing fog is settling tonight. The temazepam mollifies me and I cannot read my novel, my eyes are slow and amble from line to line, unreading. Defeated, I fall to sleep.

19th February

2007

MUM
Another day with little discomfort but so tired. Watched usual crap on day-time TV and nodded off at intervals. Alice rang

and a great get well card from Beth. I am blessed with good friends and family. John being much nicer now that I have stopped moaning and groaning (literally!) but can't take paracetamol and codeine indefinitely – the latter is making me constipated!

2008

Jess, this morning, is not good. Her face is swollen and pale, speckled in red dots where numerous blood vessels have burst, giving her the appearance of measles. She has a cracking headache and her eyelids are still noticeably swollen, narrowing her eyes. She looks very tired and is lethargic in her movements.

Dr. Floyd is on the ward and I am summoned. Susie, a nurse who I haven't especially spoken to before, comes with me. She comes in for a quick chat before I see Dr. Floyd and is very kind. The staff here do seem professional but genuinely concerned for our welfare. I have no complaints, only praise.

Dr. Floyd spends a lot of time with me, asking probing questions. She seems to have a natural ability to specifically locate the topics which I find difficult. Without these questions, I'm sure I would answer honestly and appear quite normal! Dr. Floyd tries to understand about the self-harm. She reassures me that everyone I talk to are safe. All is confidential. I want to believe her but I still have a tugging fear, too dangerous to ignore. I tell her I feel less safe here. My anxiety increases. She asks about my suicidal thoughts. I tell her I want to die; I tell her I counted out tablets and considered the garage. Why lie? She knows anyway.

Dr. Floyd says she can't see a noticeable difference in me. Everything is the same, that I know. She feels that lithium needs to be tried. If things don't change, it isn't good. Currently, I am unstable and likely to kill myself. If I start talking and it induces these fears of harming others and encourages me to ruminate on all the horrors of the past, Dr. Floyd feels I shall completely fall apart. She tells me she is worried about me, not whom I talk to, but my mental state. She says it is necessary to stabilise my mood sufficiently in order to allow me to work through events, emotions etc. I agree to the lithium. What choice? I am the same, perhaps this will cause change. My report from the nursing staff is good. They say I'm lovely and polite but never talk or say how I'm feeling.

Dr. Floyd tells me I am the best case she has ever seen of, what she calls, the "smiling depressive". I have developed such a front, a covering act, not many can penetrate. I am able to keep up this charade for long periods of time. My cover is too good. I can talk to the patients, the staff and never let down my guard. I smile and can concentrate. This isn't helpful apparently. Dr. Floyd says it is a very unsafe position for me to be in because I have no ability to express my inmost emotions. She says, if patients get angry, they are liable to break a window or throw a chair but at least the staff are aware because that is a physical symbol. With me, they have no idea. I am too well hidden. That is why she is worried. I know I am always performing but that is what my life has become. I no longer know what I am supposed to be or how I should react, everything is fake, especially myself. I don't know who to be. I lost me somewhere along the path. Where have I gone?

Susie finds me afterwards and sits down to talk. She says they have decided I need to be on level 2 obs – four checks an hour. I don't like this, the lack of privacy, it makes you conscious of every small thing you do. Perhaps they are attempting to catch me off guard, let a small snippet of the intense hatred of myself slip out, and they are there, waiting to pounce. I am also not allowed to leave the unit. I have to definitely remain until my review on Thursday and then they may reconsider. I'm hopeful they shall surely let me go out with Aunty Beth, clamped constantly by my side, on Friday, and then I must be away on Saturday. I have to be alone that evening, the day Mum was diagnosed and my life and hers became intertwined. Except she died and I didn't. I feel my existence rendered futile. I feel I am betraying Mum. She wanted life; I now want to extinguish mine.

Jess says it could be worse, there are apparently level 4 checks. Level 3 is within eyesight and level 4…within arms length! This means you are followed into the shower, toilet and someone sits on a stool beside your bed whilst you sleep. How off-putting in every respect! Jess is right, I am in a far better position than this scenario!

I have to have my bloods taken before the lithium is commenced. Two of the nurses come and escort me to the meds room – I have been highlighted as someone who doesn't like needles! They sit me down and prepare me. They know I ripped my cannulas out and have an aversion, to say the least. They have to navigate my thick, wrinkly scab crusts on the side of my forearm and elbow, but otherwise I am fine.

I watch the needle penetrate the bulging vein and see the blood rush into the syringe, three bottles. I have no fear. There is no apprehension, perhaps this is a hurdle I have jumped, any animosity towards needles has dissipated: I can do it! I want to have a go on someone else, pierce their skin and withdraw the blood, just to ensure I haven't lost that ability. I want to prove myself. I ask to take the next bloods...the nurses say no!

The afternoon wasn't so good. I hadn't felt hungry at lunch but they made me eat something so I had a yoghurt. Afterwards I spent hours feeling nauseous, not even wanting to sip water. I lay on my bed, in all my clothes, and a hoodie that Jess leant me as the ward is freezing and I only have the outfit I arrived in. They are not going to let me home so I think I shall need Dad to bring me some more clothes and definitely a scarf and fleece. I didn't think about belongings when I came. I was hoping they wouldn't make me stay.

I thought I may sleep as I turned the radio down low and my head felt heavy but staff doing checks kept coming in every 15 minutes. They want to talk and try to engage and ask opening questions but I am too knackered to converse. I can't make myself launch into tricky topics of discussion.

Dad came to see me at 7pm. He arrived in his suit with his hospital ID badges dangling around his neck. He had just come from a trust meeting. Oh, the irony; it is almost funny. From my room window, I can see the management building and the car park where Dad has a permit. Whenever I look out, I feel like giving him a wave.

The nurses on this evening were nice and I asked if I could go home to retrieve some clothes. They discussed, then said to Dad I was allowed half an hour, as long as he was with me the entire time. This was beneficial to Dad and I, conversation flows much more easily when there are physical things to be done. The dingy side rooms do nothing to encourage easy chatter. Dad was quite sweet. He doesn't understand why I'm not allowed out but said it was nice to see me. He prefers having a practical role so driving me home and back was ideal.

I spoke to darling Aunty Beth, apologised for my current state, said I really hope to be out on Friday but if not, will she still come? Aunty Beth tells me of course they are coming and will see me wherever. Such a dear family. It will be a joy to see little Zac again too but I do not want to put him through the ordeal of visiting me on this ward. There are some things you wish relatives did not have to witness, a screening programme for protection.

Lily arrives just before night time meds with a little bunch of yellow and purple flowers from her garden. She discusses lithium with me and recommends I try it, this could be a way forward. She inspects my cuts and grazes and holds my hands in hers.

Sleep doesn't come easily and I am overcome with a wild, uncontrollable desire to throw myself into the darkness. In a panic, my mind goes amok, the world disappears underneath me. I want to hide myself from life and feel the compelling need to run into the night. Flee for miles of space, of outside air, until exhaustion beats me. Trying to escape? Or be alone enough to distinguish the bad, free from the presence of others.

I stare through the window, into the blackness. I close my eyes, I have the sensation of fainting but I open my eyes and the room remains; I teeter only upon the edge of my perilous world. I am a ghost: I can stand in one life, but I can see another. I am in the real world but not part of it. My mind and body are being torn, a violent division which I cannot repair. This existence is unsustainable but that gives me a peace. The safest place, where wholeness is achieved and cannot be broken, is just a hand stretch away.

20th February

2007

MUM

Telephoned the surgery for gastroscopy biopsy results – normal, so it's back to square one! Made an appointment to see Dr. Pearce tomorrow morning.

2008

I did sleep last night, but fitfully. Nightmares lurched me awake, pyjamas twisted up and clinging to my damp skin. I threw the duvet and blankets off to cool down and then woke, shivering, and pulled them up to my chin. The cycle repeated.

This morning I see Sharon. She is a woman who is completely normal to talk to so somewhat of a relief! She suffers from anorexia and is fairly tall so her stick legs protrude like stilts from cardigans which keep her warm. She has been here a week and it is her review this morning. She is apprehensive, if she has gained weight, even a pound, then she will be allowed home, if not, then she will be kept in.

Sharon has been really trying, eating some of the food here and demolishing chocolate bars yesterday in the hope that it will tip the scales sufficiently. She still has her devious tricks, however. The nurses must keep a food diary for her daily intake, so she will take a sandwich to her room, bin most of it and leave some crusts for them to see. She picks at a plate of cooked food, eats the vegetables and bashes the rest with her fork, spreading it over the plate to appear as left-overs. She has also collected stones from the garden to fill her pockets for the weigh-in and is, currently, downing pints of water. She is desperate to go home to her eight year old son.

Before lunch, much of my time is spent on the phone, catching up on texting replies (my communication ability is distinctly lacking) and then a lengthy conversation with Uncle Peter. He is back from New Zealand so I told him to give me his news before I depressed him with mine. He had an amazing time, stunning scenery and managed to not constantly think about Aunty Maggie, although returning home was hard. He is lovely when I explain where I am and why. He has an ability to say the right things, perhaps due to his similar circumstances of loss, and says he wants to drive down straight away to see me. I say thank you and feel absorbed in his kindness. As I'm not allowed out, I feel it would be nicer to spend a day with him, perhaps early next week when Aunty Beth has left, and Uncle Peter says he would love to take me for a walk and then to lunch.

I tell Uncle Peter that I haven't really told anyone else of my whereabouts. He understands and realises it is tough. He then says, so unselfishly as I feel I have burdened him with my problems, that he feels privileged I have been able to tell him. What a lovely man. I have a family whose values are so sound, all are willing to drop everything to come and help me in whatever way they can. I am incredibly blessed. A knowledge which also enforces guilt. How can I be despicably selfish by upsetting them? I am really a horrible person.

Wendy from next door (who returned from holiday yesterday and therefore only just found out) and Isobel visit me. It is welcoming to see them and they both admirably manage normal chatter, as if we were in our street, but, with two people, my concentration wavers. When I am not asked direct questions and have to participate in a discussion, not one-to-one, the noise in my head is harder to abate. It is like trying to listen to two separate conversations, each interrupting the other. My understanding deteriorates and it requires my upmost efforts to haul my mind into the room. Such a tiring task, my head aches with sheer mental exertion. I find myself considering asking them to leave, which of course I cannot do and don't wish them to. Friendly faces are a glimmer of optimism. It is me I need to address. If only I could shake myself free, hurl myself at a wall, knock this badness out.

This is why I wear a mask, a screen for everyone I meet, because I do not know how to act. I have lost any ability to conjoin the muddle in my mind to physical behaviours. It does not fit, the connection has been breached. I am also cautious of the impostors and the false reaction they may bring. My mind's cruel conspiracy against my body: never knowing lies from the truth and constantly having to think everything is both and neither. How do you filter the rogues from the truth? And then how to develop that into a suitable, physical, emotional response? My confusion is compounded and my barriers are erected, like a draw bridge winding up as the enemy approaches.

Grace comes to see me, on her way home from work. After my begging and introducing Grace as my sensible, reliable adult, the nurses relent and I am permitted a half hour walk. Grace, as ever, is such a sweetheart. She has a knack a asking questions about my wellbeing without giving the slightest hint of prying. I, as usual, am very blunt and do not use metaphors or gentle words which only disguise the obvious. But, as soon as I see Grace, I feel my defences bracing. I am not quite hyperactive, but a flurry of talk and ironic laughter. I make light of the circumstances; I dismiss my wanting to die by locating, however small, an amusing element about which to dwell. I bob along the pavement, gesturing my arms. I am excitable and I do not know where this fizz of energy has come from.

Grace tells me that Ethan is not cross, only concerned. He has no anger towards me. This, although a relief, still floods me with blame. My little Ethan, a tower of strength, and I am bringing him down. Such malevolent acts on my behalf.

When I remember, I have to be careful, I have to be sure they are my own memories and not other people telling me what I felt. He planted death in me, like a seed. I can't let the feelings I remember about them be wrong. The difficulty in clarity comes with the distance, time can be greedy, sometimes it distorts the accuracy. But I do remember ingesting the shadow of death. It was only a tiny thing but I must have fed and nurtured it for, a dire action grows stronger, like the refraction of light. Now I am positively drowning in death's compelling allure but I must hold it back, restrain its leash, for I cannot let it take anyone else captive.

I feel I am fighting a desperate battle, spores of death are breathing out of me and I am trying to catch them in the wind, only to stand and stare as they slip between my fingers. For, when it was sown, I was desperate. My body was my only weapon and that was the sacrifice. I was fighting for my life and my life was the fight. If I gave in, the power would be broken and I would not be able to absorb all the terrors myself. I became a bone dry sponge, so parched that even the water of death became better than no water at all. I was scared that they would go elsewhere and the war would continue, who next? So I swallowed the battle and allowed them to fight inside.

After the transformation, they could not be reached for, to see them in their true shape is fatal. I became their protective shell, allowing them access to human life. If I die, I take them with me to the ground for, as a parasite, they cannot live without a host. Allowing for death makes living safe. It is the only weapon in my armoury, a weapon which I shall use. The child I had been is already dead.

Dad comes at 8.30pm, after his meeting. He dangles my mobile phone charger out of his briefcase, right in the corridor, and I quickly smuggle it into my pocket. "Dad", I say smiling, bundling him into a side room. "Oh", he says, "Should I give it to the nurses? Are you not allowed them?" His innocence is endearing but I am keeping the charger.

Dad is nice to me and we can talk, without awkward, hesitant pauses. He is really trying, he is just unable to cope or know how to react towards illness. Despite my brief explanations (I do not elaborate), Dad still appears to have little grasp on the severity that this is having on me. He asked if I could be at home tomorrow morning because the gas man is coming! I told him to phone Dr. Floyd and ask her! At the moment, I am not allowed out of the building, let alone home.

He sees my leg, tapping out of tension, and, bluntly as ever, says, "You're shaking. Can't you stop it?" It is a statement but I can feel his disapproval boring into me. I clamp my feet firmly to the floor, willing myself to be completely still but, so gently I am unaware at first, I start rocking, a small movement but an annoyance nonetheless.

It is not his fault, every person has situations which they find very difficult to be in. Usually I am able to act completely normally in front of Dad but this evening is a struggle. Dad is good with me though, and we do find topics on which to talk. He is quite cheery tonight and doesn't look so tired from work. I am glad he came.

Adam finds me, sitting on the floor, scratching my hands. He tells me to come with him into a side room. He says he's not going to get me to talk but, perhaps some one-to-one time will provide a distraction. It is hard. I am still shaky and have nothing to say. It is times like this that I need to be alone. There is too much, too fast; rampant voices and images crash into my mind but, once there, they have no way out. The increasing badness condenses so there is barely room to move. Inside I am screaming, eyes wide, mouth stretched, vocal chords straining, but externally, there is nothing. I struggle to speak and arms gently shake, concentration on restraining the tirade inside renders me almost mute. Too much for me to control simultaneously. The effort is extreme.

Adam is very gentle with me and undeterred by my limited, distracted speech. He talks and explains that it is OK when my external façade diminishes. He says, in situations like this, he doesn't want me to be alone, he wants me to be with someone who will talk to me and help me through the tough times. This is alien to me. In this state, a place of fearful unknowing and lack of responsibility for my actions, I always must get away from other people. This has to be experienced alone because, sitting in that room with Adam, my eyes are straining, on high alert, darting randomly so I can scan the entire space. I feel they are coming and only a glimpse will tell me they are here but you have to be quick, for they have exceptional speed. One tiny glance and then they disappear, back into the shadows, their safety.

This is why I need to walk into the night time. In pitch black, the world is their hiding place, they feel more exposed, squashed into the darkened corners of a room, but I am not allowed out. I get fearful and scratch and pull at the backs of my hands; I dig my nails into my wrist, still a slit from before. The blood stains the tips of my fingers.

21st February

2007

MUM

Appointment with Dr. Pearce at 8.30am. The next investigation is a scan, to check out liver, gall bladder etc – but the waiting time maybe four weeks. I can't last that long! Meanwhile, I'm to take an additional medication: antepsin. What with the co-codamol as well, this makes thirteen tablets a day! Antepsin recommended by the guy doing the gastroscopy and Dr. Pearce mentioned the bile that he'd seen in my stomach. I thought he'd said this was normal but apparently I misunderstood!

In fact, I'm feeling increasingly miserable and confused and frightened as to what might be wrong with me. Walked into town after my appointment but immediately my back ached and I felt tired. Another day of doing nothing very much. Major achievement to do some ironing!

2008

Only one real event in the night. Amy began kicking off, throwing cups which smashed and splintered down the corridor. In her rampage, she screamed at Adelle then spat in her face. This morning Amy explained and then, rather sheepishly, admitted she liked Adelle and felt bad for her actions.

Temperamental Maureen surprised me, walking into breakfast, she said a cheery hello. I was taken aback! Maureen usually adopts a face of thunder and rants about the smallest detail, in her mind, that you have done wrong.

Midday: review with Dr. Floyd. My blood results are back and normal apart from slightly raised ESR. Dr. Floyd says this will most likely be due to infected scratches on my arm. Lithium to be commenced tonight. Dr. Floyd is still unsure of my ability to stay safe. She says I have suicidal thoughts and plans, even if I'm not going to carry them out immediately. She is happy to let me out during the day on Friday and Saturday when I will be with family. I have to come back here for medications and sleep, however. I surmise that this is reasonable and will have a hefty chunk of the day with Aunty Beth and co.

I wonder about Saturday, cautiously allowing plans to vaguely form in my mind. If I trust them, they will tell me what is allowed. The first hurdle is overcome: getting myself away from here. I know that is necessary and I know how to achieve it. That is the easiest step. What comes later is more complex, more dangerous, a treacherous path full of red herrings which must be avoided. For, now Mum has gone, my Maisie can't show me the way anymore. The thought is terrifying. Should an anniversary hold such significance? But I feel I can do more good by not being, certain dates intensify the pull of death. I see my diminishing portion of life, before the descent into nightmare hallucination begins. Do I hate myself enough to defy the power of God?

I allow my head a peace. In my mind's eye, I can see Mum. We are dancing and running and laughing. It is a summer's evening and we are hosing the garden, watering the pots and, in the process, managing to soak each other. Our giggles are infectious and we flap in our flip flops and bend over, clutching our tummies, hysterical. Mum had been generous with the weed killer so our lawn was covered in circular patches of dead grass. Mum adjusted the hose to a jet stream, firing the water at the holes, doing her best to encourage regrowth. This is a happy memory. I realise it is the first time that I have actually seen Mum well. All images before were her awaiting death or dead. A solitary tear rolls down the side of my nose. I am almost scared to remember these beautiful moments. I am fearful, once re-lived, they will be taken from me.

A few years ago, Mum and I were reading the newspapers over breakfast. One article was in a question and answer format, interviewing some celebrity. We played the game and I asked Mum the questions. The one I remember was, "Whom do you most admire?" Mum said me. At the time I was honoured but stunned. Why me? But, if the question was posed, our roles reversed, I realised that I would have answered, "My Mum".

What of me now? There is nothing of myself left to admire. I am wallowing in the deathly pools. The admiration that Mum had for me all came directly from her. She tended to me, loved me, helped me grow and develop. She was my food of life. Look at the disastrous mess I have put myself in now. I am nothing to be proud of. I am nothing at all. My only strand of relief, that Mum cannot see me here, cannot observe my fall, my surrender. With her being dead, I am unable to disappoint or cause her the agonising pain of watching as her daughter disintegrates.

Later, Sophie has slashed her arm and is getting patched up. Cara (who was an inpatient but now only has to come back on Thursdays for her review) had brought her in a blade. I'm sad about this. It seems so wrong and irresponsible. It is one thing if someone chooses to get an implement to cut themselves with, but quite another if you have been given it by somebody else.

22nd February

2007

MUM
Simply dreadful night. Felt very sick not all that long after taking new meds. Very little sleep and several trips to the loo, thinking I would be sick. By 5am had given up and was downstairs with a hot water bottle and the television.

Went back to bed when John woke and proceeded to cry and groan until he telephoned the surgery. Dr. Pearce said to leave off all meds for 48 hours. John stayed off work until mid-afternoon and took another call from Dr. Pearce's secretary asking me to go for another blood test. In the event, it was a repeat liver function test and so John took me up to the hospital.

John telephoned Prue, who came to sit with me, and he went to work. Together Prue and I watched videos and I felt a bit better.

Having had nothing but sips of water and Lucozade all day, managed a small amount of supper with John. Fingers crossed for tonight. I almost dread going to bed but really am very tired.

2008

A night full of all the torments, waking sporadically with twisted sheets and discarded blankets. I remember finding myself standing upright in my room at one juncture. The fine line between being asleep and being awake was crossed so many times that I became a walking dream.

Aunty Beth arrives and it is wonderful to see her. I wrap my arms around her, nuzzle into her shoulder, smell her perfume. She holds me round my waist and leads me out to the car. Uncle Angus is driving and I clamber into the back seat with Zac. Zac kisses me and offers a brief hug as a welcome, but I see he is slightly apprehensive, perhaps doubting how to treat me. The darling thing, how much understanding does he have? Coming to hospital to pick me up, what am I thinking? How can I be doing this to my family? How can I be so hideously selfish and not put others first? Everyone is deeply affected by Mum dying, how can I be adding to their pain? I hate myself immensely. I am such a vile, despicable specimen. It is not life I hate, but me.

We go home, drink tea and then Uncle Angus collects Ethan from the station. We all have lunch. It is relaxed and easy, family together, conversation flows. They don't let my circumstances affect the banter, which makes everything appear more natural, whatever anyone is thinking inside. Ethan, without fail, has a string of stories about his capers in London and, of course, some problem on the train which he always seems to encounter! Oh, how Ethan can be relied upon to relieve pent up tension, such an attribute. He even managed to do so at Mum's funeral. Such a star.

Later, I savour a hot shower, what feels like masses of water soaking my hair and back, a difference to the bare trickle in hospital showers where I have to keep moving my head in the line of fire, just to get the shampoo out. Ethan entertains Zac and a James Bond film is put on, Zac's latest craze on the video front. I put on dinner and Dad arrives home from work. We eat.

I am utterly exhausted and only catch trails of conversation, desperately willing my mind to latch on to phrases in order to keep track of subject matter discussed. I cannot manage much food, I chew until almost a pulp in my mouth but, when I swallow, the sensation of the bolus sticking in the back of my throat occupies me. To Dad's annoyance, I don't clear my plate. Leftovers are not seen in our family and, I agree, it is a terrible waste, but if I consume any more I will be regurgitating it all in the toilet.

Post-prandial lethargy: I cuddle on the sofa between Aunty Beth and Zac, each with arms round me, competing, stroking me, allowing my head to sink into their warm bodies. I feel cherished, a prize which they both want. Since Mum has died, whenever anyone is ill or in hospital, Zac always asks if they are going to die too. Death by association. He cradles my neck in his little hand and says that he doesn't want me to die. The guilt drowns me like a burst dam. If only that was enough to make me want life. It should be but I know it is not.

Dad gives me a lift back and watches as I go through the doors. He waits until a nurse comes and I feel he no longer trusts me but not tonight, I must bide my time. I have another day with my family tomorrow.

I see Deborah is back, pacing the corridors with an aggrieved expression whilst mumbling to herself. This ward, to some, is a revolving door. They are admitted in a state, improve from drugs and time and care, are discharged, then spiral downwards until drastic enough to be re-admitted. The cycle repeats. Not much revolving door for me. I came in and they've kept me, more of a one-way access.

I feel horrendous and so low. The nurses ask, with a smile, if I enjoyed my day. They think this was a real treat for me. I say it was lovely. Is this the truth? My family are amazing and act just right, no histrionics, nothing dramatic, but calm, gentle tenderness. This is why I hate myself because, it is not them, it is me. I despise the fact that spending a day with them is so tiring. I hate feeling I need to get away, be on my own. I can't stand that I can't just be myself, relax, and be the person I used to be. Nothing is enjoyable even though my family's efforts are superb. I hate everything I feel inside and I feel a tremendous guilt that my attempts at normality fall way short of theirs. I have such incompetence; it is pitiful.

I go to bed late, knowing I need sleep, but my head is an independent entity, crammed with self-loathing, with images of family and friends, with my poorly Mum and many other scenarios and thoughts clawing at my attention. My novel does not overcome this. My eyes scan the lines, my hands turn the pages, but I have no idea on the content.

Mum died but that sounds so decisive. She was alive and then she wasn't, but the process of death was a drawn out affair. It took such a long time. I kept wishing I had the daring to kill her. She asked me to kill her. I even got the drugs, hid the diamorphine from the district nurses. Each prescription, I would secrete a box of vials to my room. No-one ever noticed or even suspected, five or six boxes were ordered at once. There was the opportunity, hour after hour I spent in Mum's room, beside her on the bed, just the two of us, but I couldn't bring myself to inject the solution of death.

I thought it odd the doctors, prolonging the suffering, keeping patients alive, for what? No-one can indulge in a life like that. It was a living torture. I saw Mum's suffering; when dead, I was glad that her pain was over but that feeling soon evaporates. It is replaced by the utter devastation of loss. I want Mum back. The agony of observing such illness diminishes, I would care for Mum the rest of our lives. I could look after her for years. Mummy, please come back. I need you.

23rd February

2007

MUM

What to write when you have been told that you have secondary cancers of the liver? Emergency ultrasound scan today and the news delivered back in Dr. Pearce's surgery.

Spent a lot of the evening telephoning friends and family. I wanted to tell them while I was in a reasonably calm frame of mind which I guess won't last. Everyone upset and crying. Phone call from Jack in Barcelona. Alice drove straight home from Newcastle. Ethan may meet us in Birmingham tomorrow at Mum and Dad's or back here on Sunday. I have lovely friends and family for which I am grateful. They will be with me to the end but I fear the last lonely journey – and the pain. Will I have the strength to cope? I doubt it. But I want to be strong, especially for my darling children. How will Ethan manage without me?

John's reaction was predictable! Busied himself with the practicalities – washing up, making food – but has also given lots of cuddles and said he loved me. I want to be so close to the family. Looking forward to seeing Beth, my dear sister, tomorrow.

I guess I'm a bit shell-shocked at the moment. Have taken pain killers and sleeping tablets in the hope that I might get a reasonable night's sleep. Almost afraid to try – there's pain and now this dreadful knowledge. I think it will be a long weekend but the news next week may be even worse. Who knows how advanced the cancer? May be too late for treatment.

Not really a Christian but, as I prayed in the Catholic church in Krakow, "Lord, give me the strength and courage to bear it". Also, "Look after my children when I am gone. Help John to foster a better relationship with Ethan for my sake. And if John remarries – which seems likely – I pray that they will embrace a new partner with the affection I have always enjoyed with Holly and Jack. I don't want to be forgotten but, for everyone else, life goes on."

I don't want to be bitter and make everyone else's life a misery. It's no one else's fault. I hope I don't lose a sense of humour. I should like to be as impressive as Maggie. She is my role model.

I don't think "Why me?", I've never thought "Why me?", I've always thought "Why not me?". It's a supreme arrogance to imagine one has a charmed life.

Last night the best night's sleep in a long time. Took the sleeping tablets and was asleep very soon. Didn't wake until 6am and for half a second I forgot, when I woke, the horrible reality. Suspect John slept less well. Wonder about Alice and Ethan and Mum and Beth. Don't want anyone to be too tired to drive today. John being very kind and attentive and telling me he loves me. At the moment, the kindness of everyone is almost harder to bear than the thing itself – but sweet sorrow.

ALICE
The evening of phone calls:
Mum – states what is wrong; she doesn't cry. I don't think she is willingly stopping herself, she just wants to put across the facts.

Ethan – agitated, asking me what is wrong with Mum and what it all means because I'm a doctor so I must know and I'm not telling him. It's his way of expressing his emotions but he's angry and I find that hard.

I drive back to Essex and almost cry continuously, save for the brief, illegal chats:
Jack – checking on me. I'm touched by how caring he is.
Holly – she's asking whether she should go round to the house tonight or should she wait? Is it appropriate? Holly and Jack always seek my advice first but how can I know now?

I get home; it's almost midnight. I see Mum, thin and pale. Is her complexion illness or a reaction to the news? She's in pain and bends over double, rubbing her back – the spasms come in waves.

Mum tells me she prayed a week ago – not to get better but that she can cope. The two things she is scared of the most: death and pain. How is she not a Christian when her motives, her actions are so right? She has taught me so many of the lessons in the bible just through her living.

2008

I didn't sleep last night. I was up until 4am and then one of the night staff (good looking guy whose name I can't remember) said to come and get a cup of tea with him. I then did snatch two hours kip until the morning bustle got into full flow.

Katy sat on my bed, enquiring as to my wellbeing. I wasn't really sure what to say. Today is the day. Exactly a year a ago, my life changed irrevocably. Katy said it was time for meds but, if I needed to talk, to come and find her afterwards. Katy, always so dear to me.

Full of remorse, but knowing I will struggle if I have a whole day stretching ahead of having to be with family, I send Aunty Beth a text, asking to be picked up at midday. It gave me the morning to try and organise my head. If I listen, if I'm careful, I will discover what needs to be done and how to do it. A puzzle is presented and I am given the clues, the difficulty is in deciphering where to fit the pieces.

I sit outside and allow my mind a freedom. It takes me back to last year. It was a normal day. I was in hospitals in the morning, shadowing a ward round. The afternoon I had free. I ate a late lunch then packed an overnight bag. We were playing hocking in Birmingham the next day (a Saturday) so were staying in a Travelodge the night before, being too many miles to cover in a day and with a match in-between.

Mum phoned me at 6pm, just before I was due to be picked up. She told me the news – cancer had been detected in her liver.

When I answered the phone, I was my usual cheery self, giddy Mum always called me, and hyperactive, getting excitable over the weekend ahead. Overnighters with the hockey girls are always a laugh. That was the last time I was happy, the last time I had a true smile, the last time I could feel wonderful to be in the world.

I grabbed my bag with change of clothes, didn't even say goodbye to my housemates, how to tell them what I had just heard? I drove home, irate at the trickle end of rush hour traffic across the Tyne bridge, and arrived four and a half hours later. This was far too quick, I must have been driving exceedingly fast, a danger on the roads. That journey, I remembered thinking about Mum's funeral. I could see myself talking in front of all the mourners, something I could have never imagined before as I would be grief-filled, unable to emit even a word but I did speak at Mum's funeral. Perhaps that car trip gave me the strength to be able to achieve what, later, I so desperately wanted to do.

Katy comes in again. She says I haven't been myself these past few days. She wishes I had some self worth. There, that simple sentence, exactly why I must die.

Aunty Beth arrives, we go home for lunch. Zac is as pleased as ever to see me. "Ali", he exclaims and runs, beaming, to hug me tight. The boys go to the football and Aunty Beth and I go for a walk. We do talk but I feel my energy seeping away. After an hour, there are silences, my mind is too consumed with other thoughts. I find it difficult to keep my focus. Aunty Beth doesn't mind. Nothing is too much bother for her. I say I'm sorry, I'm not much company but Aunty Beth replies that it is me she has come to see. My dear aunty. She wants to do everything she possibly can to help but I fear there is nothing she can do. I know how much I am loved and yet, in my head, it seems to mean little as I still long to die. Despite all the love in the world, I wish to be no more.

Dinner is a free-for-all as there is not really what you would call "meals" in the house. I scrape together what I can in the freezer and everyone digs in. Grace joins us which is great. She fits in so effortlessly with our family and is always willing to play with Zac.

Holly flies by, on her way to pick up a friend and then make their way into town for a girls' night out. Zac tells her they are dropping me back off at the hospital tonight. In alarm, Holly turns to me and I lie. I despise myself for it. I can't bear this pretence but I couldn't tell the truth either. I tell her I had an appointment yesterday and that is what Zac was referring to. A horrible, guilty lie because I couldn't face the consequences. I am appalling.

Holly knows there is something up but lets it drop. She leaves and after, there is the discussion about what should be done. I have to tell her I'm in hospital. The weeks are passing and I keep delaying the inevitable. Ethan volunteers to tell her, my treasured brother, willing to do my dirty work for me. To what depths am I sinking? I think I can't get any lower and then I better even myself. I am incredibly horrible. But no more secrets. Ethan is to tell all.

I drink three glasses of wine which frees my mind somewhat. I am able to participate and even laugh. It is all fake of course and, I suppose, inappropriate but the alcohol releases bouts of chuckles. We play a game with Zac whilst Dad and Uncle Angus watch the rugby.

9pm approaches. Aunty Beth drives me back after prolonged goodbyes. This is the hardest moment. I want to leave. I feel my skin crawling with such a drawn out departure. I cannot cope. Almost lose hold of myself but I recoil. My body separates from my mind. I am no longer there as my family kiss and hug me. I have swum away.

Aunty Beth leads me into the ward, no opportunity to run away but this is OK, I tell myself, plan B is in place. I see tears on Aunty Beth's face, she tells me to take care, look after myself. I am unemotional. There is nothing. I am a life size doll, a real physical being but vacant inside. I flew away long ago.

It was midnight, an eerie, expectant calm. I punched the tablets out of their blister packs. I had all the ones I counted before plus a packet of Ibuprofen, as you are not supposed to take these when on lithium, and a box of co-codamol. This was all I could get hold of with family staying and keeping an eye on me. I swallowed them and paced, up and down in my room, but I became too sluggish. I sat down on the floor, started rocking and then an intoxicating cloud descended upon me. I had done something wrong; they didn't like this. My head became muddled, there was no sense. I got scared. I didn't understand the torment or what the badness was saying. It is terrible to know that you should be doing something but not be able to find the courage to do it. It increases the hatred towards myself. I don't want to hurt other people and so I feel I have to obey, not break any of their demands or rituals. The difficulty comes when these are yet to be defined. That is the toughest, deciding the right from the wrong.

Flora came into my room doing checks. Apparently she saw me on the floor. She took me to A+E.

24th February

2007

MUM

11.30pm Today we drove to Mum and Dad's in Birmingham and met up with Beth, Angus, Alex and Zac. Quite a few tears and lots of hugs. I loved having my very dear family around me – and all the physical contact: stroking my hair, rubbing my back, holding my hand. I felt extremely tired and lay on the sofa most of the time but it was comforting to hear the family talking around me. Alice didn't eat much and went off for a walk by herself. And I suspect Mother was thinking, for all anyone knew, that was our last meal together, maybe the last time I would come to Birmingham. I checked out my old bedroom just in case!

Zac was a sweetie – knew I was ill but couldn't quite understand all the tears and kept talking about God and happy endings! Mother quite distressed at times, saying I was her baby and she wished she could be the one with cancer – she'd had her life etc. Beth very upset – my dear sister. She will be a great surrogate Mother for Alice and Ethan. We are all so fond of each other.

Lots of nice text messages throughout the day. Isobel and Brian said they would pray for me – and yes, I should like to be remembered in their prayers. I pray that I will find strength from somewhere.

We arrived home to find cards posted through the door. Everyone offering to help with chores, lifts, moral support. What it is to have good friends. Isobel even wrote out a timetable of when she was teaching – and put "weekends: any time". I love them all.

Poor John looked tired after little sleep and the drive last night. I guess this is taking more of a toll on him than I could have imagined.

Ethan phoned. Has gone to London to stay with a friend and will come home tomorrow. Begged him not to drown his sorrows. Could do without him hungover tomorrow!

ALICE

Dad drives Mum and me to Granny and Granddad's. Distressing and emotionally exhausting day. When we leave, I tell Granny I'll look after Mummy. I'll keep her and care for her and be strong for her. God please help me.

2008

Memories of this morning are mostly missing, as if I've only snatched a few. I do remember being on a ward which, I presume, was EAU. I needed the toilet but my body was shaking in large, unpredictable jerks. They brought me a commode and my knees protested as I stood to unbutton my trousers.

Nicola and Katy came to take me back to the psych ward and I had to talk to Donna, shift nurse, but have no idea what was said. I awoke in the afternoon, fully dressed, lying face down on my bed.

Why did I do it? It was grief of course, but grief develops, it changes. Grief spreads its meaning wide, far wider than I can see. Questions and explanations reel through my head but produce no fruits. I am taking a good firm knot and pulling at each side, willing it to unravel a little more, expose a fragment of string each time, but I am reduced to a mess of loose ends. I do not prevail, instead I have stumps of string needing to be reconnected which increases the chances of becoming tangled once again.

Ethan comes to see me some time in the afternoon. Donna had phoned Dad this morning so everyone knows. Ethan is incredibly calm and full of heart felt emotion, clinging round my waist as we go into a side room. We sit on a sofa and Ethan puts his arm around my shoulders and allows my weary head to sink into his chest. He is so tender, gently stroking my hand, soothing my physical and mental distress. Oh, my darling brother, what am I doing to you? I love you in such immense proportions. I am so sorry. Please don't worry about me, I have unbelievable powers of recovery, I always pull through, I always carry on.

Is this sustainable? Nobody realises what a mess of loneliness and inadequacy I am inside. I am a solitary island, sinking in the rising waters with no answer to escape from drowning. I am beyond help, for what can anyone offer? They don't know what to do with me. I am on six checks an hour as managed to persuade that I didn't need one-to-one obs. As much as everyone wants to help, are willing to do anything, I am a lost cause. How do you save anyone who has ingested the bitter pill of death?

After dinner, at which I managed to eat most of a yoghurt, I ask to talk to Donna again. Dr. Floyd says I must engage more so I take the initiative. Donna tells me what was discussed this morning. I had told her about Mum's diagnosis and then said I wasn't sure if I wanted to die. This is the truth. I don't believe death was my aim. I was caught in the trap and needed, had to, punish myself. I had to destroy the bad within. I had to hurt me to give them what they wanted. Damage had to be done. I was the recipient; I offered them my body. I also, apparently, saw the duty doctor of which I have no recollection. I'm now thankful that I haven't been sectioned.

At 7pm Dad arrives with Lily. He gives me a full hug, no restraint, an act of his love towards me. I see the pain in his eyes as he gazes at his daughter, deteriorating under the weight of life. We talk. Lily is good as a mediator; she asks questions that Dad and I find difficult to broach. I am open and honest and speak to Dad about real things, how I am really suffering. I have never covered topics like this before and Dad is amazing. He says things to help me. He wants to be there. I can see his concern.

I summarise accurately how I view myself – I've forgotten how to live and am too tired to re-learn the steps. It is like dying from starvation but lacking the energy to eat. You know what is required and it is offered to you but that stretch to grasp is a struggle too far. Silent tears come, just gently, only a few, but I cry. This *is* affecting me. There is a chink in my armour of indifference. I do care. Lily puts her arm around me and strokes my shoulder. Dad remains sitting. He still cannot cope with crying.

Saying goodbye, Dad hugs me twice and kisses me on the cheek. The physical affection that I have so longed for is granted and I love my Dad all the more for it because, sometimes, I need him to show his love towards me. I know he loves me but it is nice to be told and feel it. I doubt myself otherwise.

I struggled to stay awake this evening. My body was a set of aching muscles, my head too heavy to hold up. I didn't want to fall asleep before 10pm meds so I forced consciousness upon myself. I sat in the lounge with Jess, Sophie and Sharon and we watched ice skating on television.

I spoke to Aunty Beth who I could hear sobbing down the phone. Oh, how the consequences of my actions bring such guilt. I hate myself so I harm myself, but then I hate myself for harming myself. I am caught in this circular sequence and I don't know how to get out.

I allowed things to stay on the brink of my brain, aware of their presence but unable to delve into their substance. It wasn't to be touched but I was shown how to reveal their hidden secrets. I held the key and I chose to open the door, not knowing I was unable to close it. I have unleashed a rogue monster, intent on destruction.

The control I had now tossed aside. All I can do is watch the ripple effect in motion: a bad thing gaining momentum, nourished by attention, increasing in power. But how to ignore? No longer am I able to contain. What have I done?

25th February

2007

MUM

11.45pm A day of phone calls, texts, cards and flowers. Alice did some shopping for me and John made some soup.

Ethan arrived late afternoon, with flowers and in tears. I love him so much. He was very upset but so affectionate – cuddling up to me and stroking me just like when he was little. He seems so much more grown up now and lots of things he says about his life in Liverpool make me feel very positive.

Holly cooked supper for us and brought it round ready prepared. Alice and Ethan too upset to eat but I managed quite well. Holly is a dear. Then we spent the evening chatting over the TV!

I love my family so very much and, whilst the children have got to get on with their own lives, wish they lived nearer. Alice has always been a delight – but why did I ever worry about Ethan? He is growing into a fine young man and I know that his values in life are essentially very sound. So pleased to have him home.

Prue called earlier with a card and flowers. Holly brought daffodils. I am being prayed for in churches and individual homes. Uncle Walter and Aunty Joan are lighting a candle for me. I wish I believed in the power of prayer but, whatever, I am comforted by these gestures. I hope they bring me calm and acceptance and take away the panic and fear. I do not ask for miracles. Kyrie Eleison.

ALICE

I sat in bed with Mum and she got me to go through and throw away all her papers to do with Ethan: letters, assessments, all her diaries reliving the memories, years of his bad behaviour, years of Mum's torture, gone. All that is left is what I can remember. Does that mean it has all vanished? No-one else can substantiate what I witnessed.

Picked up Ethan from the station this afternoon. Driving up our street he kept repeating, "I can't do this. I don't want to go in. I can't do it." I reassure him he can. I try and calm him down. We both know what we are saying has little meaning. We know we have to do this. Ethan cried a lot and then resumed his anger, all directed at me – why didn't I phone him last week and say how ill Mum was? I don't think I can cope if he blames me. He gets angry when I don't have the answers to his questions. He says, "Why didn't I know earlier?" With my medical course, I should have been able to diagnose. I know he's upset, it's just hard. Mum says I was the only one who took her seriously. I cared and believed she was ill. I came home a few weeks ago to see her because I was concerned but, what difference does it make? I can't help her now.

Mum doesn't think Ethan will or is coping well – I tell her I'll look after him except, I know I can't do that as well as Mum.

Holly comes round having cooked dinner. No one eats much; I feel guilty, except Dad, he, as always, dutifully demolishes the lot. Holly wants to do so much to help but I'm so worried that she'll get ill again. I can't physically look after her and Mum. I can't divide myself into two, so I'm with both of them.

2008

Really disappointing night's sleep, perhaps due to my comatose state yesterday morning. I fell asleep quickly in exhaustion but then woke at 1.30am and couldn't nod off again, instead I felt wide awake and alert. I read much of my book, did the crossword and Sudoku in the paper and then decided my tummy was grumbling out of hunger so I ate an apple and bag of crisps. Although, then I didn't want to lie down straight away so I waited a time to digest my food and finally crawled into bed at 5am and fell asleep for a further two hours. I hope this lack of shut-eye doesn't make me feel worse today.

Walking to get a cup of coffee, I emerge straight into Dr. Floyd who smiles and says, "Morning Alice". I reciprocate her greeting and then disappear back into my room, head bowed. Oh dear, not sure what Dr. Floyd's reaction shall be when she hears of my exploits this weekend. Please, please don't section me. I hazard a guess that I won't be going home today.

Katy is my nurse this morning and I ask to speak to her. I am definitely better with words on the page so I read her all I have written about Saturday. She sits intently, listening to all I have to say. When I have finished, I see she is in tears. She takes a tissue to dry her eyes and I stand up to give her a hug. I am taller and automatically feel protective over her. We sit down again and Katy says how much she cares for me. She reiterates that they are all worried and were concerned about me on Saturday when they knew it was the date Mum was diagnosed. She says she wishes there was something she could do to bring back my self esteem, increase my confidence, acknowledge my self worth.

I tell her I'm not sure I want to die anymore. This, in itself, is confusing. I tell Katy I have been tentatively considering going back to medicine. Lily said, to get me actually doing something, she would talk to Dr. Floyd and perhaps I could have a few hours leave to spend shadowing Lily at her surgery. I now feel I might like to do this.

I remember how I adored patients, delighted in talking to them, excited to be entering the hospital, willing to give them so much time. Those memories and feelings are still there but will I find them again? It is cowardliness on my part. I am scared that I won't be able to be how I was. I'm scared that I have lost that sparkle which enabled me to love my course so much. I am scared that I won't be able to cope. Alice, you need to do what Zac says and "be brave". The old cliché, face your fears, but so appropriate. They tell me to look at the positives: I have overcome my recoil towards needles, a small thing that perhaps symbolises so much more.

I am almost too afraid to admit that my attitude is changing and terribly cautious to even consider returning to medicine but it is there, that first chink in a life which I thought doomed, a slither of hope, edging into my steadfast resolve.

Ethan and Holly visit me after lunch. Ethan has stayed home an extra day and Holly has taken the afternoon off work, such special siblings. They have also spoken to Jack who sent me such a sweet text. All my fears are assuaged.

Holly, on arrival, sees Dr. Burgess and ducks into the side room – Holly's consultant three years ago! The conversation is easy, Holly always relied upon to be able to talk, whatever the circumstances. I owe her an apology and profusely say sorry. There is no excuse as to why I didn't tell her my whereabouts, only my own selfish reasons. I give her a brief overview of my weeks in here. I said that I didn't tell anyone at first, it was too hard and I didn't know how. Ethan is so supportive and helps me to relay events.

They bring me gifts – grapes and strawberries – and Holly gives me a decorated notebook. Inside she has written two poems. The first by Mother Theresa and, without Holly's prior knowledge, it is my favourite verse. I had a copy taped to my bedroom wall in Newcastle and, upon reading, it is such a comfort now. The second is "If" by Rudyard Kipling, a poem Gran quotes in abundance and doesn't realise the irony of the first line as she has dementia. What a thoughtful present for Holly to bring.

I thank Ethan and apologise to him also. He has missed university and has several essays due in the next few weeks which he hasn't yet started. I get him to write down the titles, hoping I can search through the newspapers, looking for any articles on the current affairs associated with his work.

Ethan is astute and realises that, after about an hour, I am getting tired. Being with people, however understanding, is still a trial. We say our goodbyes and I am given repeated hugs and kisses and assurances that, if I need anything or want company, then to ring and both of them will come straight away. Such all consuming care. I am left, enwrapped in a warmth that only the transcending love of a family can provide.

Adam is working this afternoon. I talk to him. He knows the pretence I maintain. He says, after putting on an act for so many different people, I no longer know who I am myself. He then asks when I felt completely normal, when did I feel like me? I said when I was with Mum. She made me myself, she was such a comfort and I was real. Aside form Mum, Adam says, when was the last time? A reel of memories, I wind back the years. I cannot recall, it was too long ago.

I can imagine however, and I indulge my thoughts. I am calm, a feeling of tranquillity. Being at one with the world is what I strive for, when nothing matters much and whatever troubling is resolved. It is like swimming under water, a peace of muffled sounds, resonating together, music of the soul. There is no drag, no disruption of splashes or gasped breath, all is still. My bubble world, where moving is effortless, life in slow motion, fluidity rippling throughout my body. There is no introspection because everything is exposed, on the outside, no more smothering my face with the smile of somnolence. All has a place and that place fits; it is not angular, the square in the hole, but a fusion of oneness. Being is a gentle delight.

I am cautious to think this way, wary of allowing such a positive feeling into my mind, scared that it may turn and leap back at me, full of self loathing. But this doesn't happen and my little wish is allowed to settle, in the corner, but in my mind.

Dad comes to visit me after work. I feel quite lively talking to him. He has brought me an insert from the newspaper which has puzzles and crosswords to keep me occupied. He tells me himself and Lily are both coming to my review, arranged for midday on Thursday (Lily had rung Dr. Floyd's secretary). Lily is prepared to have me come into her surgery and so this needs to be agreed with Dr. Floyd.

I feel excitable and spiel off my plan to Dad. I can see ISS in the morning and so, if I am struggling a little or need to talk, they will give me that opportunity at the start of the day. I will then go into Lily's surgery in the afternoon and see patients. I am happy! I want to go home now. I am ready. I can face the immediate future (lets not get too carried away with long term plans!) and I can live. It is a possibility. An amazing contradiction to my previous thoughts but who says change cannot happen? I know I wouldn't have believed it, even yesterday, but today is a brand new day, even the sun has been shining and sparkling in the clear blue sky. I, Alice Addison, am happy! Praise the Lord! I find Danielle to tell her. I want this on record, just in case there is a minute chance that this feeling is fleeting. I want this brilliant emotion noted!

Aunty Beth phones me and I offer many apologies for my behaviour. How is she so wonderful to put up with me? I tell her I am feeling superb, far better than yesterday and she cries, tears of happiness. She says I sound much more like my old self. Before, I loved life. I was eager to explore, discover and learn more. There were the bad, dark thoughts in my head but they were always overcome by the bright entertainment of the fun times. Life was worth living.

I find Flora and humbly ask to talk. She was the one who found me on Saturday and stayed with me in A+E. I apologise to her. I shouldn't be doing this to other people, I am not their responsibility. I tell her I am sorry I had taken an overdose, she came in and I was on the floor, slurring my replies. I tell her the truth. When I took the tablets it was an act full of intent but, once swallowed, my attitude changed. It felt I had done something very wrong. It scared me. I was a coward. Flora is lovely and says there is no need for apologies. I am grateful she came in when she did.

Flora relates some amusing moments in A+E when I was so drowsy I didn't know what was going on and my speech was illegible! I tell Flora I no longer want to die and then, before I am really aware, I have been enthusiastically spouting all my medical student stories and placements and I am telling her how much I loved it. This is a pleasant feeling but strange, it has been a year since I could say all this stuff and really experience it as well. I always knew I did find my course great, but that seemed like a distant memory, never to be had again.

26th February

2007

MUM
11.25pm Will I have the emotional strength to keep up the diary entries? I'm not sure.

Didn't get a lot of sleep last night, despite tablets; hence stayed in bed until lunch time. Ethan, who had spent most of night on the sofa, gave the front room a really good clean. He is being such a dear.

Dr. Pearce telephoned with details of my appointment with the radiologist tomorrow – I am very afraid of what will be found (although I doubt any scans tomorrow) and that the cancer is advanced. Numerous phone calls and texts from friends and family. Beth so upset that sent home from work. A beautiful bouquet arrived from Peter and Maggie. In fact, there are flowers all over the house.

Felt sick all afternoon. Alice telephoned the surgery and Dr. Pearce has given me another anti-sickness medicine to try. Lots of TV as usual but also a good opportunity to talk to Ethan. Poor Alice is feeling very confined. Difficult for such an energetic girl to be cooped up with me for most of the day. John went into work first thing but then came home. He looks drained and doesn't know what to do with himself.

It's a ghastly situation and I'm overcome with panic at intervals. Must try and keep calm for everyone else's sake but it's so difficult. Hope I sleep well tonight.

ALICE

I sleep fitfully and frequently wake with my heart racing and suddenly eyes wide open. I'm fearful, petrified almost, although I don't know what of. I don't want to go to bed, distracting myself with writing, reading, anything but to try and sleep.

Get up at 5am and go for a walk – the fresh air so welcome. Cook Mum egg custard – Granny always made it for Mum when she was poorly and, in turn, Mum always did it for me: "invalid food".

Dad looks old and tired. He goes into work later than usual and returns after only a few hours. He couldn't cope with work. Not that he said this to me but it was the subtle things he mentioned. That's how I know. What he says has sometimes got to be deciphered. I've only seen him cry once – watching "Chariots of Fire" with Mum and I years ago. It reminded him of his father. There weren't tears but his eyes welled up. I'm worried about him. It's so hard to judge when he doesn't say anything and gives very little away with his actions and body language.

Mum is scared about tomorrow's appointment with the radiologist. She's scared the cancer is already in her bones.

Granny says it's OK because Mum has "a doctor in the house" (Granny's current favourite phrase for me.) But, how does that help? I can't help Mum with my knowledge. I can't make her better. I can't relieve her pain. I can't stop her from being scared. I can't numb her anxiety. This is what it is like to feel completely helpless.

It was a strange day today. The last three days have been emotionally draining. My exertions have been on suppressing tears because I do not wish for Mum to see me crying all the time. I can't lose my grip. But today I've hardly felt like crying. I haven't needed to control my outward expression of emotion. I didn't like it. I felt lost. I had no feeling in me, nothing to control, just empty. I don't know why this is. Of course I'm upset but I had to keep telling myself today that I was because I couldn't feel it.

2008

Katy sees me and says she is around if I want to chat. She is on a long day and is my allocated nurse. I take this opportunity. I make the decision that I am strong enough and Katy is the one with whom I wish to share. I read to her the entries I wrote in my diary the last two weeks Mum was alive. My prose was full of the horrific, unrelenting devastation but also demonstrated that exquisite bond which Mum and I formed. I am able to talk about my darling mother.

I shielded the family from her worst moments, I protected them by not telling what they imagined but never saw. Their own despair did not need to be compounded by my horrific insights but these memories have festered inside me. I do not wish to forget but having an objective listener has helped me this far. Katy is not emotionally involved, did not know my mother.

I read and do not cry. I can remember, word for word, my speech at Mum's funeral. It is a strange feeling to be saying those lines again. I had a feverish desperation before her funeral, I was adamant that I did not wish to cry whilst talking. Afterwards would be OK but not at the time. This was not out of pride or embarrassment. I knew no one would mind if grief swept me away into a quivering wreck. I didn't want to cry because I wanted everybody there to hear all of what I had to say.

I practiced, time after time, walking across the fields, speaking aloud. I must have repeated myself more than a hundred times before I could recite without my voice cracking, restrain the tears until those final words, "Thank you", left my lips.

Holly arrives during her lunch break. She has brought me the requested shampoo and also a newspaper, magazines and home-made biscuits from her Mum Lindsey – what a lovely gesture. We go for a walk in the park. It is a beautifully sunny day and, as we amble along arm-in-arm, a deer scampers out in front of us before disappearing back into the bracken in alarm. Holly acts as normal as possible, she knows I just want people to be themselves. I dislike the change I can see once they know what my circumstances are.

We sit on a bench overlooking the lake, legs dangling, basking in the February sun, too warm for coats today. She wants me to talk but I am reluctant, a shut clam. I know she wishes I could open up to her, lay my soul bare, but I am unable. It is I who has the difficulty in explaining to my family. I feel more at ease with people who do know me, but who didn't know me before Mum was ill. I try to steer the conversation off me and ask Holly about work. Usually so enthusiastic about this topic, she shrugs if off, a neglected subject, perhaps feeling discussing her job is trivial, even superfluous considering my current mental state.

Holly does ask me what Dr. Floyd is like. I realise I haven't described her yet. She is small, shorter than me and I am only 5'4". She is probably in her fifties and her hair is styled in a long bob with a fringe. She has a smile which makes you feel she can see right through you, as if her eyes are deciphering the cogs in your brain. She must pick up on the smallest, presumed insignificant, details which contributes to her brilliance. She always wears mid-length woollen skirts, tights and little ballet pumps with a slight heel. She favours blouses underneath a cardigan with detailed buttons. Her pattern is spots: black, pink, white. On any day, an item of clothing has always got her trademark spots decorated across. I like it, a friendly, familiar comfort.

We walk back to the hospital, the hour is up, and Holly leaves with a hug and kiss and makes me promise that, if I need anything or just want some company, I must ring her straight away. My doting sister. I am being spoilt. I find this an odd sensation. Mum did spoil me, on occasions, but that is a mother's prerogative. I do struggle accepting it from other people.

Late afternoon, Dr. Floyd sees me. I enter the room beaming, exclaiming that she has cured me! Dr. Floyd is pleased that I have a genuine smile (none of this pretend nonsense) but warns me not to be quite so extreme. She tells me to hold my horses. How does one hold their horses when I am feeling as divine as this?! She'll be saying I'm escalating into mania next! It is something to feel happy but so much more intense when a year has passed away in the gloom. I don't know how to control such a thing that is leaping to get out. Hold my horses? They are chomping at their bit and positively straining at the reins.

I have to explain my actions on Saturday and Dr. Floyd listens. I say I know I worked myself up to that date. It was important, almost inevitable that I took an overdose. Then she asks that key question, "Do I have any regrets?" I think and answer no. I decide that, my taking an overdose was actually beneficial. It scared me; it brought into stark realisation that I don't want to die. It also affected Dad, a short, sharp shock, an extreme measure, but it worked nonetheless. Dad now has more awareness of how dreadful I was feeling.

I tell Dr. Floyd I want to go back to medicine; I want to start work with Lily. This excites me, I have regained a fraction of that giddy energy which Mum said made me who I am. Mum also thought this contributed to the reason why I would become a good doctor. I had a real passion for purely talking to people. I am ever so tentative but this may be coming back, slowly seeping into my body.

Dr. Floyd says she is looking to discharge me on Friday, with ISS input, as long as my lithium levels are OK. I am happy; home is where I want to be.

27th February

2007

MUM

11.55pm Didn't sleep very well. Awake at 2.30am and 4.30am, after which I only briefly dozed.

Appointment at the hospital with consultant oncologist at 11.05am. Tearful on arrival because bumped first into two nurses I know. Hugs mean tears! Anyway, Dr. Mayhew had an extremely nice manner and will arrange for CAT scan and liver biopsy. Said he couldn't discuss prognosis or treatment (if appropriate!) before these results. I can hardly bear to get the results in case it's the absolute worst and I have a very short time to live. Meanwhile, more drugs – which I am happy to take. Said that the steroid would make me feel a lot better – shrink my enlarged liver a bit and increase my appetite.

Some lighter moments. There was the usual performance with the sheet to cover modesty when examining top and bottom half of the body. It got so rumpled and in the way of examination so I suggested they did away with it altogether: it was a bit silly as he'd seen it all anyway! He agreed and blamed it all on the nurse!! However, post-examination, in my emotional daze (not to mention lack of clear sight due to no contact lenses and vain refusal to keep specs on!) I made for the sheet when it was time to get dressed again! I mean, a mistake anyone could make. That rumpled sheet looked very like my grey jumper and bra!

Visitors in the afternoon - such lovely friends. More flowers from Interflora today – Aunty Joan and Uncle Walter, "every petal a prayer". So many people are praying for me. It's oddly comforting after all. More cards too and a letter from Gilly contained the most lovely sentiments – said that my charm had been always to make other people laugh – and that made me cry too. Ben telephoned (amongst several others!) – had broken news to poor Saf, completely debilitated with multiple sclerosis, and dear, what a rich and fulfilled life I have had compared with hers.

And then…by supper time I seemed to perk up. Surely it couldn't be the one dose of steroids acting so quickly? Enjoyed sitting at the table and eating a meal – although I'm attracted to some odd food. Tonight, once again fish fingers, potatoes and peas. Is it back to the nursery?! Alice made apple amber for dessert. She is proving a good cook – and also did some shopping, including vases! We're running out of suitable receptacles for all the flowers. Ethan went for a meal with his friends. It will be good for him to talk although hope he doesn't drink too much.

Spent the evening watching TV, as usual, but felt much less drowsy and more animated and was actually able to watch sections and hold conversations without thinking of cancer every few seconds.

Of course I mustn't get lulled into a false sense of security. Symptom management is not cure and I must still prepare myself for the worst – if indeed that's mentally possible. One day at a time.

Alice has been a brick!

ALICE

Oncologist appointment today. Mum petrified beforehand. Dad and I go with her and we all pile into the outpatient room. Mum is remarkably calm. She does great. I'm so proud of her. I think she's amazing.

Not sad again today. I know I should be but there was none of that feeling when you know you are about to cry. I don't really like it. It seems wrong. I'm just getting on with jobs and sorting things. Is that distracting me? Stopping me from comprehending the situation?

2008

I phone Sarah, Mog's Mum, with my news: I am better! I haven't spoken to her for several weeks as she has been skiing, so I excitedly convey my newly discovered passion for life. Praise the Lord indeed! She tells me to write this all down so I can read back and remember all this good if ever there are dark times again.

Sarah says to inform her of tomorrow's outcome and, once I am home, we can organise a time when I can stay with her. Oh, how wonderful.

I have my daily converse with Aunty Beth. She is delighted over my current mental state. The immeasurable love of my dear aunty. I am showered with such blessings.

28th February

2007

MUM

Once again fell asleep quickly last night but awake after less than four hours and then couldn't get back to sleep. Tired all day. Tonight I'm trying to cut down the temazepam to 10mg so hope I still feel sufficiently drowsy.

Quite perky first thing and actually did a few jobs. Answered some emails and Alice deleted/sorted out my word docs. Then totally exhausted by the afternoon. Isobel and Julia both came round – the former gave me a very relaxing foot massage, even though I warned her that my feet weren't in the best of shape! The choir girls popped round in the evening with flowers and a lovely soft blanket for when I'm lying on the sofa! Everyone is being so very kind – I counted thirteen lots of flowers today! – and there were more cards and letters in the post.

Alice is being an absolute dream. I hope that the strain of looking after me isn't too much for her. She's doing practically everything. When the hospital rang with details of my liver biopsy on Friday I handed over the phone to Alice – felt incapable of absorbing the information. I hope Alice will be able to accompany me during the procedure. But I am very scared – that it will hurt (despite local anaesthetic) and of what they will find. I am convinced as well that the primary source will turn out to be the pancreas. Not good news at all.

Perked up again in the evening after supper and watched TV as usual. Don't think John is coping all that well. He just hasn't got the nurturing, caring knack – but can't really blame him for not being a woman! He seems to find it easier perhaps when the children aren't around but also, I guess, he must be feeling terrible inside even if he doesn't say anything.

Spent some time in the morning writing down some ideas for my funeral. It sounds morbid but I think it's got to be done. Hope I feel better tomorrow. This afternoon I felt so weak and tired it seemed as if I was fading away. Eating well, though.

ALICE

Mum feeling better this morning. We do what is now our usual routine. I'll come downstairs and climb into bed beside Mum. We lie there under the comforting warmth of the duvet and talk.

Go on the computer. Mum wants me to go through with her, all her documents and delete any that are no longer needed or say things that she doesn't want anyone else to read.

This feels terribly premature to me but she wants to do it. She is so concerned Ethan will read things about him that aren't complementary. She doesn't want to upset him from the grave, so to speak. It's all rather morbid but I dutifully do as she asks. She's happier then, more content. It makes me feel sad though.

Mum not so good in the afternoon. She feels such lethargy, has repeated stabbing pains in her back and is nauseous. Friends of hers visit but I talk to them while she closes her eyes and listens. She likes company, even if she is vaguely drifting off.

Ethan and Dad have their first proper argument since Ethan has been home. I want to cry. I know Dad is struggling and wants Ethan and I to get on with our university courses and not miss loads of work but he is harsh to Ethan. He says Ethan isn't helping being here. Ethan handles it very well for him. He doesn't immediately start shouting or swearing and I'm so impressed and grateful towards him. Ethan fetches me and I calmly say it isn't true and he has been such a help and Mum appreciates him being home etc. I think Dad does know this really but old habits die hard. Dad doesn't like Ethan getting up at lunch time or going out late with friends. Thankfully, Mum does not hear any of this.

2008

Lily and Dad arrive at midday and we sit on a bench by the lake, waiting for my review. I almost have trouble getting my words out as there is just so much to say. I am feeling ecstatic and tell them exactly how great I feel. They try and calm me but there is no dampening this spirit!

My review goes swimmingly. I tell Dr. Floyd I am well, better than well, fantastic! I have unearthed my old self, buried deep inside, but it has now been found. I ask if I can go home today, her original intentions being to discharge me tomorrow, and she agrees. She is pleased to see me so bright, none of this half smile pretending nonsense, which Dr. Floyd saw straight beneath, but seems to think I am erring on the higher side of normal, not manic, but considerably energetic! She wants to tether this elevated mood before it escapes.

I ask to stop all my medication. I am still dubious as to how much the tablets have really affected me. Dr. Floyd says no! Lithium is to stay, probably increased depending on my bloods.

Promethazine and citalopram unaltered. I persuade her to reduce my quetiapine – it doesn't do anything anyway and is my most disliked drug. I am sleeping better, perhaps six hours a night, but now even that feels superfluous. I don't have the lethargy that invaded me, tiredness has evaporated.

I tell her that to medicine I shall return, this was Dr. Floyd's aim from the beginning, starting with Lily first thing next week. Dr. Floyd laughs and tells me to take it easy, nothing too taxing. I think this is taking it slowly, if I had the choice I would be at the surgery this afternoon! I am allowed to leave once pharmacy have dispensed my medication. I am dispatched to ISS who will see me at home and, as an outpatient, appointment with Dr. Floyd in four weeks time.

1st March

2007

MUM

11.25pm A good day! Despite poor night's sleep (only 10mg temazepam – upped the dose again tonight!), had much more energy and appetite. Isobel visited in the morning with flowers and home-made savoury cheese biscuits. Particularly good to see Isobel – so sensitive and knowing the right things to say; at the same time still enabling me to have a laugh. A tonic!

Lovely letter in the post from Aunty Joan, plus photos. Telephoned her and Uncle Walter later. Both sounded fairly frail and slower of speech – but what kind sentiments, looking upon me as the second daughter they never had. They have lit a candle for me. Never was there a better time to believe in the powers of prayer!

Ate delicious lentil soup, made by Alice, for lunch and in the afternoon John drove me to see Julia. Can hardly believe I've had a little outing. Feel so much stronger – but mustn't confuse with getting better! Sue had picked me a posy of wild flowers and gave me half a dozen eggs from her layers. And the world is still a beautiful place: blossom on the trees, crocuses, birds in the hedgerows.

Got back to find present of three jars of jam from Prue and home-made cakes from Wendy next door. The latter visited later and returned with home-made bread pudding for supper. The kindness of everyone is truly astounding. Phone calls later from friends too. In fact, my diary entries really don't do justice to the number of phone calls, texts, cards, letters and presents I have received over the past few days.

Ethan went out to see his friend Mike, in the evening, whose partner has just had a second (unplanned) baby. Ethan says it's very sweet – he's always been keen on babies! TV and crosswords in the evening. Quite relaxing, really. What a pity this is all about cancer. Sometimes it's hard to believe.

I love you all.

ALICE

I get into bed with Ma about 7am. She didn't get much sleep and has just been lying awake. She gets out one of her diaries and starts reading me extracts. She doesn't want to leave anything that may sound upsetting for either Dad or Ethan. It's sad really, as much is written on how horrible they have been to her. I feel myself forcing back tears. So many years I have comforted and calmed and reassured her.

I think she goes through most of the diary and then gives it to me. She needn't have worried, they probably wouldn't have read it anyway. No secrets – Maisie has asked me about everything and got me to discard certain things she wouldn't want others to see. She gives me her all. She is always terribly honest. She says we've always been able to tell each other and share everything. That does make me cry and I lie there with silent tears slowly rolling down my face. I feel guilty and ashamed and dishonest. She tells me everything and yet I have purposely withheld things from her. The worst part is, she doesn't know that and now she never will. Her sickness will ensure her ignorance.

I went out today for an hour to do shopping, pick up medication etc. and left Mum with friends who popped over. While I was out, I heard Mum's anguished cry. She was in such pain and was calling, "Ali, Ali". My heart was racing; I couldn't see my surroundings. Then it stopped and everything went back to normal. This must have lasted only a matter of seconds but I realised I was unprotected, vulnerable if I wasn't with Mum. They have found a way into my head, again latched onto my worst fears. They want to show they are still in control of me.

2nd March

2007

MUM

Midnight. A very difficult day despite good night's sleep. Didn't wake until heard John in the shower at 6.45am. Despite that, terribly anxious about the biopsy procedure and its implications.

In the event, it wasn't that bad. Lovely Irish nurse called Elaine who held my hand and called me "Darling". Doctor with calm and pleasant manner and who explained everything carefully. Even showed me the lesions in the biopsy jar!

Back on the day ward, went downhill. Some light moments – e.g. mega-mouth gay male nurse. Funny side wore off when I was so tired and couldn't sleep because of his volume. Never mind patient confidentiality, Alice and I knew details of everyone on the ward.

John there at beginning and collected at end; Alice for the duration. Light of my life. She is having to carry such a heavy load on her young shoulders. I am glad she is a Christian. She will need a lot of inner strength. Ethan also being lovely – did some chores and made a soup.

Beth and Alex arrived at about 11pm. Poor Beth looks very drained and had had a bad journey, with pouring rain and an accident. I MUST make more effort to be cheerful tomorrow because I am dragging everyone else down with me and it just isn't fair.

Took the outer dressing off the biopsy site before going to bed. Made me feel horrible, even though just titchy plaster underneath, thinking of the badness inside me.

ALICE

Mum had her liver biopsy today. She was so scared, not just of the procedure but more the results, even though she won't get them until next week. She was great though, so calm.

She had to stay on the ward for six hours afterwards. She lay there and I tried my best to distract her from her thoughts. We talked and did the crossword. After two hours she was allowed to eat and given some toast. She then perked up a bit and we sat laughing at the nurses.

Mum then became very tired and lay there looking so small and poorly. Lethargy overwhelmed her. My little Maisie, I wanted to protect her and look after her so much.

3rd March

2007

MUM

12.30am Slept very well last night. John went swimming in the morning – and Alice and Beth got in bed with me for a chat! Such a dear daughter and sister.

Quite a productive morning, sorting through papers. Then Lauren arrived, with flowers and lavender soaps etc., and sweets for the children. My lovely old school friend.

Tired in the afternoon but pleased to see Matthew as well, who turned up on the doorstep with a bunch of daffodils and gave me hugs. Lauren, Ethan and Alex went into town later which was nice – gave things a semblance of normality.

John's homemade shepherd's pie for supper after which I seemed to perk up! We all watched "What's Eating Gilbert Grape?" – my third viewing but such a good film. Actually managed to stop thinking about cancer for some reasonable chunks of time.

Ethan and Alex went into town late on for a drink. Beth, Alice and I watched TV and I felt quite bright and more animated. Hard to tell which symptoms can be attributed to the disease and which to my anxiety! Shall miss Beth dreadfully when she goes tomorrow.

ALICE

Aunty Beth and cousin Alex here and Lauren came for the day. Mum doing well. We all sat in the front room, chatting and giggling.

Aunty Beth slept in my room with me in the double bed that Dad built. It was lovely to be lying next to her, whispering ourselves to sleep. So comforting. I'm blessed to have a wonderful Aunty, except we were more like friends at a sleep over.

4th March

2007

MUM

11.30pm The day started very badly after fitful and insufficient sleep. Felt very nauseous and came straight back to bed after breakfast. Beth and Alex were supposed to be leaving in the morning but, in the event, didn't go until the afternoon. A miserable rainy day.

Holly here in the evening with a fish pie she had cooked and fresh vegetables. Alice, Holly and I had a long talk about John who doesn't seem to be coping well. Never good on the emotional front, we wish there was someone he could talk to now. He seems to get cross and react in an inappropriate way at times – but such a difficult situation to deal with.

Ethan is saying the sweetest things and showing such love and gratitude for everything I've done for him. All our squabbles forgotten. Alice continues to be amazing. She will make the most brilliant doctor. I am so very proud of her.

My back hurting as I write this. More difficult to get comfortable now. Apprehensive about tomorrow – but what choice? Hope I sleep well.

ALICE

Very hard morning. Mum so poorly. Me, Mum and Aunty Beth were all in tears. Aunty Beth didn't want to leave with Mum in such a state. I helped Mum back to bed with hot water bottle and radio on. She was so distressed which was extremely hard to dampen and agonizing to watch.

Mum slept and felt better. Aunty Beth and Alex drove home in the afternoon and then Holly came round. Ethan was very sad this evening and struggling a little. He told Mum she had been a mother *and* a father to him and they both were crying. I'm glad Ethan's not embarrassed or anxious to conceal his tears. He cries openly.

Dad and Ethan went to bed early and Mum, Holly and I stayed up talking, mainly about family. Holly talked about when she was ill and saying all the things Mum did and said how she has been a second Mum to her and how great that has been. It's lovely that Holly and Jack get on so well with Ma. There is no animosity.

5th March

2007

MUM

00.15am Didn't get to sleep until gone 1am last night, despite two temazepam, except I was very anxious about the CT scan. Felt bad in the morning, dozing on the sofa.

The CT scan wasn't as frightening as I expected but none the less a bit tearful during the hour before, doubtless thinking of the results and the prospect of my back hurting lying on the bed. Felt very weak.

Arrived back home to find blue hyacinths from dear Lily on the doorstep. Everyone continues to be so very kind, with phone calls and texts. Julia visited late afternoon but I could barely open my eyes and so she and Alice chatted in the main.

Very loose bowel movements all day – upset stomach, due to the illness, anxiety, the stuff I had to drink at the hospital…Alice's lentil soup?! This last item was, in fact, delicious.

Another evening of TV rubbish but nice to be close to the children; they both gave me a foot massage. John is finding things very difficult. I wish he could soften up emotionally and get closer to us all. My back is hurting too much to write anymore tonight. May have to stop writing diary in bed. Too difficult to get comfortable?

I am so very proud of the way the children are coping and I hope John will be proud of them one day too.

ALICE

Mum had her CT scan today. She was so worried this morning and in pain and terribly tired. I wanted to take all that pain away from her. I wanted it all on me instead.

At hospital Mum did so well. She was very calm and I was so proud of how she was coping. She is my shining star and now, instead of fading, she keeps getting brighter.

Dad has returned to his usual ways. He gets cross over the little, unimportant things which now seem just so trivial. No-one has anything left inside them to give any space or thought to these pedantic behaviours.

Ethan is doing remarkably well. Dad has always treated Ethan worse than me but why does he still persist now? Ethan lost his calm composure tonight though. He told Dad to fuck off and I shamefully admit I was thinking the same. Ethan then cried and I hugged him, a proper long hug. Ethan says if Mum dies he will hardly ever see Dad again. He only sees him now because Mum lives with him. Ethan says he'll stay at Holly's when he comes back to Essex. Ethan says he hates Dad.

The problem is, I know all this with Mum has affected Dad but when he acts the same, it's so hard to see how Dad cares. Dad won't even go and sit with Mum in the front room. That's all Mum wants: company, presence around her. Ethan and I spent over an hour massaging her feet tonight and she loved it, that physical contact.

Ethan and I stayed up talking. It was good to talk to him. I liked it. It reassured me that we are able to effortlessly chat about these things that are affecting us the most. I promised Ma I'd take care of Ethan. I do feel very protective towards him, always have, after all, I am his big sister.

The prospect of going to bed filled me with trepidation so I decided I needed a walk. Ethan told me to be careful. I walked in the rain but didn't notice I was cold and wet until I got back home. It's peculiar what you can block out when your mind is obsessively preoccupied by such emotion-filled thoughts. I was weary though. The lack of sleep chasing me was gradually beginning to catch up. My bed was warm and comfortable but sleep is alluding and likes to hide.

6th March

2007

ALICE

Horrendous morning. Mum was in so much pain she couldn't move. She just lay on the sofa whimpering and all I could do was stroke her, whisper to her, love her so much. It's so tremendously hard to watch someone in pain. The tears ran down my face, a silent, unhindered visible picture reflecting my inmost anguish. This was the worst time.

Mum admitted to hospital. For her, it was such an extreme effort to get there. A delightful porter got her out of the car, into a wheelchair but even that was too much - excruciating pain just to sit upright.

Mum has her own room on the ward. It's nice and clean, Mum's main concern. They give her oromorph immediately and it takes the edge off her agony. The consultant sees her: adenocarcinoma most probably from the bowel but CT scan failed to show a definite primary cancer. Chemotherapy to start tomorrow. Not curable but treatable, if she responds to the chemo. All the medication buys her time but I just want them to make her feel better. This morning she wanted it all to end; she wanted me to be able to give her a massive dose of morphine just to stop it all. She doesn't want to prolong a life like this.

I leave the hospital late evening and can't bear to go. What have I done? Maisie always says that dying is the thing she is scared of the most and that you have to die alone. No-one can share that with you. I promised her I would be with her, always there. But now I'm not. I can't bear to be apart from her. I want to be with her forever. She doesn't like being on her own. I feel I've let her down. I want to be with my darling Maisie.

Get home and Dad is telling Ethan off about such a trivial matter. Ethan doesn't rise to it. I wish Dad wouldn't. I feel very sad but then glad that Mum doesn't have to witness this. I feel sorry for Ethan. I suppose I also agree with him. Dad should be there, being strong for Ethan. Whatever has happened, whatever is still happening, Ethan will always be the son and Dad always the father. The irreversible order. Fathers should be protective. Without Mum, I can't see a family. It will all fall apart. There will be nothing.

7th March

2007

MUM

1.25pm Well, this is it. Too ill to make appointment with Dr. Mayhew yesterday and admitted to Crowhurst ward. Everyone being very kind but have felt pretty grim. Drugs regime at least sorting out the pain in my back and later this afternoon I have my first lot of chemo – which I am dreading. Really cannot cope with sickness – nausea or vomiting – so fingers crossed. And then there's always the chance that it won't even be effective. The CT scan didn't pick up the primary cancer site although Dr. Mayhew thinks most likely the bowel. Either way, he says it's a question of treatment not cure.

I am very thin and the hospital food is crap. Hard tc
that such innutritious food is thought suitable for patients. Al:
very dirty. Need a decent shower and hair wash. Oh well, gu
fact that I even care about this at all must mean that I'm feeli
better. Actually walked to the loo this morning which is an
improvement on yesterday when I had to be taken in a wheelchair
and was very wobbly and in a lot of pain.

10.20pm The afternoon turned out well. I really did perk up
after a grotty morning. Sat in a chair and received a lot of visitors!
Huge bunch of flowers from the choir and beautiful nightdresses
from Prue – plus food, flannels, hand cream. You name it! The
thoughtfulness. Dr. Mayhew also popped in to see me. My only fear
tonight is that the chemo will make me sick so I am dreading going to
sleep and the next morning. But what choice in any case?

ALICE

Go to hospital and see Mum. She is sitting up in a chair. It
is the first time I have seen her do that since coming home. "Perky
not puffy" – my newly coined phrase for Ma on a good day since
Granny said, "Steroids, don't they make you go puffy?"!!

Mum does really well. Friends come and visit. Her
chemotherapy starts: five continuous days worth. Side effects
shouldn't kick in until tomorrow. But, poor thing, she is so worried
about sickness. She hates the thought, the feeling and is obviously
anxious. That is when she doesn't want to be alone. It scares her too
much. This pains me. I want to be by her side always, to hold her
hand, offer comfort but mainly, just to be there, next to her.

Mum likes me to help her get ready for bed. Although the
nurses are lovely, she much prefers me, family. We trundle down the
corridor, drip in tow, to go to the bathroom. I stay with her while she
goes to the toilet. Up until now, I have waited outside, Mum not
locking the door in case something happens, but she is too unsteady
and in need of someone to reassure and support her. I help her
wash and put on a clean nightie. I don't show it in my face but her
frail, tiny body does affect me. She seems so little, so fragile. I want
to scoop her up, hold her in my arms and keep her there.

2008

I have been absent from medicine for a year; I feel my
knowledge may have been chipped away, reducing my brain to a
handful of facts, inexpertly hooked together. Aside from psychiatry,
an area which I was thrown into, unable to get away from, unable to
stop my brain from analysing the drugs, the diagnoses, the other

patients, my placements seem a distant memory, there but furry at the edges, not quite complete.

My mornings are still occupied by ISS – they are adamant that I can only have my medication for one day, no more. I do not mind these visits. If Carrie or Joanne come, I attempt to talk about important things. I trust them. I am still thwarted by the bad musings in my head, telling me I should not talk, but sometimes I feel I need to. If any of the other nurses come, I just smile and say I am fine because I am OK now, compared to how I was. The other nurses don't know the right questions to ask me, they don't know how to catch me out, how to get beneath my cheery mask. Only a few can do that.

I still have my secrets however. I always thought the medications had little reflection on my mental state. Since being home, I have stopped taking the citalopram. I have tried a few nights without promethazine (my sedative) but found it increasingly difficult to get to sleep. I have to take lithium as they will know, from my blood tests, if I haven't!

Afternoon in Lily's surgery. This is my first day. As I say I am a medical student, I hear my voice expel the words, thick as treacle. I am a medical student. The concept still astounds me. I feel I am an impostor, disguised as something I am not. How am I almost a doctor? I feel I have cheated somehow, snuck inside an occupation which is not mine.

8th March

2007

MUM

5.45am So far so good – although it's probably too early to tell. Got about four hours sleep (11.30pm – 3.30am), only briefly woken by poor woman – probably vomiting – next door. My fault forgetting to shut my door, having got my drip all plugged in again after visit to loo – and then not liking to bother a nurse with the bell!

Lay awake until about 5.30am, listening to Radio 3. Gentle classical sounds throughout – what could be more soothing? Some Vivaldi – but so much I have never heard before. Then rang nurse for morphine. Back aching and obviously wasn't woken for my four hourly dose at 3am – but nothing unbearable and walked to the loo. Turned down offer of dreaded commode! Also, feeling peckish! Have just had a cup of tea with toast and marmalade. Still anxious re. the possibility of nausea and vomiting but they've assured me that food won't affect this.

At the moment I feel very much at peace and full of calm. Carpe diem! Dear Alice stayed after visiting hours last night and will doubtless be worrying about my state this morning. Hope that she is managing to get sleep, knowing that I am in good hands here. My admiration for this bunch of nurses knows no bounds! Palliative care requires very special skills. They get it absolutely right. You don't want doom and gloom but not too much bustling cheerfulness either. Calm, quiet efficiency – gentleness – that's what you need. And, in general, this is a gift of a woman.

ALICE

I go into hospital early and sit with Mum. She feels terribly nauseous and just lies there, eyes closed. I sit next to her and watch her breathing. I don't think I'd really noticed how different she looked until other people mentioned it. To me, she just looked like Mum. But I look now: her face is pale and slightly drawn, her eyelids swollen, her body limp, the skin no longer taught on her arms but slipping away.

Hour after hour I sit there, alone. Mum vaguely offering conversation then returning to her slumber. She is full of tiredness but sleep evades her. I wish I could take all the pain away. I've let her down. I said I'd be with her. I said I wouldn't let her go.

9th March

2007

ALICE

In hospital early again. I sit in the squashy chair, curl up, my legs crossed, and watch Maisie. Apart from the slight movement of her chest with each slow breath, her body is still. She has no energy for anything other than respiration, like a string puppet, collapsed on the floor.

After a few hours, although I can't be sure, time seems to have taken on another dimension, Mum says she needs the toilet. She grips her drip stand and clutches my arm. We shakily make our way down the corridor but Mum is terribly unsteady. She half falls, half sinks into a visitor's chair. A nurse fetches a wheelchair and we continue down the short corridor. I help Mum onto the toilet but she is almost too weak to sit. She holds me, wanting me directly in front of her, frightened she'll fall.

Once back in Mum's room, she suddenly feels sick and, still in the wheelchair, hunches over a cardboard sick bowl, retching. All I can do is be there next to her. It's terrible to watch. She's incredibly hot and I try and cool her forehead with a wet flannel but this soon becomes too warm for any benefit. She isn't actually sick and we (the nurse and I) manage to lie Mum on the bed, fan blasting cool air over her.

The nurse leaves. Mum looks at me with weary eyes and says, when she feels as bad as this, she wishes she would fall asleep and never wake up. I fight the immediate urge to cry, fearing that, if I start, quiet tears down my cheeks may escalate into ill-controlled sobs. I can't empathise with her physical pain because never have I experienced anything close but I do know the all-consuming sensation of wanting to die. I know that feeling of enough, no more. Life no longer has a place. Except, my restless silence is strictly maintained. Mum shall never know of any of the bad thoughts inside my head. They are mine to keep. I am the keeper of the keys. These are things she doesn't need to know. I shall not selfishly share the battle of my mind.

By the afternoon, Mum appears more animated. She stays in bed but manages to, albeit briefly, chat to a few visitors who come offering their love and support. This tires her though and, as evening approaches, she is listening to me talk to her friends whilst she lies there, eyes closed. I help Mum clean her teeth and then leave. The slow trudge home in the street lamp illuminated darkness now so familiar.

Once home, I try and talk to Dad. I'm sure he's finding this terrifically hard, he just gives so little away. I then go to Ethan's room and chat. Ethan has opened a bottle of wine so I help myself to a glass and sit in the front room alone. My head is fuzzy and drifting after only drinking half my glass but I carry on and have a second drink. I like the feeling it gives my head: the distance it creates, the space between me and my emotions, the rest it gives me, the ability to just be still and let my head loll back against the chair, the way everything goes in slow motion. Wine is definitely my medicinal cure, my only comforter, my only reliever of troubled thoughts, my calm inducer, my only friend. This last thought depresses me. I don't want to dismiss my friends because it isn't them, it's me. I have no inclination to call them. I don't want to talk. I wouldn't know what to say.

Ethan comes down and we vaguely chat, crap TV in the background, and together we get progressively drunk. Normal conversation peppered with stuff related to Mum. It is relaxed and requires no effort. By this time, I cannot move. Tiredness compounded by alcohol has rendered me incapable of motion.

10th March

2007

ALICE

The mornings always bring the worst cruelties of the illness. Mum is too tired to even open her eyes. She remains in the same position, knees bent, arms folded and I watch, vaguely attempt to distract myself with a magazine someone has brought, but my eyes always wander back to Mum. Their automatic roaming, uncontrolled by me.

Mum suddenly wakes from one of her brief lapses into sleep. Her breathing quickens and she moans, eyes alarmingly wide open, looking at me, almost to check I am there. There is a rigidity in her stare which is unsettling. Mum has these frightening dreams where people sit or stand on her and she tries to move to get them off but she's paralysed and she tries to shout but she's mute. No-one notices. She feels suffocated. When she wakes, she needs to move her legs and see me just to make sure. Even her sleep instils fear.

Before lunch, Mum manages to sit on a chair by her sink and I gently wash her, the warm flannel cleansing her withered little body. Mum says I shouldn't have to see her like this but I am glad. I feel blessed to have time in abundance devoted to caring for her. I like the way that I can soothe her skin, help her into a crisp new nightie, comb her neglected hair.

Mum lying in bed once again, I sheepishly admit that I prefer the mornings. I tell Mum it's nice just me and her. It is always calm. I tell her I like it when neither of us speaks, we just know. Mum says it's that unspoken understanding between us and begins to cry. She reaches out and I hold her hand, except her fingers are stroking mine, she is the comforter, roles reversed. Tears fill my eyes. This single, simple gesture means a wealth more. Mum is reluctant to touch anyone. She can no longer bear anything near her face and shrinks away if I try and stroke the backs of her hands. She likes space of her own. The way she held my hand was so powerful.

It is I who needs the physical contact. I'm desperate to hold her, hug her, kiss her, but force myself to resist. The moment lingers and then Dad knocks on the door, comes in and the magic disappears. But no-one can take that moment from my mind. It is glimpses like this, when I catch Maisie's eye, that I hold onto. These brief acts enough to sustain my strength.

I'm the last person to leave the hospital, after our now routine teeth clean and face wash. I stay with Mum while she settles and then get home 10ish. Aunty Beth, Uncle Angus, Holly and Jack are all here and we sit chatting, laughing over a bottle of wine. It is so easy, so effortless, just like normal. I almost forget about Mum. But then the guilt comes flooding back and I wish I wasn't enjoying myself. It doesn't seem right and I definitely feel uneasy inside.

I sit outside with Jack while he has a cigarette and Jack says how odd it seems without Mum. She is always here, at home, and Jack can't remember when she wasn't. Mum is the ever-present, always welcoming, mainstay of the house. Jack finds this hard. I agree. I'm lost without her at home.

2008

Evening surgery with Lily. She put me in my own consulting room and sent me my own patients! I did not have time to worry about this, probably my largest apprehension. I was nervous as to being trusted with patients alone. I felt I had such a tenuous grip on reality and was so afraid if I struggled and let down my iron guard. This would not be right. I couldn't do that to patients; it wouldn't be fair.

However, before I even registered, a patient had been ushered in and Lily had disappeared. Lily is very good for instant decisions. I remembered my intentions in hospital: no planning, just plough in. That is exactly what happened and it was great! I was chatting away at ease and I could remember key questions and red flags. I met a patient with Charcot-Marie-Tooth disease which was fascinating. This is one of those diseases you are taught because it is a relatively easy disorder to pick up on genetic screening, but actually is quite rare so it tends to be a book-learnt, rather than patient-learnt disease. I spent a good ten minutes talking to this lovely woman about CMT and she was happy to tell me all about it (I was only aware of the *very* fundamental aspects!). That is what I love about patients, their open, trusting natures. Doctors are in such unique positions and I always find it extremely humbling.

As a medical student, patients are usually far more informed as to their illness than you are, and the majority will happily chat away if you show an interest. Collectively, patients hold a wealth of knowledge, such an educational tool. I could probably learn enough from patients in order to pass my exams!

11th March

2007

ALICE

Mum very poorly today – sickness and diarrhoea. Mentally she's struggling. She tells me she wants to shut her eyes and drift away. Externally I'm calm but it's only masking an internal furnace, violently screaming away. What am I supposed to think when my mother is telling me she wants to die?

I help Mum on the commode several times. She wants me to be the one to help her but, concurrently, she keeps repeating that I shouldn't have to see this. I shouldn't have to care for her, see my mother like this. I always tell her (even though I know she already knows) that I don't mind at all and I love being able to help her in that small way. It is all true. I think it is a wonderful privilege. I wonder why Mum keeps repeating her protests but then I change the roles and put myself in Mum's position. Of course Mum would be the first person I would want caring for me but I should still hate the fact. How much easier it is when you are the one offering – giving is so much more obliging than receiving.

The caring, in itself, a slight problem: Dad and Ethan. There is just something about women helping women. Mum certainly does not want Dad helping her on the commode! But, how can I say this to them? How can I deny them time with Mum when I'm with her so much? I've taken far more than my share of Mum's time but at Mum's request. I don't want to offend Dad and Ethan but, at the same time, I want to do what Mum wants. She must come first.

I think Dad despises me. I'm doing everything. But Mum wants me. I'm sure Dad hates me for that, even though he doesn't want to do any of the things I'm doing for Mum. Will he ever forgive me?

2008

Convinced myself I had serotonin syndrome tonight. Mentally, I'm fantastic, all is dandy, but physically I haven't faired as well. I've had palpitations, tingling in my fingers, dizziness, I've fainted and been sick. These episodes are only brief and, in-between times, I feel absolutely fine.

Tonight, I was a bit breathless as well so, with my guilty conscience in tow, I fled to Lily's, convinced that all of this was self-inflicted. I was honest with her and hurriedly expelled my predicament as if the speed would make my non-compliance less bad. Lily, of course, wasn't cross with me. She knows my dislike and distrust of drugs. I told Lily I attempted a (somewhat brief!) decreasing of the dose. I was on 40mg citalopram in hospital; I came home and took 20mg for almost a week (maybe five days) and then stopped. Lily said herein may lie my problem – those decreases are usually carried out over weeks, not days! I was most likely in withdrawal. Lily took my pulse (racing but regular) and my temperature. This was another symptom, I have been really hot, even in the chilly winds, as if someone has turned up my hypothalamus, like a thermostat.

As I felt medications haven't affected my mental state (I don't think they have improved anything, but they certainly haven't worsened me either), I was now humorously outraged. All my tablets were now making me physically unwell. Oh, fantastic! Just what I needed. Have to start taking citalopram again; Laurel said 20mg tonight and then 20mg in the morning. Rubbish! I wanted fewer tablets, not more! But I shall do what Lily says, compliance, such an issue and I am the ultimate culprit. I am secretive and have too much knowledge.

12th March

2007

MUM

3.55pm I'm not sure about the date but I know it's Monday and I guess it's something to be in a position to be writing a diary entry at all. Very tired – have dozed a lot of today – but the terrible effects of the chemo seem to be wearing off finally.

It's all been as ghastly as I feared – the pain, the nausea (although not actual vomiting), the constipation, the diarrhoea, the lack of appetite, the weakness. On this side of the fence it's all been pretty much how I imagined from my brief nursing days.

Everyone has been wonderful although, in the main, haven't had much stamina for visitors. Too much effort! Personal care from dear Alice all I want. Have been too poorly to care about loss of dignity and – although it's dreadful for her (the sights, the sounds, the smells!) – there is great comfort for me in sisterhood (general meaning of the word, Alice!).

This weekend was actually full of visitors although, must admit, didn't care whether they were here or not. But the kindness! Jack back from Barcelona. Alice said it was good for her, Ethan, Holly and Jack to be together, John is learning to move more quietly and appreciate what I need more – it is very difficult for him. An impulsive fixer, he's been left with a problem that can't be.

Small milestones. Today I got washed at the sink - a huge, tiring effort but made me feel a little less like a skunk. My hair is disgusting. As Alice said, it will soon be at the point where it begins to wash itself!

There's mention of this "first" lot of chemo treatment but, at the moment, feel that I can't face anymore. Have fantasised in the night about jumping off the hospital roof – but not nice for someone else to pick up the pieces (literally!), plus it would go against Biblical teaching and I'm not sure I could do this to Alice, Mum etc. On the other hand…a tempting quick finish. It would be fine if you could just be given a massive dose of morphine and drift off but I know all about the fine line – and it will take forever. I'll try not to think about this too much today.

Actually I should say that the pain is under control. It just takes time adjusting the drugs but all the staff are adamant that, where possible, should be total pain management. Even the wheat seed back pad that you put in the microwave is a comfort! And the lavender pillow from Grace. Grains of comfort!

Everyone seems to be assuming that I can't wait to get home but I feel I am in the best place at the moment. Too weak surely to be leaving the ward and shall miss nursing care at the end of a buzzer! Of course, there's always Alice – but what a strain on her!

<u>Room 7</u>

Room 7. The clock on the wall says 7.
It watches me so that sometimes
If I only half turn my head
It becomes the open face of a kindly nurse
A head around the door.

By my side, the digital clock on the machine
Distils the hours of sick bag pain,
Infuses nausea.
My inert arm,
Choice less,

Lies steady to receive its dose of toxins.
'There is no worse than this,' you think.
And yet you remain to think there is no worse.
Thought itself belies your words.

Out of the square of window light
The hospital roof. A detail.
Victorian moulding at the top of the drainpipe
Catches your eye and you unawares,
Invites you to black flights of fantasy.

But the ways of the roof are tortuous.
Too tortuous for this sick body to climb.

ALICE

Better day today. Mum still extremely tired and slept on and off most of the morning but not feeling quite so grim. Just before lunch she managed to get to the sink and I was able to give her a proper wash. I rubbed cream into her back and could feel each rib as my fingers rippled over the contours. I then moisturised her legs and her thin flaccid calves could fit in my one hand. I felt as if I couldn't be gentle enough, her body barely holding itself together: a little rag doll I was cradling in my hands.

Mum can now hold a short conversation in between her exhausted little naps. Tonight she smiled at a shared joke between me and her about Dad. It must be days since I last saw her smile because it had such a profound affect on me. Not only could I see, I could feel her smile as well.

2008

Went to Lily's surgery in the morning. Saw walk-in patients initially, then I had to have my bloods done for lithium levels...I am so over needles! Lily then had a few minor surgery patients and she allowed me to do most of it! It was brilliant. I injected anaesthetic and burnt off warts and saw steroid injections. I found it fascinating and good fun having such a hands-on role.

I had to leave at lunch time as Carrie from ISS had been trying to contact me. She came round in the afternoon and I did as Lily had told me – told the truth. Carrie went mad and I got sufficiently told off, a tirade of how I must take my medications, if I don't, the ISS will not be prepared to see me. I considered this, the ISS are lovely but I don't need them anymore so I felt it wasn't important. However, Carrie didn't mean this. If I don't see ISS then I will be back in hospital. Carrie has the old threat, don't comply and I will be sectioned. I certainly do not wish to return to the psych unit but surely I am not sectionable? The question, can I risk it? No, but this only encourages me to lie.

Carrie tells me that, if I stopped taking citalopram a week ago then my mood would be liable to decrease nowish, maybe towards the weekend. This meant I still have to see ISS every day! Doh! I knew I should have lied. I felt like a naughty school girl, weakly attempting protestations by nodding my head in shame. It was like being told off by a teacher! I could have been fifteen years younger. This was most likely as I was acting this age. I wondered if, perhaps, shock tactics work. Maybe Carrie getting cross will stir me into submission. Unfortunately, it seems to have had the opposite effect. Now, I am determined to take 20mg citalopram (no withdrawal symptoms, I reason I shall take half dose for a while) and not tell anyone. It will be kept to myself from now on.

The medication conundrum. Logically, I realise I am a hypocrite. I would be telling patients to take all their tablets but, I also feel that I didn't have a problem with a chemical solution. Yes, I was unwell but no, it wasn't a simple depression. It didn't have a neuro-transmitter answer, the tablets did not help. Mentally, I have felt the same, being on or off the drugs. Physically, they have sometimes made me ill! Not the best combination. Then, there are all the dark noises in my head. It feels wrong to be seeing people (ISS, doctors etc) even if I don't talk about the bad things. It is wrong to take the tablets. They don't like it; it isn't right; I shouldn't be indulging in help.

13th March

2007

MUM

6.25pm When I woke in the night to go to the loo (use the commode!) and was woken just, to have obs done (!) … both times I really did open my eyes and think, "Where the hell am I?", just like characters in children's story books always do!

Cup of tea this morning, preceded by about half a cream cracker. Seem to feel a bit hungry on waking but then, by time breakfast arrives, it's a struggle. Pomp and Circumstance on Radio 3 and I shut my eyes and I am up there on stage with the Royal Choral Society – so many happy times at the Albert Hall. Rich life.

9pm Well, I guess it was a better day on balance after meds cock-up in morning and quite a bit of nausea. Working really hard on nutrition! Prue came but no other visitors – just how I wanted it (apart from John, Ethan and Alice of course). There's some talk of Macmillan nurses and link with the Hospice, which is all very sobering – but what can you do? Think they believe I'm slipping into patient mode but, frankly, have the strength for little else. Still, managed a bit of a wash – virtually unaided – at the sink tonight. My mouth is very sore and my tongue looks disgusting, despite the mouthwashes and Nystatin.

Dear Alice looks very tired and, I expect, is surviving on very little food and sleep. John also looking exhausted. When you consider that he watched his father die of cancer and now has a sister, Maggie, and wife in the same position, it must be pretty devastating for him – although, of course, he never verbalises any feelings at all. Ethan is a calming presence in the afternoons; he has turned into such a wonderful son of whom I am truly proud.

Someone on the ward has Down's Syndrome. How difficult must that be? I can hardly bear to think about it. Imagine dear Zac.

2008

Lily's birthday – I made her a coffee and walnut cake! In the evening, went to the theatre to see Habeas Corpus, Alan Bennett. I had wanted to go and had a troop of girls with me. They found it funny, we were all laughing, you really can't go wrong with Alan, such a wonderful writer, introduced to me by Mum who regularly taught his plays in her A level classes. Mum loved his writing and I remember, when I was much younger, listening to "Talking Heads" on tape, a different play each night. Although, tonight, I did question the appropriateness – one character trying to commit suicide (overdoses, hanging etc) and another being injected with a sedative!

Good fun evening and went for a drink after. Didn't realise the time (when pubs stay open, there isn't an 11pm reminder!) so got home gone 1am. Felt good.

14th March

2007

MUM

1.30am Awoke hungry and have just asked for toast, marmalade and tea. Hope a good idea! Can only try! Midnight feast or what?!

Bit of a grim night as it turned out. Gripey pains, nausea and diarrhoea. Felt too bad to manage breakfast and the morning a struggle. However, Alice did super job in getting me bathed and hair washed – a marathon and totally exhausted afterwards, but guess it was worth it. Felt brighter and had more energy in afternoon. They say I'll probably be going home tomorrow. Frankly am a bit alarmed at the prospect because of ongoing nausea and the lack of nursing care at the end of a buzzer – but what real choice? Plus, I'm due back in two weeks – so soon! Shall I ever recover in time? – if my bloods are OK, that is.

Hard to keep positive when you're feeling lousy although everyone around me continues to be brilliant. Ange was saying what a wonderful young man Ethan is – charming, sensitive, good-looking, a real credit to me. Certainly have been very impressed with the way he has handled things. Alice continues to shine brightly in the firmament!

ALICE

Mum better this morning and, although she felt it decidedly ambitious, said she would attempt a bath. I took her in the wheelchair and she managed to sit in the luke warm water whilst I washed her hair. Once back in her room, she collapsed on her bed, overcome with exhaustion, dry pillow protected from wet hair with a towel. It's hard to watch someone usually so active take over an hour to have a bath but today, all I could think was, what a star! Such a step forward. How proud I am of her.

2008

Carrie saw me this morning. She makes me feel so comfortable and at ease that I want to tell her everything. I say I still hear the badness in my head. She asks me whether I can hear voices. Voices. Are they? I'm still unsure. I do hear words and threats but there is so much confusion and interruption that it is hard to distinguish. I just know; I feel it. I tell her about the things I see, the shadow world. But they are not formed sufficiently, not solid enough for vivid hallucinations, not quite there. They are too tenacious to reveal themselves fully. They hold the power. Being cunning is in their nature.

15th March

2007

MUM

6.30am Slept well, only waking once to use commode and then going straight back to sleep. At the moment feeling OK. Have just counted the meds to be taken every day – 33: add another 24 to account for fact that can only take paracetamol quartered (Alice says we'll try liquid!) = 57!! And this is without top-ups: oromorph and anti-sickness.

"Va Pensiero" just on Radio 3. I even sang along a bit!

10pm Well I am home – a place I never thought to see again. My best day in the hospital. Definitely felt a bit stronger, although I'm slightly anxious now about the night ahead.

A little tearful on approaching our road. The front garden looked lovely with lots of grape hyacinth in bloom. Wendy next-door popped round and lots of phone calls. Very tired as I write this. My skin looks a mess – unplucked facial hair and thinning effects of the steroids. Oh well, all is vanity.

ALICE

Mum the best I've seen her. Sit with her all morning talking, then she gets dressed, then she sits in the chair!! This is wonderful! Has lunch before Dad comes to pick us up. Mum is very apprehensive about coming back. Worried about being dizzy and unsteady on her feet. Feels OK when is discharged and walks to the car, leaning on me. I feel so strong with my arm beneath hers, as if I could carry her all in my hand.

The drive is only two minutes home but, as soon as we are on the familiar streets, Mum begins to cry. When she was admitted last Tuesday, Mum thought that was the last time she would see our house. She felt she was going to hospital to die. It is a wonderfully sunny afternoon and I feel to see such a beautiful outside world must be much to take in after being confined to a single hospital room. It is a poignant moment for Maisie.

I lie Mum on the sofa. She looks around the front room and says how lovely it is. Ma is home and I am delighted. The separation and longing when Mum was in hospital, all vanished. Now I can always be with her.

16th March

2007

MUM

6am Took longer to go off to sleep last night than in the hospital but then not awake until 5.30am? (Although John thinks I awoke in the night – if so, don't remember so doesn't count!) Kept light and Radio 3 on all night which probably disturbed him. Think perhaps he should move into the spare room. Actually surprisingly nice to awake not in a hospital environment. Feeling hungry so have taken metaclopramide and am going to have early breakfast! Wish I could concentrate to read. Everything still such an effort.

12.30pm I have had a surprisingly good morning in that definitely got a bit more energy. Had a bath, and just little things seemed easier. Alice has been an absolute gem, tidying up and seeing to my every need. As "Granny and Grandad" have always said – they broke the mould when they made Alice! She read to me some poetry she had written, which made me cry – not just the sentiments, but the actual poetry.

The doorbell has just rung – Wendy from next door with a homemade lasagne! What dear friends I have. To have been so blessed, so fortunate makes me cry.

7.30pm Lots of phone calls and texts and visits. Everyone continuing to be stunningly kind and supportive. Alice just back from supermarket for mammoth shop!

ALICE

Lovely to have Mum back home in the mornings. We sit in front of the usual TV programmes and do the quick crossword in the newspaper. I love this time: our time. Mum is tired and still curled up in the chair but she can manage this bit of thinking, interspersed with distraction from easy watching programmes on television.

In the evening, I give Ethan a lift to the station. He's going out in London and, of course, the plan is for him to get the first train back tomorrow morning and get home before Mum wakes. Well meaning plans invariably don't work out with Ethan and I'm envisaging him stumbling through the door, filthy alcohol stained clothes, pupils dilated, obviously wasted and Mum getting upset whilst Ethan collapses on to his bed and doesn't surface until late into the afternoon.

Mum and Dad go to bed early and I stay up, bottle of wine to myself and finish writing my poem to Mum. It's Mothers' Day on Sunday. Ethan and I decided not to buy anything. It all seems terribly materialistic and unimportant. Flowers from all Mum's well-wishers are still decorating the hall, front room and kitchen. Ethan and I are, instead, playing our role as children and making her a card. Although now, even a card seems superfluous. Actions are far more important.

17th March

2007

ALICE

I often find myself calling Mum "Mummy". I suppose before I would use it as an affectionate term or, rather jokingly, when I needed something, but now I seem to have reverted back to that child-like state, even though our roles have reversed and I am the mother doing the caring. I wonder why that is.

Dad is finding this all a strain. I don't think he's sleeping that well. Mum read him a short poem she wrote and asked Dad if he understood it. Dad had a shower and, when he came back, he told Mum that he had felt really upset. He then told her that he loves her very much even if he doesn't always show it, then started to cry. Mum says she's only seen Dad cry once in the whole time they have been together. That moment was so significant, so upsetting. Dad can't replace Mum. She is the only person that has managed to get him to talk, properly talk about important things. I wish I could learn how she does it. I wish I could do the same.

18th March

2007 - Mother's Day

MUM

5.50am Just in case it doesn't last....[!] to record that right now I am feeling good. Woke very early – 4.30am maybe (the birds?!) – and, after lying there for about half an hour, went downstairs and made myself a cup of camomile tea and had a couple of digestive biscuits. Even read some bits in yesterday's newspaper. A pity that John seems to be disturbed – always awake when I am now? – or maybe I'll have to try and wean myself off the bedside light and constant Radio 3?

Mothers' Day! Alice had word processed her poem, which made me cry all over again – especially the bit about the half full/half empty glass. Cards from Alice and Ethan – and Holly, with lovely message. Everything making me cry! Huge bunch of flowers from Jack. Holly came, armed with beautiful white roses in a new vase. As ever, overwhelmed by the kindness of everyone.

Alice continues to amaze, doing absolutely everything – remaining calm, being a rock. How does she do it?

11.30pm A relaxed evening. Watched "Mansfield Park" on TV. Very enjoyable. Nothing like a costume drama to soothe the spirit – and Jane Austin my favourite.

ALICE

I gave Mum the poem I wrote for her and she cried. I didn't mean to make her upset. I wanted it to be nice. Although, maybe the poem is a bit sad and depressing. I don't want to remind her again of how ill she was and, I suppose, still is.

At the moment, I don't know who I'm living for. It certainly feels like Mum, which I know is wrong. But I know that if Mum wasn't here, I wouldn't want to be here either. There will be nothing. She is the only person who has prevented me from carrying out horrendous things in my head, not that she knows this. She stopped me by just being her. That thought was strong enough to provide the resistance.

<u>My Malady Mornings with Maisie</u>

Our mornings together:
I selfishly crave you all to myself,
An unabashed desire for us to be alone,
Complete understanding of unspoken silence,
Achieved by knowing you unreservedly.

In my unseeing eye,
Your face is not that of the ill,
Sparkling history blinkers any objective judgment.
You remain my beautiful Maisie,
Present cannot change what the past has sown.

I watch your curled body,

Starfish

Painfully still bar your weary breaths,
I want to scoop you into my arms,
My string puppet limp;
How I long to be your puppeteer.

The rhythm of your hospital room,
Cacophony of background noise,
Calmly combining into now familiar sounds:
Radiator tapping, drip clicking, radio playing,
Noise to drown out the over-analysing consciousness.

The glass half full, half empty conundrum,
Matters not as neither glass is whole,
I want to pour my half into yours,
My offering of supplementation:
Take, keep, it's yours to have.

My mind obsessed with all I want to give,
But no doctor can prescribe love in abundance.
Mum, I thought we always shared,
Torn from you, I can only sympathise,
When what I yearn for is empathy.

But then, my treasured part of the day,
One moment I scrupulously capture,
You muster enough strength to look at me,
Not with empty, morphine-glazed eyes,
Instead, you offer a window – I look through and see you are still
there.

19th March

2007

MUM

5.50am Didn't wake until about 5.30am, which is an improvement. Used the shower radio last night (so automatically switched off after a time) and turned off the light; hopefully this meant that John got a better night's sleep too. Felt very rested on waking but a bit nauseous – in fact, even thought I might actually be sick – but John brought up camomile tea and a ginger biscuit, so hoping that my stomach is settling. (I dunno! Why do I feel compelled to write down the boring minutiae of my now sick life rather than wait for profound thoughts?! Exactly!)

4.15pm A poor day. Felt very nauseous this morning and had to go back to bed. Still not feeling good now. Visit from Isobel, who sat by my bed and cheered me up. I have such warm and understanding friends. More cards through the door.

6.20pm It's just started snowing – thick flakes, covering everywhere, and reminding me that the world is still a very beautiful place. The roofs on the houses opposite are white and the back garden looks so pretty. I wanted it to snow. Is it time to say goodbye, I wonder? This afternoon I just felt as though I were drifting away. At the moment I can't really imagine being in decent enough shape to receive another cycle of chemo.

11.50pm And so to bed. Matthew called round earlier and, though I was feeling lousy, since he hadn't seen me out of bed, was impressed to find me trying to eat at the table and getting up and walking around! Wish Ethan would stop staying out late at friends'.

ALICE

I found myself feeling frustrated at Ethan today. I reasoned that it was inevitable but I still didn't like it. He said it was easier for me because I've always got on so well with Mum and have always talked to her a great deal. He said he felt lonely. He also said I'm alright because my life wasn't shit before this happened. Ethan said he hated his shitty life anyway.

I wanted to comfort him, say something nice, reassure him that I still love him and am always here for him and willing to help but I couldn't speak, so I said nothing. If I spoke I was worried my concealed emotions would leak out. I may have said something about myself that I didn't wish to reveal. All I could think was what if he knew? And yet he doesn't. He has no understanding or even inkling of my inner hatred, my self loathing, my longing for death, my disguise too good, my mask too well maintained. I am two people. I wish I knew how I managed to smother the person no one sees.

20th March

2007

MUM

5.15am I feel most calm and rested at this time of the morning. Unfortunately, since I've been awake since 4.30am and so only actually had about four hours sleep, it doesn't last. Typically, I then get hungry and then nauseous and then obsessed about the way I think lack of bowel movement (BM) contributes to it…and then spend a good proportion of the rest of the day very tired and out of sorts. Understatement!

I've just made a list of things to do [!] – send Bridget a birthday card (belated!); check my emails (will I make it up the stairs to the study?!! Another first!); phone hospital re. lack of contact from Macmillan nurse; speak to Ethan! But if today is like yesterday, I shall find it difficult to muster up the energy or motivation for more than about one thing! But how fortunate to have dear Alice (et. al. – but she is my no.1 carer and chief strength) to whom to delegate.

7.25am A little more sleep. Thick snow falling now, deadening the early morning sounds as people leave for work. I have hooked back the curtain so I can watch the fat, dusty flakes fall. What is it about snow that is so magical and makes you – me, even in my present condition – feel as excited as a child? John didn't even mention it when he brought up my cup of tea! Did he notice, even?!

Midnight. Not a bad day on the whole, although morning bath and hair wash totally knackered me and I was back lying on the bed. Lily visited and suggested cutting down the morphine as it's slow-release and makes you drowsy – so, in part, responsible for sleepiness throughout the day. Shall try and cut out a tablet tomorrow. Visit also from several friends with delicious homemade coffee cake and videos. Everyone continues to be amazingly kind.

Unexpected visit also from the lovely Dr. Hamilton, Lawrence, my old GP. He had heard from Lily but also seen my name on a list at the hospital, where he is part of the voluntary chaplaincy service. What could be nicer? He will visit me in hospital as well and was very warm, holding my hand and cuddling me.

Made contact with Macmillan nurse but it sounded a bit like counselling which I don't need/want – just get my bowels moving! Suggested I met up with her at the Hospice Mon/Wed. Is she mad? Can hardly imagine putting a foot out of the front door at present – although, actually, as I write this, I am feeling stronger.

Ethan seems to have gone down with a cold and so I am now totally neurotic in case I catch it.

A terrible altercation with John at supper tonight. He took offence and was in a bad mood in general. Will not seem to let go of all the unimportant things – mainly getting cross with Ethan for crapping in downstairs loo, eating chips with his fingers etc. It's all so trivial and the resultant unpleasantness makes me very unhappy. I cried but John didn't seem a bit sorry. I can't understand why he's not overcome with pride over his children.

Alice very tired today. Do hope that she is able to sleep better tonight. Oh dear, the impact of this disease: I am the epicentre…but the ripples. Everyone is affected.

ALICE

Horrible evening. Dad came in from work tired. Does that excuse him? Everyone reacts differently to difficult situations. He got cross at Ethan, over something trivial even under normal circumstances. Thus ensued a shouting match, Mum fully aware of everything. She got terribly upset and started crying. She thinks Dad should make more of an effort. He has done around her, until tonight.

Mum thinks all the arguing is horrible and then starts thinking about what will happen when she isn't here. It will all fall apart; her fears are right, but that isn't her concern: it is mine. I will be left with the broken family. No effort is made when Mum is in hospital. Things carry on as normal when she isn't here. I'm not granted that peace, that small offering. I don't deserve it.

2008

Spent the afternoon at Lily's surgery. Really struggled. Found it an effort to concentrate and my head couldn't think of any questions to ask. I was willing the time away, longing for patients to leave. One woman was being investigated for cancer due to her pain and indigestion. As she lay down on the couch and as I palpated her tummy, a knobbly, thick lump grew in my throat, inducing nausea. I wanted to run away. I felt sick and hideous and wished the patient would just leave. It was too similar to Mum. I felt like I couldn't do it and yet I could.

Afterwards I apologised to Lily, I was sorry that I was finding it hard. Lily said not to worry, the patient didn't notice. She said I was good. I did cope. I did well. Except, in my head, I feel I am doing worse than when I was in hospital. This is the great pretend.

Seemingly normal to others, dire inside. Their biggest power. They are not going to let me have a spectacular fall, I cannot indulge in the madness, it is a solitary affair. Only I am aware of the horrors I harbour. They will preserve my outmost self so I still appear normal to any onlooker but, inside, they are biting away, destroying me alive. I am already dead. My external shell has just got trapped in the world, unable to know what to do. I am a ghost copy. I participate in things, everyone thinks it is me, but really it is all pretend. Even with help, they win. I am a lost cause. Or, not so much lost, more defeated already.

21st March

2007

MUM

6.30am Slept well, albeit only until 4.30am – but this is becoming such a regular waking time that I really am inclined to blame the birds! Whatever, managed to go back to sleep fairly quickly for an hour or so.

Again, felt rested on waking and very calm. Spent a bit of time talking to John (had left him a card last night too) and his attitude to Ethan. I know he's finding everything difficult and feels very tired but he must work on his manner and approach with Ethan. He will be the beneficiary too! A good talk, actually. Well, OK, I suppose it was a bit of a monologue on my part [!] but John not in combative mood and seemed to take my point.

Another light sprinkling of snow on the roof tops this morning. So pretty!

1pm Day started well. Felt quite energised compared with of late. Phil, my Macmillan nurse, telephoned from the Hospice. Discussed bowel movement problems with Phil who recommended another laxative – would fax the surgery so that we could pick up a prescription later today. In the event, didn't need it! But the whole episode left me sick and faint on the toilet, and then with such abdominal pains afterwards that Alice had to administer oromorph. Feeling better now because I've had a sleep too. Where would I be without my Angel of the North?

8pm Felt better after the oromorph and a sleep. More friends visited with daffodils and DVDs and hyacinths in a basket. Charlotte had breast cancer about ten years ago and so knows all about the horrors of chemotherapy. Also told me about how she'd become quite claustrophobic (needing doors open) and wanted the radio on as background the whole time! Exactly the same for me – so guess my reactions quite normal!

Neither of the children very well. Ethan's cough has developed into a cold and both have diarrhoea. Doubtless my neurosis over picking up germs will increase – but what can I do? Feeling very tired but otherwise OK.

2008 – Good Friday

Handel's Messiah at the Albert Hall. Uncle Peter had organised tickets (he and Aunty Maggie came with us a couple of years ago) and the box was full of family and friends. When I arrived, everyone was looking at the programme: there was a picture of Mum in memoriam and a few words. The conductor of the choir had asked Dad about this and Dad had chosen the photo. Ethan and I didn't know; Dad didn't tell us. I felt quite sad and suddenly confronted - shouldn't that have been a family decision?

The music was wonderful; the words enchanting. I always said it was my favourite piece Mum had sung and it still is. There were some sections that I had accompanied Mum on the piano so she could practice. I could hear her voice in my head, hear her singing, feel her smile and joy and love of music. I could hear her. I wasn't in the Albert Hall; I was at home. I was with my Mum.

Both Mum's cousin Emily and, Lauren, her best friend from school, were there and absolutely lovely towards me. They care so much and are desperate to help. They give me lots of hugs and are able to talk so well. It is a definite gift to convey what you wish, without upsetting or patronizing or being inappropriate. Speaking to the recently bereaved is a tricky but necessary task. Some people get it just right. How blessed I am to have such doting family and friends. They are missing Mum too and yet, unselfishly, they are concerned about me. Everyone finds this terrible, it is the same for all, and yet people keep telling me that I have it the hardest. I think it is all equal and all different. No one's circumstances are the same. We must adapt in ways we can. And yet, everyone else can do this, I cannot. I have stopped. Life is passing at ever increasing speeds, it is nearly nine months since Mum died and I do not know what I have done. I am rooted to a world in which I cannot participate.

22nd March

2007

MUM

Midday. I am becoming obsessed with bowel movements! – but two more this morning left me feeling a bit lousy! I've just had a visit from Phil, Macmillan nurse at the Hospice. He has an extremely nice manner and was also useful in explaining about some of the drugs and their side effects. Suggested I tried zinc supplements to help with the changes to taste buds. Plans to come and see me again after my next lot of chemo.

Gripy pains as I write this, post trip to the loo. Can't believe how this bowel business is dominating things!

ALICE

Climbed into Mum's bed at 6am. I always feel like a cheeky child trying to snuggle into my parents' bed, quite amusing as I'm twenty-three! This morning was nice. Mum was feeling well, had no pain, and we both lay there, staring up at the ceiling, chatting like we used to, before all this happened. It almost felt like normal until a thorn in my mind reminds me that nothing is ever going to be the same.

A Macmillan nurse called Phil came this morning. He was good and said all the right things. He stayed for an hour and a half and almost everything was covered from the trivial aspects to that dreaded day in hospital when Mum could see the roof out of her window and she wished she could be up there so she could jump. I don't like it when Mum tells me she wants to kill herself. It has happened before, years back, and I never thought she'd have the courage to actually carry it out, but now, I'm not so convinced. If she was offered the choice, I'm no longer sure which way she would go.

2008

Felt dreadful today. I haven't slept for two nights; I have been awake for three whole days. Insomnia is torture. I don't know how I can still function and yet I can. This is the worst. If I couldn't do anything I wonder if I would be in a better position. If I can do things, albeit badly, people think I am OK. The psych nurses say it is good; I am able to keep busy, I am eating, I am being active but, I always ponder, why is this positive? I am giving life a go and yet I still do not want it. I long for death. My day is filled with thoughts of self-harm, ways to damage this body which is suffering. I want to die but I know I have to be OK for tomorrow.

Dad told me off for blocking the drain because I was sick. I didn't mean to be sick. I didn't really know what to say to him. Apologising seemed daft. I went to Lily's. She kept me safe. I talked to her, I explained why I felt I was still sinking.

23rd March

2007

MUM

6am Not really sure why this compulsion to commit such daily trivia to paper! Anyway, despite waking a couple of times in the night, still seem to be getting a reasonable chunk of sleep – usually about 5 hours between midnight and 5.30am. And I'm still blaming the birds some of the time which, after all, is quite a nice way to be disturbed!

1.30pm Felt quite down this morning. Went to the hospital for bloods. Felt a bit wobbly. Phlebotomist had a go at vein in one arm and then had to use the other. Nothing is straightforward now and I'm just so tired. Everything is such an effort and I just want to nod off the whole time.

ALICE

Mum mentally low today. She seemed quite down: speaking softly, her replies slow, her eyes staring into the distance, unfocused. I want to say something that will lift her but I know there is nothing to say. I can't make any of this go away. Instead I sit, just with her, and stroke her feet. I don't want her to feel alone.

Dad and I took Mum to have bloods taken. Mum was a star and, despite not being anxious about the actual procedure, was duly worried about the results: low red blood cell count = transfusion; low white blood cells = delayed chemo. Going back to the hospital evoked strong emotions and Mum cried walking up to the entrance, her arm wrapped around mine.

2008 - Easter Sunday

Leave early for Aunty Beth's and drive through London to collect Ethan. He is still asleep when we arrive – typical! – so we wait while he hurriedly throws on some clothes and then takes twice as long in the bathroom, gelling his hair etc.

It is lovely to see everyone initially. I haven't seen Granny and Granddad since Christmas, and that I can't remember, I must have been in a state. Aunty Beth, as always, has made so much effort and we all indulge in a feast of roast lamb, Yorkshire puddings, and vegetables. After lunch, Zac excitedly wants to dish out Easter gifts. Dad got everyone a present except me and Ethan. I'm not sure if I'm upset or think it is to be expected. He really does hate us. This is such a small, pathetic detail but why would Dad do that? It seems to hold meaning but maybe I am reading too much into it, this is a daft Easter egg after all.

We went for a walk in the afternoon – it was freezing! Ethan and I didn't bring enough clothes so we were both sporting a collection of Aunty Beth's coats, scarves and gloves! But, by the evening, I really am struggling. It is as if I no longer have anything to say, even answering questions requires effort. All I want is hugs. Zac, as always, mauls me constantly and this is such a comfort. He has an ability to mould himself to your body; he is the best hugger there is. When I arrived, he said, "You're not in hospital?" and I said no but he needed to be sure, "You're not going back to hospital tonight?" No, "Or back in hospital this week?" No, darling Zac. I am home. What a sweetie. He doesn't like me being ill.

I help Aunty Beth with tea. At the table, all I can think about is Mum, where she would be sitting, her smile, what she would be saying. We are now an odd number. The table seating isn't symmetrical. We are all wrong.

We leave at maybe 9pm and our goodbyes are thankfully brief. The drive home is torture. Ethan and I resume our positions in the back. It is somehow odd to sit in the passenger seat, where Mum should be. Ethan soon drifts off to sleep and I lie back and can see Mum. I can feel her sitting in front of me. I can lean forward and stroke her shoulder, like I did on those trips into hospital. I can see her reflection in the wing mirror, her smile at me on journeys to visit family. I can see myself stroking the backs of her upper arms when there was shouting and arguing and she would end up in tears on all car trips of any length. The four of us could not be together without unrest. It horrifies me seeing her. She is there and I am petrified but transfixed. I cannot move; I am pinned to my seat.

Dad doesn't notice Mum is there; he is falling asleep himself. Ethan and I can see his eyes closing in the rear view mirror. We always say to stop; I always offer to drive. Dad refuses so we endure the car drifting out of lane or lurching and braking alarmingly. Dad refuses to listen. I often wonder if he cares, for himself, for his children in the back, for all the other travellers in their cars. He is likely to cause an accident. It is not safe.

I remain rigid for two hours, until we drop Ethan off at his shared house. Once Ethan has gone and we have had a brief toilet stop, the activity seems to have disturbed Mum. She has disappeared.

Once home, the horrors return. I remain vividly awake. Pacing the house is scary. I resort to outside.

24th March

2007

MUM

10.30am Writing this as Aunty Beth and Alex are on their way. They may be some time in arriving as the M25 is closed. Didn't settle as quickly in bed last night but maybe because I finished my book before usual thirty minutes allocation for temazepam to work and gave myself too much non-drowsy thinking time?!

4pm So very tired as I write this. Just want to fall asleep the whole time. I really am in very poor shape.

11.15pm Rather unpleasant conversation with Ethan. Feel he cannot continue staying at home, getting up late, doing no work for university and then going out with friends at night. It's not going to help anyone

ALICE

Mum had an argument with Ethan tonight. Ethan would not just leave it, kept pressing his point, kept berating Mum. He didn't shout and he didn't swear but, aside from that, his attitude was that of before. All I could think in my head was be quiet, stop talking. I wanted to get up and silence him. I didn't. I stayed next to Mum, sitting on the arm of her chair, stroking her back. She got upset with Ethan and then cried. Tonight was how things used to be.

Once arguing had stopped and everyone was watching the film, I stared for ages out of the window. In my head were numerous occasions jumbled about when Ethan had been vile to Mum. All I could think was how that time was spoilt, never to be recovered; how he'd taken so much of Mum away from me. And now, these all too obviously precious moments were again being snatched from me. Not time of happiness but time of upset. The echoed picture from before: me comforting Mum.

I selfishly think of what we could have done together which, instead, was replaced by Mum talking and crying to me over Ethan. I don't want this anymore. There has been enough hurt in Mum's and Ethan's relationship. I wish he would stop. I no longer want to be the intervener. I have had enough. I know I'm being terribly self-centred and not seeing things from anyone else's perspective. My selfish desire for solitary time with Mum to be spent talking about anything other than Dad or Ethan.

2008

Didn't do much in the morning, only slept two hours last night. Feeling very slow.

In the afternoon, Holly and I went to visit Gran. I found this extremely hard. I could not keep up our aimless conversation. Gran is now confabulating all the time. Holly is great as she can talk about anything. I try to join in but it is a struggle. I resort to reading poetry, starting with "If", Rudyard Kipling, Gran's ironic favourite. She has a poetry book which Mum bought her. My darling Mother, always so thoughtful.

<h2 align="center">25th March</h2>

2007

MUM

4pm Another day of total exhaustion – and more pain than usual too. Got up for breakfast but then back to bed until lunchtime. Sometimes I think I'd just as rather stay in bed the whole time, flicking between Radio 3 and 4. Holly came round at lunchtime, and then Beth and Alex drove back to Bristol.

Ice skating is on TV which is very beautiful – the music also. Dear Alice is plugging away at her uni presentation *and* seeing to my every need. My Angel. I hope it goes well for her next week and wish she didn't have such a marathon drive up to Newcastle.

6.20pm Feeling a bit better although the pain not good today. Had short walk around the garden with Alice; it looked very pretty. Beth has rung to say they are safely home. Lovely phone call from Lawrence too.

11.35pm Hope I sleep well tonight – try not to think about tomorrow. Poor Alice looks very tired and was back on the computer, working on her presentation. John, Ethan and I watched interesting programme about Jo Brand taking up the challenge of learning the organ and ending up performing Vidor's Toccata at the Albert Hall. Then Ethan and I watched "Northanger Abbey". Really enjoying this Austin series.

2008

Joanne from ISS sees me at home. I explain how, fundamentally, little has changed. I am different in that I am able to function, I can do things, I can enjoy myself at Lily's surgery, I am able but still, all the dark, bad, lecherous horrors are there. I can keep them at bay, to an extent, but night time, when alone, they come at me with vengeance. The same picture from before: I appear to be coping but really I am sinking further.

26th March

2007

MUM

9.30am Got to sleep easily last night but then awake early and thinking about the day ahead. Have just phoned Crowhurst ward. The bloods are OK so I am to go in this morning.

1.20pm I have been admitted – back on Crowhurst ward and my own room again, which is great.

3pm Drip set up, after three unsuccessful attempts at finding a vein! Feeling the best I have done so far today so hope the chemo effects aren't as ghastly this time; only saline flush in the line at the moment.

27th March

2007

MUM

8.30am Not a very good night! 3x one hour sleeps. No heat pad to settle niggling pain and new digital radio went off and wouldn't switch back on. Wrote a poem (for John) in the near darkness in the early hours. At 6am woke for third time, feeling nauseous and constipated. Can't help thinking, "Here we go again!"

1.15pm Things actually not too bad, especially considering how little sleep I had last night. Feeling nauseous as I write this, set off by lunch! Otherwise, an OK morning. Alice came as usual and thought I seemed much better than last time, and I got washed at the sink.

Starfish

Visit from Lawrence who has Bell's Palsy. Said he felt very self-conscious about appearance but I didn't even notice – admittedly not wearing specs! Besides which, all is vanity to me nowadays. Anyway, enjoyable conversation as ever. Lawrence hasn't had an easy ride with his children – and it's not over. Nice to have frank exchange. Asked if I had a faith. Guess I have one of sorts.

For John:

You said I was your best friend.
And that's what counts, I guess.
Not what was spoken but what was not.
What passed for words
When you couldn't heave your heart into your mouth.
It's difficult for alpha males like you.
Stiff upper lips, brave faces
Who deny and hide behind the mask.

And then it splinters.
You say, "I love you".
The words I want to hear.
You say, "I love you, even though
I do not always show it."

And the tears come,
Held back through a quarter century of love.
You, sobbing in my arms,
I remember Dedham days
Before these darker hours.
Take strength from me.
You cannot fix it every time.
Not this time.

Tidy not my life away,
The future's in what's left behind.
And who'd have thought from inauspicious starts,
A hair shirt and a plague of locusts
Would bring to Job in hour of need?
What joys would spring?
Give words of love.
They will reward
In comfort blanket and angel wing.

ALICE

Mum's poem – Ethan and I were the hair shirt and plague of locusts when we were little…clinging to her and constantly buzzing around!

Mum poorly. Started seeing flashing lights this afternoon and her vision went all blurry. She said it felt like the migraines she's had in the past. Doctor said it most likely a side effect from any number of the drugs she's taking. So many problems.

I got upset with Dad tonight. The problem when someone upsets you is that you start thinking too deeply about it. Dad is the only person who hasn't asked me how I am doing, how I am coping. This made me sad. And then I thought, the only person who Dad really loves, really cares about, is Mum. I'm glad about that. Mum certainly deserves it. But then I think, why doesn't he love his children? Why doesn't he love me? And I don't know what I have done wrong or what I can do to gain his affection. Unfortunately, I fear the answer is nothing. I cannot buy his love. Love is a feeling that is there or not. Why don't you love me Dad?

Thoughts led unhelpfully onto next thoughts. I ended up crying, sitting hugging my knees on the cold tiles of the kitchen. Dad was in bed, Ethan was out with friends. I felt a wave of loneliness shiver, quite literally, through me. I was all alone. I felt I was seeing a glimpse of the hideous future. Mum had gone; I was left. There was nothing. All family life has irreparably fractured. My task in maintaining some sort of unity, dismally failed. I wish I was a better person and not so flawed. Maybe you can have too much life. Mum, when you leave, please take me too.

2008

Had to see ISS doctor and Joanne at the psych unit. The doctor says it seems like I haven't improved despite my attempts at normality. They want me to go back into hospital. I don't. I have to talk my way out of it. I am going to Sarah's tomorrow in Chichester. I say I will be safe. They are dubious but I know I will be OK. I have never done anything bad in front of other people. I still possess that element of control. They relent. I have a few more days of freedom. Am I running away again? I don't know.

Spent afternoon with Lily seeing patients. It was really good. Delightful patients, all willing to chat and explain and wishing me luck with my course. I enjoyed myself.

I showed Lily my arm. Slashed myself last night. Bad head, had to make sure the badness was on me and not anyone else. Lily steri strips it. Probably needed stitching but certainly don't fancy trip to A+E. It will suffice. I am not bothered by scars. I would have told ISS this morning except, as they were considering hospitalisation, I thought it would seal my fate!

28th March

2007

ALICE

Really bad day. Mum terribly ill. Nauseous all day. Late this evening, Mum was then sick. I find it so hard, not to watch, but because I can't do any of the things I would normally do to comfort someone. Mum can't stand being touched, won't even let me hold her hair away from her face, and she wants silence. I can't talk: no words of sympathy. Instead, I sit there rigid. Why do I feel the need to stroke Mum and speak to her? Maybe it's because these comfort me, alleviate my distress, give me a use, a sense of feeling needed. Except, I'm superfluous.

I help Mum onto the commode. She is in so much pain. I want it all to stop. Watching her is devastating. Each time I feel like this, when everything is tremendously tough, I'm so scared that I won't be able to keep it up. But each time, I keep going, I stay strong. It doesn't matter how many times this happens, the fear is still there. What if I fail?

2008

Carrie from ISS sees me. She has been asked to see if I will go into hospital voluntarily. I tell her I am too busy. I have Lily's this afternoon and then I am driving straight to Sarah's after. Carrie thinks I will be safe but has to make sure I am going where I say I am going. I give her Sarah's number, hoping Sarah won't mind and instantly feel the burden I am placing on her. Carrie says I must talk to ISS everyday. They will be phoning my mobile.

29th March

2007

MUM

5.30am The fact that there's no diary entry for yesterday says it all! Largely dreadful. Sick last night, after an afternoon in which experienced migraine-type visual disturbances. Apparently several of the meds can produce this effect. Fortunately Alice was here at the time – otherwise I really didn't want to see anyone. Feeling very nauseous and ate barely anything – although, I guess, nothing like the nausea experienced first time round? Hard to make the comparison once it's gone but suspect an independent observer would deduce this! A better night with nozinan!

Holly made lunch at home for Wendy and Peter, Arnie and Jane (John's sisters and their partners) – and the girls came to visit in the afternoon. Unfortunately feeling too nauseous and dopey from the nozinan to be bothered. By the evening I was back with a sick bowl but then, finally, managed a bowel movement – which made me feel a whole heap better. Movecol from now on it is then!

ALICE

Mum much better today: more animated, happy to talk and feeling less sick. She managed to get to the sink so I could give her a wash. By the afternoon she was sleepy but otherwise doing well. I felt so much happier about going to Newcastle. I still didn't want to go but then Mum wanted me to go so I wanted to go because it was what Mum wanted. I just didn't want to be away from her.

Drove up to Newcastle – all fine. Went to see Catherine. It was wonderful to talk to her. She is so lovely. Actually being with someone is so much nicer than talking on the phone. I wished we lived closer.

I didn't want to go to bed. I knew I wouldn't. I knew it would be hard but it was 2am and everyone else was sleeping. The night was horribly disturbing. Horrific things dancing through my head. They were out to play games with me. I couldn't stop the maddening racing of muddled voices. I didn't sleep at all. There is no rest for the wicked.

30th March

2007

MUM

5.30am Another good night's sleep – well, at least five hours. No disturbances and feel OK this morning.

Do hope that Alice had a good night back up in Newcastle and that the presentation is a stunner! She deserves to do well – what a star! – although I shall be glad when she has safely driven home again. (Likewise when Holly and Ethan are back from Liverpool at the weekend. More to worry about!)

Just thinking about how great Ethan is now. Stayed around a long time yesterday afternoon; it's so wonderfully effortless just chatting to him. Should have always known he would come good. Now he readily admits that he was pretty awful when he was younger – when I was trying to do my nursing course, when Jack was living with us etc. Hope he doesn't beat himself too much over the head for this! Lots of OK teenagers go through ghastly periods and, whilst I know I thought it was grim at the time, it's now faded into total insignificance. As far as Ethan goes, it's probably been an important formative experience and made him the sensitive, lovely young man he is today.

I feel very lucky with my dear children and only wish their relationship with John were better. Oh well, you can't win them all – and it really is down to *him* now. They have made so much effort whereas John seems incapable of deviating from type.

9pm A bit nauseous after washing this morning and struggled with lunch – but food total crap today! Lots of visitors in the afternoon. Ethan came in with lovely (pretty) notebook from Gilly, full of photos and good memories from Butlins/Austria/Italy trips etc. What a sweet and thoughtful idea.

Well, I am now on my last bag of chemo for this second cycle. It's due to finish at gone 11pm. Certainly the experience has been far less ghastly second time around but still this whole business is the hardest thing I've ever done and you do wonder, some of the time, if you have the strength to continue because, even when you're feeling OK, it's not great. Total invalid, really. Radio 3 is playing beautiful, soothing music and the staff are very kind….but basically, you think to yourself that this is your lot in life and it's not what you wanted.

ALICE

Presentation at the medical school in the morning – all fine. Then met up with a few friends. I love friends. I wish I lived closer. Then I tried to pack as many of my belongings as I could. It was a strange, sad feeling, knowing I wouldn't be living there again, knowing that I probably wouldn't ever be back in Newcastle. Drove home. Arrived gone midnight. Calmer tonight. I know I'm near Maisie. That thought made me happy. I stayed up for a few hours though, just in case they were waiting. I had to be really tired before I could sleep.

31st March

2007

MUM

6pm I am home. Felt pretty grotty and nauseous at lunchtime and extremely tired this afternoon. Slept. Otherwise suppose this is a big improvement on last time. Alice is being amazing. I don't know how she does it!

Have just practically had a row with John. Don't know where I found the energy! Started off trivial but John's response – to blame Ethan. I don't care!! I don't want blame. Why can't he just say OK? Anyway, ended up with my shouting and crying, "Leave me alone! Get away from me. Don't ever shout at me again." John still defensive to the end. I mean it: get away from me. I don't want him anywhere near me if he's going to be like this.

ALICE

Mum came home at lunch time – feeling very tired but otherwise OK. I love it when she comes back. I feel she's safer somehow. I don't know why.

This evening not so good. Mum asked Dad to do something (I can't remember what) which resulted in an argument. Dad shouting at Mum. Mum in tears pleading with him to just get away from her. All rather depressing. I don't understand. How can Dad shout at Maisie? She has only been home a few hours. Why does he do it? I wish I could see inside his head, watch how it works. Then I may understand why. Everyone went to bed. I felt sad.

1st April

2007

MUM

6.45pm April Fool's Day. No joke! Palm Sunday and I am watching "Songs of Praise". This hymn from the Albert Hall so I'm probably there somewhere!

Bad day. Felt dizzy and totally exhausted. Asleep for most of it. Plus, hair is falling out in handfuls, despite Dr. Mayhew's assurances. Eaten very little. Alice goes to such trouble to try and tempt me and then it tastes terrible and I feel nauseous. Got to eat to get the meds down but mainly there seems no point.

ALICE

Mum not good today: in bed mostly. Then, tonight, she curled up in her chair, groaning and sighing, terribly nauseous. Again, all I was doing was watching, sitting by her. The desperate desire to be able to make her better crushed by the depressing knowledge that there was nothing I could do.

At 11pm, Mum was much worse and began being sick, vomit streaked with blood. I phoned Crowhurst ward and they said to bring her in. Mum started crying, saying, "I don't want to go back to hospital. I'm so poorly. I'm so ill." I stroked her hair. I wanted to tell her she'll be alright, except I know how ill she is.

I woke Dad and told him. He didn't move, just lay in bed. I ran round the bedroom, collecting a few bits for Mum, putting them in a bag, got Mum into her dressing gown, helped her put her shoes on. Mum asked where Dad was. "Just getting dressed", I lied. I went back into their bedroom – Dad was still lying there, eyes open, sighing. He said he was tired. I wanted to hit him. I wanted to grab him and punch him in the face and scream at him. That would wake him up. How can he do this? Why can't he do it for Mum? I hate him. I know I'll find him so hard to forgive for doing this. I shouldn't have told him and just driven Mum to hospital myself.

Mum re-admitted – drugs injected, drip hooked up. She was feeling slightly better. Dad went home and I lay at the bottom of Mum's bed, stroking her feet as she became increasingly drowsy.

I finally, reluctantly, left at 1.30am. The nurses were concerned that I was walking home on my own. Dad had left me so what choice? It was chilly outside but it felt nice, the cool breeze taking away some of my pent up emotions. I phoned Ethan who was in Liverpool with Holly collecting his belongings. He started having a go at me, getting angry, crossly demanding to know why Mum is so ill, shouted when I said Mum was feeling better now she's in hospital. Ethan said mentally she's not better and is really messed up and said about her wanting to jump off the roof. He said she would never have said that normally. I got upset. He was cross with me and I was finding it hard to cope with.

Ethan has no idea. In the past, when he has been exceptionally vile to Maisie, she has told me she wanted to jump off a bridge, she has told me she wanted to die and it was all because of Ethan. I don't tell him any of this. I know it would upset him but I don't like Ethan telling me what Mum is usually like. I know Mum far better than him. Maybe Mum wouldn't have told me so much if Ethan had been easier. Maybe there wouldn't have been the need but, for whatever reason, Mum has always told me exactly how she is feeling.

I felt upset but I couldn't cry. If I cry I think I may fall apart, or at least a bit of me will break. I've got to be strong, hold it together, as I'll be back in the hospital in a few hours. I go for a long walk, tiptoeing along the silent and still pavements.

2008

April Fool's Day – no joke. Isn't that what Mum said? Had to see ISS in the morning. I wasn't very good, quite low and no motivation to do anything, despite liking seeing Sarah at the weekend. I was still in my pyjamas and it was 11am – I had been awake for hours.

They said I would have an evening visit as well as I obviously wasn't doing too well. I finally showered and dressed and had something to eat (ISS suggestions!).

I went shopping but my mobile doesn't receive signal in supermarkets. I realise I have a whole host of missed calls and voicemails from Francis, my social worker, and ISS saying, "Alice, we are outside the house, will you please come and let us in". Oops. I then get a call from Dad. Apparently two doctors, Francis and an ISS nurse were banging on the door thinking I was hiding inside. Dad finally answered and they spoke to him. He is great for them to talk to as doesn't have a clue what is going on and told them I must be out but didn't know where! They had come round to section me! Ahhh! Great move that I wasn't home.

ISS always ring before they turn up, although maybe under the circumstances, if they had told me who was coming, I would have legged it anyway. Obeying Dad, I dutifully phone ISS and they say I have to see a nurse at home. She comes and by this time it is 8pm. She stays for at least an hour and I find this really tough. I have to talk about lots of things which I find ever so hard to do. I'm scared about discussing the bad things. The threats in my head get worse. Must not talk, Alice. But everyone tells me it would be helpful to talk. The people I trust who know, Sarah and Lily, think it will be helpful.

The ISS want to help and do their best. They try and get me to elaborate. Part of me knows I should but then the voices get so much worse. I am scared of what they can do; I am not scared of ISS or friends. Silence seems a safer option.

Night time was dreadful. I ended up slashing my arm and the backs of my hands. I could hear Mum again and several hours were spent walking the streets, hurriedly trying to trace Mum's voice. I ripped at my hands, scratching, destroying the skin. Flesh is only flesh. It is me but it isn't. Part of me but also separate. I didn't sleep at all.

2nd April

2007

MUM
1.30pm Well, here I am back in hospital, on a saline drip, after having thrown up late last night and been re-admitted. Pretty grim end to the day but the nozinan sorted out the sickness and, eventually, two bowel movements this morning too! Still very tired – slept on and off most of the morning.

ALICE
Mum feeling better today. Very tired but no nausea or pain. In the evening, I lie on her bed, curled up at her feet, stroking her legs. I love the physical contact and Mum likes this as it's nowhere near her face. She is talkative and we softly chat. She traces my nose with her finger – it's the most gentle, comforting feeling.

Ethan comes back from Liverpool. I get home about 10pm and we have an argument. Ethan shouts a stream of swear words at me. I get cross, then upset. I then wish I hadn't. I sit hugging my knees and rocking in my bed, nails digging into the backs of my hands. I want to drag knives over my arms and stomach. I want to cut my flesh and look deep into the wounds.

When I go back downstairs, Ethan has gone out. I wanted to say sorry to him.

2008

I spent an agitated morning in the house, flitting from room to garden, on edge, never calm. I had to see the consultant psychiatrist from ISS, at the psych outpatient unit at 11.30am. If I didn't turn up, the police would be called and I would be sectioned.

I did go and I was honest. The doctor said they wanted me back in hospital. I am not safe, I hurt myself, I have suicidal thoughts, I wander off into the night, sometimes with no realisation. This is true. It is quite scary to find yourself outside in the small hours, with no recollection of how you got there. The doctor says she won't section me, I can be an informal patient, just stay for a few days. I agree. Not really sure what else to do.

Well, here I am back in hospital, returned to the delights of the psych ward. I have to wait until I am allowed into my room so I go outside into the lukewarm sunshine of this spring day. I phone Ethan, Aunty Beth, Sarah, Lily and explain to each my whereabouts. I then catch up with the patients who recognise me. Sharon has just stormed out of her review (I'm not exactly sure why) but she is OK and has lots of leave and overnight weekends so she can see her son. She is still desperately thin and all angular as her clothes do little to disguise.

Phyllis gives me a big grin and says hello. She looks definitely better and her face is animated with peachy cheeks. She is much more able to chat at a normal speed and isn't rocking anymore. It is lovely to witness improvements. Sammy skips past and remembers my name which I'm quite touched by, I didn't talk to her all that much before. Ann is back, wearing a flowery, linen summer skirt instead of her trademark leggings. Rote has a new addition to his outfit: a cotton baseball cap with flaps at the side looking similar to floppy, long dog ears. The cap is covered in badges reminiscent of that 80s trend. Apparently Sophie is still here but on overnight leave today. It will be good to see her.

Helen takes me into my room, yet a different one. She asks me if I have brought anything I shouldn't have. I confidently say no and then Helen watches me unpack. Oh dear. As I grabbed the same (unemptied) bag from Sarah's, I had forgotten most of what was in there. Like a magician, I conjure a string of contraband material from my rucksack: mobile phone charger, I shoved in at the last minute as knew my phone would be well used; antihistamines, completely forgot they were in my sponge bag; Lemsips, I have a cold, am very snotty and have a cracking chesty cough; razor, just flung in with my toothbrush. I didn't mean to lie. Oops.

After confiscating those belongings I then had to see Dr. Floyd's registrar. He says I'm not allowed to leave the building and I am on level 2 obs. He does a physical examination and I return to my room to unpack. I knew the most vital items: a radio, to clear the suffocating silence; mobile phone, always a must; notebooks and pens.

Ethan and Grace come in the evening (with Grace driving her parents' car – I hear from Ethan already a few close misses…she only passed her test two weeks ago!). It is great to see them, hugs and Ethan strokes the back of my hand. We chat away with Ethan updating us with his antics in London and the latest on all his potential boyfriends/just speaking/being friends/ignoring each other! I never can keep track.

Lily comes by later, as promised. I talk to her about the things I hear, I say I am sorry as I feel I have let her and the surgery down as I was meant to be working today, I say how much I was enjoying it. Lily is fantastic and she talks lots about medicine and my course and I feel that eagerness creeping upon me, the fascination at the human body, the delight when you understand why. I want to re-learn what I knew, go over my notes, grasp what I once could because everything is familiar but I know, at the moment, I can't quite explain and elaborate as much as I was able. I actually want to revise. It is so interesting and I want to learn, recapture that knowledge.

3rd April

2007

ALICE

Mum not so good today. She is so tired that she can barely move. Just reaching for a glass of water consumes all her energy. She lies there and says that opening her eyes is too much effort.

2008

Awake with a clinging dampness resulting from the dire dreams flinging me into the plumbs of darkness. My pyjamas are sticky and my hair matted to my forehead. Another series of hideous expeditions that I fought through.

In the morning, I am escorted to the main hospital to have my bloods taken. They won't even let me do this on my own, I am supposed to be an informal patient but they are treating me as if I am sectioned. I then have my review. Dr. Floyd is away so her registrar takes charge instead. It is brief, not much is discussed. I ask for leave, he says no. Even if I am with someone else who picks me up? No. This isn't good. I don't wish to be stuck here for days with no escape.

I sit outside, chatting to Sharon, and meet Jas, a cheery chap with hair that sticks up and jeans rolled up to his knees like an advert for a 1950s seaside postcard. He is very friendly and says he has calmed down since earlier this morning. He could hear his brother calling, "Let me out. Let me out" and Jas thought he was stuck inside the comfy chair in his room. He asked staff for scissors (they said no) so he ripped the chair with his teeth, grabbing great handfuls of stuffing and reducing it to a bare frame. His brother wasn't there.

Dad comes at lunch time to drop some stuff off from home. It is OK except his opening is to launch into a telling off over my hands. "No wonder you are back in here if you are going to do that" etc. He gets annoyed. He doesn't understand. We do talk a bit, he only has a short while as is returning to work. He then looks at me and says, "You've put on weight". Well, thank you Dad, lovely to see you too! What a thing to say. Firstly, he has only noticed now, even though I am living with him; secondly, Ethan reassures me that I look lots better as was too thin before. Honestly, Dad just does not think ever before he opens his mouth.

Dad says he will come back this evening. Why? I am thinking. He doesn't have anything to say to me (bar negative comments). He comes out of duty. He assumes it is what others expect so he does it for that. Seeing him once in a day is quite enough for me. Dad then makes me feel guilty about him going to Seattle. He won't be at home so he is wondering what I will do. He seems to place his presence on a pedestal. Dad being home or not affects me very little. I hardly see him anyway. And now, Ethan is back which is lovely. I talk to him lots.

Ethan and Grace pop in around 6pm. They bring me apples, dried fruit, nuts, magazines. So dear. Grace gets cornered by Maureen, initially for not closing a door! Maureen then harasses her for fags and follows Grace as she gets a cup of water, which

Maureen grabs off her and declares, "I'll have that". Poor Grace looks petrified as Ethan and I laugh at her, Maureen has trapped her in a corner. Grace thinks she is about to get soaked as the water is brandished at her. Karen sees what is going on as she walks past and so distracts Maureen whereby Grace escapes! I keep telling them that there are some characters in here.

The evening is pretty dreadful. I hear Mum, her cry, her call for me, "Ali, Ali". I spin in circles in my room. I know I can't leave. Mum stops calling. I don't know where she is. With disgust and frustration, I rip the plaster off my arm, snatch the steri strips and dig my nails in deep, into my flesh, the wound gaping, me tugging at its edges. I sit huddled on my bed and I quickly calm. The world returns to normal.

It is 9pm and staff handover but Katy sees me and I say I may need a plaster. She looks at my arm with Duffy, another nurse, and they say stitches look necessary. The night staff take me to A+E where I wait for two hours to be sorted. They clean out all the gunk, stitch and plaster me up, then prescribe a course of antibiotics. My arm is pretty infected and looks rather suspect.

I return to the ward gone midnight and receive a text from Aunty Beth asking if it is too late to phone, Zac wanted to talk to me. I phone back and Zac answers and I chat to him about Egypt (they are going on Saturday), college and being home. He is such a dear but definitely struggles on the phone – answers in the main are "Yes" and "I don't know"! Zac then passes me onto Aunty Beth who says he suddenly got tearful and said, "I want to talk to Ali". I ask if Aunty Beth had told Zac I was back in hospital and Aunty Beth says no. What a darling Zac is, and he really can pick up on people's emotions with such astuteness.

I tell Aunty Beth about my A+E trip and then it is time to bed. But I do not feel sleepy. I read but do not feel my eyelids tire, I urge my brain to rest but it is a flurry of activity. My body finally slinks into sleep gone 3am.

4th April

2007

MUM
Back home again, after having been readmitted to Crowhurst ward on Sunday evening, after a day of nausea and finally throwing up. Don't feel I've got the heart for my diary at the moment.

ALICE
    Mum home. I'm happy. Mummy is where I like her to be.

2008

    The morning seems to be eaten up quickly. I wake late, have meds, eat breakfast, drink caffeinated coffee that Dad brought in for me, spend a while in the shower washing my hair, read the bible, ask to use a hairdryer, return my razor (they were reluctant to give it to me after yesterday's exploits) and finally talk to Katy (my allocated nurse). She is lovely and I explain about last night and hearing Mum. I also say I don't want to be here and she understands. They are surprised to see me back but realise I may be unsafe at home.

    I don't know what to do. I don't think any of these feelings or voices are going to disappear by spending a few days in hospital, although I am dubious as to this length of time, Dr. Floyd is away this week and next and I'm not sure about my discharge without her. I must take each day as it comes and try to see this in a positive light.

    Lawrence arrives at 2pm. I play the GP card once again and the nurses allow me out for a walk with him. I am surprised. I haven't been given any leave so I thought they would say no. It just demonstrates that it is always worth a try! We walk to the lake and pause, sitting on a wooden bench. I briefly updated Lawrence on my situation and he is such a wise, understanding, calming person to talk to. He listens and replies with such sensitivity. He has a pocket bible with him, reads me a psalm and his favourite verse, Philippians 4, then places his hand on my back and prays for me. We sit in the spring sunshine warmth, my eyes close, my surroundings forgotten, and my mind is transfixed on Lawrence's words.

    Isobel pops by. I told her I was back in hospital and she isn't teaching as it is school holidays. She brings me chocolate and a newspaper. Mum's friends really are superb, they treat me with such fondness because they respected Mum so much.

    Soon after, Ethan, Grace and Holly arrive and we sit outside on the bench, Holly regaling us with stories from her week in the Peak district with her young people from work. It is nice to see them all but, with three visits in a row, I am so tired and flagging with all the talking I am required to do. Holly keeps repeating she thinks I should live with her. I don't know. Perhaps I could stay occasionally.

Dad phones for no reason and I try to tell him (nicely) that I don't want him to come in tonight. I am exhausted with visitors and have to make additional effort for Dad as conversation does not flow. He was asking pointless, non-questions and then wanted to speak to Holly because he didn't believe she was here! Dad appears to have successfully annoyed all three of us today.

6.30pm and still light. As they let me out earlier, I try my luck and ask to go for a walk. Initial reaction: no! I plead my case and Roy checks my notes and relents. He says I seem OK and was out earlier so it should be fine. Am I going to do anything when I'm out? Where am I going? Will I buy blades or tablets? Be no longer than half an hour, Alice. I felt like a change of scenery so had a pleasant wander alone; I didn't have to concentrate on talking.

Adam is my nurse and I ask to talk to him. We go into a side room and lock the door as Maureen is on the march – she has already screamed a page of swear words at me and keeps stomping from room to room accosting unsuspecting staff and patients.

My opening question to Adam is, "How do I get out of here without lying?" because I want to be able to tell the truth but I also want to leave hospital. If I don't lie, how is this possible? I don't see how I am any different from when I arrived, or last week for that matter. They want to stabilise me. I am all over the place and my emotions switch quickly and erratically. I can be easily distracted and enjoy things but then one bad voice in my head can hurtle me into the depths of despair and cause that desperate search for death. It causes me to lash out and harm myself. I find myself repellent. This, when considered, is all rather confusing. How can I think such contrary things, experience feelings that are the polar opposite of one another? It makes my head hurt.

I talk to Adam about Mum and hearing her. He then asks, do I feel guilty about enjoying things without her? Guilt. A feeling I am all too familiar with but no, I don't feel guilty about enjoying things because that is what I know Mum wanted for me to do. I knew she wanted to see me happy and enjoying medicine, as I used to, and engage with all the disabled adults I worked with. This is what Mum wanted. I feel guilty when I cannot do all these things, when life seems too hard, too tiring, when I do not even want to leave the house or get dressed or washed or eat. That is when I feel bad because I know Mum would be so saddened to see me in such a way.

I tell Adam that I don't know how to help myself. I have no idea what to do. It is not that I don't possess the inclination, because

I do sometimes, but I don't know what I should be doing in order to improve my state of mind. How do I help myself? What can I be doing? That is what I need help with. They (the doctors and nurses) always ask what they can offer, what they can do, what do I want from them? The honest answer is, I don't know. I'm not trying to be awkward, I just have no ideas.

5th April

2007

ALICE

Mum had a bad nose bleed. Blood was everywhere – all over her bed sheets, her pillows, her nightie. It scared me. I don't know if I should be scared. Mum was surprisingly calm. She is amazing at coping. I ran her a bath and then washed her hair. The whole process was exhausting for little Maisie. She sat in her chair and had a nap.

I washed the blood out of the bed linen and the sink filled with a pinkish swill. The blood swirled in loops, then dispersed, tinging the cold water. I watched and felt sad. Mum's blood was on my hands. I rubbed her sheets gently, almost stroking them, as if the blood was still a part of Mum, but it ran away, curling down the plug hole, washing through my fingers. I couldn't catch it, couldn't stop it. Don't slip away from me Mummy, please don't slip. But I know you are already on that slide.

2008

Awoke frequently throughout the night, hideous dreams jerking me awake, blankets strewn on the floor, sheets twisted, pyjama bottoms up to my knees, sleeves of my top up to my elbows, sweat drenched. It was the day before Mum was diagnosed, I was the only one who had foresight. I knew what we were about to embark upon but I could not tell Mum she was dying. It was terrible. Mum, despite feeling poorly, was trying to carry on as normal and she didn't quite understand why I was home. I was crying and crying and didn't know how to tell Mum how awful the next months would be.

Then, all the characters in my dream jumped to the next day, a Friday. A doctor, a nurse and, bizarrely, my social worker, arrived at the house to break the devastating news to Mum. I knew what they were going to say and I hated myself for having divine knowledge and, with absolute certainty, know what was going to happen. I had already lived through it once and now I had to do the whole thing again for I knew it would all be the same, I had seen it before. I panicked. I didn't think I could do it all again. I was scared. Those months were emotionally exhausting. It was almost too much, but not quite. I lived on edge, the very brink of my capabilities, for such a long time that now I have collapsed, concertinaed into a flat mess on the floor.

And herein lies my problem. In dreams, I am emotional, I can cry, I can weep, I can physicalise devastation, but here, in real life, there is nothing. I cannot feel sadness, although I tell myself that Mum dying is terrible. But I am nothing, lukewarm water, neither hot nor cold, a hovering being so far removed. I want to cry, I want to scream, I want to express, but I am hollow, an intact eggshell, but the forces are pushing me from above and below so I do not break, great tension but no relief. I do not crack.

Dad turns up this morning before 10am; I hadn't even showered. It unnerves me when people just appear, with no warning. I'm unsure why. It makes me feel better, perhaps in more control, if I know roughly when to expect people. We talk but our conversation is challenging and topics do not come easily. We arrange lunch tomorrow, with Ethan and Holly, if I am allowed out, and then Dad leaves.

After lunch, I feel an increasing lethargy. I try distractions, reading, writing, cups of tea but am compelled to lie down. I fold onto my bed, lying on my tummy, face turned to the side and am aware of the ward noises (music, slamming doors, raised voices) for only a moment until I fall to sleep and remain so, dream free, for an hour.

I awake, drowsy but refreshed and splash my face with water, put on my shoes, gather my coat and wait for Lily. She arrives and drives back to her house and we drink coffee and talk. I try my best to describe the major hurdle I need to overcome in order to properly express myself. I am so scared of hurting other people. If I talk about things that are forbidden, the threats in my head intensify and tell me that friends and family and other people I know will get hurt. So I choose to keep quiet. It feels much safer that way. But this does not help me; I harbour the brooding demons and then abuse myself. Lily listens, she understands what I am saying even though I do not make logical sense. She comforts me and then picks a lovely posy of fragrant flowers from her garden for me to put in my hospital room. Holly phones me and so Lily phones the ward to ask if I can return an hour late and then drives me to Holly's house.

Lily leaves and Holly and I sit on the sofa in the gentle hue of her scattered fairy lights. We talk about lots; I am updated on Holly's Mum Lindsey (whom I haven't seen for a while). She is currently in Amsterdam. We talk about Jack, whom we haven't had contact with since Easter. He is apparently coming back soon but no one knows when and he seems to have told each of us different things. It is lovely to see Holly, she is so caring towards me. She bought grapes and strawberries and twiglets! Armed with my goodies, she drives me back, half an hour late but with no interrogation by the staff.

Late evening I am ridiculously buoyant, dancing around. I feel great and happy and not tired in the slightest. My mood is so erratic and this is what they find hard to deal with. I can change within minutes; there is no stability. Now, I have no desire to die, I love life and everything in it. Each day to me is extremes of emotion, depths of despair to heights of ebullience. I have a bipolar disorder which, instead of sustaining a high or low, flings me throughout the day. I feel like a soft toy being thrown high into the air only to come tumbling down, gravity taking hold.

I finally settle, three hours after taking my sleeping tablet and read my novel, as always, to induce drowsiness.

6th April

2008

I awake early and try to force myself back to sleep but fractions of my dreams penetrate my consciousness. Peculiar dreams last night. Mum and I had gone to a play at the theatre but the performance was dire. We were then entertaining back at home, perhaps a meal as some family members were there. I went to put my arm round Mum's waist as she was cooking on the hob but I was unable to touch her. There was a force field of only a few inches surrounding Mum which I could not enter. I didn't understand this is my dream. I was observing the prize but wasn't permitted to touch. Waking, I open my eyes and am confronted by confusion: where am I? I thought Mum was still alive. Reality dictates: I am in a psychiatric unit.

Looking out of my window cheers me up somewhat. It's snowing! Little pinhead flakes but they've settled and the grass has a white carpet, the bushes a fluffy moustache. I go outside in my flip flops so I can crunch through the untouched grass, toes tingling against the freeze. When I was born, the following morning brought a blanket of thick white snow. Mum could watch from her hospital window, new baby in her arms. She tells me it was magical.

Exhausted, physically and mentally. I am unable to keep going so lie down on bed and fall asleep for half an hour, until Dad arrives at midday to take me home. Ethan has just got up, Holly has made delicious lentil soup and the four of us sit down for lunch. The conversation is animated but Dad appears unable to participate, jumping up from the table as soon as he has finished, not waiting for the rest of us. He doesn't have anything to say to me so why does he insist on visiting me in hospital?

Dad gets cross, Holly smoking in the garden, Ethan wearing Dad's fleece to keep warm as it's freezing outside, sighing when neither Ethan or I want dessert being too full on soup.

Dad goes out for a walk but then, on leaving, rubs my back and gives me a kiss. He does care but this is so confusing. He kisses Holly too but ignores Ethan. How have we deteriorated to such petty behaviour? If Dad wants to see me and talk, why doesn't he stay and postpone his walk for half an hour? It's all the time I have left. Holly drives me back, such a sweetie, and arranges a time to see me tomorrow.

Faintly amusing evening on the ward, although I am already weary of this place. Maureen still kicking off, accusing everyone of being social services and then asking Roy if he was the underwear department?! All Ann's lighters were confiscated yesterday. Frankie didn't realise so gave her a spare one. Ann is now the ward's arsonist and setting fire to whatever she can.

Night encroaches and I feel very anxious, simmering badness in my mind. My room is claustrophobic so I brave the cold and I sit huddled in the shelter.

7th April

2007

MUM

2pm A difficult few days, characterised by nausea and exhaustion. What's new?! Macmillan nurse Phil visited with more advice about Movecol – so hopefully I can break the constipation/diarrhoea vicious circle eventually.

Visits from…can't remember! – but everyone continuing to be really supportive. Yesterday Wendy came round in the morning with dinner! In the afternoon, Ange came, who spent about two hours massaging my feet, which was relaxing.

Beth's 50th birthday on 5th April and I didn't even get it together to send her a card. And the pair of us were going to go away somewhere together. This weekend she and Angus are walking near Anglesey; Alex is looking after Zac and, I think, spending Saturday night in Birmingham with Mum and Dad. Beth says the accommodation's OK but not up to my standards!

Otherwise, feeling a bit better today. Jack is back from Barcelona for the weekend and Holly is cooking tonight.

9pm After supper felt increasingly sick with back pain. Not good at all.

ALICE

Holly and Jack come round. Holly, so sweet, brings all the food for dinner. We're doing a roast and she has prepared everything. It's fun, her and me cooking in the kitchen together. Mum stays in the front room but the rest of us eat round the table. Everyone is quite noisy and it's just like old times, each person vying for attention.

In the evening, Mum feels sick and is in pain. Her back aching with sudden jerk-inducing spasms through her side. She's leant forward in her chair and I try and rub her back gently, try and hold the heat pack in the right place, try to relieve part of the pain. She looks at me and says, "I can't go on. I can't keep going like this".

Mum calms slightly and I slowly take her to bed. She lies on her side. I wrap the hot water bottle around her back and tuck her in, the way she used to tuck me in as a child. I sit on the floor and rub her legs. I give her oromorph and temazepam then stay a while longer, waiting for her to drift off to sleep, waiting for her not to writhe in pain, waiting for her body to relax, just waiting. I creep out, leaving the door ajar. Mum has her bell. If she wakes and needs me in the night, she rings her bell so I can hear her call.

I go downstairs and the tears ease themselves through. I don't try and stop the crying. I feel sad but slightly underwhelmed. Mum tells me she wants to die now. I should at least have some passion in my anguish. Should I shout, scream, run? No. There is no frenzy of activity, just calm, still. I sit in an unmoving silence.

2008

Somnolent day. There is no hot water all morning so I don't shower. My hair is greasy but who cares? I am a skunk, as Mum would say. Holly picks me up at lunch time and we go home, drink coffee with Ethan and see Dad when he pops in. I walk back to the hospital, feeling fresh air and exercise will do me good, and bump into two old friends from school. I talk to them but it is a strain. I seem to be exhausted by the presence of others today. I hate myself for it because everyone is so nice and wants to be with me. I spend my days avoiding drawn out affairs and limiting visits. It is too much otherwise.

Evening arrives slowly, darkness seeping through the windows. I want to die. I don't know why, nothing has triggered this sinking of my mind. The world is the same place. There is no reason. I cannot explain. This is what is difficult – why? I never know the answers. I want to kill myself but such drastic action does not have a basis. Life just seems too dark and, without consciously realising, I am once again staring into death's gaping mouth, an endless tunnel devoid of life.

I do not despair. I am calm, unable to function. I cannot write; I cannot read. Even walking requires effort so I sit on the floor, back slumped against the wall. This is the time when they say I should talk, seek a nurse, get help, but I cannot contemplate these things. I need someone to come to me. I don't possess the skills for such sensible actions. There is nothing there. I remain still until the floor hardens my bottom, the wall grips my shoulder blades and I am aware of pain. I rise, tingling with pins and needles as blood flows back into my weary joints.

After sleeping much better last night from the inhalation of cannabis, I enter into the drug induced world of no care. I have no resistance, a whole joint is mine. I want to feel it in my mouth, my throat, my lungs, have the satisfying aroma on my fingers.

I smoke but I am now an unwitting participant in the corrupt business of illicit substances on the ward. A nurse is the supplier, no doubt heading a roaring trade. While a patient gave me my quota, he, in turn, received it from the nurse in question. The nurse smokes crack, not at work, but got a patient to do a piss test for her so she would be clean. The twisted underworld of psychiatric care. This is what people don't see. Everyone hears about the prison drug networks but not here. We are the forgotten area, a taboo subject.

We languish on the very outskirts of public awareness. It's not that people don't care, it's that they don't know. A conspiracy of silence.

8th April

2007– Easter Sunday

MUM

6.30am Went to bed earlier than usual and Alice sat with me and was very comforting – after having given me some oromorph. Slept well, really: woke briefly at 3am and then 6am. Feeling OK as I write this. Am coming to the conclusion that, whilst much of the initial sickness is related to the chemo, at this point it is probably more to do with the disease itself. It feels as if my whole digestive system is fucked! All badness inside. Hence, I tend to feel best first thing in the morning when I haven't eaten for a long time. Also I guess I'm most rested then. Either way, the days continue to be a struggle to get through and I really don't know how much longer I can go on. It seems pointless somehow – delaying the inevitable. If only death could be guaranteed as painless drifting off to sleep. Bring on the morphine?!

ALICE

Easter Sunday - a sombre affair. Not much done today. Mum in bed until late afternoon. I lie with her, stroking her feet. She feels sick and is in pain. My utter helplessness is all consuming. Why am I so useless?

I made Mum some Easter biscuits yesterday and she managed to try a piece of one. I put lemon icing on top as lemon is a flavour that Mum can still just appreciate.

Mum has her hair cut early evening. The effort to sit in a chair for half an hour was almost too much for dear little Maisie. They said she wouldn't lose all her hair but, every time I wash it, great handfuls fall out. It certainly looks very thin. Mum has said she wants it cut very short (easier to manage when she can't wash for over a week).

This change in appearance does affect me. It's a physical, so obvious reminder. A manifestation of how this cruel illness is taking over her entire body. The steroids have induced a false sense of wellness. Her body is desperately thin and wasted but her face has maintained its fullness. She doesn't look drawn, her cheek bones don't stick out in that sickening, death-awaiting mask. But now, her hair acts as an all too obvious physical symbol. It is not that her hair is grey or boyish short, it is the change, the difference. That is what is hard to see. I know I must allow time to heal, to patch over my insecurities. Next week, I shall not even notice. But tonight, all I have is her new image imprinted in my mind.

2008

I wake up and am out of bed and in the shower before I realise what I am doing. The water is scolding but I don't touch the dial and let my back and neck grow pink from the heat. I wash my hair twice as it feels so dirty, then quickly dry myself before shoving pyjamas back on, dripping hair soaking my top. I ask for a hairdryer then dress in yesterday's clothes. I wonder what the point was in showering.

Outside, I speak to Leo. He tells me his story. He was expelled in Year 9 and, with no other school willing to take him, went to a behavioural college. He left at sixteen and spent the next four and a half years in and out of prison, various misdemeanours, drugs, assault, violence, robbery etc. He only ever managed a few weeks on the outside before breaking the law once again.

Leo is now twenty-two. He has been out of prison for a year and says being here has helped him enormously. He says he has grown up and wants to get his life back on track. It is wonderful to see hospitalisation really benefiting patients. I pray Leo can transfer this dogged determination to the outside world, once he is discharged.

Lily comes to see me at midday. She has brought: flowers, pretty pink and white, cheering up my room; seeds, so I can plant some vegetables at home; a jar of frogspawn[!], only Lily would bring that in: she wants me to watch new life forming. Lily tells me I am doing well, despite moments of deathly longing. She tells me to compare now to how I was. She is right of course. Lily reminds me how, two months ago, I did not want to go out, I didn't particularly want to see anyone. I wanted to die almost continuously and I was sleeping very little. Yes, I am improving and yet the bad is still inside, crouching, hiding, leaping out only at choice moments. I swallowed death but it has still yet to be digested.

Through the window, I see Jas in his seaside rolled trousers. I slowly turn and walk back to my room. The radio goes on,

I feel tiredness bite me like a mosquito, but force myself to sit at my table and write. I must not sleep in the day but this lethargy is exhausting. I drink coffee to stay awake, chew a sweet for distraction and watch my pen as it squiggles and loops and clean white pages are filled with my words. It's like the sentences are waiting in my mind, pausing for the paper to be presented, just hovering.

Katy comes in to talk to me. I say I feel dreadful and I just don't know why. She says this time I have been in hospital, I haven't been my usual smiley self. The staff had noticed. I was always chirpy before. What does this mean? I have given up pretending? Or I lack the energy and ability to be nice anymore? I wish I knew why I felt like this.

Dad picks me up after work and drives home. We encounter Ethan who was on his way to see me. Ethan and I have a drink; Dad eats dinner. I go to my room to exchange dirty clothes for clean ones.

Mind led body,
To the edge of the precipice.
They stand in desire,
At the naked abyss.
If you love me, said mind,
Take that step into silence.
If you love me, said body,
Turn and exist.

Anne Stevenson – Vertigo

Except I do not love my mind; I do not love my body. Each I show hatred towards, loathing of the badness, despicable elements inside. So, if I love neither, what is the solution? By dying, do I give in to mind? The hideous tangle, will that win? My taming efforts will come to very little if mind is the victor. I have heard of the appalling things that will occur. Indecision. How to untangle, obtain the sense, defy the logic which always tugs in my well-educated brain?

You are a scientist Alice, so why the confusion? The voices, the threats, the terrors. I don't want to believe them but I have seen what they can do. They wreak disaster, they can hurt and I do not wish anyone else to fall victim. I punish my body in the hope that the damage is sufficient. No more hurt on other people. I can't bear it. My head dissolves into agony. Please, please, let only me take the blows. I do not mind for I am only a shell. There is only so much one can be abused until subsequent abuse no longer matters. I am not made worse; I am not made better. I am a china doll.

I do not smoke tonight. I do not want to be involved in this corrupt network of drug supply. Why did I smoke cannabis anyway? To give me a rest, if fleetingly, from the turmoil that my poor head contains. But my morals are still, if tenuously, in tact. Don't perpetuate the problem Alice, you are just as guilty as them. Supply and demand: no demand, no supply. Trust in your prescription drugs, despite their apparent indifference to you. Work with the doctors, not against. They are there to help you.

I now have six tablets I take at night time meds. It is a horrible sensation swallowing them all, it reminds me of taking an overdose. I am a bit drowsy after half an hour or so. I get ready for bed and then read but it is odd. I know I am tired but this isn't a drowsiness where you think you are on the brink of falling asleep, this is a spaced out state where you feel distracted from the world because you become internalised and the replaying noise inside your head is all you concentrate on.

9th April

2008

More devastating nightmares. I was on the floor, curled up beneath my bed at one point. All too distressing to even write about. I got up at 7am, there was no more sleep to come.

I feel pretty dreadful. I tidy my room, walk outside, read the newspaper. All distractions. Helen is my nurse, she comes and gets me for a brief chat. She tells me distractions can be good because then I can focus my mind on something else. I should go into the lounge so I am not alone. The problem is, it feels like I have the capacity to delay the badness within. In company, I can hold it together enough but it doesn't mean the shadow land passes, instead it hovers, a smoky aura, patiently waiting to descend.

After lunch, unable to function, I fall face down on my bed and, despite unrelenting drilling outside, I quickly fall to sleep. Helen wakes me after an hour and asks if I would move rooms. I'm currently in room 2, close to the nurses station, always noisy, so I am glad to change. I scoop clothes into my rucksack, gather my books, throw toiletries into my wash bag and shove my feet into shoes.

The flowers on my windowsill from Lily have not yet withered: they come too. The frogspawn don't look good, perhaps they were too warm. The squiggly iris of jelly eyes look limp, the mass has sunk to the bottom of the jar. My frogspawn are dead. I have killed them. Unceremoniously, I tip them onto the soil beneath the bushes. I thought they might block the sink or toilet. I feel sad. I didn't want them to die. I was going to add them to the hospital pond with the ducks and swans and moorhens.

Maureen is stoned. Fred gave her a joint. I'm not sure she realised what it was. The patients and staff seem relieved. Maureen is chilled out and doesn't raise her voice. This isn't good. If Maureen doesn't understand then this is bordering on abuse. I pray that cannabis doesn't make her ill or react adversely with her medications.

Holly collects me and drives to Tim and Flo's house - we are greeted by darling little Mia in a Minnie Mouse costume complete with ears! Carol, Tim's Mum, is also there and here is our Barbados reunion. Truth time and I explain my recent escapades and the true reason I joined them on holiday. Everyone is lovely. They are such a delightful family and include me with incredible ease. It is hard to believe I have only known them for that week.

They laugh at me in flip flops: we're not on the beach now Alice! But I forgot to change into my proper shoes. The ward is controlled by under floor heating – no radiators allowed here, we would burn ourselves on them – so the lino becomes very warm, seeping heat into your feet. Flip flops are the best footwear.

The food is plentiful, the conversation jolly and Flo is amazing considering she is due to give birth in three days time! I enjoy myself. I laugh and smile and eagerly participate in the chatter. Holly and I stay almost four hours. This is quite an achievement for me.

We all exchange hugs on departure, already arranging the next meal we shall have together. Once in the car, I feel my body loosen and sink into the seat. I enjoyed myself immensely and yet I can feel the tension and concentration in my body. It was a long time to remain normal, control my ravaged body, prevent the noise in my head destroying my pleasure. And yet I did it. I do enjoy parts of life. I do not think everything is dire. Some things are amazing but then some things are desperate. My mind undulates between the two. Indecision, for which was to go? Fleeting, contrasting emotions. How do I stop myself from experiencing such extreme emotions? Life is glorious; life is erroneous. I no longer wish to be flung between the two.

10th April

2007

MUM

7am Really am losing interest in this diary. Everything such an effort. Anyway…Ange came round on Sunday and cut my hair – *very* short. It looks fairly terrible: chicken's bum meets chipmunk cheeks! First thing in the morning sticking up all over the place. However, it is quick and easy to wash and, hopefully, it will improve with some regrowth!

Yesterday John drove to Birmingham to collect Mum and Dad. In the evening, Mum, Alice and I watched DVD of "The History Boys" which was an Easter present from John. Thought it excellent. Ethan went to a barbeque – and then the King's Arms with live music – in the afternoon, and gave me a bit of a foot massage before I went to bed. Lily visited – always a tonic.

ALICE

I called the doctor out this morning. I was probably over-reacting but, the problem with knowing too much medicine, is just that, I know too much. We are taught the most serious things so that we don't miss them. Mum had a sore red patch on the back of her hand last night. This morning I see (unnoticed by Mum) rather alarmingly, thick purple lines wriggling their way up to her elbow. I go from thinking it's cellulitis to septicaemia to neutropenia…the severity and ludicrousy increasing with each diagnosis. I wish I knew more. I wish I'd seen more. Knowing only half is perhaps worse than knowing nothing. Ignorance can be comforting.

Dr. Pearce came round and said it's unlikely to be any of my suggestions!! Most commonly, it is the effect the chemo has had on Mum's poor veins, gradually destroying them. The body is just attempting to repair itself. Mum's arm looks like a snake, the patterns developing into diamonds, purple lines criss-crossing.

2008

Dreadful night. I was up and down from my bed continuously trying to shake myself free, rattle my senses into the real world. In my dream, I was trying to hang myself. I had to find a suitable place where I was high enough to leap and snap my neck in the fall. I succeeded and remember dangling, staring at my limp feet, suffocating.

Once the morning arrived, I peeled myself from the sheets and stood under the shower, washing the demons away.

Francis, my social worker, popped in this morning to see how I was doing. She is very caring and sympathetic but practical too. Effy came by to check if I was OK. My miserly existence from all else hasn't quite gone to plan yet – too many people invading! Roy collects me for my review. Dr. Floyd is still away. Her registrar is nice but brief. He says I'll need bloods for lithium levels on Monday and he reduces my quetiapine (on my request). I am told to see how this week goes, plan activities to do once home and I should be discharged next Thursday.

Late afternoon, I walk home. What should be a pleasant stroll turns into a trek of supreme effort. My pace slackens and I feel a creeping tingle ripple through my shoulders, down my arm. I am too hot but then, with rolled up sleeves, no coat and a biting wind, I am cold. Feeling two opposite sensations simultaneously is peculiar. My breathing seems wrong, almost gasping. My head begins to ache and the scenery on my periphery blurs. I develop a musty aura and feel my mind floating.

I focus on a bench ahead and grasp it with outstretched arms, feeling the contours, locating where to sit. The bench supports me and I lean forward, the earth rotating in my sight before disappearing into a mottled greyness. Slowly, the sensation passes. I ease myself up and loll on the bench, successfully avoiding fainting. Minutes pass, I am chilly but too concerned to tug down my sleeves or put on my coat incase this encourages my body to collapse on me. I gently amble home, each step an effort but each step closer.

Back at hospital, the evening seems to drag, each hour eeking out its worth, the sun straining to prolong its widespread rays. I feel fidgety but too tired to move. My body does not obey my demands. But then the terrors come, not slowly but with vengeance. Voices compounding voices. They are too fast, too ferocious, all sense is lost. They ravage my mind like lions destroying prey. I don't want to listen but I have to. There is no choice. I know what they are saying is true. I am despicable; I am filthy; I am brimming with badness. I must give them something. They do not go away.

I grab the blade and strike out, a slice of my arm, food for the fiends. The blood is red and thick and flows round my elbow before falling onto my pyjama bottoms where the light blue material openly receives its offering, spreading across my thigh. My head is ambushed. I am hurtled into confusion. I shake and, with a last effort, strike my hand down on my arm, a deep gash, two parallel lines now obliterated by a mat of red, unrelenting blood. I stumble into the bathroom, clasp a wad of tissues and stick them to my arm. A soggy mass of blood tissues go in the toilet. I repeat. And again. Blood is ample.

I climb into my bed but cannot settle. My ears are straining, seeking out the slightest indication of any roaming badness. My eyes are wide, alert, piercing through the darkness. I want to get up, walk around my room, anything but to lie here. I allow reason, sense and those I trust dictate my actions. You are safe, Alice. There is nothing there. Do not be afraid. You are safe. I remain on my back in bed, willing myself to believe these words.

11th April

2008

Pretty dire night. Didn't get to sleep until gone 1am and then I kept waking, nightmares flinging me into consciousness. I saw all the even hours: 2am, 4am, 6am, 8am but I did sleep inbetween them. At 9am, Katy woke me for meds. I felt groggy and unrefreshed but Katy was a dear, checking how I was this morning, showing concern. I really am being cared for.

After breakfast, I had a bath. I allowed my weary body to soak into the bubbles, down to my shoulders, submerged, further until the water lapped into my ears. Sound was distorted and pleasant, my watery wonderland. I felt safe, protected. Naked but bath water was my shield, soap bubbles my sword. I washed my hair and rinsed it with the hand held shower attachment. I remembered when I was little and Mum washed my hair, always checking the water temperature with her hand before carefully dousing my head, ensuring water didn't run into my eyes.

I remembered when Dad slipped in the bath, tearing his arm on the shower attachment, a huge, open wound, blood smeared over the tiles, filling the bath, spreading over the floor with such speed. Dad crawled to the door to unlock, allow access. I heard him shouting and came running, scene out of a horror film confronting me. I was fifteen years old but I knew first aid. I called Mum. She saw and ran down the road to fetch Lily.

Dad had torn an artery. I grabbed the nearest thing to hand (Dad's dirty shirt) and tied a tight tourniquet. Dad was lying on the floor on his back. I knelt beside him, both my hands around his forearm, gripping as tightly as I could, and held Dad's arm up. You should elevate the wound above the heart, I knew that. Mum returned with Lily who was a comforting, knowledgeable presence.

Mum carefully placed a towel to cover Dad's modesty! In the circumstances, I had failed to register Dad's nakedness.

Mum and I carefully dressed Dad and drove him to A+E, Lily following. He was seen straight away and, when the doctor cleaned and washed and disinfected, half the skin on Dad's forearm was missing, peeled back revealing skeins of muscle fibres. They gave Dad painful injections and then instructed us to take him to a different hospital to have surgery as they had the plastics department there.

Dad was admitted, evening arrived and Mum and I went home. Cold and hungry, we put some food in the oven then, together, tackled the bathroom, trying to clean as much as possible. We found a postage stamp sized piece of fat and skin hanging on the bath. We sat in the front room, open fire lit, and talked together, both relieved to be in one another's company. Together, Mum and I could do anything. Mum asked me why I used Dad's dirty shirt, she had just washed all the towels so they were extremely clean!

In the bath, the plasters on my arm come off so I seek out staff. Susie and Katy take me to the meds room. Katy says I don't look well and I reply that I'm not great but it is all so non-specific, I just feel completely run down. Susie is lovely and carefully cleans my arm. She wants me on more antibiotics as it is all infected and discoloured. She is ever so gentle and cradles my arm as if it was something delicate.

Susie is concerned about me. She has read my notes and knows I ended up in Casualty after Mum died, anaemic and dehydrated. I was staying at Sarah's. We went to church and, when we got back, I could barely keep awake. Unsure as to what exactly happened next, I am relying on Sarah's account. She took me to A+E, think I was reluctant to go (actually, I can remember this – I wanted nothing to do with hospitals!). I ended up on a drip – lots of fluids – I was a bit dehydrated, anaemic, low blood sugar, nothing too specific, just run down with exhaustion. I spent the afternoon in casualty and caught up on hours sleep, much to Sarah's surprise! (It wasn't exactly the most peaceful environment.)

Susie says she'd like me to have my bloods done, just so they can be sure it is not a physical problem which can be easily remedied. I get properly dressed, dry my hair and then Susie comes into my room. She is my nurse today and wants to talk. She spends a lot of time with me and listens. I feel she really wants to know what is going on in my head. She understands. I don't know why, I think I trust her, but I elaborate much more frankly than I have before. Susie says things that are exactly right. She describes the problems which I find difficult, she really seems to know. I feel quite amazed. In many respects, she is like Dr. Floyd. Susie catches on without me having to explain in great detail. I am so grateful for her time.

I start to think that maybe this hospital stay won't be pointless. I do still feel the same but at last someone understands. Susie appears genuinely interested and wants to find something that will help me.

Before Dad picks me up, Susie checks my blood pressure and blood glucose to ensure I am alright to leave. Dad drives to the supermarket where I pick up food for lunch and then home where we eat together with Ethan. Dad suggested this. He is being kind to me so I should just enjoy it but everything is odd. When I'm living at home, Dad wouldn't think twice about not seeing me for days on end – he didn't notice that I was in hospital – but now, he wants to see me every day. It is nice, I'm not denying that, it's the change that is strange.

Back on the ward, Susie takes me to see the on call doctor who takes my blood, four syringe fulls. I think I must still have "Afraid of needles" in my notes as the doctor kept ensuring I was OK!

Gone 11pm, sedative filled, I should have gone to bed but I felt agitation grip me like a straight jacket. I paced around my room feeling nervous about today. Perhaps I told Susie too much. It is wrong to talk, Alice. I started to think Susie may get hurt. I don't want her to be a victim, that would be terrible. I don't hear the badness, the threats, the curses but I know what they've said before. I wanted to cut myself just to make everything safe in case. I was frightened and confused but I was sensible. I tried to think of Sarah and all the truths she has told me.

I walked out of my room to the staff room and asked Adelle to talk with me. She was absolutely lovely and listened to my plight, understood how I was thinking even though we discussed logical (opposite) reasoning. She gave me time to relax slightly. We stayed talking and I felt the need to damage myself abate. Adelle said she wouldn't let me back to my room until I was calm. She stayed with me and said she was quite happy to talk all night! Adelle wanted to help me. I felt encouraged by her company.

Warm mug of tea later, I wiggled into my pyjamas and into bed, drowsy head appreciative of pillow.

12th April

2007

ALICE

First day on placement with Lily. I haven't done any medicine for six weeks – it feels even longer. It's agreed that I only go in for a few afternoons, mornings are too hard with Mum so poorly. Today, I remembered how much I adore being a doctor or rather, I don't remember because I'm unable to describe it, but I just know. It is a feeling that seeps through my entire body. I feel right. I feel in place. It is not necessarily happiness as patients are ill but it is a oneness, a wholeness, a contentedness. It is somewhere that I fit.

But then I leave the surgery and remember. I'm never going to be a doctor. This makes me feel sad. My life is no longer mine to lead off the path. I am now being led and I have been told the ending. But this gives me peace of a sort. It is calming to know that my life will soon be over. Every night, lying awake in bed, I see my suicide. Although the methods vary, the outcome is always the same. And it's OK because I have done what I have needed to do. I have looked after Mum, my dearest Maisie, but she is dead too. I was there when she needed me the most. But, with her gone, there is nothing.

2008

I wake at 6am and can't get back to sleep so I make myself coffee. I wash and dress and swallow my morning meds then Susie comes to speak to me. We sit in my room and she offers firm reassurance that she is OK. She feels I'm doing well being able to talk to her. She knows I find it incredibly difficult but, perhaps now I can see no harm has come to her, we could talk some more. Susie doesn't want to distress me but she does want to help. I do feel calm and safe with her. She is on a long day tomorrow so we shall have a discussion then, giving me time to think. Susie redresses my arm and says she hopes I have a nice day off the ward which isn't too exhausting.

I walk into town and meet my friend Claire for coffee. It is lovely to see her and we talk at ease. Claire is a doctor in Sheffield and currently on A+E which she isn't particularly keen on – she wants to be a GP - but, because of her knowledge, it is effortless to talk to her about drugs and diagnoses without explanation or lay person misunderstanding. I am back in that secret doctor world, shielded from innocent civilians.

Claire says it is extremely insightful talking to me because I can explain myself so articulately. Psychiatric inpatients, in general, do not have sufficient awareness of their illness for analysis. But, sometimes, I think this is a hindrance. I can analyse myself almost too well but to what endeavours? Ignorance seems like bliss to me.

I arrive back in hospital at 4.30pm, go to my room, unpack clean clothes, more notebooks and pens, nice food and then sit, edge of my bed, and feel dreadful. My whole body shakes, a resting tremor of small amplitude. My breathing feels wrong, slightly too shallow, rate increased but I can't seem to tame it. My physical surroundings are distanced and I enter into that pre-fainting aura.

Katy comes to see me. I try and explain but descriptions escape me. I just feel odd and poorly. My temperature, blood pressure and oxygen stats are taken, but they are normal. What is wrong with me? I doubt myself; I think I'm making it up but I don't wish to feel like this. Katy reassures me. She takes time, talks in my room, says I haven't been myself, I'm no longer smiley, my tiredness is obvious. Katy is gentle and kind and cares so much. She puts her arm round my shoulders and I want to loll my head against her and fall to sleep in safety.

We are interrupted by my phone – Dad ringing saying he is outside but no one is answering the ward bell. Katy lets him in and Dad and I sit in a side room. Words are stilted, we struggle to converse. I suggest driving home so I can pick up some non-important item I had forgotten. Driving, a practical thing and being in the car is a more normal situation, not quite so forced.

Driving back to hospital, Dad brings up Mary. He says he is going to invite her to dinner and thinks I should talk to her, apparently Mary's daughter had a break down. I tell Dad it is an idea and I would like to meet Mary but I do not want to discuss my recent psychiatric history with a stranger! I tell Dad to arrange a date; I'll be there. I have to make the effort too. Dad wants me to get to know Mary.

13th April

2007

ALICE

No sleep gives me a strange, distanced, slightly spaced out view of the world. I'm cushioned from everything around me, as if I'm watching through cling film. I actually feel tired, or what I imagine tired should feel like.

Mum into hospital to get her bloods taken. After the last two days of being very poorly and unable, really, to leave her bed, Mum manages this trip so well. We also go to Crowhurst ward to see the doctor as Mum has now developed a red rash covering her entire body. She also shows the new doctor her arm of purple wiggly veins.

Later, in the afternoon, the doctor rings back with Mum's results. Her white cell count is fine so chemo definitely on Monday. Her red cells are lowish but no transfusion needed yet. Her LFTs are slightly worse, the numbers creeping up. The change isn't significant but Mum does think, is it worth it? Why bother with the chemo? The medical response is unchanging: too early too tell if chemo has improved things.

It is now six weeks since Mum was diagnosed. I thought of the patient I saw in Lily's surgery yesterday whose cancer story had only just begun. It was too close to home for me really, her presentation too similar to Mum's. She had indigestion, abdominal pains and slight weight loss. She lay down and I palpated her tummy. Immediately I felt the all too obvious cancer. It was a hard lump. It made me feel sick. My hands got clammy and I was uneasy inside. I wanted to run, escape outside, breathe fresh air but I couldn't. I think I wanted to cry. I didn't. Professionalism prevented the personalised response. Is it professionalism? Or is it that thread that I must keep hold? If one bit slips then I may unravel, completely collapse. Breaking down doesn't happen in parts. It's all or nothing. Maybe that's why you have to keep pretending. If one part gives in, everything comes tumbling down.

The thoughts over-ran my head. It was late, maybe 2am, and I was sick. Badness in my head seemed to make me sick. It splashed on my t-shirt so I went downstairs to wash it but then I found myself outside, walking. It wasn't aimless walking, it seemed to have a purpose. I walked along the alley - up to the top then back along until I reached the road at the other end. I kept walking, up and down, back and forth. I felt like I was pacing but maybe I was dawdling. I don't know. I think I must have been tired. Memory doesn't work properly.

I must have been a while because, when I got back to my bedroom, the glowing alarm clock said it was 4.07am. Time is curious sometimes.

2008

Another restless night with appalling dreams. I was eating dinner with Dad and Holly which escalated into an enormous row. I ran away and, with such conviction, carried out my suicide. I took a massive overdose, pills in their hundreds, then swam out to sea and drowned. It worked. I am even killing myself in my sleep. Why can't I do it in real life?

I phone Aunty Beth who is on her way home after a week in Egypt with Uncle Angus and Zac. They had a brilliant time, great food, lots of swimming and snorkelling, amazing reefs and Zac appreciated the mini disco in the hotel – dance competitions every night! I'm so pleased they had a relaxing and fun holiday. Aunty Beth deserves a proper break. Lovely to hear her voice again though, my darling aunty.

Susie comes to find me and I begin to read extracts from that which I wrote when Mum was poorly. I think this may be the best way for people to understand what those months were like, gain some insight, really know what Mum and I were like together. I read and am without emotion. All the events I remember with crystal clarity but this does not force laughter or sadness upon me. I am a mouth piece with a barren body. Roughly half way through, I stop. Lunch time is called and a break is needed – I have been talking over half an hour. Susie thanks me for sharing those words with her. The feeling is reciprocal. She is helping me.

It is OK to read to Susie because she is distanced from the events. The people I talk about, she doesn't know. I couldn't talk to anyone at the time. It was all too awful. I didn't want to burden others with the horrors that I witnessed.

Susie, on a long day, comes into my room again for story time. She sits in a chair and I resume reading her extracts. She cries in parts and yet I feel nothing. I can remember all the events, remember how I felt but I no longer can feel it, tap into that emotion. Susie thinks I have dissociated. The mind is very clever and has mechanisms to protect itself, prevent events from becoming too damaging. But I don't want this. I don't care if everything is all horrific, surely to be able to feel is better than nothing at all.

I have done a spot of reconnaissance work and decide now is the time to disclose. I tell Susie about the drug network, who's supplying, who's distributing. The staff have had their own suspicions but have no proof, just hearsay. I say, "Would it help if I had the private mobile number of the member of staff who is bringing the drugs in?" Susie smiles and says it may help. I'll get the number from Fred. It's all getting round now though, nurse under suspicion phoned in sick today, she knows they are on to her.

Later, I descended into a pit of self hatred over the things I had spoken to Susie about. I kept thinking, over and over, about Mum. She wanted me to kill her. I wanted to kill her, to end the horrific suffering, to relieve her of a hideous existence. Mum begged me, again and again, enough morphine, Ali, enough morphine. I couldn't do what she asked, I couldn't bring myself to inject those millilitres of poison. Mum asked me but it was the only thing I could not do for her. But then I got confused. What atrocity was I thinking? Killing my own mother, I was almost her murderer. How can I even imagine such a thing? I hate myself for it. I nearly killed my Mummy. My head jumpily swirled with conflicting words. I felt guilty for not killing Mum when she asked; I felt guilty that I even contemplated killing her. I didn't know what to do.

In my head, rage built up, damage this pitiful human specimen. I took the blade and slowly sliced my ankle, feeling the sting tingle my leg. Blood dripped and pooled and smeared.

At some point, I calmed. I walked to the staff room and got Susie. She came immediately. I said I had cut myself and she ushered me into the meds room. I tried to explain but my words tumbled out. I kept saying that I was sorry. Susie sat an agitated me down. The indentation of my heel in my flip flop had filled with bright red blood. Susie kneeled and lifted my foot onto her lap so she could clean and disinfect. My whole body was shaking, my leg waggling, hindering Susie's steri stripping efforts.

Susie was so lovely to me and tender. She washed the blood off my hands with alcohol soap and talked. She told me I was OK, today had been really tough with me reading so much about those ill days with Mum. It is my reaction to it that Susie wants to help me to change. She took me to my room, a shivering shell, and got a verbal order for lorazepam. She sat next to me and tried to offer a distraction that might help. I usually go for a walk. Susie knows this but said she can't send me off the unit now, it was dark, late and I was in a mess. I understood. I knew I'd calm down soon.

Lily phoned shortly after then arrived at 10pm to see me. She brought me chocolate and grapes and nice coffee, all the things she knows I'll enjoy in here. I hugged her tight and didn't want to let go, I just want to hold on and never break from her arms. Lily took me for a walk outside, around the hospital pond. The night staff allowed it, "You must stay with Dr. Hatfield all the time, Alice". The authority of a doctor saving me again.

Sleep is hard to come tonight. I am unsettled and, even though tired, this does not help.

14th April

2008

I awake feeling dreadful and have no idea why. Both my sheets are knotted on the floor so I am lying on a sticky, plastic mattress with a blanket coiled around me. I am freezing and feel sick. I drag my aching body into the bathroom and retch but nothing is produced. I fall back into bed but no more sleep will come. The day has started.

After meds, I sink into a bath, swirling the too hot water around my scarred knees, too many hockey matches. My legs turn pink and relax into the water appreciating their lack of supportive use. Once out and dry, Duffy comes to take my blood – checking lithium levels yet again. She also patches up my arm and ankle. I think of Mum's veins and how hard they were to locate, small and thin and collapsing. My poor, darling Mummy.

At 5pm I walk home, cold but sunny, and see Ethan. I get the weekend newspapers, some clean clothes, put dinner in the oven for Dad and take more coffee – I have got through a jar in a week.

Dad arrives home and has a slight disagreement with Ethan. Ethan found blades in my room (the ones Lily gave me so at least I didn't get infected cuts) and started saying how Dad hadn't even looked. It transpires that, after this, Dad did go through my room and removed all my tablets. I get annoyed. I hate anyone going through my things, I understand the reason why, but at least he could have told me. Dad lies. He says he hadn't been through my room. Why does he lie to me?

Ethan has thrown my lithium tablets away and I get the other medications off Dad. This is what the ISS gave me, have been signed for, the tablets I am currently on. They both get cross with me, I should know why they did it. I do, but it is the callous, secretive way it has been carried out. I want Mum. She would have sat me down, calmly explained, tried to help, not lie. I know Dad was doing it for me, for my safety, but he doesn't ask. He wouldn't know that blades were there so I can hurt myself in a minor way, not too drastic. He doesn't know Lily gave them to me because he doesn't talk. Communication thwarting us again.

I grab my rucksack and run out of the house. I can't stay. I walk and the tears come, dribbling down my face, stinging my eyes. I want to run away, run and run, go anywhere but here. I know why I am reacting in a such a way. Having tablets made me feel safe, it was a reassurance, but now that's gone, I am scared, no get out clause. I don't know what to do, where to go, rain starts to fall. I remember my anatomy, I remember the craft knife I have at home. I see myself, right hand destroying left, slit down the artery, never across, it is not enough. It plays over in my mind, I can even see the blood.

I do make it back to the ward, over an hour late, tear spattered face, eyes swollen, red cheeks. I run into my room.

15th April

2008

I awake at 6am feeling such lethargy but unable to force myself back to sleep. I get up and the mirror reflects a spectacle: eyes, the whites of which are covered in tiny red lines, squiggling like a road map; eyelids, swollen and puffy; crusty bits of sleep stuck in the corners; hair, a bird's nest on top, straggly tails beneath. I look how I feel.

Long, drawn out day. I don't know if I'm bored but lack little motivation or inspiration to do anything. Dad arrives at 4.30pm, after work and before he goes to some work's dinner. I say sorry about yesterday, I just wish he wouldn't lie. He decides to take this moment to have a go at me for how messy my room is. I look at him incredulously. What does he expect me to do? Tidy it from here? I ask him not to go in my room again. He goes on about how it's his house and he can go where he likes.

Dad doesn't understand why I want to die. He launches into how we've got to cope and how it's my fault as I'm not doing anything during the day. Accusingly, he demands to know how I've spent today, what doing? I shrug. He says I've got to get on with life, with university. He's getting on with everything, he says I know what

Mum would want me to do. Dad says he spoke to Mum about what he should do. I wince when Mum is mentioned. Dad continues, how he remembers all the good times being with Mum. He's conveniently developed a fucking selective memory. I have listened and comforted and hugged Mum for years and years when he has been despicable towards her. I've listened to Mum when she said she wanted to die because of all the vile things Dad has done, when she wanted to run away.

Dad progresses, he has no guilt, only happy memories. He's either in denial or is more ill than I am or just damn arrogant how he's been all his life. I tell him that, if I was him, I would feel tremendously guilty. Like a horror film, the way in which Dad treated Mum plays in my head. She was dying and he still shouted at her, still made her cry, still was so unbelievably selfish. But I am silent, I can't remind him of those things, I am stopped by the thought that I really may hurt Dad by telling him these things. I want to though. I want him to acknowledge his behaviour.

I begin to cry. Dad can say anything about me and I remain, externally, unemotional but what makes the tears come are the recollections of Mum being so hurt by him. I let the tears dribble down my face silently, drip from my chin to my top, I can't move or speak. My mother was wonderful and Dad just brought her down. I sit there, tears still coming, and Dad sits too, opposite me, arms crossed. He doesn't move, just looks out of the window.

Eventually, I go and get some tissues from the toilet. I return and ask him to leave. I can't talk to Dad. I am prevented by saying all the dreadful, hurtful things I want to. Is that my conscience stopping me? Dad tries to kiss me as he leaves, I shrink away from his touch. Get away from me Dad. I can't even look at him. All I see is the pain in Mum's eyes as she lies there dying and the indifference of Dad as he gets cross.

I run to my room, tears still flowing. Up and down I pace until I stumble into the bathroom and am sick in the toilet, foul smelling, bitter, lumpy. It makes me retch again and again. Tears mingle with snot and bile. I collapse against the toilet bowl, face smeared, and want to die there and then, oesophageal varices, brain haemorrhage, willing any complication of vomiting to claim my life. Nothing happens. The nausea wanes, I stagger to the sink and splash cold water liberally on my face. It soaks my top, my bra. I shiver but the chill is a relief.

Composing myself, I go out for a walk, just walking. I'm only allowed an hour. I want to die, the feeling so intense. Do I jump in front of a bus, car, train? But all these things would result in trauma for someone else. I can't allow my actions to have such an impact on some poor, unsuspecting participant. I decide the best place to die is in hospital. Staff are used to witnessing horrors, more immune than lay members of the public. People die in hospital everyday. My damage would be limited. But then, of course, the staff are trained to save you. It would have to be carried out properly. This is what I'm scared of. Death holds no fear but killing myself does. What if I only half managed it? What if I was left unable to do things for myself? I then would not be able to finish the job, complete my suicide. That is what I am afraid of.

When I get back, Katy finds me to talk. She knows Dad makes me worse. She knows some of the things he's done so she understands my devastation. I am honest with her. All I do is talk about death. I explain my hospital suicide. I promise I won't do it when she's on shift! She laughs and puts her arm around my shoulder. She longs to help, to make me feel different. Katy is ever so caring towards me. I am now on level 2 obs again – fifteen minute checks. I suppose it's to be expected.

I phone Aunty Beth who's worried about me. I have a rant about Dad. Aunty Beth knows, Aunty Beth understands. Mum was always in tears on the phone to her about Dad too. My lovely aunty. She says she wants to come at the weekend. Poor Aunty Beth, she has so much work to do and yet, unselfishly, she wants to drive to see me. I'm unsure through, sometimes when people are so wonderful to me, afterwards I am worse. It's almost too hard, my head doesn't understand it. Sometimes it's best if I'm just left to me. It is so tiring being in company, too much of a struggle.

Ethan phones at 10.30pm. He says he is sorry he hasn't made it to see me today, he could come now. Er…no, Ethan! I don't think the staff will be too impressed and I've just been drugged up so will soon be drowsy and slurring my words. I tell him not to worry, we'll chat tomorrow. Sleep well Ethan, take care.

16th April

2008

Largely dreadful night, thrown from one nightmare into the next. Woke at 2am, leapt to the sink and was sick, vile tasting fluid flowing from my mouth. Waking again in the morning, still felt grim. Stayed in bed for an hour reading before I could summon enough energy to face the day.

Katy encourages me to eat breakfast so I do, a bowl of cereal, hopefully not enough to unsettle my stomach. Lily phones for an update and is, as always, lovely, caring and sensible. She says there is always a room at her house. We could arrange, when I am allowed out, for me to live there. I am so grateful to have Lily for support.

Katy takes me into a side room to chat and I find myself becoming so frustrated with Dad. How does he have such a selfish, blinkered view? Looking after Mum, I know I did everything I possibly could, I couldn't have done anymore for my darling Mummy. Thinking about Dad, I don't see how he could have done any less. He was crap. I feel so upset about the times he was despicable, Mum deserved much more than that. She deserved the absolute best because she was so wonderful and caring herself.

The alarm goes off, wailing, pounding your ears, doors automatically slam shut, magnets releasing. Everyone carries on as normal, us patients are so used to this occurrence. Must be a false alarm or disturbance on the other ward because our staff calmly return to their jobs. The alarm continues for a painful length of time.

Management are all down on the ward this afternoon. The nurse selling drugs, Sabrina, has been in for a meeting. Fred has phoned the ward and grassed her up because she owed him £40 and has now stopped answering his calls and requests. Sabrina has been suspended since Monday and now we think they are trying to obtain sufficient evidence to sack her. The management look alien down here, smart suits and ties. All the normal nursing staff wear casual clothes, comfortable, relaxed, fits in with us. The way management dress is also the only clue we have to determine who they are.

Tea time comes and I have no appetite. I ask to go for a walk instead. Almost as soon as I am outside, in the open, the tears come and I walk and sob and don't care about the looks people throw me. One of the benefits of being in the hospital, for all strangers know, someone could have just died. I walk, not knowing where. Cul-de-sacs, alley ways, all blurred from my tear-filled eyes. I want to die. It is an all-consuming feeling that can't be controlled or reasoned or dampened. I feel horrendous. I can't describe, just so low.

Eventually I meander back to the ward, crying ceases and I grab Susie to talk. She comes and sits me on the bed, beside her. I try to explain but I cannot. All I think of is death. I want to die.

Sometimes I don't even know why. I take Mum's book and ask to finish my story. Susie sits in the chair, cradling a cup of tea; I sit on my desk stool, shakily clutching my book. I read the last few weeks of Mum's life and what I said at Mum's funeral. Finished, I cry. Susie is crying too and she comes over and hugs me. I can't move. I cling onto Susie tight, feeling all those memories of pain and anguish and desperation. For the first time, I feel once again how bad it was.

I have been extremely honest with Susie; I have admitted to thinking of death and ways to achieve it. She knows I'll at least try and cut myself if nothing else. She says I'm not safe and I can't disagree. I am emotional, unstable, impulsive and suicidal. I'm not surprised they want to check on me.

Ethan and Grace arrive shortly after and we sit and talk and it is easy and calm. They also see Sophie, whom Ethan hasn't seen since school. I say to Ethan, lets get a flat together, anywhere, just not here. He says he'll look. Will he want to live with me though? His crazy, disturbed, older sister, meant to be protective but really just a burden. Ethan brings me fruit and newspapers and ice creams! I feel better for being with him, more serene, calmer in my own body.

By bed time, I feel the itching, self-loathing come upon me. I scratch the backs of my hands until they are red and raw and bleeding. I want to slash myself. I told Susie I would try and talk to someone before I did. I find Adam. He takes me into a side room and gets me to speak. Adam is good because he can talk to me at length, even if my replies are short, non-committal and vague. I don't cut myself, I suddenly feel too tired. I crawl into bed gone midnight, read and am asleep before 1am.

I had told Susie that, if Dad showed up, could she tell him I didn't want to see him. He isn't the cause of my problems but he certainly compounds them. Susie agrees, she thinks he does make me worse. I decide a bit of distance is needed, a break from one another. I need space without being berated by him. I needn't have bothered with my precautions, however. Dad hasn't come today, he hasn't even phoned.

17th April

2008

Awake frequently throughout the night in varying positions in my bed, blankets strewn around me. Get up not feeling dreadful for once. Drink my coffee and read the bible. Both Adelle and Nadia say to me not to go out before my review with Dr. Floyd (at

12.30pm). This doesn't bode well. I'm getting the distinct impression that I'm not going to be allowed any leave at all.

The morning I spend agitated and shaky, trying to write, trying to read the newspaper, trying to do the crossword, trying to do anything but with little success.

Review with Dr. Floyd, just her and Roy. I prefer this, it is more intimate, less like an interview with all eyes on me. Dr. Floyd says I am depersonalised, holding my own life with little regard. It is good to speak to her again, she describes me so accurately and yet concisely. She changes my antidepressant, citalopram has done little and trimipramine (a tricyclic) will also be sedating. The sleep I am getting has no quality and is now becoming morbid. She increases my lithium to 1000mg, my bloods still show a level less than 0.6, the effective range. Alarmingly, she also mentions ECT as a treatment, not for now, however.

The depression has overtaken how I view life, my feelings, my responses, everything. Dr. Floyd says this is dangerous. The staff want to keep me safe. I do think about dying for a large portion of the day. Dr. Floyd was dubious about giving me leave. Will I keep myself safe? Who knows. I want to die. Sometime I will try. Dr. Floyd says I'm allowed out if I am accompanied. She knows I will not do anything too severe if I am with family. She asks about voices. Mum definitely, but also the muddled, dark ones. It is great that Dr. Floyd is back, I do feel safer, more understood with her, but the review is hard work and I leave with a full head of additional thoughts, grasping for my attentions.

18th April

2008

I awake at 6am but soon return to unconsciousness and only stir for 9am meds. Impressive! I didn't have any dreams (or, at least that I can remember) and I don't think I woke a particularly large number of times. Maybe this new medication is going to knock me out sufficiently.

I drink coffee and eat an orange for breakfast and then Holly arrives to take me out on "accompanied leave". I am allowed an hour. Holly drives to her favourite walk through the bluebell wood.

Dad phones me shortly after I arrive back. It is awkward and his initial questions always manage to annoy me: "Where are you?", almost always in hospital; "What have you done today?", usually not much. I never have lengthy answers to these comments and always reply in near identical ways. "How are you?" is always the worst. I can remember cringing when people asked Mum that. How do you answer? Dad states he is coming to see me after work. He doesn't say anything of how we last were together. I say no, perhaps not. Dad says, "Oh, why not?". How do I tell him that I don't want to see him? That he makes me worse? That I need some space? I say that maybe I shall see him next week. He is going away walking in Norfolk this weekend anyway and I need time to think.

He hangs up, back to work, and I slide down the wall to the floor, knees up, wondering what to do. I now feel really bad, I hate thinking these things of Dad. I hate how horrible I have become. I hate me. I think of the pleasant walk with Holly and how that should have been nice. It was, but I was just acting, a learned response, knowing how to behave. None of it is real. Life is real but I am not. I'm desperately trying to act how I know I should but I can't feel any of what I am doing. If I smile or laugh or sigh, they are purely physical actions. There is no longer a connection to my mind, my emotions.

I am in a continuous, exhausting play, always acting, never feeling right. I have become a puppet, only able to function from what I have learnt before. It is a place in which you think you are never going to escape from, never run free, for that, to me, is unimaginable. I cannot form the picture in my mind. All there is, is a swarming, self-loathing. My body oozes badness and I want to strike out. Such animosity towards my physical being. I want to slash and burn my skin, fight against how hideous I have become, damage, destroy, anything in an attempt to abate the black demon that I am becoming.

I am shaking and I stand, pacing up and down my room, scratching, as hard as I can, the backs of my hands. I feel it stinging which trembles up my arm. Scratching, scratching, walking back and forth. Adelle comes in, calms me slightly and says Susie is coming to have a chat. I can't even remember all the horrible things that Dad has done and I would never hurt Dad, all the rage and anger is purely on myself, on this odious creature. I want to cut myself, deep enough to see the bone, stare into the depths of tissue that makes me, the layers of form, the constituents. Susie comes, I cannot stand still, I cannot even look her in the eyes for fear that this heinous monster will jump and hurt her in some yet defined way. She says she has called the doctor, she wants him to see me, prescribe lorazepam, dampen my anxiety. Susie says I appear worked up, agitated. Medication will help me to get through this.

The evening was odd. I was feeling far better and able to do various things but then, with no warning, my head was engulfed by a vicious self-loathing. It was agony to be inside my own body. My skin crawled with disgust but I couldn't run, I couldn't get outside, I couldn't escape from my physical being.

I locked myself in a toilet, head-butted the wall, then unsheathed my blade like a sword and swiped hard across my hip. The blood was instantaneous and, as I pushed harder, it ran down to my pants, spreading laterally, bulging with that quiver like tears almost ready to spill. I looked in the mirror but all I could see was a body of death.

I cut myself again looking at my reflection instead. I could only see the mirror me, there was no pain, I wasn't real. I stopped. I wasn't real, all was meaningless. If I wasn't real then to die was safe. No-one should notice. I would be an enigma. My eyes glared painfully hard into my mirror eyes, desperately searching for a glimmer of life. But all was lost. I was a china doll, no substance inside. I felt I was about to cry but couldn't because I was not real.

God's ink
Mere existence
Hidden within

The silent provider
Held internal
Should remain concealed

But I am
The keeper
Of the keys

Necessity dictates
The unseen
To be revealed.

19th April

2007

Haven't written for a while. Fourth day Mum has been in hospital. Hardly slept. Found myself walking in the early hours of every morning. Head too full of morbid thoughts. They're torturing me again. Finding it hard to hold it together properly but when I see Mum, all of that evaporates. She makes me feel right, feel normal. How does she do that? She is amazing.

When I got to the hospital this morning, Mum had an "accident". I don't like that euphemism usually saved for children. She had diarrhoea and it was over her pants/nightie/sheets. She managed to laugh about it and remain jolly but I know she finds it hard. I washed her and she contorted her body into a fresh nightie – chemo drip and now syringe driver and all their attachments having to be passed through the correct sleeves. I asked Mum how best to wash the dirtied clothes and she told me what she used to do with towelling nappies she used when we were babies. She felt guilty that I was doing this but I say it's reciprocal: you did it for me, I do it for you. But she says it's the wrong way round. She expected it with babies. Mother takes care of child. Role reversal, although I think that's happened before Mum got ill. I think our roles are interchangeable. Mummy, I still want you to look after me, even though you are too ill and you must concentrate on looking after yourself. It's the thought that you will never be able to care for me, help me, hug me again that makes me sad. I'm strong enough to look after you Ma, however long that may be. But where does that leave me when you're gone?

When I got home, I decided to not be so bloody sentimental about everything. I was just scrubbing clothes to make them clean. It meant nothing more. Take everything literally, Alice. Take them one at a time. Dirty clothes + soap + water = clean, fresh clothes. Full stop.

More 3am walking. I don't seem to remember actually leaving the house but I like the crisp, fresh air. It is very relieving. The less sleep I have, the less I seem to need.

2008

I did wake and dream last night but nothing as disturbing or distressing as previously. Weekends are slow and laid back here so I remained in bed before rising to collect my morning meds.

The morning seemed to pass, time eaten away by little chunks: breakfast, shower, dry my hair, get dressed, read bible etc. Before Holly arrived at 2pm, I went to speak to Donna (charge nurse) as Duffy had indicated I may not be allowed out. Donna says I'm not leaving the unit, they can 5(2) section me if I try. I do my upmost at pleading, begging, telling them I will be safe. They get me to come into the staff room and close the door. After what happened yesterday, they do not want me going out for fear of my safety afterwards. I have to stay here. I do my best at trying to win them round but it was always going to be a losing battle. There are four of them, one of me, and I do feel quite overpowered.

After tea, Susie takes me to a side room so she can document all that I've said on the drugs front about Sabrina. We go through our conversation and then flick through my diaries. There is a point of writing – I can give her unequivocal dates! Official stuff done, Susie then gives me the time to explain about yesterday, attempt to describe how I felt, why I was scared for her. It's really hard work and I feel anxious just remembering.

Lily then arrives and I embark on a last ditch attempt to get off the unit, pleading at how good I've been all day, playing the GP card etc. They're not having any of it! Oh well, you can't mock my efforts! Susie has a long chat with Lily, I said she can say anything to her, Lily knows most anyway. I stand, clinging to Lily, almost in desperation, just to feel that warmth, that cuddle, that love. I need physical affection.

20th April

2007

Ma doing so well which was lovely to see. I was beaming when I walked into her hospital room and saw she was sitting up and reading! Usually she can't concentrate enough to read – she's never sufficiently alert. Although she did notice a few things tonight which panicked me slightly. She said I was shaking and then pointed out the little cuts on my hands. I have scratched my hands rather a lot these last few nights. I passed them off dismissively and we were soon chatting about something else.

I must have let myself slip. People don't usually notice anything. I'm too good at hiding. Must improve my external disguise. Wouldn't want Maisie worrying about me. Shaking can be a tricky one though.

2008

Kept waking last night in confusion. In separate dreams I managed to kill myself by hanging and then by taking an overdose. When I woke, my initial thought was, "Where on earth am I?" and then, on realisation, utter disappointment that I was, in fact, still alive. I hauled myself out of bed, I had to get outside. The morning greeted me with a thick mist and grey, overcast sky. I felt it physically weigh on my shoulders.

Susie asks me if I'm OK. I have that distant gaze in my eyes. I explain about last night. She asks the method I used to kill myself. I answer but should I be so honest? I am not allowed out again today and Susie laughs as I try my best to obtain leave. Alice, you are not safe enough. This is true but I still want some leave, go for a walk, be free from here, just for a while, go home, go to a shop, anything to obtain blades and tablets. Swallow then cut, slit along the artery, at least give yourself a chance to die. I do feel terrible and I just want to die. Thinking about how to actually kill myself, commit the deed, is exhausting and I am thwarted by my now limited options.

After a shower, Susie looks at my hip and re-dresses my cuts. She says, when I am on my own, I seem worse. She is right but there is also that need to get away from other people sometimes, to keep myself to my demons. Susie asks me what I would feel like if I was with someone constantly. This would be awful and I am certain Susie is hinting at level 3 obs. I would hate it. This really would send me loopy, staff wherever I go.

Again I feel the self-loathing, all-consuming, so much bad within. It is like I have body dysmorphia but, instead of hating an outside aspect, I hate all that is within, mind dysmorphia perhaps. I see a blunt bit of plastic on the floor, clench it and unevenly saw away at my outer wrist. But this is not enough, I hardly feel it.

Susie knocks on my door and I try to explain, desperate to get the words out but I am shifting my weight, one foot to another, shaking and I can't seem to form sentences in my mind. Susie guides me to the meds room where I am given lorazepam. I tell Susie I am scared and feel I have done so many bad things. It is wrong to talk, Alice. Susie reassures me that she is OK, I haven't managed to indirectly hurt her. Logical reasoning, Alice, use your scientific mind. I do calm down and the shaking ceases.

I spend the afternoon with Holly. First, a fashion show, the dear thing has bought me some new clothes, comfy for in here. I am being showered with gifts and I am so undeserving. I should be the one giving the presents, except I now cannot go anywhere to get anything! Holly knows my size, my style and they are just right.

We then play table tennis. After my first lesson yesterday, I have improved slightly, although am still mildly dazed from the lorazepam so my coordination and speed are slightly delayed! Holly teaches me how to serve and she still beats me but it's not quite such a thrashing! And, I am learning a new sport. All good.

When we've finished our last game and just mucking around with trick shots, Katy comes in with Isobel. She was visiting her mother-in-law who is in hospital after a fall, so popped in to say hello to me too. How lovely. She brings me tulips and, when Isobel goes, Katy finds a plastic tumbler that I can use for a vase. They really brighten up my desk. What a difference flowers can make. They do cheer me up purely by being there.

Soon after Holly departs, Dad and Ethan arrive. I told Ethan I wanted him to be there too, seeing Dad alone is too hard. I should be supporting Dad, it would have been their 25th wedding anniversary yesterday, so I want to feel nice things instead of languishing in all the atrocities Dad has done. They don't stay for too long but the conversation is much easier with Ethan there also. I feel relieved of some of that pressure. Dad is nice to me which, in itself, is confusing, but good because we talk without that strain in the atmosphere.

For tea, I have Lindsey's home made soup which Holly brought in for me – yummy! Far superior to hospital grub. After, I feel the need to be prepared. I am entering into a battle but my equipment is haphazard. I need everything that I can scrape together. I then stuff my box of Lemsips (found at home) into my jacket pocket. In the locked toilet, I methodically rip the sachets and empty all twenty of them. I wrap my discarded evidence in newspaper and throw it in a corridor bin. All the time, my head is calculating, twenty sachets is equivalent to forty paracetamol tablets. I need more but I am not allowed home where I could find, I'm sure, paracetamol, ibuprofen and maybe, if I'm lucky, co-codamol. Bitterly saturated Lemsips will have to suffice, one potent drink to wash down my other, equally hurried together, medications. I'm not entirely sure what's there but plenty of quetiapine and citalopram and perhaps the odd promethazine tablet. Everything now is ready. I feel calmer, safer. They are there if I need to use them.

I look outside my window, into the black. Rain has quickly arrived, pelting the bus shelter with fat blobs, hounding my ears with rhythmical splats. I run outside, to be underneath that water. I open my arms, hold them up, and let the rain soak through me, cleanse me.

21st April

2007

Arrive at the hospital in the morning and Mum says it's been a disturbed night. The woman whom she shares a room with (Caroline) had a nurse sitting with her as she was so agitated – rocking, climbing in and out of her bed, shaking her legs, lying down, sitting up. She looked so distressed. Mum said Caroline seemed confused in the night but, because of the curtains, Mum couldn't see her. Mum heard her fiddling with her syringe driver, though, so rang for a nurse. Nurse arrives, realises Caroline's drunk the contents of the syringe driver and bleeps the doctor. The sedative that they give Caroline just makes her agitated and her confusion seems to mount.

Mum ends up sitting in an armchair, early hours of the morning, trying to talk to Caroline about her family etc. How did Mum do this? She is just incredible. This is Mum who was struggling to sit up and yet, when Caroline really needed her, Mum was there. My Mother is marvellous.

I think another doctor then came and, once I'd arrived and it was morning, they managed to sedate Caroline enough so she fell asleep. Mum did find this all terribly distressing though. Mum is scared that she'll end up not being able to recognise people or understand her surroundings. Mum was also alarmed at the quantity of drugs Caroline was taking – similar things to Mum, just in much higher doses.

Granny phones me in the evening. This afternoon, Granddad was knocked over by a bus which then drove over his arm. She says he's OK, is in surgery and that's about it. Her medical detail has always been sparse. He's smashed up his elbow and has deep lacerations to his arm, I managed to coax out of her. Granny sounds calm but of course I'm concerned about them both because I know I can't be there. I know that, to me, Mum will come first. Is that selfish of me?

2008

Kept waking. Killed myself again in my sleep. Got up still distinctly drowsy and bumbled about dropping things and bashing into them, as if my proprioception had been tuned in slightly off centre.

At 11am I walk straight into Dr. Floyd. She says she wants to speak to me, Susie will be there too. We all walk into a side room and Dr. Floyd spends nearly an hour talking with me. She uses her time so unselfishly and is extremely thorough. Dr. Floyd asks me about cutting myself and the suicidal thoughts. Now, there is no rest from the wish to die, it is constantly there, just varies in intensity. Susie is really good and helps me to explain and answer some questions. Susie knows a lot and I do struggle sometimes to accurately explain.

Dr. Floyd increases my antidepressant (trimipramine) and says I'll need bloods done again for lithium. When I'm in a mess, she has doubled my lorazepam.

Dr. Floyd says she wants to keep me safe. Susie reiterates that my moments of madness come at no particular time, there is no pattern to my behaviour or mood. Usually, I don't even know why, at points, my head gets too much to bear. What is going on? Dr. Floyd says I am not allowed out – I am too unstable. True. I do say that physical activity may help. I enjoy being active and it seems to release some frustration. I am usually quite energetic so, being cooped up here, does me no favours. Dr. Floyd is great. She understands and realises this is important. She says I can have half an hour of accompanied leave. This means a walk with a staff member. I feel happier after that, seeing the outside world is important, it does make a difference.

I have my first appointment with a clinical psychologist tomorrow. Susie says she will take me and we can walk there. I think it will probably be tough and Susie will definitely be a calming presence. I am so grateful towards her. I've decided I am also fond of Susie because of the words she uses. I find language fascinating as Mum taught me such a great deal.

Dr. Floyd also said that I was sensitive to others, picked up on their feelings, so everything (especially with Mum) was heightened and affected me greatly. Dr. Floyd is right, sometimes I can feel the pain that others bear as if it was my own.

Holly came after lunch and we played our, now routine, game of table tennis. It was fun and Holly is such a good teacher. We managed a few half decent rallies! Holly left to go to work and I returned to my room and had a feverish two hours writing. Not really sure what possessed me but I couldn't stop. I carried on through tea time, pangs of nausea putting me off any food.

Zoe, from Newcastle, phoned me, always so caring. I related some of the more amusing moments of being in hospital. It's not all bad being here. I reiterate how lovely the staff are.

Once 6pm meds were dispensed, Susie took me for a walk off site – yippee! We walked quickly and I lavished the freedom, bouncing along by the lake. Pausing on the bank, we were mesmerised by a carp leaping, wiggling from the water. Excited, we ran around the lake trying to follow this carp. I was laughing. This was fun and I was so relaxed and able to enjoy. This was real.

Walking back, we exchange stories of working with learning disabled adults (Susie's previous job) and it is interesting and means something and I want to listen and I want to talk because I adored my job in Newcastle and I adored the outreach work when home. I loved listening to Susie's own stories. This was a good time. I was happy. See Alice, you can give a true smile, a real laugh. You can see the good in the world, don't despair. You can see how wonderful life can be; don't let the dark times overtake you, don't be swamped by all the badness within. Take a stand, Alice. Grab that glimmer of light and hold on with all your strength. Don't let go; don't slip. Just keep clinging.

Dad comes after a meeting. It is OK, brief but I can see Dad is tired after a long day. We mainly talk about table tennis! Spoke on the phone – Sarah, Aunty Beth, Ethan – and then the day was up. I seem to have kept busy and have prevented the boredom that can seep in. I must try and be active everyday as everyone tells me it's good to be occupied.

22nd April

2007

Mum is very sleepy and Dad is around as it's Sunday so I go running. I run for over an hour and it feels good. Each time my foot hits the ground, I squash some more bad down, I fight them away, I stay strong for Mum. They can't get me now – my love for Mum surpasses any of their devious trickery.

2008

Dreadful night – perhaps two or three hours sleep. Initially couldn't sleep because I could feel Mum gripping onto me. When I lifted her off the bed, her spindly arms would attempt to cling to me but, in reality, didn't have the strength. I could feel her little hands fluttering on my back, her limp elbows tucked into mine. I could sense that delicate pressure of her chin on my right shoulder. I tried to close my eyes tighter but I re-lived the events. I could hear Mum, begging me not to leave her, calling out my name, crying out in pain. This was endured for several hours, I couldn't move.

Once asleep, I then committed suicide. I was on top of the dunes, white yellow sand but an enormous tirade of waves swamping most of the beach. People started running away in a panic to avoid the engulfing waves. I ran towards the water and jumped beneath its surface. All at once, everything was calm, serene and I was floating in a watery underworld, tropical fish in their hundreds. I have never felt so free or untroubled. I continued my downward plunge as if being drawn to the blackness below. I knew I was going to die; I knew I was becoming one of them. The darkness consumed me and I was no more.

I woke at 6.30am and was oddly confused but, my surroundings making sense, I was then disappointed, the realisation that I was in hospital and not dead.

I had a clinical psychologist appointment in town which Dr. Floyd was very keen for me to attend but, not being allowed leave, I had to go with Susie. We set off, sun shining but I was distracted. I didn't think I was nervous about where we are going but I did feel uneasy. Susie wanted to know how I killed myself in my dream and what methods I think of now. I was honest. I said overdosing then crawling into a bush somewhere, hiding from everything or perhaps, more dramatically, jumping into water. When we walk across the bridge over the river she keeps an arm on me!

Seeing the psychologist was fine but hard repeating myself again and, in the end, I got bored. It was only an initial assessment so lots of summarising was required. After this, they shall decide what they can offer to help. The latest craze is "Cognitive Analytic Therapy" which is what they want to do to me, goodness knows what this entails.

Susie and I walked back and the cool breeze gave much needed refreshment. But, halfway, my mind turned in on me, too much, too fast. My head hurt with the sheer exhaustion of following all that is in my brain. Inside, everything was too busy, too horrific, too muddled. I felt like I was inhabiting two worlds: a physical one and a mental one. Keeping track of both is near impossible so I struggled to clasp bits of each at once, desperately forcing myself to stay in the real world, not get taken by my abhorrent mind.

Susie asked if I was OK. She put a hand on my back. This helped. If I have a person to hold, it helps me to not lose too much sight of what is real. I gripped her arm, hugging it towards me, willing myself not to be taken to the depths of my horrific internal voices. I tried to vocalise what is happening. Susie wanted to help me. She was so marvellous. It is always terribly awkward to explain when I am in a mess. The entire world takes on such a penetrating appearance, as if it is too real to be real. All colours and sounds and movements are tremendously exaggerated, they pierce my eyes with an intensity that hurts. It greatly pains my head, not like a headache, but a deep, internal rumbling.

I tried to close my eyes, momentarily pausing on blinks, then shutting them completely, relying on Susie to guide me. Susie stopped, she told me just to breathe, stand, no more. She was so sensible and ever so calm and reassuring. We got back to the ward and I gave her a great hug, almost desperate to convey how much she has done for me.

Lindsey then, unexpectedly turned up early afternoon. Her opening statement was, "I need a diagnosis! Give me a kiss". We went to sit outside because indoors here is too warm, stuffy and artificially heated. Lindsey is right of course, just overly dramatic in declaring that outside is far superior (probably more organic etc.). Lindsey has brought me gifts: the new Sebastian Faulks novel, whom Lindsey knows I like (so thoughtful); a selection of nuts and dried fruit, all in handy little snack packs. She then turns to me (my role is now Dr. Alice) and describes the problem with one of her fingers. It sounds and looks like "trigger finger". Firstly, I say tape it to the adjacent finger, to act as a splint ("Oh, Alice it feels better just talking to you"). Secondly, take ibuprofen to reduce swelling ("Oh, I don't take tablets"). Thirdly, if it persists, may need a steroid injection into the tendon ("Oh, Alice, can't you do that?")?!!

Swiftly moving on, she explains why she needs her finger to be better – she has just bought a house! What?! She dangles the new keys in front of me, obtained this morning. The reason? She wants to extend her garden. So, Lindsey has bought the property next door so she can nick part of the garden, more space for her crazy plants and organic veg!

Lindsey is lovely to me and, I must admit, it cheers me up just listening to all her extravagant activities. She then waves a radio around with four dangly cords, the ends of which jingle blue plastic beads. She says it is great because it is a shower radio so Lindsey hangs it on her handlebars (she cycled here) and has music while she peddles! Half the time I think, if Lindsey walks in here, she will never leave – they'll keep her! Oh, and I'm reassured this is OK because Lindsey puts rechargeable batteries in the radio so no environmental issues there. She soon leaves in a flurry and I am left trying to make sense of what I've just heard.

Dad came after work and brought me a bag full of stuff: food, post, notebooks, newspapers etc. He was trying to be nice but really struggles. "What do you do in here?", "Why don't you actually do something?" "Why can't you think about the future?" I can't even contemplate tomorrow. "Why not?" "Do you want to get out of here?" The problem is, when nothing seems to matter, I am indifferent to where I am, what I am doing or anything. Dad then says the clinical psychology thing doesn't sound that good and it is not what I need. I've got no idea whether it will help or not but I trust Dr. Floyd implicitly so will at least try whatever she suggests.

Ethan and Grace turn up later and we sit outside in the shelter as all the rooms are so hot. We laugh about Lindsey but then I express my concerns about Holly to Ethan. He is the only person I can talk to now. Today, Holly had been preoccupied by work, reeling off problems and line managers and her boss and all the things that dramatically intensified when she was ill. Now, I don't think Holly is getting manic but it is still concerning to see her distressed over work when I am all too aware I can do very little in here. Ethan tells me I shouldn't be the one worrying, I have enough to deal with myself for the moment.

Ethan is lovely, we have a bit of a laugh. Leo briefly joins us (elated by a football score) who knows Ethan and Grace from school. Ethan wants to come to my review with Dr. Floyd on Thursday which I say is fine. Ethan really is such a big support to me. It gets late; they leave.

23rd April

2008

Was woken at 9am to take meds. Could hardly believe the time. I was incredibly drowsy and stumbled around in my pyjamas, straining to see through sleep-filled eyes, burning myself as I made a much needed cup of coffee. Half an hour later, Adam came to fetch me for meds again. I had already forgotten the reason for being woken!

I tuned the radio from Radio 4 to Classic FM. Loud and dramatic and God inspiring, the Hallelujah chorus suddenly streamed into my ears. Handle's Messiah, sung every year on Good Friday at the Albert Hall. This was Mum's choir on the radio. This was Mum singing. I was taken aback. I adore the Messiah, my favourite piece that Mum has sung, but hearing it with no warning startled me. I sat unseeing and almost became part of the music. I didn't want it to end, I wanted the music and Mum to capture me, wrap me up and never let go. Please don't run away from me. Please don't stop. Please stay.

Adelle was my nurse today so, as soon as she says hello, I responded, "Can we go for a walk?". As always, I am desperate to get out, even if it is briefly. She laughed and says she will arrange it once the morning is in full swing and everything has calmed down a bit. Brilliant! I am going out.

Firstly, however, Adelle asks if she can take my blood as has only just learned and needs to practice. I am eager to help and happily agree. Adelle was so good at venesection and liked the tips I gave her, all learnt from my course and other doctors. I tell Adelle she can have another go tomorrow – I am her designated pin cushion!

Dad arrived so I immediately led us into the table tennis room. I think, from now on, this will be best. Sitting in magnolia square rooms with nothing to say is something I want to avoid. Dad is good at most sports and has played table tennis sporadically. The first game he won but then I seem to get into my stride and know his shots – I won the next game! The first time ever in beating Dad at a sport (except running). I was pleased because I feel so drugged up half the time I'm always amazed I see the little ball well enough to play.

Ethan came shortly after Dad. We played table tennis (again!). I will be an expert by the time I leave here. We then sat outside on the bench in the sinking sunlight. Maureen came out and so I talked to her to demonstrate to Ethan how lovely she is when well.

Come 11pm, meds dispensed, lights dimmed, the strip lights were glaringly all switched on again. Ann and Maureen, who were engaged in a shouting match, progressed to a fight. Ann smacked Maureen with her walking stick; Maureen swung her handbag round Ann's head! They were separated and calmed and perhaps sedated some more. The lights went down and I could settle into bed, reading the new novel that Lindsey brought in for me.

24th April

2007

Lucy phoned – I asked her to find out what's going on with Granddad as she still knows some of the physios at her old hospital. Granddad has had internal fixation to his mashed arm and a lot of the tissue was damaged. He's in plaster from his shoulder to his wrist and the wound is all open underneath. He'll need more surgery and probably a skin graft. He can't move as his back is terribly bruised and he's got more bruises and cuts to his face. He's already had three blood transfusions for blood loss and then anaemia. He's in a bit of a mess.

I'd love to go and see him but, of course, I can't leave Mum. She is my main priority. It's sad. Before, Mum and Aunty Beth would be there, rallying round but now, there's just Aunty Beth, on her own. I feel desperately sorry for her. She must be lonely, helping by herself.

2008

Very perturbing night. Couldn't get to sleep, fidgeting and turning. I was far too hot, the stuffiness and heating of the room seemed to intensify. I wasn't even covered by sheets or blankets. I reeled from one nightmare to the next, waking then sleeping. I properly awoke at 7.30am, probably in total snatching a handful of hours' sedation.

Ann and Maureen were still at each other this morning. Ann brandished a pair of scissors which were quickly confiscated by staff. I waited to have 9am meds and then sank into an almost too hot bath.

Holly arrives at lunch time. We sit outside, coffee in hand and then head to the games room for table tennis. The staff all tease me saying it's had more use this week than the previous year. I don't mind, even though I find it hard to concentrate sometimes and my eyes don't process their visual content quick enough, it is something that I can almost enjoy. It allows me to channel some of my wrought mental energy into a physical manifestation. It certainly aids my restlessness.

Review today so all the kick offs were really thrashing out and, funnily, managing to annoy each other with their multiple outbursts. Maureen (of course, good mood can't last for that long), Sammy and then Ann stormed out from Dr. Floyd, slammed the door, stomped outside to light a fag and scream angrily at the ducks, other patients, birds, anything moving really.

Ethan visited. We played table tennis and then sat in the last of the sun's rays. Dad came with a bagful of fruit for me but didn't stay long as I was exhausted.

Adelle asked if I wanted a walk earlier as I was badgering her so much. She is so kind, trying to help me. We walked round the lake but Adelle noticed I wasn't with it. Everything was too much to concentrate on. I kept drifting out of the real world. It no longer made any sense to me. I stayed close to Adelle. I knew she would be safe so I kept near.

When we got back, I lay down on my bed. My head was hurting, its fullness unbearable. I curled into a ball, shutting my eyes to lose that sense. I could still hear though. I think this is what they mean when I dissociate. I seem to leave the real world and enter into the murky shadows of the infinity of my mind. The real world becomes false, too extreme, and all I have are the demonic chants within. This time I was too weak; I listened. I swallowed all the tablets I had, just as in my dreams. It was so similar to my subconscious that I suddenly doubted myself. Had I overdosed? I didn't know. I got scared, petrified even. How can I do these things without being fully aware? I am terrified of me. How is that possible? But it is true.

I needed to know whether I existed or not. I stamped on my razor, took a single blade and slashed my hip, hard. It stung and bled and turned my fingers red. I concluded that maybe I was real, contrary to what I felt, this was actually happening. I needed proof. I weaved to the staff room and Vicky came to the door. I asked her if she was real. She said yes so I showed her my hip. Is that real? Vicky led me into the meds room and steri stripped me up. This was where everything then got terribly confusing. I don't know what's going on. Is this real or not? I don't remember any more.

25th April

2008

Only vague and incomplete memories from EAU. Adelle came and was sitting in a chair next to me. I wanted to talk to her but she kept saying, "I don't understand what you are saying, Alice". This I couldn't fathom as I could hear the questions very clearly in my head. I needed the toilet but no one understood so I started tugging at my cannula and ECG leads to get unhooked so I could do a wee – all the saline running, quite literally, through me. Adelle took me to the toilet; she had to come into the cubical with me.

I had to answer some questions posed by a doctor but I kept losing consciousness. I know this because he kept rubbing his knuckles across my sternum to wake me up again. It got quite sore and annoying; I just wanted oblivion.

Adelle must have walked me back to the psych unit. I don't remember. I do recall her holding my discharge notes, however. For some peculiar reason, I grabbed the papers and screwed them into a ball. Adelle took them off me and tried to uncrumple them. She said they were to go in my notes. I remember feeling suddenly guilty. Why on earth did I do that?

Once back in the psych unit, I must have gone straight to bed because I then remember being woken up by Dr. Floyd's registrar and Adelle. The doctor did a neurological exam and spoke to me but my memories of these are all hazy. I do know I had to walk up and down my room and this was very difficult as I was so wobbly and jerky. Once they both left, I lay down exhausted and cried and cried. Fat, unhindered sobs, no holding back.

The evening was spent in a daze. Holly, Lucy and Dad all visited and all at once. I have no recollection of what was said.

26th April

2008

Didn't sleep well at all, probably because I slept so much during the day yesterday. Finally decided to get up at 7.30am. I was still shaking with the occasional jerk. It was a struggle to shower and get dressed and I couldn't even write, my pen just made incomprehensible scribbles.

The ward was on lock down as Neil kept trying to escape. He was then later transferred to a higher security unit so he wouldn't be able to get out.

As the day evolves, I get more and more agitated. Susie is my nurse; she takes me for a walk around the lake. I explain how confused I was, real or fake? I wanted to give the tablets to Susie a few days ago but got too scared that harm may come to her. I tell

Susie I'm petrified. I am scared of my own self, frightened of what I am capable of doing without even realising. How can you be scared of yourself? Somehow, that is a conundrum I need to solve.

I can't eat lunch, my throat feels burnt. I try yoghurt but even this feels hot and tender as I swallow. I went back to bed, just lay face down on top of my covers and I dissolved into that transient state between not quite sleeping nor fully awake. Reciting thoughts and reeling memories clamoured for attention.

Like a sword dispersing all the confusion, I see a clear image: Susie falling from a great height. The impact as she hit the ground, lurched me upright, eyes as wide as I can make them. I run to the staff room and hammer my palm on the door. I can see Susie. She takes me to my room. I thought I'd hurt Susie. I would never do such a thing. Susie calms me, she tells me to look at her, she is OK, nothing bad has happened. Everything is so perplexing at the moment. I don't want anyone to get hurt but I think they have been, which I try to stop. I then get told the bad things didn't even occur in the first instance. It all pains my head and exhausts my mind. I am caught in a trap and running in circular motion. How to break free from the unrelenting spinning?

I discover that Adelle isn't here today because she called in sick. This sends me into a panic. What if I caused this to happen? Or what if I said or did something bad? I don't want to hurt Adelle at all. I have lost any ability to rationalise. Helen takes me out into the unseasonably hot weather and we sit on a bench. I explain that I'm scared I've hurt Susie and Adelle and didn't want to at all. Helen goes through everything logically with me and reassures that I haven't done anything wrong: I haven't hurt anyone. I believe her but there is always is that hint of doubt like a pea underneath all those mattresses. I can still feel it.

Shaking abated somewhat, Ethan and Grace pick me up at 6pm. We go to Holly's. It is a beautiful evening and we sit outside on the decking, sun still glowing, each cradling a glass of wine. Red wine, my vice but so delicious to taste after three weeks abstinence. Holly, the sweetie, had got crisps and cheese and grapes. We all greedily tuck in, especially me. This is the nicest food I've had for a while!

I have a dear chat with Aunty Beth, upstairs lounging on Holly's squidgy bed, who wants to come and see me next weekend. I am so blessed with such a doting aunty.

I had to be back for night time meds but half an hour late – they didn't mind. Meds swallowed, teeth cleaned, pyjamas on, book read, light off, I hear it, "Ali, Ali". Sit up Alice, open your eyes, remember none of this is real, Mum can no longer call. Scan the room, "Ali, Ali", I run down the corridor, through the ward doors and up against the locked external entrance. I can hear her calling me and she is out against the nigrescent light and I am held by the transparent glass door, listening. That is all. "Ali", I sit on the floor, knees up, hugging arms, "Ali", I squeeze my eyes to see a fraction further into the watery light, "Ali". Mum is dead Alice, this isn't her, "Ali", I look towards the ceiling, "Ali". Alice, you've got to walk away, forget, do not hold on anymore, "Ali", my darling Mummy I love you so but this is a ghastly torment. "Ali, Ali", I want to help you so much Ma, but you are beyond my grasp, I can never find you and the experience is harrowing.

Except tonight, I cannot go out and search. I cannot walk in the coolness of the night time air. I cannot be proactive. So all I do is listen. I talk to you Mummy, so that you know I am there. I said I'll never leave you but this time my words of comfort are not spoken out loud, I say them, repeat them, rephrase them in my mind. Mummy do not fear for I am with you, beside you. Please stop calling me Mummy. You are dead.

Flora eventually finds me. She leads me back to the ward and gives me lorazepam to try and still my overactive mind. After this distraction, I can no longer hear Mum. She has gone away. I crawl into bed but discard all my sheets and blankets. I am burning to the touch, even pyjamas are superfluous, adding to my almost unbearable warmth.

27th April

2008

Awake late and groggy but with no recollection of any disturbing nightmares. Adelle seeks me out and the relief I feel is instantaneous. I explain how I was so worried about her, thought I had done or said something terrible because I couldn't remember what happened. Adelle sits me down to reassure me and fill in the gaps of my patchy memory. She arrived just after 7am on Thursday in EAU. Adelle said I was mumbling so much she could only catch the odd word and didn't know what I was talking about. I tried to climb up the bed as I was treating it as a deck chair and wanted to lower the head section. Adelle pulled me down and reclined the bed, using the hand held remote control!

The doctor apparently wanted to get me to walk up and down the ward to assess my gait. Adelle says I took this as a signal to leave, so got my jumper and started walking away! Adelle turned me back but I was too confused to understand. Cleverly, Adelle said, "Follow me, Alice" and, dutifully, did as I was told so Adelle joined in my little neuro assessment.

Walking back to the psych unit, Adelle held my hand to steady me. She is such a darling. I am so glad that she was my nurse. As it transpires, I did screw up my discharge notes. I said, "That's rubbish", then crushed it between my hands, much to Adelle's amusement. She said she had to flatten it out in order to squash the paper into my notes. Adelle tells me that her being ill has nothing to do with me; I did nothing wrong. I am so relieved. Adelle is wonderful, I'd hate to hurt her.

Dad comes in the morning before some lunch thing he is going to. He brings me my post and newspapers and it is nice to see him. We play table tennis which detracts from our contrived conversation. And, it is fun. Dad enjoys teaching me and I enjoy playing.

Lily arrives shortly after Dad has gone. She drives to a different wood (we go via Lily's house and her husband comes out to give me a hug). I hold onto Lily's arm. Even this tires me. We sit by a pond and watch the spectacular reflection that the plants and trees make. Lily asks me lots of questions. I don't mind this. Lily knows how to help and I want to tell her, I want to feel understood.

Driving back to the psych unit, it is as if my consciousness is giving up. The drone of the car siphons off any grip on reality that I have. I disappear into the depths of my mind.

I think I am grateful that Lily didn't get me flowers, although they are beautiful, I seem to have become adept at killing the things with remarkable speed. Such a shame.

The bad thoughts infiltrated my mind, self-perpetuated introspection resulted in rumination. I had nothing to hurt myself with so I scratched off the strips of scab and dug my nails into the flesh wounds on my hip. The blood was thick and tacky like runny honey. It stained my top, my trousers.

I sought out Susie. She sat me down in my room and I tried to explain this absolute urge to damage myself. I'm so exhausted keeping track on all that is within and yet I'm afraid of sleep and what that may produce. A lie down is the horror option for me.

The evening is lengthy and I am restless, skipping from one place to the next. I can't stay still. Maureen is babbling on in the small garden only accessible from our ward about how a helicopter landed here and she was going to be taken away by air. I can't see the ducks as we are no longer allowed in the communal garden. I think about running through the locked doors; they are magnetic, so a well timed launch can pop them open. You get a few bruises but do end up outside. I do my best to persuade the staff to let me out for a walk but to no avail. Alice, you are only permitted accompanied leave. I try and get out when the night staff arrive but they quickly corner me.

Before meds, I have my nightly converse with Aunty Beth and then slip into bed, exhausted by the day, and read until my eyes object and the words grow blurred and smudged across the page.

28th April

2007

I'm losing interest in writing. It's been a ghastly week and, if I ever were to read this again, I'm not sure I would want to be reminded of how horrific it all is. Mum is so poorly – in pain, feeling sick, dreadfully lethargic. She falls asleep during the day and then wakes suddenly, fear-filled eyes darting around, drenched in sweat, breathing rapidly. Terrifying dreams leave her disoriented. I try to calm her, talk to her, let her know I'm there but it is not enough. I see her glaze of fear.

Mum has become more confused. Yesterday morning, I took breakfast to her in bed and she stared at the tray, the vacant expression on her face dissolving into a fazed look. She clumsily picked up a knife and attempted to stick it into her bowl of cereal. Admittedly, I was rather alarmed, and hastily guided her hand to the spoon. She got distressed because she knew she was making mistakes, she just couldn't quite comprehend what she was doing.

She also has episodes of forgetting the words for objects. For me, these are the hardest things to cope with. Dealing with vomit, diarrhoea, blood etc. are not particularly pleasant, especially when it's your mother, but the certain physical way in which you can sort them must provide a thread of comfort, as there is knowledge that you are helping in a small way. When Mum has been confused and I've led her to the correct words, the usefulness is short-lived, as she realises she couldn't think properly which, in turn, compounds her anxiousness. I feel it's similar to Gran when she was in the early stages of dementia, except her mental state gradually deteriorated over many months. With Mum, however, it only happened when she woke up that one morning. There is no time for adjustment or coping strategies. This is it.

Mum's nose bleeds have been getting worse. One night the bleeding wouldn't stop and Mum was getting increasingly worried, grabbing tissue after tissue to mop her nose. I tried to explain how she just needed to hold her nose but, even though she was listening, she didn't seem to take it in as couldn't follow my instructions. Her anxiety was becoming more marked and, through all this, Dad was lying next to her, falling asleep. He said nothing and did nothing. I don't understand how he can let all this pass him by. I felt sad.

Eventually, I got Mum leaning forward, pinching her nose, breathing through her mouth. I told her she needed to leave it for ten minutes so she grasped the clock to time it and wouldn't let go until exactly ten minutes had elapsed. These small, pedantic behaviours are becoming more the norm. Mum is terribly apprehensive about taking tablets even quarter of an hour late or early, despite reassurances that it's not going to make a difference. The ten minutes lasted the usual seemingly longer time when clock-watching. This was of benefit as Mum relaxed considerably. Her nose almost stopped bleeding, bar little red patches on the tissue, and she was happy to have her temazepam and go to bed. I checked on her, as promised, a bit later and she was fast asleep, with no blood to see.

There was discussion of Mum going to the Hospice. Selfishly, I don't want her to. I want to be able to care for her at home. I want Mummy to stay here. I don't want to let her down. I don't want to fail her. I don't want her to leave.

2008

At lunch time, Dad picks me up and drops me home. I have lunch with Ethan and Grace. Ethan isn't very well so is lounging on the sofa. I then decide to walk back, I need the air and exercise and freedom. I know I'm not allowed on my own but family don't know that.

Walking tires me out but it was certainly worth it, until I almost reach the hospital. The Trust buildings are situated just prior to the main hospital site. This small car park is where Dad has a permit. On the handful of occasions that Mum was at the hospital, we would park there. In my mind's eye, I was painfully hit with the sensation of sickly Mum. I had my Maisie, leaning completely on me, our arms intertwined. I felt that weight now. I walked through the motions – the blood taking room, the CT scan waiting area, the liver biopsy and the day surgery recovery room where I waited for hours with Mum. I was almost being drawn with a powerful force to retrace those steps that were walked a year ago. It made me feel sad. I wanted Mum. I wanted to see her. I didn't want to be walking past things that hurt her, things that I couldn't control, things where she should have been but, to me, she was invisible. I couldn't see her.

Eventually I go back to the psych unit and slump, exhausted, on my chair, swigging water. I think I'm dehydrated.

Holly came in the afternoon and we walked to the lake in the hospital grounds and sat on the bank in the sun. We watched the wildlife: eleven fluffy ducklings swarming mother duck, a couple of moorhens and a large, white swan, sitting serenely.

Holly went back to work and I fell onto my bed, exhaustion claiming me. I slept for four hours, until 9pm when I woke and couldn't penetrate the unconscious state anymore. I had more dreams of Mum being alive. She was poorly and Ethan had completely broken down. I was trying to care for him, be protective, shelter him, but this, coupled with doing everything for Mum, was proving too much. Ethan was falling apart and all I could do was watch. My little brother, how I so wanted to help. I felt useless and completely drained.

29th April

2007

Light always overcomes darkness. How easy it is to agree with this during daylight. Is that why the darkness brings the demons into my mind? Is that why they run riot at night when I am able to suppress them during the day? Oh, that longing for the morning star. My night time wanderings of deserted streets yearning for the light to return. The frightening reoccurring thought, that darkness shall capture me and never let go. I can only imagine that day when I shall fly away.

2008

Awoke at 9am and, despite so many hours sleep, I found myself in an over-tired delirium. Meds, breakfast, shower, all carried out with uncoordinated fumbling. Adelle cornered me and asks how I got back to hospital yesterday. I gave a wry smile, she must know. How does Adelle find out everything? She is turning into Dr. Floyd who also has a sixth sense in detecting my misdemeanours.

Adelle reminded me that I was allowed accompanied leave only. Alice, you are not safe on your own. She says whoever takes me out next will be made fully aware. How annoying! I much prefer a walk on my own. I was hoping no one realised after almost getting away with it yesterday. Sometimes, just being with people is such an exertion, my mind struggles to remain sufficiently alert.

Francis, my social worker, arrives at 11am and says she has come to take me out, have some respite from the ward. How wonderful of her. She drives us to a little familiar village and this brings back memories. The day before Mum's funeral, everything was ready. There was nothing left to organise but we all had that desire to be occupied. Aunty Beth et al and Dad, Ethan and I went for a long walk, finishing in this village where we ate lunch at a civilised pub, a place we used to love as kids due to its ample garden equipped with swings and slides and tunnels.

Mum and Dad first lived together here, in a tiny house just off the high street. When we were small, we would go on the row boats down the river and then play cricket and rounders and bat and ball on the green. Mum would have prepared a picnic and we would all tuck in, legs crossed on the rug, waving our food filled hands as wasps tried to eat out snacks.

Francis parks and we go into a converted church which has an array of arts and craft materials for sale. We look at paintings and garden gadgets and expensive decorative crockery. We slowly peruse various items before sitting in the quaint little café and Francis treats me to coffee and scones. Francis is such an amiable woman and she talks about herself which I like, it takes such an intense focus off me. She was born in Finland but has lived here for nearly thirty years. Her husband sings in the Essex choir, he must have known Mum, if not well, then at least by sight.

After looking at the handmade greetings cards, we then return to the car. This is where lethargy catches up with me. I sit and speaking is a tremendous effort, I can't even hear properly so I have little idea of our conversation topic. It is almost a relief to be back, in hospital, where I know I can escape to the silence and solitude of a room that is only mine.

I chat to Adelle shortly after returning. Sometimes, after excursions, I have a rebound effect which sends me very low indeed. Adelle helps me to stay real and understands what I say. She also distracts me by taking my mind to consider other things. What do I want from my review on Thursday? To be discharged. Adelle says I really have lost touch with reality! Not yet, Alice, you are not safe or responsible enough.

Adelle is pleased that I like the relief I get from table tennis but why aren't I doing any other group sessions? After successfully avoiding any participation activities last admission, the OTs have, thankfully, ignored me his time! I don't want to do group therapy! Adelle says it is part of being here and I should do some. She is going to talk to the OT – ahhh! As long as I don't get roped into "Creative Writing" or board games or jigsaws, it may not be quite as bad as I imagine. I would like to use the gym, although I haven't seen what's there. Physical activity gives my body more of a sense of balance: tired mind, tired body. If my mind is tired but my body restless, I find it tricky to handle.

I phone Granny – her 82nd birthday today – and have a short chat. I do find it hard being in here and talking to her as normal. She is praying for me everyday and every week at their fellowship (which is tonight). Granny always makes a cake for everyone but today someone else is doing the baking. Granny will get even more birthday cards, she insists on counting them and then telling me the total! So sweet and so wonderful that she and Granddad have such a wide network of friends and flourishing social life! More so than mine at the moment.

I chat with Becci; she threw a chair at Dr. Rand (her psychiatrist) in disgust. I'm not entirely sure what this poor guy has done wrong. Meanwhile, my love affair with Dr. Floyd continues. She can't do anything wrong in my eyes. I voice this opinion, at which Maureen squares up to me, invading my personal space, and emits a tirade of hatred. Oh well, her view is certainly not going to change mine.

At 7pm, Holly picks me up and we drive back to her house and sit in her softly lit front room. Holly gets all her potions and lotions and gives me a foot massage. Glass of wine in one hand, this is terribly relaxing that it feels wrong to be so indulgent. Holly paints my nails and we talk and watch one of those daft fashion programmes on television where they teach people how to dress. Somehow, they really are watchable.

I come back (late) but just in time to catch the tail end of meds. Drugged up, I then check my ignored phone. Darling Sasha had left me such a caring and considerate voicemail. She is a fantastic friend, willing to come and see me straight away (despite the 300 mile distance). She is desperate to help in any way. I am so blessed with friends; how I love them dearly. I phone Sasha back and talk with my lovely friend, in the teaming rain, still wearing flip flops and ambling around the grass, soaking my feet, my hair, my clothes. It matters not, all these senses offer a physical experience.

Too soon, the doors are locked and I take my soggy self back to my room to dry and change into pyjamas. Once I completed the pre-bed banalities, I am struck by a shudder of fear. I couldn't hear anything but I found myself concerned that they would launch an attack on my unsuspecting mind. I want to be alert, ready, but I am so tired. Would I be strong enough? I also felt naked, all my blades had been removed, no offering can I give. I am worried that I will start hearing Mum and try to escape to find her. I am so scared that by some unknown, indirect way that I will hurt other people.

I get Nicola. She sits me down and talks to me for a long time, reiterating the logical argument, showing me a glimpse of clarity. Nicola is ever so patient. She says that tonight, try not to cut myself (no materials so probably unlikely) and she will give me lorazepam.

30th April

2008

Slept but largely felt dreadful. Can't remember what I did in the morning but come lunch time, having forgone breakfast, I felt hungry so sat in the dining room eating a cooked meal (some sort of tuna potato thing) to prove to staff that I am eating. The problem is that, the majority of the time, who wants hot food at lunch? It seems an old fashioned notion which my grandparents follow but that I am unused to.

I am putting on weight, which is unsurprising given all the treats people bring for me. The irony is, the more weight I gain, the better people say I look but the worse I seem to feel. The inverse relationship. Perhaps this is just another of their powers over me.

Each addition only makes my mask grow thicker, more ingrained, still smothering the darkness within.

After lunch, I still felt hideous and then too full. I lay face down on my pillow, blankets cradling my stomach, and slipped into a post-prandial nap. I really am getting old before my time. Two hours sleep but not at all restful. More dreams again. Mum was poorly and Ethan was falling apart. I was trying to support him and care for him as he didn't move from his bed but, at the same time, do everything for Mum. I was dashing all over the house, doing my best but failing. I couldn't cope; it all imploded. I didn't manage, but I was agonizing to succeed. I wanted, so acutely, to be able to look after them both. I felt such a weight of disappointment.

Paulo sits outside being philosophical. He then likens each of us to a clock, fractionally out of time. We are the ultimate time keepers and we need to learn how to adjust our hands to become synchronised with the real world, a place where we must inhabit. Hospital is only a haven for those who have lost track of the time of life.

The evening is harrowing. I am overpowered by the macabre, abominable, penetrating thoughts. They catch me in such a terrific impulse that they require release. I shakily take my last remaining razor blade and pull it down on the side of my wrist. The skin bursts like a pod cracking open, the blood streams down to my palm before collecting and drip, drip, dripping, a pulse on the floor. The split skin makes an eye, gaping widely in the middle, a red pupil of the devil. The white of my wrist eye, is a yellowing cream, like off milk. I see the tiny fat globules jostling together, squeezed into the sac, like ball bearings in a children's rattle. I see inside me, what this skin hides, I am bursting with badness, my exterior taught, and yet relief seems impossible to find.

Nadia talks to me after a trip to A+E but I'm not sure that is it helpful. I do not assist, I can no longer describe, and words escape me. I don't know what I feel, all is awful. Nadia wonders how being here is actually benefiting me. I agree. I don't think I'm different and all I can think is, yes, good, let me out, then I can kill myself properly. Incarceration, for me, heightens the heinous voices in my head. Let me out; let me free.

In bed and Sarah phones. She is reassuring and a darling. I ask her to get me out of here. I know she cannot, I just feel so desperately sad. Sarah says it is the best place for me at the moment. I am unsafe and can't look after myself, this I must learn. I cry. I feel as if I can go on no longer. Sarah prays for me, she talks to me, she offers hopeful words. Why do I feel so dark and bleak?

1st May

2008

Wake at 9am, just in time for meds, but my face looks drawn and tired. Puffy eyes highlight my emotions from last night. I ask for an antihistamine to hopefully lessen the bags and prevent my eyelids from itching and swelling more due to spreading eczema.

Maureen is her usual Thursday review self, flying around, bag swinging, mismatched dark auburn trousers and a turquoise top with olive green trim. Her and Ann engage in their elderly, mentally ill brawl and are separated by staff. Paulo joins in and starts winding Maureen up. He really is encourageable, sending Maureen into a rage.

The weather is spectacular, illuminating lightning flashes followed by terrific rumbling thunder, drum rolls indeed. The rain pours and makes thick, shiny puddles on the path, to the delight of the ducks. People say it is more depressing with weather such as this but I disagree. I love the darkened skies and exciting noises. It has that element of difference from the norm. It makes me appreciate our fascinating world.

At lunch time, Ethan and Holly arrive and whisk me off to eat soup and crusty bread at Holly's house. Ethan didn't mean to hurt me but, in justifying his excessive spending this year, he retorts that it is understandable, "Look at the mess Alice has got herself in". So, it is my fault and everyone agrees.

Audrey is outside. Her shaved head is now sprouting clumps of baby soft hair, in spiky turrets. She does not get even growth because, years ago, she doused her body in petrol and put a lighter to it. Her torso and arms bear spreading white plates of scars; I've never seen her legs. Her face remains relatively unscathed but her scalp is a freckled patchwork. Darling Audrey, I cannot imagine what you must feel like to do that to yourself.

You can tell it is review day as tensions are escalating. Maureen is the key initiator: "Fuck off Dr. Floyd", "I'll screw her neck off" etc. The more animated Maureen gets, my sympathy towards her increases. How it would be lovely to see Maureen in a state of sustained wellness. She has been here over a year, will this ever be achieved? The depressing reality of incurable mental illness.

I try to distract myself for the remainder of the afternoon. Dr. Floyd (wearing a polka dot blouse) sees me at 5pm and keeps me for an hour. She is extremely thorough and generous with her time but that sixty minutes is an endurance. She is not pleased with me to say the least, especially overdosing and cutting myself. I seem to have got worse. I agree but when they say that I am the one who has to help myself, I don't know how.

I am asked lots of questions but answers elude me. I don't know. Stop thinking about dying, Alice. How? I feel I have no control over my own body, my mind, anything. Dr. Floyd then mentions Dad and Mum. Apparently I see them black and white, good and evil, very childish Alice. But this is not true. I am just realistic: I know their traits. I can't stand it when people tell me what to think of my parents. No-one has any idea of what it is like to live in the house. I start crying. Dr. Floyd says Dad cares and I am damaging him and all my family. This I know and feel a sinking guilt about but, that simple fact that Dad cares about me, makes the things he has done even worse. If he hated me acutely, then his actions would be more understandable.

After this, I struggle. I can't stop the tears, which render me particularly useless. Alice, at this rate you won't be able to do medicine, become a doctor, go back to Newcastle. All these threats are empty, they mean nothing to me, so how can I strive towards them? I want to run away, a new town, where no-one knows me, no-one knows anything. I can change my name, grow into my pseudonym, no-one would ever know.

Alice you are here as a patient, not a doctor or medical student. You are too observant of others and get too involved. Their behaviours will become yours. This isn't true. I have more integrity than that and nothing is as powerful as the battle in my mind. If a patient could penetrate, I would be so astounded I don't think I could even begin to believe. But why don't they see this as part of my problem? I have too much insight. I don't like it. I don't purposefully go out to become patients' mentors, advisors, counsellors. This doesn't happen. Patients talk. That is it. Surely that is normal, expected? It is I who then seem to recall intricate detail and awareness, my perception has intensified. This is a fundamental obstacle of mine, life appears too real to actually be real. Too much rather than too little. Life is putting on too great a show which, to me, highlights its falsity.

Medications are discussed. You shouldn't have overdosed on lithium, Alice. I don't think I did. I didn't have any spare lithium because I was taking it regularly. Everyone disagrees with me, you must have taken it Alice. Maybe I did, I should believe my doctors, but I am convinced I didn't. I still think the other drugs I took augmented the lithium effect, but maybe this isn't possible. I don't know enough pharmacology.

Do you want to start on lithium again, Alice? Did it make you feel better? I don't know. Not good enough answer Alice, yes or no? Yes, because you (Dr. Floyd) think I should. No Alice this isn't about pleasing me. I don't know. Why does no one believe me? I feel worse, how can I tell if lithium is making a minute improvement? My head hurts, bursting with confusing and conflicting thoughts, encouraged by emotion, tears tiring me out. I thought Dr. Floyd understood but now, dramatics on my part, I feel she has no idea at all. I cut myself even before Mum was ill. I can prove it: I'll show you the scars. Why do they think these are new, maladaptive behaviours?

This could go on for years Alice, we are not getting anywhere. Do you really want to be in hospital for a lengthy period? I don't care. I don't want to be here, I don't want to be at home, I don't want to be anywhere. Alice, what do we do with you? Lock you up in a secure unit so you can no longer harm yourself or give you leave because that is beneficial? I have to answer so I say leave because I think that is what they want to hear. Now, I am granted outside access on my own. I am neither pleased nor depressed by this, I am indifferent. All is meaningless. I then think why don't they just discharge me? I am obviously a burden. How I hate myself with such intensity. Right now, I am suicidal. Which is it Alice, thinking about dying or actually intending to carry it out? Both. No, that isn't an answer. That is the truth though. Mostly I have a morbid aura but, on occasions, it develops and I do believe that I could kill myself, take drastic action. Why can't it be both?

I have taken up much time, sorry Dr. Floyd. No apologies Alice, I wanted to spend this time with you. Thank you Dr. Floyd. No praise Alice, I want to help you. I am grateful of her time, however. I know I am a nightmare, a disgrace, an awkward patient. I don't want to be, honestly. Goodbye Alice, I'll see you soon. Escape.

Feel ghastly. Go to my room and splash my face (and t-shirt and hair) with cool water to try and rinse my tears away, still brimming with emotion. Go outside, hole myself up against the fence and chain smoke three cigarettes, my arms growing goose pimples, my teeth developing an independent chatter. More crying, it couldn't be halted, but these were more controlled tears, condensation dribbling down a cup. I sit shivering and just feel shit. Sorry I cannot be more eloquent but sometimes descriptions escape me. Maureen, of all people, then makes me smile. I cannot remember how but her chesty titter encouraged me. A fellow comrade: we share in a joke together.

Later, I speak to Donna who was the nurse in my review. She is lovely to me and said it was awful seeing me so upset but it was also a good thing to see me do. I never show them my emotions, sometimes it is OK to cry. This I know, it certainly feels more normal. Donna offers suggestions but, the problem is, I have already tried everything. This is why I result in feeling beyond help, because well-meaning support still offers little change.

2nd May

2007

Mum felt better this morning. It was lovely. I sat at the end of her bed, rubbing her feet and we just chatted. I forget how delightful these moments of wellness are. It took us hours, but I managed to bath Mum and wash her hair and put cream on her, get her dressed and, finally, take her downstairs. She has spent a week and a half in bed since returning from hospital.

Unfortunately, Mum's improvement in health is marred by Ethan. As Mum could engage in conversation, it deteriorated into an argument with Ethan. I don't understand how he shouts and gets cross anyway, but now, knowing how ill Mum is, I think it is almost unbelievable. Mum got upset and cried.

I managed to get to Lily's GP surgery in the afternoon for a few hours. Lily let me do some of the minor surgery: I burnt off warts, helped to remove cysts, took out stitches. I really enjoyed it and, its not that I forgot about Mum, but I didn't think about her. When I got home, the guilt poured in. How can I get pleasure out of something in the knowledge that Mum is home, suffering? I didn't like myself very much.

By night time, Mum is again very poorly. I end up giving her more morphine and anti-sickness tablets. She keeps repeating how she can't go on like this. She tells me she wishes she will fall asleep tonight and never wake up.

2008

Sleep was fitful and infrequent. I felt so hot that, lying there, in only pyjamas, sheets kicked past my feet, I became more and more overheated as if thinking about it increased my temperature even more. I became so worked up that I went to the sink and splashed cold water on my face and arms. This didn't work so I soaked my t-shirt and bottoms, hoping damp clothes would cool me sufficiently. I later woke, freezing, curling around myself to preserve warmth.

I walked home at lunch time, forcing the freedom upon myself. Being allowed to leave, I felt I should. I sat in the kitchen with Ethan and Grace, drinking coffee, reading newspapers and talking. An hour later, I walked back, knackered and feeling crap. Fell onto bed exhausted.

Dad came without warning after work. He was doing his best – bearing strawberries – but his downfalls are his lectures. "What's that?" (my cut wrist) and then I endured a telling off. He sighed when I said I don't care. People never like the truth, I should revert to lying again, putting on an act, pretending. Dad said it's progress (his favourite thing) that I am allowed out alone. Is it? I'm not convinced. Awkward visit, hovering in reception; awkward departure, rigid kiss.

Emotionally dreadful day worsened. I briefly talked to Duffy and said I wanted to discharge myself. I don't want to be here as a burden, I don't want to cause nurses distress, I don't want to only be a hassle. I feel the same and I am just as safe wherever I am. What is the point in taking others down with me? I want to hide away, stay alone, so I come into contact with no one, then I can't pass the badness on.

Duffy said to wait to see Dr. Floyd, an on-call doctor won't know me and will listen more to the nurses. Just wait Alice, only the weekend, which also means Monday as it is a bank holiday. Duffy was kind to me, a reassuring presence, a sounding post. My anxieties were eating my insides, destroying myself from within. I wanted to escape but you can't run away from yourself.

Evening disintegrates. I have a clear image of hanging myself from the window. I feel I have no control. I've already seen my actions, as if I've carried them out before. I remain sitting, staring. I'm scared; I'm petrified. Don't move Alice, remain. Stop thinking Alice, don't follow, Alice resist. Inside I am screaming, yelling without restraint, hollering with no resistance. It is so loud and so painful and so consuming that I feel it is unsustainable. My head can't cope; it is going to break. Alice, do all you can to keep still, don't move, don't initiate the action, for by starting, it must be completed. Chain reaction. Stay Alice, just stay.

3rd May

2007

Ethan's anger and aggression has turned on me. He shouts and yells. He is like he was before, except he no longer treats Mum as badly. I am filled with a deep sadness. I spend the day feeling I am about to cry at any moment. I think I am mourning, mourning for all the lost time I had with Mum. All those years of sitting and consoling her after Ethan's dreadful behaviour. I think of how many hours Mum and I must have spent discussing Ethan and then I think of how we could have otherwise spent that time together.

I normally try and reason that, if there hadn't been so many problems with Ethan especially, but and Dad, then Mum and I may not have been so close. Our intimacy, our knowingness may not have been so powerful if we did not have that bond, that solidarity that was caused through upset at family life. I have to try and believe this is the case. Perhaps Mum and I would not have developed such a unique relationship if Ethan and Dad hadn't caused her so much mental anguish.

But, today, I could not think that way. My mind, my thoughts and feelings, wouldn't allow it. All I could see was all the time that I could have enjoyed with Mum, was taken so cruelly from us. And now, my Maisie is too ill. We shall never have any normal time again. It is a most distressing thought. And no one will believe me. Everything to do with Ethan that she has ever written she got me to throw away. It's all gone. I think even Ethan has forgotten much of what happened. I am the only one left but, Alice, no one is listening, there is no one to help you.

2008

A night full of horrendous dreams and little sleep. In one, a friend of mine was terminally ill and I was her carer, no-one else seemed to be there, except the doctor at the hospital appointment who brutally drilled into my friend's back to show me the rapidly spreading, mound of cancer, bumpily progressing down her spine, a distressingly obvious humpback of bubble-wrap skin.

In another, I was scouring a hospital, having lost my baby. I was a mad woman, frantically searching cupboards, beds, bathrooms, outside, under bushes, beneath trees. Somehow, I ended up in A+E with my blood being taken. A young doctor stabbed my finger with a needle and, mistakenly, hit an artery. The blood spurted, a great fountain, strawberry red. My finger was misshapen, dislocated in fact, and it was forcefully snapped back into position, stitches joining the split skin. I still couldn't find my child.

A third was the all familiar suicide, successful as always, free and peaceful and painless.

In the early hours, I woke, my arms pulled my head and shoulders to the sink and I vomited, thick and sour and vile. Brown sludge blocking the plug hole. More sick and retching later, I cleaned the sink, sipped some water and wearily slumped beneath my sheet, lethargy overwhelming but sleep avoiding me, like a naughty child running from its parents' wrath.

When I finally, reluctantly, got up at 8am, I felt just as disastrous as I did in the night. I forced myself into the shower, washed my hair, cleansed this despicable body. I read the bible, furiously slurping cup after cup of black coffee. I couldn't face any food, the strong coffee banishing the foul taste in my mouth.

Lily sees me briefly in the morning. I explain to Lily my hard time with Dr. Floyd last review. I say I want to discharge myself. Lily says to wait until next week and then she can come in with me and Dr. Floyd and we can arrange something together. Lily says she'll take me back to her house, be my surrogate Mum. How she is so wonderful to me. I am surrounded by such love and kindness.

At midday, I walk home. Aunty Beth said she would collect me but I feel the fresh air and benefits of a stroll are needed. It took me longer than usual due to the unhindered sun, heat and my still feeling a little queasy, but I was glad of the decision.

So mentally soothing to see Aunty Beth. She is ever so dear to me. Holly is there too (as well as Dad and Ethan) and we sit outside on the patio, before deciding to have lunch outside. The table is haphazardly made, as that goes with outdoor dining, partly why I enjoy it. Glasses are filled with chinking ice cube filled water and food is produced. I eat tentatively but needn't have worried, my lunch did not reappear after being swallowed. It is a lovely time, followed by a cafétiere of coffee (Ethan on his green teas after coffee refusal!). We sit in t-shirts and strappy tops, the weather truly gorgeous.

The badness suddenly takes the breath from me. I excuse myself, bundle through the back door and then half fall on the floor. I lie rigid, out on my back, close my eyes and stay there until the sheer dizziness of life wanes, until I can reinhabit the world that everyone else is in. My breaths are slow and feeble, I consciously inhale deeply and curl up to my knees, then kneeling, finally standing. I venture into the kitchen and sip orange juice.

Aunty Beth drops me back in hospital at 6pm. Adelle comes to me and stays in my room for a long time talking. I try to explain what happened when I had to get away from everyone this afternoon. It's like a panic attack without the panic. I'm calm, not distressed. How can I do things normally because I always need an escape route, a flee plan? How could I possibly work anywhere if I'm suddenly gripped with a power that I can do very little about? Adelle steadies me, employment is not a pressing issue currently, Alice. You did well, you managed the symptoms, you got through it, that is your coping mechanism. There is nothing wrong with that Alice, day by day, you handled today, in time it will come.

I tell Adelle about the bad thoughts, the bad dreams. I reiterate me hanging myself. It's not that I want to think of these things or that I then dwell upon them, they just intrude with such force and no warning. I'm not thinking, it is just there. Adelle must have handed this over to the night staff because a woman, whom I've only known by sight, came to talk to me. Her name is Gill and she wanted to know if there was anything she could do to help. The staff here really do attempt to do their best for patients.

4th May

2008

Sleep remarkably well, can't remember waking once. Aunty Beth arrives at 10am and meets the lovely Adelle who reminds me to enjoy myself and not to worry if I get tired or have trouble coping. She says she'll see me again tomorrow morning and to take care until then.

Aunty Beth and I go from hospital to church. I needed someone to go with as I am still apprehensive with strangers if I'm alone and Aunty Beth wanted to come too. We like church, especially together. Aunty Beth wishes I lived with her so we could both go to her new church. We went once, with Zac, a short time after Mum died, and they began playing a children's worship song. This was only the second time we had heard this. The first was back at my church, the summer before Mum died, when somehow Mum, I and Aunty Beth were up on the platform, singing and teaching the congregation the actions! The second time the song was heard, Zac loved it and Aunty Beth and I were so confident that people were watching us for the hand movements! The song begins with laughter, by the end, Aunty Beth and I are in tears. Happy memories.

As it is communion, the service is lengthy. After an hour, I feel my mind buckling. I pray desperately to be able to stay. The voices crescendo and become distorted, my sight disintegrates, blurring of the edges, too bright in the middle, my body feels feverish and then distant, as if only partially connected to my head. I have a rippling tingling throughout my legs, as if they are about to give way but I am sitting down so they cannot, a contradictory sensation. My head is too heavy for me, a weight on Aunty Beth's shoulder.

A hymn begins, everyone stands, Aunty Beth threads her arm through mine, across my back, and leads me outside. I stumble, staying tightly stuck to Aunty Beth. We reach the car and I collapse inside, seat back, head lolled, arms dangling, eyes shut. Aunty Beth I'm so sorry, I wish I could cope, I wish this didn't happen, I wish I could control or have some influence over it. How I adore my aunty and her unwavering care and love.

We pick Ethan up, go via the florists for lilies for Holly and the adjacent shop for little chocolaty biscuit squares for dessert. By the time we reach Holly's, I have recovered and feel fine. I begin to doubt myself. Am I just making all this up? Why couldn't I stay in church? I wanted to. Pull yourself together, Alice, everyone says that you are the only one who can help yourself.

The four of us sit outside on the decking, admiring Holly's garden and then eating a delicious lunch. I enjoy myself, the weather could be summer and the company are my wonderful family. A fabulous lazy, prolonged Sunday lunch.

Slurping coffee and nursing full tummies later, I feel it. The girls notice too: Alice you're shaking, you look very pale. It is there again, my senses too extreme. I sink lower in my wicker chair and close my eyes, one sense down. It is like being hit by an overhead wave of exhaustion. It flattens then tugs you away in the undercurrent. You are fighting for breath but have to wait for the immeasurable power of the sea to spit you back out where you can find your feet once again. However much you struggle, you cannot win, you have to wait.

Departure in the psych unit reception. I grip Aunty Beth with love, thankfulness, endurance, our bodies entwined. Drive safely home my incredible aunty. I deposit my bag in my room and sit outside in the still hot sun with the patients who have recently returned from weekend leave.

Later, deathly intoxication descends. I sit in my room, crying, shaking, immensely suicidal. I don't know what to do or how to control it. Talk to the nurses Alice, that is what you are instructed. Nadia, my nurse this afternoon, comes from the office and sits in my room. I perch on the end of my bed, attempting to explain, elaborate but descriptive words are sparse and not adequate. I want to cut myself. Nadia asks if I have tried elastic bands on my wrist, clenching ice cubes etc. but these do not work. There is something in cutting, the damage, the blood, the gaping slit, I don't know what but I have to cut myself, there is something in the sacrifice.

Nadia mentions that I have said that walking helps me. She is right, perhaps I needed the reminder. I walk automatically down the grass bank towards the lake. Once there, I sit, looking but unseeing. I discard my flip flops and submerge my feet, water half way up my shin. I can't decide if I can feel the water or not. My senses aren't engaged. I need to feel real, I need to understand the textures through my toes, over my feet. A fish jumps, I see and follow the diverging ripples. Ducks are playing across the lake, flapping the water. I am beginning to appreciate, once again, the greatness of creation. I am seeping back into my body, experiencing the beauty of life.

I shake my legs dry, wiggle my feet into my flip flops and begin walking, full circle around the lake, then to the top of the hill where the view stretches into town: the water tower, the town hall, the tallest buildings, all can be seen. I phone Sarah. She eases me into sensible choices. It is not necessary to harm myself. She helps me to see what is real and how to distinguish that from my gripping, resolute, evil power in my mind. None of that is right, Alice, don't believe them.

I am much calmer and the sun has gone, so I weave my way through the, now darkened, tree lined paths, stumbling, no artificial light. I see two deer appear then disappear with equal grace. Rabbits litter the ground, bats flap in the deep navy sky. Everything in outlines. I reach the road, softly illuminated in the warming orange glow of the streetlamps, walk across, and am back, two hours later, on the ward.

Alice Addison

5th May

2008

Particularly ghastly night. I could see the devil in me before I went to bed, head bent over the sink to splash face, eyes glance up and it's then I see the fear in the mirror. The shadows dance behind the pupils of my eyes, the white surround extenuates just how low, how vile I have become. You can't clean, wash away, scrub your insides. I scratch my cheeks but I know I am nowhere near.

I walk home, overfull rucksack increasing the heat, and see Dad and Ethan. They are having an argument over some trivial point. Nothing changes. I add Ethan's washing to mine and put a first load on. I realise the towel in the downstairs toilet is filthy so I chuck that in too. I check the tea towel and hand towel in the kitchen as these are the most used, often fairly grim, and Mum always said needed doing far more than once a week. Dad sees what I am doing and launches into a rage. "What do you think you are doing? This is *my* house. Don't you dare just come home and start..." etc. It went on. "It's my house, I decide".

I feel my eyes dampen, not quite tears but swilling, threatening to tip over my lower eyelashes. I have an hour out of hospital in which I can spend at home and Dad chooses to shout, get angry and tell me off over something pathetic. I should be grateful I can do my washing in his house. I am, I didn't know I had to ask. I was trying to be helpful by doing towels as well. How do big disagreements stem from such trivial actions? All I think is, I ran this house when Mum was ill and after, I did all the washing and sorting and tidying. It was all taken for granted. If Dad had offered, just once, to do some household chore when Mum was ill, it would have helped me enormously. Now I'm not at home, Dad is doing some of these things himself and now shouts if I am doing anything "interfering".

He goes on about it being "his house". This is so upsetting, I think he does it on purpose. And why is it his house? Oh, yes, because Mum died so Dad no longer has a mortgage because of the life insurance. Does Dad go out of his way to upset me? Dad is still grumbling and going on at me. I don't want to listen to this. Being locked in hospital is shit so I am not prepared to spend my little freedom trying to placate Dad and calm and resolve everything and then apologise. I would have to do this as Dad never says sorry, he is incapable of admitting any fault. He still refuses to say he did anything wrong when Mum was ill. What an arrogant bastard.

I run out of the house. Ethan calls, I say sorry but will see him another time. I don't where to go so I retrace my steps to the place I walked when Mum died. Then I cry, walking across the fields with no direction, I cry and cry. I am suicidal. Yes. Right now. Need distractions. If only I was on a bridge. I am shielded, physically, by all the things in my head by being in the middle of a field, soft earth beneath my feet, birds twittering above. I'm too low to die. I have no will or energy to plan anything or carry it out.

I spend the next hour walking well trodden paths and grazing my feet on the bracken in not especially terrain sensitive flip flops. Eventually, I start walking in the direction of the hospital. The sun was encouraging me to stay though, be outside in creation to appreciate this wonderful day. I hadn't eaten anything so I bought a sandwich and a drink and took them to the woods. I nestled into a patch of grass, overlooking the lake. I had calmed somewhat. My private picnic, what could be nicer? My own company is something I long for, others can still be too great a quantity for my mind to bear. After Mum died, my greatest companions were dogs and babies: loving, caring, physical and, most delightful of all, didn't speak. We could just be. Humans very rarely just are, someone always talks and the moment is lost.

Eventually, I arrive back. The mirror welcomes me with white eyelashes. I blink then splash my face with water, eyelashes black once again. I have washed away the encrusted tears and all that was before.

I briefly talk to Roy. He wasn't in my review last week but is one of the few nurses who can read Dr. Floyd's handwriting (doctors' illegible scrawl holding true). I am still quite confused. The nurses say I am giving mixed messages – enjoying myself one moment, harming myself another – but can't they see that this just reflects my inmost turmoil? I am incredibly muddled as to why I am up and down with such intensity and velocity. Roy says Dr. Floyd has put "no eye contact". I laugh, I was crying almost all the way through!

I speak to Aunty Beth (again!) after our earlier chat when I was in tears over Dad. I feel far better now and darling Aunty Beth is all for driving down tonight to collect me to live at their house for a while. She is willing to do anything that will help but I have to stay in hospital until Thursday. My fabulous aunty.

6th May

2007

Aunty Beth here for the weekend so I take the opportunity to visit Gran. I have been home over two months and still haven't seen her which I feel quite bad about. I know Gran won't remember but I will. Mum gets very anxious if I'm away from her for any length of time but, obviously, she's happier with Aunty Beth than any of her friends.

Holly comes with me and offers to drive. This means we have the whole hour there (and also back) to talk. I've been slightly concerned about her mental state and Lindsey asked me yesterday to speak to Holly as well. Holly does talk to me and I feel honoured that she does. I don't think she lies to me or tries to bend the truth. She is impressively open. She said her boss had spoken to her this week because he felt she was working too many hours, which is true. Holly goes through the warning signs that she and her psychiatrist worked through. Holly hasn't slept properly for the last week, she is noticing her hair falling out more, and she is working twelve hour days. She knows she probably won't recognise if she goes manic so I'm just terribly impressed that she is being so sensible and talking to me about it.

Holly is anxious and seems scared of becoming very ill again. I do my best to reassure her that, by telling me, she has done so well. We discuss her taking the mood stabiliser again. I wish she had never stopped taking all her drugs in one go and hoped she would stay on the sodium valproate. She didn't like how her anti-depressants and anti-psychotics made her feel. She was numb to many emotions and had little energy. We go over again how the mood stabiliser is unlikely to do that because people with epilepsy are on it for life and they function perfectly normally.

We eventually reach an agreement that Holly will phone her psychiatrist after the weekend. I tell her I will check up on her! She appears committed now but I know that means rather little. Her memory is still quite poor and she is liable to find an excuse for not doing so. I think it's wonderful that she can talk at such length. Rightly or wrongly, she also respects my knowledge about her disease and her drugs and so listens to my opinions. I'm glad we had the car journey together but I'm all too aware that my time with Holly is restricted. I think about her becoming dreadfully ill again and wonder what would happen. I would love to, but know that really I could not look after both Holly and Mum.

Everyone now looks to me. I can no longer share the responsibility with Mum. I don't want Holly to be ill. I can see she is scared. I want to protect her, make her better. On the way home she drives through two sets of red traffic lights. I should have driven.

Holly drives me to Dad's and Ethan is up, preening in the sun. We all sit outside, ice cubed drinks, until Holly leaves to go to work. Ethan has his first exam tomorrow and hasn't done any revision. I say that we could scan through a text book for relevant topics but Ethan reasons that, if he begins trying to work now, it will just stress him out about how little he knows, so he has opted for the calm, laid back option, not to do anything. "Well, it's too late now", says Ethan. Instead he goes to the gym.

I potter in the house, sorting clothes, opening my mail, checking emails that are now over a month old. Unfortunately, Dad comes in for only a moment, I don't know why. This wasn't the plan. Startled, I look at him and there is an awkward pause. Dad then adopts his head-in-the-sand, oblivious to all, falsely cheerful, sing song voice. This immediately annoys me. Yesterday we parted, me in tears, him shouting, and now Dad is pretending that nothing happened. I explain this to Dad, how I find it hard with such personality shift. It makes no sense and I can't keep up. Dad doesn't let me finish, he defensively talks over me, a rant, then walks off. I wanted to be calmer than yesterday but Dad never gives me a chance. He won't listen and because I have said something bad, it makes Dad mad. He goes to work after collecting whatever he came for. How, even when I only get a short amount of leave, do arguments weed themselves in?

Ethan comes back and we eat lunch outside in the sweltering heat. I have on my new skirt and a vest top courtesy of Holly and am still deliciously warm. I spread the newspapers and enjoy these moments of luxury. Rucksack bedecked, I then slowly walk back to hospital, skirt flowing, flip flops flapping. I take the longer route, through the park, and take my time, too warm for energetic marching.

Aunty Beth sends me a text saying she is proud to be my aunty. This makes me cry. I am a mess and destroying our family. I am nothing to be proud of, a flailing body of incapacity and ineptitude.

Later, the life was sucked out of me in one hit. Nothing made sense. I couldn't see or hear properly and nothing seemed real, as if my senses had given up. Bin liners had been celotaped to the windows as the curtains aren't back from being cleaned. I saw myself crawl in one, face first and asphyxiated on the bed. I got scared. I had seen it but I felt as if it could have happened, like a premonition that I was about to fulfil. I silently battled, my mind tormenting itself.

I'm unsure how long later, but my body triumphed. Like a crazed woman, I ripped the bin bags down, stuffing them with a force of magnitude that was far more than necessary, underneath my arm. I ran and thrust them into the furthest communal bin from my room, panting and shaking.

Back on my bed, I didn't understand what had just happened. I could have killed myself but I didn't. My head was a mess. I no longer know what I want or feel. I was agitated but exhausted. I sat on my bed, leaning against the head board, knees hugged. I couldn't allow myself sleep. Sarah phoned me. I like hearing her voice, sometimes it doesn't even matter what she says, it is just her voice. I know Sarah is real. I was monosyllabic, partly because I didn't know what to say and partly because the thought processes of generating a suitable response and then verbalising it were too much for me. I couldn't coordinate the necessary mental tasks.

After our one sided conversation, I felt calmer, more subdued. I possibly could attempt to read. I lay on my front, propped my arms on the pillow and willed my brain to focus sufficiently on my novel. This quickly tired me, my eyelids drooping heavily. I turned off the light and prayed myself to sleep.

7th May

2007

Terrible day. I spend the morning crying. Dad has been horrible. I don't mean to cry but I dissolve into heaving sobs, unable to contain them. Mum curls around me, her hand stroking my hair, and we remain like that for ages. Dad shouts at me, he then gets cross with Mum and then storms out of the room, unwilling to listen to either of us. How can he do this? How can he be so harsh, especially to Mum?

As I cry in Mum's arms, all I can think is, please don't leave me Mummy. We've always been a team, in it together, supporting each other. Dad and Ethan have been vile in the past but Mum and I are always there for the other. I can't do it alone. Don't leave me Maisie. I want to go with you. Life without you is my most horrific dream. I don't want to do it. I am unable. Maisie, you mean such an incredible amount to me. You are my most favourite person in the entire world. I don't want to live without you. Please don't go.

2008

Up early, packed, breakfasted, showered all before 8am. At 9am, Adelle comes to take my blood for lithium levels. They like doing me because I've got easy veins but perhaps not anymore. Adelle firstly misses then has another go. No joy. I tell her not to worry, try the other arm. Still no luck even though I wiggle the needle a bit. Adelle is now doubting herself. I always did this, missing veins is essentially confidence destroying. She doesn't want to have another go, as I'm becoming a pin cushion. I ask how she'll feel next time she attempts to take blood. I say I don't mind and she should at least have one more go, otherwise she'll be even more nervous and doubtful if she tries on someone else.

Adelle gets a new needle, applies the tourniquet above my cubital fossa and has her final attempt. Result! The blood flows into the syringe and Adelle is chuffed. She thanks me for being calm and not minding multiple stabbings. I am only too pleased to be able to do this. I was incredibly grateful to patients when I was a medical student, I'm glad to provide that role reversal. Everyone needs to learn and then practice. You cannot become an expert in a medical field overnight. It takes skill and knowledge, teaching and learning. I was acutely aware of this on my placements, favours are always being asked of patients. They have to be brave to agree to a fumbling but eager medical student.

I walk home to avoid the mad cleaning upheaval on the ward and catch Ethan before he leaves for London. He has his first exam today. Grace is giving him a lift to the station. I make sure Ethan has got a bunch of pens that work as, knowing him, he'll lose half of them en route. A hurried goodbye and then they are gone. I busy myself at home and then sit in the garden, newspapers spread, and drink lemonade and suck an ice lolly I found in the freezer. I phone Granny as can't face speaking to her in the hospital.

I walk in the midday heat, via the shops to buy some lunch, and am relieved at some shade on arrival, my arms are already pink from yesterday and I forgot to put suncream on this morning. My hospital room is ready, pristinely cleaned and I decide to embark on a touch of furniture rearranging. I shall probably be told off for this but sometimes you need a change. I put my desk on the wall furthest from the window, hopefully I will be cooler. My bed is now longways against both windows which should give me a breeze at night. My room even feels different. Furniture in place, I unpack my things. There are still no curtains and, as the sun descends in the sky, my room receives these boiling rays. Paula finds a curtain but we cannot locate the hooks so we manage to tie up each end, at least providing me with some shade.

Ethan phones me having just completed his exam, "Not as hard as it could've been, I was writing the whole time so that's good, isn't it?" It transpired he had to buy some pens once in London: he'd left the load I gave him in Grace's car! So typical.

I have been feeling low all afternoon, non-specific but just generally tired of life. Katy takes me outside and we sit on the furthest bench away. She knows I'm not right, not my usual self, although what that is I no longer know. We talk and I cry, not sobbing, just silent streams of tears. Katy puts her arm around me and that touch of comfort is so welcome and nice that it makes me cry even more.

What is wrong with me? Why do I feel like this? I feel rubbish, there are no elaborate descriptions. Katy soothes me with her understanding and, once we walk inside, she says to find her if I am going to do anything. Are you planning on hurting yourself, Alice? Are you going to do anything now or later? Please try and get me first. Thank you Katy, I will try.

8th May

2007

Mum had an appointment with Dr. Mayhew, her consultant, this morning. He says Mum's blood tests show that her liver function is much the same, no improvement. The chemotherapy hasn't worked so she is having no more. Prognosis: weeks, perhaps months.

This is what it must feel like when people say time stands still. I remain in February when Mum was first diagnosed, when it gets dark at half past four and I put on my scarf and gloves in an attempt to keep warm against the cold wind and rain. I do not understand how the weeks have elapsed. All has stopped. Nothing else matters; it all has paled into insignificance.

2008

Rough night. I awoke feeling as if I hadn't even gone to bed. Hauled myself into the shower, then got changed in the corner of my room which is half shielded by my tied up curtain. If anyone walked by close enough, I'm sure they could see everything but I am beyond being concerned.

Annoyingly, someone had taken the fuse out of the hot water tank on the wall. We aren't allowed kettles – too risky (the cord, the plug, scalding water etc) – so I pleaded to the staff and got a steaming cup of coffee from their supplies.

I had an early appointment with the clinical psychologist which was in town so I left straight after breakfast. Still felt lethargic but decided the walk would do me good. I listened to music for the half hour stroll, too hot for my usual power walking but I seem to have an ability to walk anywhere slowly. The psychologist was called Rachel and I liked her. I felt she understood what I was saying and didn't draw conclusions which were frustratingly false. She said she wanted to help me and, even if I do go back to Newcastle in August, we could at least start to discuss some things. She'll see me for an hour each week which I think is plenty. These sessions are tough, just because I am so unused to talking about myself in this way.

Katy comes to find me, checking if I was OK after this morning's appointment. She shows such awareness. I say the psychologist was fine but I am captured in a hole at the moment, too weak to climb out. I don't know why. My emotions no longer follow physical events, they command my mind which doesn't tally with life circumstances. If there had been enough staff on, Katy wanted to come with me. She said these things can usually take their toll because it is hard work. I said I would be able to get to the psychologist myself. Katy is so lovely.

Possibly developing a nervous rocking as time passes and my review looms. Half an hour now, providing Dr. Floyd isn't running late which is usually the case.

Review went surprisingly well. I came out with a calming satisfaction, reassured and less likely to despair. Dr. Floyd is fantastic at giving explanations. The more knowledge I have, the more I understand, the less I am scared. It stills my unrest.

Firstly, I did explain how I felt Dr. Floyd had undermined me last time by giving her view on my perception of my parents. I found this the hardest and then apologised for my uselessness at answering or explaining any further questions once I was crying. Dr. Floyd said that sometimes, when people die, the living elevate all that person's attributes to a falsely high level and she was wondering if this is what I have done with Mum. Dr. Floyd knows this is not the case, as I keep insisting and am certain is true, my relationship with Mum is unchanging. Before Mum was ill, when she was ill and after she died, my view hasn't changed.

I explained a little about Dad and say, at the moment, I am not strong enough to just accept hurtful comments as Dad's way. I feel I am too vulnerable so any of the negative things Dad does, I will take them out of proportion and too personally. This is why I decide some distance is required, only for a short time, but a break from each other. Dr. Floyd said this sounded sensible.

Dr. Floyd sees I can enjoy myself but also, conversely, the very low points. She said I am doing better, going in the right direction. It is good I am able to do things but what we are striving for is a sustained elevation of mood. I describe how, on occasions, I see me acting out my suicide and it feels real and then I have to stop myself from replicating it. Dr. Floyd said this is déjà vu and, as soon as that phrase is mentioned, I realise she is exactly right.

She thinks I am still experiencing intrusive thoughts because bad things are in my head but I don't want them to be there, I don't want to think about them but I don't have a choice. Also, Dr. Floyd said I have obsessional ideas of dying. It seeps into everything, is always there, prominently or niggling in the background, but always present. Dr. Floyd thought it would be a good idea to mention this to the clinical psychologist as she may be able to help in this particular area. She doesn't know, however, what my periods of heightened senses are. Hopefully they will decrease as I'm more able to participate in activities.

My lithium is staying at the same dose; my trimipramine is to be increased. I am to say to the nurses if side effects are apparent. I am given overnight leave on Saturday and will stay at Holly's. I walked out feeling so much better than last week. I understand what has been said and can see how I have improved slightly. That old question though, "What does the future look like?" is still tricky. I say I cannot see ahead. I am very much in the here and now as if a barrier has been erected. Even planning tomorrow is a challenge. One day still at a time it very much is.

At 6pm, I plug in my headphones and walk in the still bright and hot day to Lindsey's for her Cancer Research fundraising evening. It takes me just under an hour and I am refreshed by the evening air.

Different stalls are set up: plants, pots, jewellery, bags, clothes. I am whisked, by Lindsey, to the drinks stand where Holly has made jugs of Pimms with plenty of fruit and mint and elderflower cordial. On a table in front of us are bowls of home-made houmous, tortillas, carrot sticks and other bread and dips. I serve the drinks whilst Holly runs back and forth to the kitchen, refilling the jugs. I am then transferred to the raffle where I sell tickets and write names on the back of numerous stubs. I find a creeping claustrophobia hinder me: lots and lots of strangers in a confined space. The raffle helps distract me and focus my mind to an extent but I begin to feel decidedly odd. I slurp down my second tumbler of Pimms.

The raffle is finally drawn at the end of the evening and everyone remaining flocks onto the decking. I squeeze out and into the kitchen. I pour myself a large vodka martini but then get roped into assisting with prizes. At this point, Ethan arrives having got back from London. Him, Grace and I weave out way to the back of the garden and sit on wooden chairs beneath the trellis. I drink too quickly but assume the alcohol is calming my tightened muscles and churning brain.

Finally, everyone leaves, Lindsey and Holly join us and Lindsey embellishes collapsing into a chair. Holly drops Ethan and then me off.

I telephone Aunty Beth to update her on events. I think she is so pleased to hear me happy and then am called (the last one) for meds. My increased dose of trimipramine is a nightmare. They only have it in 25mg tablets, big white ones the size of paracetamol, so I have six! Plus two lithium tablets which are even bigger. I don't mind taking tablets but this is going to prove rather a feat every single night.

I put on my pyjamas, lie on the bed with no sheet, it is too hot for covers, put the night light on and open my book. I can barely prop myself up to read and, as my eyes hit the page, insects scuttle back at me, across the leaves, over my hands, a zoo of letters. Defeated, I throw my book, switch off the light and lie, eyes closed. I have no thoughts. It is bliss, just a spinning sedative, waltzing me to sleep.

9th May

2008

Woke at 6pm but I did sleep right through, or I passed out into oblivion. Either way, I received that prized commodity, sleep. Felt excitable all morning, almost frivolous. Maureen's birthday today. We had a big card that everyone had signed and also a cake. Maureen was chuffed and ever so sweet, thanking everyone individually for their writing on her card.

Then, innocently drinking a cup of coffee, half my tooth crunched out. I went to the mirror to inspect. My lower molar, which has been particularly active, had again chipped off. This is the same tooth that I had capped, got an abscess, root canal treatment, part fell off again etc. It isn't painful but my tongue is drawn to root around. A big hole in your mouth is always an odd sensation.

The problem started when Mum was still alive. A bit chipped off but I left it as didn't want to leave the house. A few weeks after Mum died, I was staying at Sarah's and woke up to one side of my jaw being big and swollen, accompanied by a terrific pain in my teeth. Decided I needed to go home to see a dentist and insisted I got the train, much to Sarah's disapproval – she wanted to drive me. This possibly wasn't my best idea. Getting the tube across London nearly finished me off.

I got home and collapsed. Ethan found me hours later with an even fatter face and talking but not making sense! Think I scared him rather, poor thing. He wanted to phone for an ambulance but, within my incomprehensible jumble, I conveyed that I was not about to go back to hospital! He got Lily instead who came round straight away. Our family could pretty much keep her practice going. Ethan half carried, half walked me downstairs and Lily's husband drove me to their house down the road! I stayed the night there: Lily looked after me and gave me lots of drugs! Next morning I went to the dentist...abscess!

I went to Adelle and open wide for her too see. She said, "What do you want me to do about it?" and laughs. I say, "Fix it!" She said she thought a dentist would be better qualified, well, just qualified, as Adelle has no experience with teeth. I was being a bit pathetic and didn't have the number so Adelle phoned up directory enquiries and retrieved it for me. I gave them a ring. My dentist surgery is lovely and I explained what had happened. She said the dentist can see me tomorrow. I was really impressed, firstly because it is a Saturday and, secondly, that there is an appointment available. I assumed I'd be holey for the weekend.

Holly, taking annual leave as is owed a few days holiday, picks me up at 11am. We go to the supermarket and then drive home to make sandwiches for our picnic. I leave a note for Dad to say I have overnight leave on Saturday and will stay at Holly's and also to hope that he enjoys tomorrow. He is going on a cookery course, his Christmas present from Ethan and me. I feel this is the best move, I don't want to phone him but I also don't wish to be quite so petty as to ignore him completely.

Holly drives and we meet Johnny (Holly's uncle) in the boat yard, a funny little place owned by a guy who lives on his own in a two storey houseboat which sits on the bank. There's a lot of evidence of tinkering going on, paint jobs, repair work, spare oars etc. We pile into the row boat, picnic basket in tow, then transfer to the yacht. It's a lovely boat but apparently four berth. I decide yachts are very similar to tents – four man tent comfortably sleeps two, six man sleeps four etc. The weather is undeniably fantastic: glorious sunshine and cracking winds. We sail pass at the places we went as children: the infamous paddling pool (a concrete square which fills with sea water as the tide comes in), the beaches we paddled, the places we walked.

We moor up and put the kettle on in the little hull cleverly equipped with kitchen essentials. It's nearly 5pm but we are still able to bask in the sun in vest tops. Boat tidied, we row to shore and quickly drive to Johnny's house for a much needed toilet stop! Then I am dropped back, windswept, bronzed (well, possibly burnt), freckled, after a fantastic day on the water. There is something incredibly soothing being afloat.

I deposit my bag and excitedly tell staff of my activities today before having a well needed shower. I keep the water fairly cold and stand, appreciating the coolness on my skin. I wash away all the salty deposits and shampoo my hair which is thick like a rope. I bask in my cleanliness before getting dressed and walking through the ward where, no doubt, the dirt will soon jump on me.

Susie is my nurse and we sit outside on chairs in a grassy corner but still in the sunshine. I talk about my review, my guilt over last night's pathetic behaviour using drugs and alcohol. I am almost self-medicating, not helpful Alice. Susie says I shouldn't dwell on yesterday's antics. It is OK Alice (not official advice of course) but everyone does that sometimes. You didn't do anything bad or out of control.

I say what a good day I've had and how I've felt excited, free, happy. These are good emotions; Susie is pleased. Talking about drunken behaviour, I tell Susie the story of Mum's music exam. In her forties, perhaps ten years ago, my mother decided to take up the violin. The problem with being musical, especially string instruments that can sound dreadful, is that you can hear when it is out of tune. My Mum's ear was far better than her bowing skills. Anyway, Mum did make it to her Grade 1 exam and I was her accompanist.

On the day of the exam, Mum was the first student after lunch. She was so nervous she didn't notice the examiner arrive. I did. He was fairly elderly and came in late, greeted the receptionist and explained how he'd been for lunch with some old friends. He disappeared into the examination room, stinking of whiskey.

Mum and I were called in. I started playing the first piece but Mum, shaking profusely, couldn't bow the opening phrase so stopped (I followed) and panicked. At this point, the examiner sauntered over, placed both hands on Mum's shoulders and was flirting outrageously. I was watching in amazement. He concluded that all Mum needed was a glass of wine before the exam, sufficient for calming the nerves. Finally, this charade was over, I played the three pieces and left them to it although now I was rather nervous as to what would be going on behind that closed door. I didn't want to leave Mum with him!

Exam over, walking home, Mum didn't even notice any of the alcohol smelling, inappropriate touching etc! I couldn't believe it. How could she not?! When I explain, Mum then said that yes, it was quite odd, she was just so overwhelmed with anxiety that she could think of nothing else. Nevertheless, she did well. Grade 1 violin: merit.

Susie says it is really good that I can talk about the funny times I had with Mum. She is right but I still have difficulty in seeing her animated. The picture still in my mind is Mum lying in bed either dead or horrendously poorly.

The evening ticks by quickly which is always a relief. I speak to Aunty Beth, our almost nightly chat, and the conversation steers to the future. I tell Aunty Beth I still struggle to plan or think about anything beyond tomorrow. None of it feels real. I ask Aunty Beth what I did between Mum dying and Christmas. This is six months that I have almost no recollection of. What did I do? Aunty Beth says, very little, most days nothing. How did I spend such a long time with so many hours of inactivity? It is quite disconcerting. My Aunty Maggie died, I remember that and I remember seeing her in hospital, but very little else. I took two overdoses but the details of which have faded from my memory. Maybe this is also, partly, why I am writing now, otherwise I will forget great chunks of my life.

10th May

2007

    I phone Holly in the evening. She sounds upset and I probe her to tell me why. I think it started with an argument with Lindsey over putting her ill dog, Dina, down. D-day is now, apparently, tomorrow. Holly says everything is horrible at the moment, especially with Maisie being so poorly. Holly tries not to cry but I hear her voice breaking and she does. I do try and comfort her, let her know I care and that I'm here. She seems lonely.

    I ask her about talking to her psychiatrist. Holly hasn't phoned. She says she's OK now. I knew she wouldn't phone. I'm extremely dubious as to how she is OK but I don't press it. Now is not the time to be firm with her. I suggest she phones tomorrow, before the weekend. I don't like to think of her alone in her house but I can't go round this late. Mum needs me here. My duties aren't split. My priority is Mum and always will be.

2008

    Woke up, not with horrific recollections of the night but blurred and non-descript images. I showered then filled my rucksack with necessary items for the weekend. As I was doing so, I saw a vivid image of myself in Holly's house. It was dark, probably night time. I was on my own in the kitchen. I took a knife from the metallic magnet where they are kept on the wall. I located the brachial artery on my left arm. This is a pulse doctors take in babies as their wrists are too small. I flexed my bicep, found the artery in the indentation of my muscle. I scored the knife down the length of my upper arm. I held my arm at right angles, like a wing, and my feathers grew deep and bubbling and red. I watched and realised how simple my own mortality was to control. I watched, mesmerised by my own body. I watched and couldn't move. Everything had already been decided.

    Someone reminds me of today's date. I have been in hospital thirty-nine days. Calculating the days always makes me feel like a prisoner, counting down my sentence, except I do not know the length, an undetermined entity. Five and a half weeks: the period equal to my last hospital stay. I have written more than last time. Is that significant? A concern? Am I slowly edging into seclusion, withdrawing myself from others even further? Writing is a solitary activity but that is why it is appealing. It gives me quiet time, a rest from the rush of the world. I'm not troubled by it but others tell me too long writing alone is not helpful, perhaps even detrimental but no discussion, I'm not stopping now.

Before I leave, Susie talks with me. We go outside as the temperature of my room rises as the day matures and becomes terribly humid. I'm unsure whether to say about my strange premonition but that implies it will happen which I don't want at all. I never involve anyone else but, if I tell Susie, will I still be granted leave?

Well, I'm crap at lying so of course I do end up explaining. Susie is great. She's on a long day so I can always phone the ward this evening and speak to her. She says I've had this before and not carried it out, which is a good thing, it shows I'm fighting apparently. I wish it felt like that, though. I still feel I'm out of control and not making any decisions, good or bad. My perception of right and wrong has been so distorted that I no longer know the difference. I am blindly leaping from one day to the next and the days are ticking by but I'm still in the air, being pulled along by some unknown force. None of this is me.

Susie says to try and enjoy one thing and not to worry if I find some things too much. It is OK, Alice. Susie checks my meds and says I've got lorazepam as well so, if inside my head becomes too furious, I can take it to hopefully calm the thoughts somewhat. I stuff the tablets in my bag and am let out.

I walk in the scorching heat, my back quickly sticky from bearing a rucksack. I listen to music which slightly separates me from the speeding cars and bustle of people. It means I don't take so much in, my attentions are already heightened from all there is to see, hearing life as well sometimes becomes too much to assess all at once.

I walk straight to the dentist, insufficient time to pop home first, and sit in the waiting room, cooling down. I flick through some celebrity magazine which always entertained Mum and I whilst waiting. I loved this as a medical student too. If ever we were early for teaching sessions or surgery or appointments, we would join the patients and indulge in a spot of daft celebrity gossip. Always great to pass the time but rather dull on one's own.

My tooth is temporally filled in, at least my hole has now disappeared. I have to leave it for a few weeks and, if still sore or causing problems, then the dentist will pull it out, if it is OK then he will crown it.

Walking home, I pass Lily gardening and we go into her kitchen for a much welcome glass of orange juice. I update her on the last few days and also see her daughter who is going to Swaziland on Monday for her medical student elective. She had asked me to go with her. I feel sad seeing the excitement in her eyes on preparation. I was meant to be going to Africa last summer. I was full of naïve good intentions and then Mum became ill and I feel I have aged significantly, far more cynical about life. I don't wish to be but how to change?

Armed with my overnight stuff, bottle of wine, tonic water, barbeque food, I trek to Holly's with aching arms as the weight of the bags slowly indents my shoulders. On arriving, bags are dumped and water greedily consumed in attempt to cool my overheated, over exercised body. Holly and I cook rice and new potatoes whilst chopping vegetables to make salads. We light the barbeque and then make a jug of Pimms, helping ourselves to a glass. A few friends arrive, as does Lindsey who brings her freshly made cheese scones. Dad also comes (he'd spoken to Holly).

I decide Dad and I are better off in the company of others. I haven't seen him since the unfortunate event and I do my best to act nice and normal. Dad prefers it when anything occurring before is forgotten. Today he went on the cookery course. He seemed to enjoy himself and even brought his certificate[!] and recipes achieved. Because the weather was so impressive, he also barbequed different types of fish.

After the food was eaten, Lindsey then Dad left. I am grateful to Holly because I have seen Dad, which I know I should, but am struggling too much with him on my own. It was very non-committal and conversation was diffused.

We sit outside, drinking wine, until gone midnight. The evenings are so mild. We have a big, liquid candle on the table which successfully deters the mosquitoes. Finally, the food is tidied away and we sink into the sofa and comfy chairs in the front room. Here is where I begin to feel odd, I'm not quite there, as if I have departed, just slightly from my body. I can move my arms and legs but more like a puppet as if they are attached but only by strings. Voices and sounds and colours and shapes swill in my head, a jumbled round-a-bout of senses. Perhaps I'm drunk but I've only had two glasses of wine and coffee and water since. I need to go to bed, life is too big, too complex. I want all the friends to leave. I want to scream for them to go. Restraint is such an effort.

Finally, I am able to escape to the bathroom, clean teeth, go to the toilet and don pyjamas. I say a hurried goodnight to Holly, then lie in bed. Reading relaxes my taught muscles, lulls me into a false sense of security, real enough to put me to sleep.

11th May

2007

Disturbing conversation with Holly, who is talking non-stop. Not really a conversation, more of a monologue with me trying to interject. Dina the dog has been put down but Holly is now OK with the whole performance and she is telling me how it was best for Dina. Holly has worked late again tonight and then reels off all the changes she wants to make at work and all the extra sessions she has eagerly volunteered to do. She talks about Jack, then Ethan and then proceeds to tell me that I can be manic as always have lots of energy and rush around doing things. She tells *me* to be careful because *I* am likely to escalate into mania. I find this rather hard to even imagine as my life with all its circumstances is particularly depressing currently. But this is so concerning. This is Holly, seemingly normal to onlookers but, to those who know her well, the subtle signs are there. I feel she is beginning to get ill again. I feel desperately sorry for her. It must be such an ordeal. But I also know that I am now the one in charge, the only sensible person to help her. Except, my time is for Mum. I know that, if Holly is really sick, she will be sectioned. I know I should not worry about events that have yet to happen but it does play on my mind. I do not know what else I can do.

Later, Mum is weeping. Dad and Ethan arguing, then getting cross with Mum when she begs them to stop. I do not understand them. How can they do this to Maisie? How? Why? Unanswered questions which I shall never know. Please don't make my Maisie cry, especially now.

2008

Slept well. Possible reasons why: medication compounded by alcohol, coolness of room with windows wide, complete darkness, relative quiet. In fact, everything that I can't replicate in hospital. Oh well, appreciate things when they are good.

At 9am, I tiptoed downstairs, put the kettle on and ground a generous handful of coffee beans. Holly joined me soon after and together we did the mammoth load of washing up left from last night. Clean, tidy kitchen, we sat outside, the beginning of another glorious day. Over a week now, we have basked in ideal British sun. Always a breeze but hot enough to imagine being on holiday.

We pottered in the garden (I don't have a clue but, under instruction, I can just about cope!) and I helped Holly with the jobs needing two pairs of hands. Holly then retrieved all her feet lotions and soaked my feet in an old washing up bowl, still outside, me reclining on the decking, before giving them a massage and painting my nails. Always erring on the side of tomboy, this felt funny and unnecessary but massaged to relax me to a degree. I don't keep immobile for long enough however, so smudge my toe and finger nails and they have to be re-done.

Somehow time has passed and we are in the afternoon. I re-pack my rucksack and, at this point, I am ready to leave. I don't know why, I must be on my own. Holly says she'll give me a lift but I decline. I want, need, to walk. It doesn't matter that it is hot and I have to cut through town and the hospital is almost an hour's walk away, all of these pale into insignificance. I need to be outside, on my own, walking. Then I may feel more real.

I decide to go through the park, take the path that snakes around the edge, longer but shady in parts and much preferred view than main roads and shops. But my perception is heightened to an intensive level. My world looks like a film in slow motion, where the camera pans 360° and all is viewed except I am walking straight, my head slightly bowed. I fumble to put in my headphones. I have found this helps. If I can see and hear the same thing, the senses combine exponentially, producing even more intense multi-dimensional images. Now, my ears are preoccupied.

Sunday: the park is full. I am inundated by my inquisitive eye. There are running and skipping children, wearing shorts and t-shirts and, the youngest ones, hats to protect from the sun. Some inexpertly attempt handstands and rolypolys whilst others play cricket, Frisbee, bat and ball. A tennis ball is thumped over my head but I want to duck because, as it approaches me, the yellow becomes luminous and the size increases and I probably can't but think I hear the whistle through the air. Everything that moves seems to grow before my eyes. Parents either join their children or sit on rugs with babies or eating picnics. Teenagers race around on bikes which, in my eyes, look too fast, too big, too close. The guys go topless, scrunched up t-shirts in fist; the girls wear exceptionally short shorts and prance in their bikini tops. Everyone is either applying sun cream or burnt.

I walk around the pond, full of row boats and pedalos. Splashing, laughing, shouting, I see great waves instead of ripples, the boats are going to sink, danger instead of pleasure, bicycles zoom past, they are going to fall in, drown. I see the spokes on the wheels but not a blur, in detail. I see everything. There is a queue to the ice cream van – old, young, men, women, children, grandparents, white, black, Asian, fat, thin, happy, angry. It's like a cross-section of our whole society, each has been represented. Three geese fly overhead but they are huge and I'm sure a wing will slap my cheek because I can feel the compression of the air made by the bird's flight path. They are coming at me, we are going to collide. They pass without incident.

I am spat out at the bottom of the park, along the river where I see a swan, and onto the pavement adjacent to the road. I try and look at my feet and listen to the music continuously playing in my ears. Cars flash by but I see the colour, make, driver as if I was closer and the cars were stationary.

I make it back to the hospital, relieved to have got here, and dive into my room, space, alone, quiet, free from human activity. I lie on my bed, sunglasses still on, and disappear into the colourless living silence of my head, resting from the madness of the real world. I will be OK, once the exhaustion of senses has recovered.

I feel safe once I've spent an hour or so alone, bonus is, my bedroom is now tidy. I go outside to the garden. The wards are back to normal after the deep clean and we are permitted to mix once again. Leo comes bounding up, chuffed to see me, thought I'd gone. He is being discharged on Thursday and eagerly tells me how much better he is. He tried to cut himself the other day, locked in a bathroom, blade prepared, but couldn't do it. He stopped himself. It is such a wonderful feeling when you hear of other people's successes and improvements. Perhaps that's why I wanted to be a doctor. I'm honoured to be able to join in with the lives of patients. Thrown together, they are your immediate friends, they have much more understanding than others, purely because we live together.

I stay in the garden and stroll the perimeter, phoning Sarah, who is going sailing for five days, and then Aunty Beth, who has just returned from a weekend in Oxford. As Mum always said in the throws of illness, life does go on.

12th May

2008

I did sleep but woke up several times petrified. My eyes would be wide, breathing rapid, heart pounding, body drenched in sweat, pyjamas clinging and had to be peeled off. I was so scared that sometimes my arms would be waving, batting away unknown demons from my face, for, every time I awoke, I would not know what I was frightened of. I had this when Mum was ill. I would be jolted awake into an unknown fear.

I got up at 6.30am because I didn't wish to be woken in such a way again. It is unnerving to be so afraid and not know why.

Helen gets me from my room and says Dr. Floyd has come to see me. It seems so early for a visit. I'm not about to say how little work psychiatrists do because that isn't true, they may start their day later but they finish later too. As a medical student, we didn't mind this, anything to get out of 8am ward rounds. Nevertheless, the trooper Dr. Floyd seems to live here and today, on form, she is wearing a black skirt with white polka dots and pump shoes with a ribbon tied into a bow sitting snugly on her toes.

We sit in a side room and Dr. Floyd wants to know how I am. Because I feel much the same, she breaks it down into more specific questions. When you're in the middle of a struggle, it is quite hard to be objective and say, with certainty, that yes, you are getting better. Dr. Floyd thinks (and I agree) good points are: sleeping more, less tired in day, enjoying some things, less time considering death or planning suicide. She says she still thinks I have intrusive obsessive thoughts which hopefully the lithium will continue to help with. Keep drinking lots of water Alice, especially in this heat. Your lithium levels were too high after overdose, whatever the reason, and we don't want that happening again.

Dr. Floyd says that, in depression, you get more REM sleep and so, if you have morbid thoughts as well, these develop into nightmares. My increased perception should decrease over time, become normalised as I get better. As Dr. Floyd always tells me, it is a lengthy recovery, no quick fixes, be patient Alice, this takes time. Thank you Dr. Floyd. She makes me feel safe because she can give me accurate explanations and I like being able to understand. I feel more in control then.

At lunch time, I walk home to see Ethan. We sit outside, browning our skin (Ethan is already dark from sunbeds and I'm not ghostly pale as got some colour from sailing) and then Dad drops in, unbeknownst to me or Ethan. This time, it is fine to see Dad. He calls me "Ali" which is always a good sign. I talk to Ethan about his London weekend. He is back there again tomorrow for his last exam. Again, he has not even lifted a book, let alone read one. You never know with Ethan, he may cannily be able to blag it.

Sad and lengthy evening in hospital. I keep thinking about Mum. I feel sad, sad because I miss her terribly. Giles's wife comes to see him in the evening. He is still very quiet, barely talking or eating. He is a short man, slightly overweight, middle-age spread. He has large facial features which are more pronounced under burnt nose and cheeks. I see his wife looking at him, looking after Giles like a child. She wipes a tear from her eye as she leads him to an outside bench. There, she hugs him, patiently talks and there is so much love in her face, in her actions.

I need my Mummy. She would look after me so exquisitely. I want her; I need her. I'm not strong enough alone. I need my superstar Maisie, my starfish. Then I'd be loved and cared for. Mum gave me my strength. Now I have been sapped, a shrivelled leaf no longer attached to its stem. I'm carrying on, seemingly progressing but is this real?

Life without Mum is still a treacherous place. Life without Mum is still a goal that I do not want. I must be kidding myself. So what if I can do things? I do not want to be in the world, however much enjoyment gained, without my darling Maisie. I sit in my room and look at a photo of Mum and me, gaze into her twinkling eyes, smiling face. Oh, delightful Mum, this was a good day, a fun time, our smile of togetherness is real.

I am called for meds and dutifully obey, despite the queue, but then I hear Mum. Alice, this isn't real, you've brought this on yourself but I am compelled to check. I ask to get out, I need to look to ensure Mum isn't there. No Alice, it is far too late, no walk tonight. I go back to my room agitated, jumpy but cannot keep still. I go into the garden, walk the perimeter, scanning all the time, but I know Mum won't be here, this is a place she doesn't belong. Don't listen Alice, Mum is safe in heaven, these are just games in your head.

10.45pm outside doors will be closing soon. Paul guides me into a corner and offers me a drag on his joint. Perhaps this will calm my brain, lessen the torture, remove the agonising voices. I suck in deeply, willing the drug to enter my bloodstream. Subject less chatter, little thought required.

Doors are locked. I'm extremely tired now, a clumsy exhaustion, but too afraid of sleep to be able to go to bed. I slowly perform night time tasks and find myself in bed but lights still on. I focus on the book I am clasping but my mind is elsewhere. Mummy, I love you. My novel is rendered useless so I sit in the dark, eyes wide, unsure as to what they are prepared for.

Time ticks by on my illuminated travel clock. 2am: I leap from bed, rush to the sink and vomit, again and again, dinner coming back. It's still dark and each object in the room has a hazy outline so I stay, hands gripped to the sink. I walk my fingers along to locate the tap and splash cold water across my face and swill sickly bile water round my mouth several times, attempting to rid my tongue of the taste. The badness in my head making me physically ill. It is like I cannot harbour all these dark, morbid thoughts. Something must be done. Maybe I expel some of the bad through being sick, like when bad escapes through blood on cutting myself. I sense an improvement after being purged, not quite so much to handle in my mind.

My head seems to increase its weight and is relieved and calmed to be sinking into a pillow. After this, sleep does entice me; I allow rest to my fighting but tired body.

13th May

2008

Woke early, consumed with fear, drowning in my own frightened rigid body. Felt exceptionally tired but too afraid to attempt the climb into unconsciousness once again. Missed breakfast, drank coffee instead which was probably not the best for an unsettled stomach but the smell and taste too enticing.

After showering, I spent the rest of the morning writing. I also read things I had written about Mum: it helped me to remember them more clearly, tried to ease any picture of her, aside from death, into my mind. I liked re-living little anecdotal events, sometimes I can even hear what Mum said. Such a comfort.

I met a new patient; we are accumulating them. Her name is Esther and she is only twenty-one. She is very small, thin and shorter than me. She was smiley and chatty but emitted frequently a nervous laugh which perhaps betrayed her calm exterior. Her face was eager and I think she enjoyed talking to me. She followed me when I went to the kitchen so I made her tea and we talked some more. I know I'm not much older but I feel my life experiences have already equipped me to an extent to be in a place like this. The younger you are, the worse it must be.

Dad arrived at 4.30pm. He phoned earlier to say he was coming. I wanted to play table tennis but Dad insisted on a walk. He was annoyed that I hadn't been out today. I don't know why, I just didn't want to, couldn't face the real world. Apart from initial frustration, it was fine with Dad. We walked around the lake and he asked me what Dr. Floyd had said. Dad likes knowing definite dates and numbers so he must find this unknowing really tricky. I, conversely, don't mind. I hate planning. I'm far happier taking each day as it comes, see what happens next. We talk about anything: Ethan, Holly, Jack, sailing, anything to fill the silence.

After, I am left thinking that this meeting was good. Dad made the effort and I learned not to rise to unthoughtful remarks because it is only detrimental to the both of us. We kissed goodbye.

Holly comes in the evening. We sit outside talking. Holly looks very tired. I do still worry about her, especially with this new job but I just feel particularly useless for, what significant thing can I do to help from here?

Holly leaves and I feel anxiety slowly growing. I don't want a night like last night. I'm apprehensive about getting into bed. I turn my phone to silent and a wave of loneliness engulfs me. I feel depressed about certain friends. Some have been brilliant, others have ignored me completely. They don't return my calls, which are infrequent because it takes so much effort. I know I was useless at phoning when Mum was ill but now I do not have a mother to care for or to spend all my time with. I don't understand why I have become this object of avoidance. It makes me hate myself even more.

I know about the stigma of mental health but some of these friends are going to be doctors in the summer, graduates like I should be. Surely they cannot hold such prejudices? Perhaps they don't know what to say. People always find bereavement hard, but how can this be? We are taught. Doctors have to break bad news the entire time. I am not only bereaved but mad also, what a combination. However, by far, the worst thing to do, is nothing.

14th May

2007

Mum has a green folder that she told me to put under her bed, on the trunk so she can still reach it. She said not to open it or read it. This morning, as we were talking, me cross-legged on the floor, rubbing her feet, Mum says that she wants to ask me something. She tells me that, in the green folder are all the things she has written down for her funeral. She has been too unwell lately to add anything to her folder so she wants me to read through and help her to sort her notes into a proper order. Mum says am I feeling strong enough to do this with her now? Strength. That word keeps being said and yet it has little meaning to me. How do I know if I am being strong? I am doing what needs to be done and I am doing my absolute best to care for Mum. I love Mum so tremendously that I want to do everything possible for her to feel calm, unanxious and as contented as she can be under these trying circumstances. All this is driven by my unwavering, unchanging, absolute devotion to her. It doesn't make me weak or strong. It is just what happens. I didn't feel I would cry this morning and Mum wanted to arrange her funeral. If Mum asks for my help, then I shall gladly give it.

Talking about the funeral was not as I expected it to be. I can't contemplate Mum not being around, so planning her Order of Service was not as hard as I imagined. I was talking to Mum about it, so she's still here, I can still chat to her, just like we've done for years, everyday, amounting extortionate phone bills. I have no idea of what it may be like when Mum dies. My head cannot develop these thoughts, all it makes is a white space in my mind, a blankness, nothing. There is no life without Maisie.

We talk about music and flowers and hymns and poems and bible readings and venues and donations. I feel as though I am acting out a role. It is almost surreal. Mum is calm. We talk about the beautifully sad music she has chosen and that is when Mum sheds silent tears. I hold her hand. I feel like crying to show her I care, to show her how much she means to me, to show her how hard this all is, but, at that moment, I couldn't cry. There were no tears to come.

2008

I allow my mind a certain freedom. I want life. I do want to live and I think this might be real. I loved being a doctor, perhaps I can make it. Only a year Alice, well less than a year, nine months to go. Can you prepare yourself for August? I can envisage studying; I can imagine working. Strange feelings, an unsettling notion but nonetheless there and particularly prominent.

In the evening, everything went wrong. Living without Mum? Don't be so stupid Alice, you are weak and pathetic and won't last a day if you try to live. The badness encroached. I was spinning but too tired to maintain my balance. I slipped; I fell. Coffee jar wrapped in plastic bag; coffee jar hit on wooden bed post; coffee jar splintering in my hand. Shard is sliced across my hip but the glass isn't sufficiently sharp. Sawing, digging, depressingly pathetic: resulting mess of cuts and grazes. None of this seems right - plate spinning continues in my head.

15th May

2008

Woke at about 2am and 4am, absolutely petrified. Fell asleep again each time very quickly, though. Very groggy waking properly - 9am so absurdly late. Hurriedly dressed, cup of coffee, teeth cleaned and left at 9.30am to go to my clinical psychologist appointment in town.

Another good session with Rachel. I do like her and feel she understands me. Hard work talking for an hour but I did get through it. Said about intrusive thoughts and obsessive death images. Rachel already knows this as that is what the initial guy I saw said in his assessment. I feel secure in the knowledge that all the professionals are coming to the same conclusions.

Walked back via the sandwich shop to buy my tasty lunch as a reward. Still keeping headphones in as a precaution. Life is less intrusive and intense if I can use some of my concentration on music.

Signing in at reception, I am handed a note. It's from Lindsey. She is in the day unit today having a mole or something removed. Walking down to the ward, I meet her standing outside, stitched up. She says she is OK but wanted me to be there to hold her hand but I was too late. The sweet thing. It's all been very quick with no hanging around post-procedure. In honesty though, I was glad I did not have to return to the day unit. That was the ward I sat in with Mum for hours after her liver biopsy.

Lindsey also waggled a bandaged hand in front of me. She told the surgeon about her finger and asked if he could do a steroid injection at the same time. I looked alarmed and hoped Lindsey wasn't just going on my diagnosis but no, Lindsey said I was right, it was trigger finger. The palm injection, she says, was by far the most painful bit. I felt quite chuffed. I haven't forgotten all my medical knowledge.

Afternoon: review with Dr. Floyd. She thinks I am doing better, much more energy, enjoying things. I can see my future but before I saw it as something which could happen but I would be acting in a role. Now I can actually feel myself doing things, wanting to participate. Dr. Floyd thinks there are times still when I depersonalise. She says people can self harm when in this state because nothing seems real and by cutting, it reassures and proves you are real. I agree emphatically. Yes, that is right.

Dr. Floyd says I can have weekend leave and then we need a discharge plan. I say discharge next week. Dr. Floyd laughs and says that is perhaps too soon. Next week, maybe, she will give me a week's leave so I will have a further review and, therefore, talk to her again, just so she can be sure I am still heading in the right direction. Meds to stay the same but Dr. Floyd has added diazepam to take at 6pm. This should help with the derealised feeling, the racing nature of my thoughts, and will hopefully cease self harming because my worst times are in the evenings, especially when bed time approaches.

I see Ethan straight after my review. The generous thing has walked here, in the rain. He is soaking. We vaguely hit the table tennis ball back and forth whilst talking. Esther blunders in and is a sweetie but hovers in the room, getting in the way. Ethan and I talk to her and I am always so impressed with the ease that Ethan speaks to patients in here, some of which are quite ill.

Dad phones me to say he is coming after work. Usual annoying questions: "Where are you?" "Hospital" "Oh" How is that surprising?! "Why aren't you out?" "Because I've already been out" "Did you go home?" "No" "Oh" and more boring annoyance to follow.

Dad arrives and we head straight to the table tennis room. Activity is definitely a must. Dad is quite sweet. He asks about the review. He seems pleased that I am allowed out but asks what I'm going to do over weekend. I don't know, probably not so much. It's exhausting enough purely being at home. Dad halts the game; he looks tired. I'm doing this to him. I feel guilty. Sometimes I just wish everyone would stay away, have no involvement, then I would be unable to upset them. I want to be a lone ranger, then I could damage others no more.

Sophie's friend, Cara, is back again on the ward. Revolving door. She's got plasters on her forearms but the flesh you can see is mottled with scars, like someone's dropped pick-up sticks across her arms. She has been fairly quiet but always appears at the staff room requesting meds.

Aunty Beth phones after her dancing class and I update her on today's events. I then phone Ethan who has sent me such beautifully caring texts but with a distinct air of a psychotherapist and who follows with a postscript: "Be under no illusion that from now on you'll be experiencing a bombardment of psychological texts – I promise I will spare you of that!"

I stay outside until 11pm when they lock the doors. I feel a brewing unease in my stomach so pace around the garden, toes tingling in flip flops brushing against the newly mowed grass which is now wet and cold. I see Mum smiling at me. I smell her perfume.

Keep the routine, Alice: pyjamas, teeth, toilet, night light on. I wrap the blanket around me, tucking it in at my feet which are icy cold. I prop myself up on my elbows and submerge into my novel, forcing myself to read right up to the moment that my eyelids can no longer stay open. I place my book on the bedside cabinet, turn the clock to face me and click off the light, switch conveniently located an arm stretch away from my bed.

16th May

2008

Woke twice, each time in a state of terror. The first time, about 2am, I went for a wee; the second time, about 6am, I debated getting up but so drowsy, I managed to fall back to sleep until the more reasonable hour of 9am. Coffee, washed, dressed, meds quickly as I was given my blood forms and meds card, the latter to be handed into pharmacy so I could get my meds for the weekend. I then went to the main hospital to get my bloods done before 10am as it was a pre-dose lithium level.

Susie comes to talk to me about the police statement I am to give about Sabrina and the cannabis distribution. Dr. Floyd asked if I would give an account to the police as I am articulate but, mainly, because my perception casts a keen eye over the activities on the ward. Dr. Floyd says that, if I don't go back to medicine, then why not join the police? I have always been interested and I say I was working in psychiatric prison before I came home. I do find forensics fascinating.

Susie says they want to talk to me at the police station either Monday or Tuesday. Do I feel comfortable with this? Also, if possible, they want to see what I have written in my diaries about the whole debacle. Slightly unnerving having people read my words but Susie assures me it will only be sections specifically relating to the cannabis trading. A member of staff will come with me so I won't be doing it alone. To be honest, none of this fazes me. I do not mind talking to anyone about things which don't directly relate to me.

Susie says she hopes I enjoy my weekend at home but reminds me that, if I struggle, I can always come back. Alice, we are always here, ring if you need us. It is OK to do that. She knows I won't phone but, thank you, Susie, thank you for caring.

Just after lunch, meds arrive. I grab my rucksack of belongings, plug in my (well, Mum's) ipod and march home as, wearing too few clothes, I am chilly. I spend some time with Ethan, Holly pops in and then I shower, savouring the delicious jet of warm water. Ethan and I change, showing each other going out gear, before Grace and her sister, Liz, arrive.

Ethan walks me to the restaurant where all the hockey girls are having their end of season meal. It is superb to see them all again, my fabulous friends. I feel relaxed and at ease and I do offer some explanations to their questions but I don't feel pressured. We laugh lots as well. I enjoy myself enormously and giggle and relish the company.

We meet Ethan, Grace and Liz in a bar before heading elsewhere. I dance and dance, spinning and spinning, not wanting the feeling to leave, wishing I could stay in that smile of laughs and twirls. Don't stop the music please, instead stop the time, so I can capture a second which lasts an hour. Care free dancer I shall be, dance all the worries away. Death fled tonight. It could not intrude. It held no place. Life was the victor.

Home at 2.30am. Tom pours me a glass of water, then stumbles to bed. I carefully crack my tablets out of their blister packs and manage to swallow them despite wanting to ignore my medications all together tonight. I try to read but alcohol and tablets combined render me senseless. I sink an exhausted body into a wonderfully soft and cosy bed.

17th May

2008

Ethan comes into my room at 11am to check that I am OK – I was still asleep! This is terrible to say but I am so tempted to drink every night if it provides me with such decent rest. I still wasn't hung over though. I cannot ever remember a time when alcohol has made me ill the next day.

First chore of the weekend is to tidy my room. It is a complete mess of clothes and papers and books and shoes all in unhelpful mounds of mismatched items. It takes me over an hour but I do manage a reasonable order and my carpet can now be seen. The problem is, when I have limited leave, I just run and grab, failing to replace anything as it consumes valuable time.

Breakfast is a leisurely affair with papers spread. Fresh fruit, natural yoghurt, granary bread, fresh orange juice, all willingly eaten and deliciously tasting. I stay in the kitchen and cook some vegetarian meals for Holly, which I place in Tupperware boxes, enough for one meal, so she can freeze them. Because of her new job and odd hours (including evenings) she rarely finds time to cook properly. I wanted to do this for as a thank you. She has been so great with me in hospital.

The early evening, still bright outside, brought a drape of darkness upon me. I considered my medical career, my fascination with the human body, my amazement of its functions, my wonder and joy of being with patients, my being humbled by acting as a patient's confessional, they would disclose the most intimate details of their varied lives to me, only a trainee. Did I still want to do this? Did I still want to be a doctor? I know and can remember the positives, but my uncertainty blighted any enthusiastic thoughts.

I tried to bring to mind that initial decision, that university application which would determine the course of my life. When was that defining moment when I approached Mum and said this is what I want to do? I attempted to filter through the years, methodically working backwards. Surely there must have been an ascertainable moment, perhaps not some major event but maybe a smaller, almost insignificant occurrence. Not one was realised. I did not know. What does this mean?

May, I would be taking my final exams now, starting work as a House Officer in July. I would be Dr. Alice. I had emotions at opposite ends of the spectrum thwart me at the same time. I felt bombarded with no outlet, my own over-active mind was working too fast, I couldn't keep up. I was tiring but mentally I was speeding at an unsustainable pace.

Being possessed by confusion, I threw my wardrobe door open, hinges straining, and yanked clothes from their hangers and threw them onto my floor, shoe boxes and a mess of other belongings followed. Eventually, I found it. I thought they were hidden, still there, but I hadn't the nerve to check. I unwrapped the paper pharmacy bag and peered inside, Mum's morphine tablets glinted back at me. I slumped on the floor, handling my goodie bag like a greedy child unwilling to share their sweets. That bag, holding the near-certainty of death, wrapped me in a deep serenity. I felt safe, protected. The tablets nuzzled against me, my heart rate slowed and my mind calmed, focused purely on death. None of the other complications got in the way. Death was my companion. In dying, I would be cured.

18th May

2008

I did sleep without waking but dreamt I killed myself again. I was driving Mum's car, foot on the accelerator, faster and faster, engine growling under the speed until I steered myself directly into a concrete wall. The bonnet concertinaed but I was transported between car and wall and felt myself be flattened on the impact, a glass thin person peeling to the floor, dead.

Morning was spent re-sorting my washing, packing bag for hospital and speaking to Aunty Beth. Ethan and I jointly washed up and cleaned the kitchen. Dad had gone out walking and said to Holly he would be late so Ethan and I walked to her house together, me carrying my hospital necessities, Ethan clutching the food I cooked for Holly and the fresh bread I made this morning. Aunty Jane (Dad's sister) and Uncle Arnie arrived, then Dad, and we sat down to a delicious lunch, prepared by Holly.

I found this event OK, probably assisted by two glasses of wine and a particularly alcoholic dessert. I just felt sad with no Mum there. Dad was distant throughout and cold towards me when I said goodbye.

Back in hospital, the evening runs quickly away, night time meds, doors locked. I feel particularly awake and ask Adelle if I could speak with her. I tell her about my weekend and describe what I'm finding challenging at the moment, the extreme nature of my mood, the joys of Friday night and the depths of Saturday. It is hard to understand such a thing, let alone control it. It is the contrast that I find hard, how can I love life one moment then wish to eradicate it the next? Adelle is, as ever, willing to listen and help and reassure me that the fact I am able to enjoy myself sometimes is a definite positive.

Our conversation develops into easier territory and I find myself explaining why I want to go back to Medicine. Then, I feel more sedated, not so on edge and realness is apparent. I no longer wish to cut my arm. Adelle says to come and find her if I begin on that downward spiral. I definitely feel more secure in that knowledge. And I feel cared for, Adelle has that nurturing knack.

19th May

2008

Initially I couldn't get to sleep, kept reading another chapter of my book then trying again. Woke at some point every single hour. Exhausted, I dragged myself out of bed at 9am as no longer could bear being supine.

Dear Kelly from church turned up quite unexpectedly. She was clutching a bouquet of flowers, white, yellow and red, and gave me them along with an all-embracing hug. We sat down and it was delightful to talk; Kelly is ever such a patient and responsive listener. I am always impressed with the ease that people externally show when visiting me in here. Sweet Kelly has had her own share of difficulties, alcoholic ex-husband and the trial of endurance which entailed, but always treats me with such love and importance.

Holly arrives at lunch time, an hour with me before she goes to work. We go straight to the table tennis room and play for the first time in two or three weeks but it feels much longer. I'm shaking, though, which is more annoying than concerning. Getting a cup of water, I spill it over the floor, pausing between serves, my bat is trembling. I could still play but did feel distinctly uncoordinated. I could hit the ball with some degree of accuracy but my hands had a high frequency shake. Perhaps a resting tremor? This is where my knowledge desserts me. How can I play a sport needing steady hand and concentration when I can't even pour a drink? Holly beats me but not by much, I am improving.

After, we sit outside alone. Patients seem sparse. Holly hands me a letter that Mum wrote to Lindsey when I was six years old. Holly and Jack stayed weekends with us when we were little and there were problems even then, mainly surrounding Dad. Mum, in her caring way but not wishing to interfere, wrote a letter hoping to explain a few things to Lindsey. Dad was the same with whoever, he treated Ethan and I as equally as he did Holly and Jack. I suppose from an outsiders view, however, it may have appeared Dad showing favouritism to the children he lived with. This was not the case.

Mum knew Dad in most depth. She was attempting to explain some of his traits. Even then, almost nineteen years ago, Dad remained the same. Holly was ill one day and, apparently, Dad showed little care and responded thoughtlessly, upsetting Holly. Mum writes, "He [Dad] dislikes anything to do with illness and would never show concern unless it was terminal". This is what distressed me the most when Mum was dying, Dad didn't alter. He had made his stance and that was ignoring or dismissing anyone who was unwell. When it came down to it, the terminal nature did nothing to sway his opinion.

Mum was dying, I had Mum in tears, asking me why Dad was avoiding her, telling me that Dad didn't believe how ill she was, distressed in the knowledge that she was wrong about Dad, when things really mattered he wasn't there. It was devastating to see Mum's disappointment, her loss.

In the letter, Mum continued, "I tend to feel sorriest for myself when I'm ill. No one to fuss over me". I was only six years old and I already must have had some insight into how Mum was perceived. That is why I had to go home, that is why I had to stay with her, day after day, because I could not trust Dad to be with her for any length of time. I love my Mum so much and, aside from the suffering of disease, I could not let anyone add to that.

Mum's endurance tactics: "To survive life with John you have to be a strong, confident and fairly self-contained character...which is why I think I'm going under. The same seems to go for the children". There it is, the essence of why my relationship with Dad has plummeted. I am no longer strong but a weak, pathetic individual. My confidence disintegrated as soon as Mum died, I no longer knew what to do. I needed to be told decisions I could not make. Self-contained I certainly am not. I always kept quiet, allowed the wrongness to remain in me but I am told I should share, should disclose. I have said so many things which never before I would even have contemplated saying. So, there it is: my mother who possessed great insight into other people has diagnosed and explained once again. Dad, I am going under, Dad, I've already gone.

Dad phones me and I am filled with guilt and remorse as he is actually rather sweet and asks none of his seemingly rhetorical questions. He changes so much from one day to the next. I always feel so mean when Dad demonstrates care as I've said such hurtful things about him. I have a bath to calm down, soothe my mind rather than my muscles.

20th May

2008

A good, thorough night's sleep. I was up early, breakfasted, showered, dressed before 10am when Adam accompanied me, in a taxi, to the police station.

The woman who interviewed me was called Claire. I don't remember her rank but she had terrific people skills and a friendly but assuring manner. The recording room was prepared, tape, sound, all videoed which omitted the need for any notes to be written. Claire started by asking me about my course, perhaps medical student is a far more reliable witness than psychiatric inpatient! Then followed the expected questions where I said all I knew about Sabrina selling drugs to patients but of course had no proof. I had accurate dates, however, because they wanted to see my diary. I typed up all the relevant bits and they kept a copy. I said I smoked dope which was how I got involved and then considered if I really should have said this. I don't need anyone else, I incriminate myself as find it incredibly hard not to tell the truth, the lies end up tangling.

Claire wants to know how the situation arose initially. How do you sell drugs to patients? I did wonder about this. It all started before I was admitted but I did ask Fred. He said Sabrina had caught him with a joint one night so put it out and confiscated the drug. Later, Fred really wanted a smoke. He pleaded with Sabrina who gave him back the joint on the condition that he'd buy it from her next time. Thus, dealing was commenced.

I was probably only talking for forty-five minutes. It went fairly speedily and finished with the specifics: what type of cannabis? how much money? size of the lump in oxo cubes? other patients involved? etc. Job done, Adam and I waited outside for the taxi back to the hospital. I was glad Adam came with me.

Lunch time came and went with little upset. I then had a surprise visit from the vicar and his wife who had such an air of quiet calm. They are ever so caring and unfazed by difficult circumstances. We sat and talked and then they prayed for me. I felt distinctly tranquil.

Lawrence arrived a while later, having been on ITU in the main hospital in his chaplaincy role. As always, a joy to see him. I have had such a spiritual day!

Dad phoned and said he could come at 5.30pm if that was OK with me. I said yes. He arrived and we went to play table tennis. We didn't engage in a game, just a knock-a-bout but, for some reason, the repetitive nature helped us to talk. Dad was gentle with his tongue. He seemed genuinely interested in me and how I was doing. We talked about things happening now, not seeking desperate topics on which to make comments. It wasn't awkward to be with him. I didn't feel edgy or concerned. While I couldn't tell Dad any plans (Dad likes to know, except I don't have the answers), I could explain how I am better than before and Dad listened instead of rebuking me. This was a good time; I saw Dad's potential gentleness.

Dad left to go to some meeting and I sat on the hard lino floor in my room. I felt dreadful. I've said such horrible things about Dad; I've hated so many of his actions. I've seen the worst in him and, at those times, not even contemplated any of the good. I am such a vile, hate-filled person. And now, I am a mess of confusion. I don't understand. Dad can be nice and obviously does care so why, in the main, does he act in a dismissive, detrimental manner? I don't know, I can't untangle the muddle and, now, I don't know what to do, where to go, how to act.

The all too familiar self-loathing descended like a sheet smothering me. I wanted to strike out, slash my own hideous monster, destroy part of my body to end the blackness, for some bad to be taken away. I remained sitting and smacked the back of my head against the wall. Bang, bang, gone.

21st May

2007

Mum in tears and all fretful. It has gone 1pm and bathing and dressing has taken so long as Mum needing frequent rests on the bed to renew her. She is sobbing and repeating how she just won't be able to make her appointment with Dr. Mayhew tomorrow. She won't be able to manage. I tell her it doesn't matter. I tell her I shall phone him. I try and prevent her from panicking.

I telephone and cancel the appointment and ask if he could phone me instead. The secretary seems dubious and says he should really speak to Mum. I explain how poorly she is and how she wants me to ask all the questions. Patient confidentiality is escalating to ridiculous proportions. All the same happened when Holly was ill. They would only speak to the patient. What has happened to taking charge and caring for someone else?

2008

After lunch, I see Stephen, the chaplain, and have a chat. He is pleased and thankful that I am improving. I also see poor Maureen who is in a state. She was so irate this morning that the staff pinned her down for an injection and she could be heard hollering a variety of obscenities inbetween heaving sobs. Everything went quiet so she finally had some rest. Awake now, her eyes are red and hugely puffy, narrowed to small slits. I do pray she has a better afternoon.

Restless on the ward, I embark on a two hour hike, weaving through the fields, walking as fast as appears sensible. I look at the wildlife and plants and trees and squirrels and appreciate the wonderful world. I phone Sasha and Sarah and talk excitably and at length to both, my concerned, supportive friends. I arrive back at hospital refreshed and jolly.

I am suddenly taken by the too real unreality. The bad fills my head and I am trapped inside, a prisoner of my mind. I am a hostage within. I look at my hands, there but not mine. I am not attached; I have been taken. My pen won't write, the connection has been broken. I want to hurt myself, fight against the badness. Subconsciously, I have been scratching, deep and repetitive, a burn on my skin, blood smeared. I want to die. Overwhelming desire for death. Die now Alice, die now.

My diary sits open at my desk, mocking me. I want to rip, tear, destroy. My hands shake and will not cease. I throw my cup of coffee instead, soaking the paper pages, saturated black. The mug clatters to the floor. Walking is a feat. One foot in front of the other, my legs are not mine, I am not me. I stumble out of my room and encounter Susie who scoops me up and takes me outside. I cannot stand, a fidgety walk in a metre square. My words are coherent but senseless. I don't know what I'm saying. Is Susie real? She is there but her voice is distorted. I can't think. I hear the questions but my head cannot distinguish the meaning.

Susie leads me into the kitchen where we gather armfuls of paper towels and then to my room where we mop up the mess. Susie calmly sits me on my bed. My head is agony; the hurt is blinding. Susie says this is when it is especially hard, when I am depersonalised. She hugs me. She knows physical contact is beneficial. Exhausted, I fall into her. The silent tears come. My head is unrelenting and I am too tired to follow the unpredictable paths. The weight of the pain in my head is too much.

Susie explains that, in my world of unreality is when I am most dangerous. I want to kill myself now, wherever, however, anything to stop my vile mind. Torturing oneself, the only way to cease is always death. I am the torturer, it comes from within me, therefore I must be obliterated. I don't have the concentration or sensibilities to find out how to commit suicide in here. It takes thought, time and planning, none of which I possess.

Susie takes me to the meds room and disinfects my arm before plastering me up. I wash my hands, get the blood from my nails, but I cannot feel the water, only watch. I do not know if it is hot or cold. All I see is the pink tinged stream falling from my fingers. I am given more diazepam to slow down the unrelenting, racing, ill-controlled thoughts in my head. Please, just a little rest before flooring exhaustion takes place. Help.

I was given extra sleeping tablets. I fussed around my room, avoiding going to bed, scared of the horrors that await when I am so vulnerable and unable to fight. My body finally won the battle and could function no more, buckling at activity.

22nd May

2007

Dr. Mayhew phones. He is very good and understanding. He increases Mum's morphine: she shouldn't be in pain. He tells me to phone back with any problems or concerns. I say thank you and he apologises. He says he is sorry that he couldn't have helped more. He is sorry that the chemotherapy had no effect. He is sorry that he can offer no more treatment. That must be such a hard thing for a doctor to do. I say thank you again. I know he tried all he knew how. It is not his fault. And that is what this horrid affair comes down to. There is no fault. There is no one at blame. I nor Mum look for anyone responsible. Things just happen. All there is, is a debilitating sadness. Nothing more.

In the afternoon, Lawrence comes round to see Mum. He asks if he can pray with her. This is amazing: Mum says yes! We sit either side of Mum and hold a hand each. Lawrence says some lovely words and has the right phrasing. He does not ramble, like me, and asks God for all the appropriate things that Mum wants. She has not been wishing or placing hope in a miracle, she just wants the strength to be able to cope and, physically, to be comfortable. She wants to be calm and not afraid of dying. Lawrence asks all these things and prays for God's protection over her.

Maisie is crying by the end. I bury my head in her lap as I begin to cry. Mum has been the best demonstration to me of how a Christian should lead their life. Perhaps unknowingly, she has taught me so many lessons directly from the bible and she, herself, is just such a wonderful example. She is a person who I can only dream of becoming half as good. She has led such a selfless, caring life. How can someone teach me such fundamental Christian beliefs without being saved herself? I know you're hearing this God; please lift her up in your arms. My marvellous Maisie, please fill her with your strength.

2008

Awoke feeling lousy after several frightening awakenings. Considered phoning in sick to the clinical psychologist as couldn't face the half hour walk followed by the draining interrogation.

I did go to see Rachel (psychologist). The fresh air invigorated me and, actually, the hour went swiftly as wasn't too mentally tiring. We spoke at length about depersonalisation and perhaps more safe ways to test reality ie anything other than cutting myself.

As soon as my bag is thrown in my room, Roy collects me for my review. I was feeling much better at this juncture and could sense the rising excitement of departure. We discuss last night which I am slightly apprehensive about. I don't wish for one incident to mar my whole profile. Dr. Floyd feels moments like those I am still most dangerous so will increase my diazepam, lunch time, tea time and night time, so I receive a sustained effect. Otherwise, Dr. Floyd is pleased with me. I still get racing thoughts but this is during a distinctly low mood. I feel horrific at these moments. Dr. Floyd was ensuring I wasn't going manic due to high dose antidepressants. I'm pretty confident I'm not bipolar, however, would I have sufficient awareness if I was?

Good news, I am going home. Dr. Floyd wants to keep the other medications stable but I am not to be discharged just yet. She gives me a long weekend leave (Thursday to Tuesday due to the Bank Holiday) and says she will see me on Tuesday and we can discuss discharge then. Thank you Dr. Floyd.

I skip out of the room. I conclude that I am certainly better. I can enjoy enjoyment rather than tell myself what enjoyment is. There are still the occasional bad times but Dr. Floyd tells me that this is to be expected, it is how I manage these that is important. Be patient, Alice, everything takes time, give your body a break from insistence. Eventually, my mind dominating phases should go. I will be left alone. Dr. Floyd tells me one step at a time, Alice; Mum told me I always tried to run before I could walk.

Afternoon spent hanging around for my leave meds which didn't arrive until 5pm. Rich and I spent probably two hours, on and off, playing table tennis, a brilliant past time: engaging, fun and physical outbursts channelled into the ball. That is one thing I will miss, being on the outside.

I carefully pack my bag, using every available pouch and cranny to stuff the odd sock or slide down a bottle of shampoo. I still end up with bulging rucksack and two carrier bags balancing me, one in either hand. I am given enough regular meds for the five days but only two extra diazepam (one day's worth) as they still don't trust me, my record with drugs isn't perhaps the greatest.

I arrive home, hot, sweaty and with aching arms. My fitness has plummeted living in hospital. This does not bode well. I soon am changing into hockey gear as the girls have asked me to play in summer league. They laugh at me as the only time I have run in these last months is away from nurses! I manage though, fifty minutes pitch time, exhausted but amazed at my ability to still play, if badly. I was just pleased I could run and sustain the speed!

Going home, I feel my big toe throbbing in my shoe. I know even before I look that my foot will be bloody. My sock is red and I peel it back revealing a cracked toe nail, only still attached by a few millimetres. Mum always said hockey was such a rough game and despaired at my passion despite a string of injuries: broken bones, torn ligaments, stitches etc. When Mum was at school she was always picked last for, whenever a ball came near, she used to run away! If there were too many players, she would be relegated to the edge of the field to hit a ball with her equally hockey-phobic cousin. Mum never did understand how I enjoyed such a thing.

Tonight, a satisfied lethargy filled me. I was in that pleasant state where physically I was tired but in a good way. I had achieved something. My body ached with a bed awaiting longing. I slid into my room, familiarity soaking the atmosphere. My bedroom for sixteen years.

On my bedside table there are two small, double photo frames. The first has passport photos: Mum and me, Aunty Beth and Mum in the seventies; the second, chopped photos: Mum as a baby in her Granddad's arms, me as a baby in Granny's arms. I always look at these before I turn out the light. Daft sentimentality but I look at Mum nonetheless, grinning back, an exquisite eye smile, my sensational mother.

23rd May

2007

Terrifically hard day. Mum so lethargic that getting her to the toilet was a supreme effort on her behalf. She was hanging onto me, with her shrunken legs, quivering below and her neck desperately trying to support a lolling head. Most of the day she was too tired to open her eyes. Exhaustion consumed her.

Mid-afternoon I attempted a quick flannel wash in bed. Mum made a valiant attempt but, even rolling from one side to the other, swallowed all her energy and exacerbated her pain. Cleaning teeth in a cup had to wait until Mum had recovered.

The Hospice was again mentioned today. I recoiled at the word which I immediately rebuked myself for. Hospices are wonderful places full of admirably caring staff. I feel my brief stint working in one last year equips me to have reasonable insight. But, it makes no difference. I want Maisie at home with me. Mum said today that, ideally, she doesn't want to go. She much prefers the home comforts (however limited now), the familiarity, the routine, her own belongings, the surroundings we've lived in for fifteen years and the family at home, me looking after her. Please don't deny her this. Please don't take that away. I don't want to let my Maisie down.

I had been sitting with Mum all day, either by her feet or sprawled on the floor, reading her letters and emails, talking to her. The entire day she had been fretful, a string of panics from one anxiety to the next: each I took and tried to assuage her fears. Although I eventually calmed her, I knew it wasn't enough. She was never peaceful.

By 7pm, Dad and Ethan were both home. I needed to pop out on various errands and, in truth, the fresh air of outside was so enticing. I felt as if I needed to leave the house to prevent me being suffocated from within. I know I should want to be with Mum at all times, and I do, but sometimes I also experience a powerful need for escape. It is only ever a short while. Is this very bad of me? Should I not be feeling this way?

I wish I could do better because then tonight, the guilt was all too evident. Within ten minutes of leaving the house, Ethan phoned me saying Mum was panicking and desperate to talk to me. I spoke to her and her voice was wobbly. She was in a mess. She felt frightened. She didn't know what to do. Where was I? Why wasn't I with her? I talked to her softly. Whether this effect was transmitted over a mobile phone, I don't know. I asked Ethan to sit with her and, five minutes later, I was back home, rubbing Mum's feet.

There is very little I can do practically but now my presence is a comfort in its own right. I have become Mum's safety blanket. The words I offer could be said by anyone but it does make a difference. It is me Mum wants. I look at her longingly and realise that our feelings towards one another are mutual. She has always been my comforter, my safe place, my rest. No-one else can fulfil that specialness. Her radiating love and affection is all consuming. This is how I know that, when she is gone, the world will seem a much darker and terrifying place. It will, of course, be the same, for this world is a tumble of atrocities, but I will no longer have my devoted comforter. I will be left all alone, in the dark.

2008

Had a slip up today in the supermarket. Grace drove Ethan and me as, still being classed as an inpatient, I am uninsured to drive. I was able, in the first half an hour, to cope with the blinding strip lights, bustle of shoppers, rattle of trolleys, hum of fridges, every colour, shape, size of item, the nauseating variety of products, but then, without warning, the mass of senses caught me and I was trapped, trapped inside a body which was not real and was not mine, trapped down an aisle which was a distant interpretation of how it should be, trapped and I did not know the exit.

I hung onto the trolley, I know that. I could see a pair of hands which looked like mine, wrapped around the metal bar with some plastic advertising. I could see them holding fast, prominent knuckles. Everything: people, objects, sounds, were too close, too near, and yet remote because I was not part of this snapshot of living, this moment in time, I had been taken away.

I did recover, a while (ten minutes?) later. Slowly, reality oozed into my body, like hair gradually saturated in the rain.

24th May

2007

Despite increased morphine, Mum still in pain. She either screams out or emits a pitiful whimpering sound which strains my entire body. There is not much I can do. I watch her rigid body, hands clutching at stomach. I didn't think it would be like this. It is not supposed to be like this. Mum shouldn't be in this much pain. That's what all the doctors said; that is what I said. And yet, the agony is all too apparent.

Watching another person suffer is, I'm certain, by far the most mentally anguishing activity. Seeing Maisie like this makes me feel pushed almost entirely to the edge of my emotional capacity, as if one more whimper, one more scream, will throw me completely into a quivering wreck. I want the pain instead. Please take it away from undeserving little Maisie. I am her willing recipient, give it all to me.

2008

Bad dream. In an act of suicide, I chopped off my left hand at the wrist. I was left with a bloody stump. I wanted to crawl into a dark space, maybe a cave. I would die by the rich, redness, drowning in my own blood, but I continued to walk, just walking, arm dangling. It was almost as if I couldn't stop.

Next episode in this horror story, some unidentifiable person put me in the passenger seat of their car. All they could say to me and repeat was, "You can't be a doctor with no left hand because you can't take blood". Why this should matter when I wanted to die is as equally bizarre as the dream itself. Morbid nightmares still dominating.

Today I fulfilled a cliché spectacularly: freedom is when you are on a bike. I decided this after jumping on mine and cycling. There was no plan or route or destination. I took a road and followed its tarmaced surface until a direction choice had to be made. Left or right it mattered not. This was liberation instead of enclosure. I and my mind were fleeing with the wind. Escapism.

Dad left in the afternoon for the airport – a week in Seattle for a conference. Ethan and I have the house to ourselves.

25th May

2008

Unsure what possessed me but had to go for another bike ride this morning. The rain was crashing down accompanied by terrific winds that, at points, it felt like hail on my bare face and hands. The very edge of roads always collect the water and I was streaming through, a soaking from all angles. The rain hurt so my eyes were just perceptibly open but, head bowed, I saw very little.

Arriving home, half an hour later, conditions getting the better of me, I walked through the garage. My trousers were so wet they didn't feel there, stuck fast like tights to the contours of my legs. My top was peeled off, even t-shirt, bra and pants were saturated. I slapped into the house and swiftly to the bathroom where a delicious hot shower awaited.

The afternoon brought a selection of Mum's closest friends to our house. They were all brilliant with Mum and have been so kind to me. Ethan and I wanted to say thank you so we had a tea party!

I knew this would be a lot for me to take in, especially as I was "hosting" however laid back the atmosphere. I had diazepam before people arrived and I did manage well. I could talk to everyone as I circumnavigated the room, there were no moments of dissociation. I was real, the people were real, the house was real, and, I had a lovely time. Ethan and I are exceptionally blessed to have such mother figures: good fun and terribly caring.

The evening was more of a struggle. I felt myself slipping. Mum's friends had all gone but Holly and a few of Ethan's friends remained. I felt I was mute but performing the necessary physical tasks of engagement: nodding, eye movement etc. My attention was escaping and I could not remain. Be practical, Alice. I cleared, washed up, tidied, hopefully not in an annoying way. People got progressively drunk and they were the hardest to converse with. I only had two (slowly sipped) glasses of wine so did not compete with their high spirits.

At all stages there are temptations. I had choices. By drinking more, and quickly, this distance from others would decrease as alcohol would lessen my perception, my notice of every single detail. I would calm. More diazepam? Get hooked on prescription drugs? How about illegal drugs? Cocaine was being snorted off the kitchen table. Join in, Alice, get wasted and forget. Life is just one decision to the next.

The socialising became unbearable. I put the kettle on, made coffee and holed myself up in my room, door ajar to keep an ear out just incase something went amiss, alcohol and drugs never being the best combination. I had to be away, be alone, be on the floor, something solid, just be.

26th May

2007

Mum very weak today. She stays in bed until 4pm when she valiantly agrees to attempt a bath. I help her into the bubbles and her tiny body disappears beneath the surface. I cradle her head; she lies back and shuts her eyes. No hair wash today, the effort is too extreme. I kneel beside her, dip my arm in the water and stroke the back of her hand. She likes to feel my presence; it makes her feel safe. She still has visions of sinking beneath the water's surface and being unable to haul herself out.

Mum stays there until the water turns lukewarm and she starts to feel cold. I help her out, wrap the towel around and she staggers to the bed, whereupon she collapses on it, her body half sprawled across the towel. She is little and naked and utterly helpless. I gently rub her dry then drape the dressing gown over her. Her eyes are closed. She is too physically exhausted to even be able to open them.

Then comes the horrific pain. Mum grasps at her stomach and wails. Her body writhes, attempting to find a position to ease the crippling agony. She screws up her eyes, her face contorted, her desperate grimace reflecting the internal suffering. I decant oromorph into a syringe and give it to her. There is no effect. I repeat the dose: she is still in distress. I give lorazepam to calm her. Pain induces anxiety but Mum is barely aware of what I'm telling her to swallow. She is desperate. She wants me to give her enough morphine so that she'll become unconscious and never wake up. She wants me to kill her. And in that split second of chaotic madness, I want to do what she wants. What am I doing? What am I thinking? With shaking hand, I stroke her legs and tell her that she'll be OK in a minute. Hang in there Maisie, you'll be OK.

I sit there for over an hour, my heart racing. Mum quickly calmed and soon was asleep, the drugs committing her to a deep slumber, not easily awakened. But, I have to run. What was I thinking?

I get outside into the woods and gulp in the fresh air. I feel I've been almost suffocated. How could I even have contemplated killing her? And yet it was what she wanted. I imagine a suicide pact, except it is unbeknownst to Mum that I want to die. We both drink down the morphine and say goodbye. There is nothing left for Mum and, without Mum, there is nothing left for me. But, Maisie, I can't do that to you. You are my most wonderful Mother and friend. This is the only thing that you ask of me which I cannot do. I am petrified, that fleeting moment, when I felt I could kill you, will haunt me for a long time. The day I wanted to kill my Mother. What monster have I become?

I phone Mog. I know I shouldn't bother her but I do not know what else to do. She talks to me for a long time. She thinks I've taken on too much. But, even if I was willing to delegate, who to? Mog always makes me more sensible, so I go home.

Mum is still fast asleep; Dad is nowhere to be seen. He hasn't woken Mum to take her tablets. Everything is all very late. Why did I leave? It falls apart when I'm not here. I should have stayed at home. I gently rouse Mum and she launches into a confused monologue of rhetorical questions. She is all muddled but laughs her way through, intermittently repeating that she isn't confused.

I don't understand what she is telling me. She can talk but all sense is lost. My efforts to decipher her words, dissolve into fits of giggles. I can't speak for laughing and Mum joins in. Except, it isn't funny. I'm laughing and I don't comprehend why. I start crying. The sensation of both emotions together is bizarre. Mummy, it is so hard to see you like this.

Just before I put Mum to bed, she is suddenly sick, just a tiny amount, but she retches a lot and feels rather dreadful. It passes but leaves behind anxiety, trepidation that she will be sick again. Mum is too scared to go to sleep now – the dread of waking and immediately being sick is too fearful. I just sit with her, stroking her arm with my one finger, an almost imperceptible touch. Mum doesn't like physical contact when she is nauseous.

I begin to feel lonely. This is what no one can see. No one knows about this. Everyone sees the practical side of care, not the actual love. Even Dad and Ethan can't know what this is like. I am the only one who sits with Mum for hours, watching her. It is such a solitary activity that my thoughts run in a continual stream in my head, almost like observing a film from a distance. Time doesn't behave in its normal dimensions. Its speed undulates, as if it has been warped. Is that what overwhelming care for someone does? Or is it the deafening silence of solitude?

2008

A black day. The dark, depressing weather reflected my own self, inside, protected from the wind and rain, lashing at the window. Was I suicidal? I knew I wouldn't attempt anything but did I feel that death is what I wanted? It was an option, certainly. When you enter into this state, it is as if your entire consciousness shifts beneath what you imagine is the lowest point possible. This fundamental alteration causes life to feel very different, my eyes no longer see the world as it is. Happiness is a sensation that only others can experience, and even that is fake. It is as if I hold the only key and am alone in realising the falsity of the world, a secret no one else has discovered.

My struggle through the hours culminated at bed time. I turned off the light but could not close my eyes. I stared into the blackness and my room became dark and scary. A frightened child. What of? Monsters under the bed? Ghosts behind the curtain? No, only myself and the blackness inside. I wanted my hospital room back, never dark only dimly grey, light streamed through the door, outdoor lights illuminated the windows. Everything could always be seen. I wanted to be severed from reality, slip into unconsciousness, but my eyes remained firmly open, eyelids refused to obey.

27th May

2007

  I wash Mum's hair. She gets out of the bath and sits on her bed. I ruffle her short crop through my fingers and wave the hairdryer above. Mum doesn't like her short hair but I think she has the most beautiful head which was concealed before. Her hair tapers into a delightfully sweet point at the nape. It is lovely to touch.

  Mum is tired, however. Her head gently falls towards me. She leans on my chest, her weary body needing rest. And our roles are fully reversed. I cradle her, Maisie's head lying in the crevice between my breasts. This is such a maternal position. A mother wrapping you up is the safest place in the world. Except, I am the daughter. I want to protect you so much Ma. I don't want you to be scared. Seek comfort within my enveloping arms. I will never let you go.

2008

  Lily pops in mid-morning, arm in cuff, broken collar bone after falling off her bike. Poor thing. She tells me I now really will be rather helpful in the surgery as she has only one functioning arm, thankfully the right. I do get excited at this prospect. Seeing patients, once again isn't so daunting. Lily has sorted a placement for me, including a project I can do.

  I cycle to the psychiatric unit at lunch time. I have an appointment with Dr. Floyd at 2pm. I have no belongings bar keys, money and bike lock. I enter with the distinct air of never being admitted again.

  On the ward, I see Sharon and give her a hug. She is in again after slashing her wrist and then refusing to go to A+E with the paramedics. All the usual suspects remain: Maureen yelling, Audrey sleeping against the vending machine, Duncan swearing, Felicity preening, Ann cackling, Gloria floating, Scott impersonating cartoon characters. I find Rich and his face lights up, a cheerful baby smile. We run to the table tennis room and are away.

  Dr. Floyd opens the door, perhaps an hour later. "Alice, I've been trying to find you" and then, "Why didn't I check in here first?"

and teases me about this ward table tennis obsession. We talk, I am doing better, still up and down over the weekend but, on the whole, the very bad times are becoming less frequent. Self harm? Dr. Floyd looks at my elbow which I sheepishly have to admit was a hockey injury. She smiles and writes some more in my notes.

Alice, you need to pace yourself, take it easy, don't do everything all at once. If you expand so much energy, the rebound effect is tiredness. I do not want you so tired that you become suicidal and then end up back in here. I do not want to see you crash. I understand, Dr. Floyd. Don't be tempted by drugs, post-cocaine depression is the hardest to treat. No, Dr. Floyd, I won't. This is the truth, I have an inability to lie to her.

Please can I drive now? Eyebrows raised, you better not be wanting to crash the car. Is driving absolutely necessary? Yes! Why? So I can get to Lily's and help her. You are planning on going back to the placement, when? Tomorrow. Alice!! What happened to gradually acclimatising? Lily has broken her clavicle so may need me. Hang on, you want to be able to use your car so you can drive Lily to house calls then you both see the patients? Something like that. I think Dr. Floyd is thinking we are the terrible twosome. Not terrible but symbiotic, I like to think. A pause. Only do half days with Lily for the moment and you can drive next week, leave it for seven days, Alice. OK, Dr. Floyd, thank you.

You want to be discharged now? What about until Thursday at review? NO! Please, I don't want to stay another night. OK Alice, I'll discharge you, follow up with me in four weeks, CPN visit within 72 hours. Compliance Alice. Yes Dr. Read, for sure.

I leave beaming, not actually dancing but feel I should be, they might drag be back in though. Dr. Floyd gave me my prescription and looked at me sternly as it is for two weeks. Alice, can I trust you? Yes, well, I think so. Scary prospect, especially now I have the green piece of paper in my hand. No overdosing, Alice, you can do this. It is that shiver of temptation that still grips me; it needs subduing.

Cycling back, it played like a mantra in my mind, "No overdosing, no overdosing". The pharmacy was reached, the meds dispensed in their colourful boxes. I got home and carefully unwrapped them, placing each drug in the draw of my bedside table.

28th May

2007

At bedtime, Mum can no longer stay awake to read. I always go in to check on her about half an hour after she has taken her temazepam but, she is fast asleep - her book open the page she started on, bedside lamp switched on, glasses slipping down her nose. I try and rectify all these without waking her. She must have read the same opening chapter for the past several nights.

Mum and I decided that maybe poetry would be better – poems are much shorter! Except, even these are now unmanageable, so I have started reading to her. Bedtime story: it's a very calming end to the day.

2008

Little sleep last night due to cracking thunder and eye straining lightning. It felt like the entire house had been captured and shook and compressed with each throw of nature. Being in the attic room, I felt special, closer to this inspiring weather. I did as I used to do as a child and scrambled upon my desk, face as close to my sloping window as I would dare. It was like a fireworks display but better, more dramatic and mesmerising. The storm had caught me too.

Lily's surgery in the morning. I cycled, thankfully the rain had ceased leaving only puddles as if to prove it was there for the skies had cleared. The staff, all women bar one male doctor, are compassionate and offer me warm smiles and hugs. And then: the patients. No dramatic first moment, no apprehension, in fact, I was confident. I sat beside Lily (arm in sling) and listened attentively. Patients capture my attentions. I did blood pressure and stethoscope stuff (heart, lungs etc) because these are tricky with only one hand. I could translate a patient's words into the doctors' jargon. Despite fuzzy knowledge lingering in my brain, I did understand. Perhaps four years of study do not just disappear.

I didn't wobble as such, I kept my calm, hopefully encouraging, composure but perhaps it reinforced my vulnerability. Obtaining a family history from a woman, she told me her mother died aged fifty-four of cancer and she had TB as a teenager. I think this took me by surprise. I didn't feel tearful or run to escape, but the similarities caught my overactive senses. Mum was three weeks shy of her 54th birthday; she had TB aged thirteen. This was ridiculous. One in three people die of cancer, many have had TB. I was drawing comparisons which weren't there. The moment passed; I asked her about her Dad instead.

I did OK. I was fine, it was my brain that was over-analysing. Perhaps it will be beneficial that they never found the type of cancer that Mum died from, even though I have my suspicions. I won't be able to identify with others quite so readily, a talent I shall need in order to stay sane in the world of the sick.

A few bits of minor surgery were next: a cyst in the lower breast and a fungal infection in a big toe where some of the skin surrounding the nail had calloused and needed removing. I got to inject the anaesthetic, sliding the small needle in and then watch as the skin swelled into a bubble. I can do this. Unsure as to where my boldness came from today, but the session was complete. After so many months and years of practical placements, a few hours appeared pathetic but I knew, for me, it was quite enough.

29th May

2008

Usual clinical psychologist appointment in the morning. Rachel is lovely but I'm quite tempted to stop going. When I was in hospital, seeing Rachel was a relief, a chance to get off the ward, witness a different environment. But now, I think I'm finding it slightly boring. Talking about oneself can be so tiresome.

Francis, my CPN, saw me in the afternoon (72 hours follow up) and sees I'm managing, coping at home, so doesn't stay for long.

Hockey in the evening was enjoyable. I was absolutely exhausted, lack of fitness catching me once again, but I played better. It is as if my brain needs to teach my body how to perform the skills once again. They are there, just need to be coaxed out, persuaded into a real life action.

30th May

2008

Odd simultaneous hot/cold sensation again this evening. It made me irritable. I snapped at Ethan. I took some diazepam, which I now only seem to take when I need it rather than every afternoon. I was on 10mg a day but some days I've managed with none. The last thing I want is a benzo addiction just as I start back at university. I had to confirm I was taking up my place today, only an email but there was a decisive air about it. Dear the Dean, I will be commencing 5th year in August. Purely writing it increases my heartbeat and blurs the letters as if all of this is not real.

I still have moments of complete stillness, the feeling when you inhale and leave the air in your lungs. I laugh at myself, Alice, this is ludicrous, you think you will be able to cope on your course without Mum and after all you've seen? I'm setting myself up for a spectacular crash in Newcastle. Patients will run from you, Alice, and that is not fair on them. What are you thinking? I don't know, I'm being pulled along by that unknown force which insists on dragging me with it.

Today, I played the piano for the first time since Mum died. Daft sentimentalities but I felt like crying. Mum's choir music was still laid out across the top of the piano, her carefully sharpened pencils for annotations, the box of tissues she thought great as the cardboard background was white with black silhouettes of musicians playing various instruments.

I used to play the piano for Mum so she could learn her part, alto always alto. I loved listening to Mum sing. When I was younger and went to her concerts, I always told Ma that I could hear her. I couldn't but managed to convince myself I could because I studied her face, her mouth and willed my ears to detect her voice. Mum always laughed and said it was a bad thing if I could hear her – it probably meant she was out of tune! Choirs are one voice.

I played the duets we used to sing together but couldn't sing, my voice cracked like a pubescent boy. I made mistakes, fingers out of practice, concentration flitting from the sheet music to my hands to Mum's presence to the right of me, just behind my shoulder, where she used to stand. I was locked in. I couldn't turn around, of course there was no one there, but an eeriness kept me rigid. I banged out the notes until the spell was broken and I was set free. I ran from the piano and panted at the sink, running the tap for really cold water.

31st May

2007

Argument between Dad and Ethan this evening. I try to dissipate it as this upsets Mum terribly. I attempt to reason with Dad.

I do feel he is being pedantic and unnecessarily fussy with Ethan. Except, Dad will not listen to my attempts. I cannot quell the unrest within him. He turns his back then suddenly faces me and yells, "Do not tell me what to do. This is my bloody house." I have no response. The sadness I am filled with physically weakens me.

Consciously, the thoughts this induces, are presented in my mind, not with startling clarity but not with confusion either. The thoughts aren't in order, but they are not muddled up. They appear one after the other, as if a pre-programmed slide show. I never wanted to come and live here again after leaving and always wanted to save Mum from here. Of course, I always did come, too often probably, according to Dad, but I needed to be here for Mum. However unhappy I felt, it would always be overcome by the wonderful happiness of being with Maisie. No matter how dire the situation, Mum and I could cope together, precisely because we had each other.

But what now? I have the unenviable realisation that, without Maisie, home is not the place I will want to be. I see myself, dutifully paying my Father visits but making them fleetingly brief. They are duty bound occasions and this makes me squirm inside. I despise the thought of doing what is right and not because I want to do it. I hate that it will be a chore.

Most of all, I hate myself. I hate my sliding relationship with my Father. I hate the way I have so obviously disappointed him. I hate that I cannot find a way for him to talk to me about important things. I hate that I have little patience for him. I hate myself for expecting and longing for more from him. I shouldn't want to change other people, I should want to change myself for the better. Perhaps I need to be stronger. Dad sees how I dote over Mum. He sees only a fraction of what I do for her and all his eyes show is how pathetic he thinks I am. I am not strong enough to keep the powerful feelings of abundant love for my Mother hidden within me, they escape with each movement I make, but, for this, I am unashamed. Love for Maisie conquers everything.

2008

Awoke very late which Lily thought was good – get my rest, get my sleep. I went straight to the kitchen and baked bread for Lily. It is a privilege to be able to cook, make food which you have chosen, you like, handle the ingredients, appreciate how the finished dish arose. Hospital food wasn't inedible but, slopped on your plate, holding very little aesthetic value, it was rather tedious and too similar for a lengthy stay. Bland tasting but holding alarmingly bright colours, reminiscent of childhood food colouring days.

Lily gave me a folder of contact details for the patients I am going to follow up: this is to be my placement project. I handle the documents with almost too much care, a delicate object to which I have been put in charge. I have started back, studying to commence today.

Late afternoon, I developed a full body tremble. Thoughts of everything flashing and combining, subjects linking which had no connection, faster and faster, not just images but complete with their own sounds and smells and actions. My external surroundings became my tormentor, hideously bright colours, edges too sharp, sounds resonating, my head painfully sensitive. I was screaming but no noise could be heard. I split the diazepam box in my haste and uncoordination. I swallowed the tablet then lay down, you cannot fall further than the floor. I let the world go past, fly above me, while I was a coward and hid silently still.

1st June

2007

Maisie has her syringe driver fitted. The district nurses won't or can't give her a port for extra top-up meds so I do it. Phil (Macmillan nurse) said this would be OK. But I do wonder how others cope. If district nurses can't inject extra drugs then how come I am?

A few hours later, we realise the syringe driver isn't working. I suggest re-siting it and Lily comes over to check. It gets sorted. But then Mum in severe pain as she has had less pain relief. I give her some extra diamorphine: snap the glass vial, make up the solution and inject it into Mum's arm. I am extremely calm but this betrays my turmoil inside. Today I have been mentally low. It takes supreme effort not to stab myself with the drugs and end it all there and then. Instead I calmly give Mum her much needed diamorphine then retreat to the kitchen, panting as I wash my hands.

I am scared of myself. Scared of what I might do. Scared of what I am capable of. I know I can't stop here, torn between that agonising wish to die and the knowledge that I cannot die until Mum does. Of course, my desire to care for and my love for Mum will always win outright but, on brief occasions such as this, I feel I may succumb. I may be sapped of all strength and give up the fight. The thought that I may do that to Mum is terrifying. How could I let her down in such a way? But the battle is ongoing: each day is afresh with temptation. Calculations dance in my mind. I have a wealth of drugs to choose my deathly cocktail from. Diamorphine may be termed "controlled" but I am the one in charge. All drugs go through me. Everyday is a reminder and, dare I say it, a comfort in the knowledge that I could be dead by taking whatever medications are left. This makes me less afraid.

2008

In the afternoon, I went into Mum and Dad's bedroom. The reasonings behind this, I am not sure. I haven't been in this room for a very long time. It looked all wrong and incredibly empty. I hadn't thought about what to expect, I just turned the handle and was then inside.

In my mind's eye, ironic I know, the room has life: Mum's pressure mattress on the bed so the sheets don't quite fit, commode wedged into the corner when out of use, transparent bag of hundreds of pink mouth sponges, a couple of containers of baby wipes, soft toy dog Raffle perched somewhere, vials of drugs in boxes, suppositories, hot water bottle, radio, cardboard sick bowls, dressing gown strewn. This is the room, not how it is now. It looked sterile, sanitary. It looked dead.

I think Mum's anniversary is building inside, slowly gathering momentum, each day, more debris is added. I feel I may do something extreme. At the moment, I don't know if I want to or not, all I know is that I am scared, terrified incase my actions are not mine, I may be lead and unable to resist. I'm too panicky to tell anyone, they might put me back into hospital and that is not a place I want to remember darling Maisie.

2nd June

2007

Terribly straining day. Mum wakes in pain. I inject her with diamorphine. Her poor little body is in such distress. She writhes around, then is still: alternates between the two physical states, unable to relieve the agony. Eventually the pain dulls, but it is still there, probing her belly, unwilling to allow her to settle.

In the afternoon, the diamorphine in Mum's syringe driver is doubled. Later she feels increasingly nauseous, culminating in a dreadfully weak retching effort. Having not eaten all day, all that comes up is a fine thread of stringy saliva. The effort to lean over the bowl is almost too much for her.

Once the retching subsides, I inject her with metaclopramide. This has no effect and Mum remains nauseous. I give her a second injection, this time nozinan, which helps ease the situation but then the pain returns with vengeance. I give Mum another diamorphine injection. The cancer is torturing Maisie. All I can do is rub her feet, watch her limp body, eyes closed but awake. She says she doesn't want to live anymore. She hasn't the words to describe how grim she feels. She wishes to die. She wants enough diamorphine to end it all. I cannot do this. I cannot kill my Mother.

2am – Mum asleep. The sheer responsibility suddenly hits me. I am the only person who can give Mum her medication. The district nurses won't go near the port because they aren't trained and haven't used them before. If I wasn't here and able to administer the drugs, Mum would be in the Hospice. I feel an overwhelming, compressing weight upon me, suffocated almost. How am I the sole carer? The one with the ultimate responsibility?

Of course, I don't want anything different. Mum doesn't want to be in the Hospice, but now I feel the fear creeping in. Am I really able to manage this? I know I can because it is all for Mum. I know the strength does not come from me, but there is still that nagging feeling of doubt, tugging away within me. I can look after other people so why can't I look after myself? There, I am incompetent. All I do is slice open my skin and watch the blood grow into a reddening blob, run across my tummy, dribble down my hips. The contrast is stark.

Alice, you can do this. You can look after your beloved Maisie. This is what you have trained at university for, all the years are for these days, nothing more. The knowledge you have gained is all for now. That is the reason you have lasted this long. The undeserved years at university, the exams you shouldn't have passed…all this achieved so Maisie can be poured over and cared for in the best possible way. This is the meaning.

2008

Tidy of the house that was meant to be frantic but Ethan and I turned it into a more leisurely affair. We've done our best, at least it has a "top show" as Granny would say. This week with Ethan has been lovely and I feel beneficial. First, I adjust to living, once again, outside of hospital and, second, which is to come, I teach myself how to live with Dad. A step by step approach, one thing at a time, as Dr. Floyd would say.

Dad arrives back in the evening, just as I am stocking the fridge with food after being to the supermarket. He gives me a rigid hug, "How are you" etc. I ask Dad about Seattle, his replies are brief and he isn't concentrating as grabs the dish cloth and begins wiping down already clean and disinfected surfaces in the kitchen. He then systematically unpacks his suitcase and gets things in order. This is OCD, Tom and I are convinced. While frustrating, Dad also refuses to acknowledge his obsessive tidying, which manages to cause a lot of tension.

Later, Dad's rituals over, Holly comes round and this diffuses the awkwardness. Ethan is in London so it had just been me and Dad. I think Dad is trying, he bought us coffee beans and Ethan a rucksack. He goes to bed early, night time travelling and time difference taking its toll.

3rd June

2007

Better day and, surprisingly under the circumstances, Ma and I even have a giggle. Mum is able to have a bath this morning, however, we have to plan ahead and negotiate the syringe driver. I root around Mum's store of plastic bags and find a long thin one, used for carrying wrapping paper. I cut the end off the bottom, then thread Mum's syringe driver through, followed by her arm. Mum is then in the bath, plastic bag like a plaster cast, covering the length of her arm which she keeps elevated by resting it on the side of the bath tub. I have an elaborate towel arrangement to prevent any water getting in. The whole thing is a performance but funny, and Ma gets her hair washed. I'm so glad we can still laugh.

The whole debacle does leave Mum drained and she rests on the bed. Eventually she gets up again to clean her teeth. She suddenly coughs and frantically leans over the sink. A gold crown falls out. I retrieve it. Mum is admirably calm but does despair at the number of minor additional complications that seem to plague her. She opens wide and I inspect the stump of tooth that remains. She isn't in any pain.

I phone the emergency dentist as, typically with all these things, it is a Sunday. Lovely, helpful dental nurse who answers. I explain Mum's precarious situation and she is incredibly understanding. She says someone will come to the house tomorrow morning but to phone back if there are any problems. I am touched by such delightful people. I wonder if they realise that, especially now, a nice voice on the phone is such a strength.

Little encouragements like this each day are a dot to me. Every day is join the dots. My challenge is to get from one dot to the next. The closer the dots are together, the easier it is to draw the picture. It gets harder as the dots become few and far between. Maybe that is why it is impossible to be a lone ranger. No-one can do it alone. Other people are needed to provide the dots, to show me the way.

2008

Afternoon at Lily's surgery – a teaching session with her third year medical students. I join them around the big, circular table, five students, a school girl on work placement, Annie (the education administrator) and Lily. I feel daunted and sink low in my chair.

Topics are discussed, diseases, diagnoses, signs, symptoms, tests, results and all the words rush at me like dominoes toppling unable to stop. I know these, they are familiar but I am intimidated by the sheer number. Each word forms a spider diagram in my mind and, from that, more mental words are pictured. It becomes too much and I can't remember enough. Explanations linger but aren't sensical, I know this, I have learnt all that was said, but it seemed to dazzle my mind into submission, internal spinning, externally a simple sentence of words almost linking.

Late evening, Ethan and I in the kitchen discussing his 21st birthday, and Dad walks in. He actually stays a while to talk with us. This is almost proof that the three of us can be civil. There is no arguing or anger. Ethan wonders how many people he can have to his birthday meal (Dad paying, of course) and Dad is asking if he gets to bring someone.

As soon as Dad has gone to bed, Ethan and I discuss. Surely it's not Mary he's thinking of taking but surely it will be. Ethan doesn't want her there but then thinks Dad might be better to cope with if he has someone to entertain. Dad has been nice (for him) over Ethan's birthday, so we can't really complain about this. Anyway, it's Ethan's decision and I'm not persuading him either way.

Pre-bed routine complete, the darkness lying in my bed brought a horror slide show of ill and dead Mum, taken from different angles, at different stages. I couldn't banish the images, they would not go, wouldn't allow me to think of anything else. I writhed in bed, thrashing out my internal screams.

4th June

2007

The extra diamorphine really affecting Maisie. She was terribly drowsy today and rather dizzy. She only made it out of bed to go to the toilet and, even then, was drastically clinging onto me with both hands. She was confused and vaguely entering into disjointed conversations, intermittently drifting back to sleep, unable to keep her eyes open.

However, by the evening, Mum was in a pleasant state: still spaced out but drunk, almost. She was giggly and everything was said and done at length. She wasn't quite in slow motion but each word spoken or movement made had that fractionally delayed quality. Mum proceeded to entertain me with a puppet show consisting of playing games with Raffle (her soft toy dog from the choir girls) and had me laughing uncontrollably. My Maisie, still shining bright.

After that excitement, her weariness returned and it was time for bed. The usual routine was followed by the request for me to read to her. I think Mum fell asleep on the first page but I continued through the entire chapter, just to make sure. My voice changed with the various speaking characters, just how Mum used to read us bedtime stories. I loved her wonderful ability to give each character a voice, an accent, pitch. It was such a comfort to fall asleep to the beautiful sound of her reading: a blanket of safety.

2008

GP appointment in the afternoon. I had to change from Lily after the psych team deemed it was breeching patient-doctor relationships. New surgery, new GP, she was lovely, hit just the right tone and was easy to talk to. I realise I may be slightly biased when it comes to doctors, but all the ones who I have been involved with have been great.

5th June

2007

Dad shakes me awake. Mum has woken early to discover she is soaked in blood. She is lying, still curled on her left side, blood seeping through her nightdress and pooling on the bed sheets. She tugs at her sleeve and, together, gingerly but purposely, we peel off her clothes. Mum's arm is a deep crimson colour, the blood tacky beneath the transparent square of plaster keeping the syringe driver in place. But the blood has forcefully squeezed itself out, dribbling across the sheets, uncontained. Mum's liver, overgrown with tumours, is struggling to produce the necessary clotting factors, resulting in prolonged bleeding.

Mum is understandably agitated and begins panicking. Mopping up the area with tissues, I calmly tell her the bleeding is stopping. The soothing tone I use thankfully betraying my inmost alarm at being woken into confrontation of such a situation. I adjust the syringe driver and take an excessive time ensuring it is working. I do this to reassure and pacify Mum but it actually has a calming effect on us both. This excitement has a rebound soporific effect on Mum, who lies back, exhausted by the morning's events. I sit beside her, stroking her rhythmically until she lapses into a welcome sleep. I stay there for hours, watching.

Lily, delightful as ever, comes at lunch time and checks over Mum. A now much more settled Maisie is willing for me to wash and change her. I roll the sheets from underneath and give her a fresh nightie.

Downstairs, I scrub the patches of now deep red blood with Vanish, remembering to use cold water as Mum said. My hands tense with dislike at the water temperature and this feeling ripples up my arms to my head, where physical impressions digest into mental turmoil. Blood induces many complex, confusional states in my mind, but it is always *my* blood. Having Mum's blood wash through my fingers instantly crashes these thoughts, like a playing record becoming stuck. I cannot repair.

My mind becomes a devilishly knotted, mis-shapen ball of thoughts, whose origins are unknown. The relenting question: how are they in my head, these thinking patterns, when I did not put them there? They are not mine and yet they belong to me. Afraid that my question will remain unanswered, I return to Mum and my head is peacefully quiet, all possible activity directed towards my wonderful Maisie.

2008

Woke several times throughout the night, myotonic jerks in arms, jumping with fright. My breathing was heavy and quick but I never knew the reason why. Perhaps dreams but the memory of which escapes me.

Lily's surgery in the afternoon. I didn't want to go in. Tiredness had invaded my body but not my mind, I wasn't sleepy. Debated not going but forced myself to do so, distraction may prove helpful.

Saw many patients by Lily's side but my brain wasn't quite functioning. I would miss great chunks of conversation and would only realise when I was engaged once again, but with no clue as to what had been said. Almost a relief once the ordeal was over.

In the evening bad thoughts escalated. I found myself alone in my room, a heap on the floor, silently sobbing. The tears pricked my eyes and stung like vinegar. I wish I could say I was sad about Mum but I didn't know the cause or reason. Throwing on a coat, I flung myself out into the rain, walking the streets as fast as I could, pavement pounding. I reached the fields and my face was wet, raindrops and tears mingled and neither could be distinguished. My shoes soaked up the muddy puddle water and I could feel my toes turning ice cold. Being outside is always, if fractionally, a relief.

Calming myself somewhat, I phoned Aunty Beth and had a long talk with her. Aunty Beth is like Mum, she can keep you entertained for ages re-telling amusing stories that have happened. They both have a knack for making incidents funny. The chat with Aunty Beth brought me home.

6th June

2007

I've stopped Medicine – officially, they have given me a year off. I tell Mum. She feels guilty. She says she doesn't want to completely disrupt my life. But she also says she loves me being with her the whole time. I tell her I've wanted to stop since I came home. Mum is far more important than anything else. I feel so privileged to be able to look after her.

Dad doesn't like me stopping and starts hassling me to do a placement in Essex. He thinks I'm being silly. He has absolutely no idea of all the things I'm doing at home, of my desire to be with Mum, or how hard it is to be involved in medicine right now or, indeed, of the practicalities – Lily might be lenient, a hospital won't be. Of my supposed six week placement with Lily, I managed a grand total of probably five afternoons: Mum too poorly, she needed me at home. I told Lily not to sign me off. It felt like a joke. I felt guilty about it but she did, saying I've done far more medical stuff at home than any placement would achieve.

Dad says why don't I do my placement with Lily? He said that Lily knows everything I am doing with Mum, couldn't I just do that? I cannot believe he is even asking me this. He wants me to do a project on my dying mother whom I should then have to do a presentation on, most probably after she has died. How is he even considering this? He has absolutely no idea. I tell him I am stopping Medicine. I no longer care what he thinks. This is all for Mum.

Is it lying to Mum saying I'm only having a year off when I don't think I can ever go back? Does she really need to know my intentions? That decision will be made when she is dead.

2008

Frantically busy morning at Lily's surgery but I was so glad I was there. Numerous patients who actually cheered me up! Lily got me to do some examining and I felt that this went well. I was also able to diagnose. GP is fascinating for such variety of patients, everything is covered.

I cycled because the day seemed nice but, come lunch time, the rain was falling and I got soaked. The ride back nearly finished me off. I was incredibly tired, my body so heavy my arms were struggling to keep myself upright. I collapsed when I got back, legs shaking, as if my very last energy resources had been sapped. I had to stay on the floor a while to recuperate.

In the afternoon I managed to type up some documents for Lily. This, at least, was sedentary. In the evening, Dad arrived home and actually came to find me before he went out for dinner. He asked about my day and was kind. I like Dad when we can talk.

I felt dreadful which seemed to get worse as the skies darkened. My head hurt with a deep, internal throbbing. Getting on for 11pm, Lily came round to say goodbye to me. She is off to Costa Rica tomorrow morning. I felt like crying when I saw her.

Lily gave me a one-armed hug and I wrapped my arms around her back. She can tell I am feeling a bit wobbly. She says sleep is still very important so take diazepam tonight. Lily tells me I'm doing so well, really throwing myself into life, trying so hard. I wish it was easier. Another hug and kiss and Lily had gone. I shall miss her dreadfully even though it is only for two weeks. She has become my tower of support.

Suicidal thoughts. I had sunk to what I thought was the bottom but there is always further to fall. The darkness and loneliness of the house engulfed me so I ran into the night, breathing in the silence and stillness of the alleyway, overgrown weeds catching my legs, my arms, grown so high.

The alley spat me out into the harsh illumination of street lamps. I retrieved my phone from my pocket and phoned Sarah. She got me to tell her of all the activities I had got up to this week, these are the good points. Don't worry about a little slip, Alice, you are doing really well. Compare the difference between what you are able to do now and what you were doing in hospital.

On the other side of the road I saw, in the distance, a man stumble and fall before pulling himself upright, his unsteady balance unhelpful. I said to Sarah I had got to go and make sure he was alright. The guy was middle-aged; he could have been my Dad. Then, in my head, I was going over all the medical problems which could present as a supposed drunken state (hypoglycaemic attack, perhaps a muscular dystrophy of some sort etc.) but the man told me he had too many beers and will be OK because he lives down here. I was fairly dubious as to how he was going to make it but I was not about to carry him. He staggered off, clutching garden fences for support.

I got home gone midnight (after returning via drunken man street to check he hadn't passed out or knocked himself out - he'd gone) and still felt dreadful. Swallowing my tablets produced an uncomfortable lump in my throat, as if they were all stuck.

7th June

2008

Awoke at 3am, ran to the bathroom and was promptly sick. My energy had been taken; I sat slumped against the toilet bowl, nausea gripping me. I finally, shakily, made my way to the kitchen where I got a glass of water and the blue plastic bowl which Mum always gave us when we had a poorly tummy. I climbed the stairs, collapsed into bed, and lay there, unable to move but unable to sleep. At 7am, I could hear the beginnings of the morning traffic and this, miraculously, was the sleeping draught I needed.

I woke up at 11am, slightly disorientated by the time. I forced myself into the shower, tentatively ate a yoghurt, did a few, very sedate, activities and that was it, my body would not obey my commands, I couldn't even sit to read a newspaper. I crawled back to bed and slept for the majority of the afternoon.

The evening was depressing. Dad arrived back from his walk in Suffolk but, before I even had a chance to ask him how his day was, Dad had launched into a tirade about how dirty the house was, how everywhere was a mess and just a load of general crossness. He then turned on me, why was I at home (I had told him I was going out), what am I still doing here etc. He dismissed my reference to illness, he used his derogatory tone of voice.

I went into the kitchen to did the small pile of washing up Dad was referring to. I picked up a mug and wanted to throw it, with all my strength, onto the tiles, smash it to pieces, demonstrate to Dad what a mess actually is. Ethan joined me; he was sweet. He said I shouldn't be doing this when I was unwell. We did it together: I washed, Ethan dried, but each item of crockery was a temptation to crash to the ground.

Kitchen cleared, I walked past Dad to the front door and went out. He didn't say a word. I walked for a while in the dark and then tried to phone people who could help: Aunty Beth, Sarah, Mog but no one answered, they all have lives, their own occupations. I was suicidal. Empty streets are lonely places.

8th June

2007

Putting Mum to bed tonight, she leant upright and gripped my hand in both of hers. She told me she was ever so grateful for what I was doing. She said she really wanted to write me a lovely long letter, reinforcing her thanks and love for me, but can no longer manage to write. I know she can't write and I also know that whatever she puts on paper shall be nothing new. Since Mum was diagnosed, our bond has not strengthened or weakened, just stayed the same, for there is no changing such a relationship.

She wants to write to me so I can keep it but, I tell her, words on paper is only a physical thing. It has no value. What is most important is our time now. Writing on paper is meaningless if the reader can't feel the words. But I can feel all that Mum says. I can feel her love. I feel how close we are to one another. No page of writing can even attempt to recreate that exquisite sensation.

No longer reading to Mum at night. She can't concentrate on my words for long enough and can't remember the characters, let alone the story line, from the night before. We now just have a little chat in the dark before I creep out.

2008

Start the morning afresh with medical books. I am going to familiarise myself with the knowledge once again. I am going to revise. Always a daunting task, initialising, there appears too much that could possibly all be learnt. But, that first step has been taken.

Dad has got a table tennis table from some of our friends who live in the next road. This is a kind gesture, something we can all use together but I feel a niggling annoyance that now I have to be nice to Dad even though I don't feel like it.

Holly comes round in the afternoon and we all play table tennis outside in the garden. Perhaps this will prove to be a family bonding exercise after all.

10th June

2007

Mum confused. She no longer has any awareness of the time or day. She is easily muddled and speaks out loud things she is imagining or dreaming. Conversations are stilted with Mum latching onto certain words or topics, these tenuous links diverting our chats in all directions. I spend hours talking with her but she needs breaks for naps.

Mum gets frustrated if she can't convey what she wants to tell me and this takes much prompting, coaxing and encouragement. I suppose some would call it patience but I don't feel like I am being patient. Patience implies it is an effort for me and treats Mum like a child. This is not so. It is upsetting to see Mum like this but I will gladly, unreservedly, give her all my time.

But once it is dark and the early hours of the morning creep upon me, the fear becomes almost too much to bear. I can't force all the negative thoughts from my mind; they hang there, like a parasite, feeding off my intense self-loathing. I feel lonely, a stranger to myself. Irrepressible blackness consumes me. The single moon reflected light catches the razor blade, in an eerie, half attempt at illumination, almost a reminder that the darkest hours cannot be recovered. I abuse myself in all the ways I can get away with. Maisie shall not find out. She will be spared the knowledge of my demons. Suffering in silence is a powerful weapon they hold against me.

2008

I went for a run today, only half an hour, but this was something I haven't done for a long time, possibly even since Mum died. Running helps a tangled head. Somehow, the rhythmical stamping of feet demands a structured, ordered view of the world. I arrived home and, in post-hours run, felt a distinct notch better.

A terrible altercation with Dad in the evening. He gets cross and indignantly says how I don't tell him anything (ie things to do with hospitals and CPNs and medications etc). I tell him that, in order to be informed, I need to respect him and know he cares. I then say (and now possibly regret it) that he demonstrated his level of involvement by getting angry when I told him of my initial overdose and then not ringing or even noticing I wasn't in the house for five days, including my birthday, when in fact I had been taken to a psychiatric unit. I say this sums up his concern towards me.

Fleeing the house in tears, I swerve my way down the back routes of alleyways and quiet residential streets, gulping in half caught breaths through heaves of sobs. I want Mum; I want to explain all these things to her. I need her to hug me; I need her support with all the psychiatric stuff. I want to die right now but too late for shops and medication is at home, a place I am not ready to return to. I walk through the devastating mental lowness and loneliness. I walk myself out of all energy I have left.

11th June

2008

I had my tooth taken out – the same one which has been causing so many problems. Now a big, swollen hole. I'm not allowed to take most painkillers because they interact with lithium but

Lindsey does suggest some herbal remedy! I went round to her house because she has just taken care of a delightful black labrador. Lindsey has become a foster dog carer so gets the neglected animals for a few weeks. Ethan and I now have a dog to play with too!

Evening the same as the last few nights. Walking in the dark for hours, ways and means of suicide playing a game of chase in my head. Too low for any meaningful description. I feel grim and yet do not know why. Nothing makes sense; all is black. There is nothing of life.

I talk to Mog, she says I'm not a lost cause, there is a way. It is evasive to me though. How can I feel like dying so stubbornly when I still cannot locate a definite reason? Mog, I don't know how much longer I can keep this up.

12th June

2008

Appointment with Rachel (clinical psychologist) in the morning. This was actually a really good session. She had printed off for me a detailed report on dissociation. Rachel explained how all my, seemingly random, symptoms link together under this one title. Obviously the not feeling real but then it went on to list increased sensitivity to light and sound, loss of concentration, nocturnal panic attacks etc. I feel more comfortable when I am offered an explanation, the tricky part is how to overcome these and be able to act normally.

Talking to Rachel, I think I worried her as everything had a morbid edge. She spoke to Francis (my social worker) who came to the house in the afternoon. I was honest to an extent. I said I had been struggling, walking at night which seems to be an indicator of me going downhill. I felt very tired and sad.

I have developed a new symptom since leaving hospital. It has only happened a handful of times. I am walking along and then, as I look at my surroundings, I recognise absolutely nothing, as if I am walking in a completely new place, never seen before, but these are the streets I grew up on, a familiarity. I carry on walking, bemused, and a short time later, I seep into reality and all is restored. I know where I am. This is jamais vu (the opposite of déjà vu, an expression I remember from medical student days). It doesn't scare me being a stranger but it is decidedly odd.

Francis says I have to see Dr. Floyd tomorrow. I can tell they are worried and I am enduring the rapidity of appointments. It makes me anxious.

13th June

2007

At night, alone in my room, Mum safe asleep in bed, they come. I see them, shifting between the shadows, contorting their shape of indistinguishable outline. They are only visible for splintered moments. They are too quick for my eyes. I see them but they have hidden within the dark spaces before my vision is able to focus but senses work together. Although my sight betrays me, I feel and hear and know they are still there, waiting, biding time. For what? Something stalls them. I can't do this, but something does. They must break down some unknown barrier before they get to me but, they will get through.

I am unable to move. My knees hugged, I wait, transfixed, paralysed, fearful. My unseeing eyes are blinded by the darkness. They hide, they build and then they pounce. I have no defences. My soul lays exposed, naked, unprotected from inevitable attack. They have come to steal my memories. I am no longer my own. Fractions of my mind are taken and abused, deformed into a partially real and partially false recollection. Distortion is their quest. I still have access to my memories but they gain the control. They fire them back at me: memories too intense, too tangled, too horrific. Remembering is a dangerous activity. The memories are too hard to handle alone.

They out number me and I am weak. My head hurts with almost physical exertion. Sometimes I am not allowed to expose, relive the memory fully. Instead it is left to fester, masked in an engaging dread. It lingers on the tip of my mind, an occupying presence but one into which I am unable to delve. It is ghastly to be afraid of locked up secrets in your own head. A person shouldn't scare their own self and yet I am terrified daily. The thing I am most petrified of, is me.

Please, please I beg - to whom? Please don't take my memories of Mum. Please don't change those beautiful images. Please don't hide them from me or offer them at a price. Please leave them alone. These are the most precious memories I have. If they take them, I shall be thrown into a weightless, suffocating place. Is it not black or dark because, in order to know that, you have to understand light. In this place, there is nothing: a colourless, senseless, grave of empty souls.

2008

I walk to the psych unit for my appointment with Dr. Floyd. On approaching, I see Katy coming in for work and my face lights up. I hug her and it is wonderful to see her smile, if fleetingly, again.

I am called in by Dr. Floyd and am a picture: black eye and swollen cheek from removed tooth. Whenever I see Dr. Floyd, I always manage to give an initial bad impression! Dr. Floyd gives me so much of her time, far longer than the allocated half hour. I am honest. I tell her of the suicidal thoughts. I'm not exactly planning anything but, conversely, at points I want to die and have the means to do so. I can enjoy things when I'm not tired but, as soon as the bad thoughts infiltrate, all positives seem meaningless.

Dr. Floyd is still striving for sustained enjoyment. She adds an SSRI (another anti-depressant) to my drug cocktail, to increase the serotonin in my brain, in turn to lift my mood. She doesn't think I am particularly safe and there is talk of hospital but I do not want to return. Dr. Floyd says she is going to see me next week and she will phone Francis who will see me two times before that. I know Dr. Floyd is thinking I may do something drastic if things deteriorate further. I don't blame her, I agree.

14th June

2008

Gran's 87th birthday. We drove to Aunty Jane's with a variety of presents: flowers, sweets, ginger wine (Gran's favourite tipple) and a cake. As Gran's dementia is so far advanced, she won't even realise it is her birthday and we all introduce ourselves with our name and how we are related which helps her somewhat in the recognition process.

I made the cake which proved a success on the taste front but it was a disaster in the cooking process. Gran has a dairy free diet as this was upsetting her tummy so I had to find a recipe without eggs or butter! The cooking time stated thirty minutes but it was still raw so I had the cake in the oven for over an hour and a half! I was, understandably, dreading people eating it but, actually, it wasn't so bad, sort of ginger cake consistency.

Cousin Dan was down from Reading for the weekend and it was, as ever, great to see him. He is such a charming guy and we share in our devastation, his Mum dying six weeks after our Mum, we have that bond of lost mothers.

Aunty Jane cooked dinner and we stayed until gone 9pm. I had managed successfully, with no hiccups in my head, an entire day. I wasn't overtaken by unruly thoughts, my concentration held fast. This must be an achievement of sorts. And it was a good day, great to see Gran more animated than of late and she appreciated sitting in the garden with everyone, blankets and shawls wrapped tightly.

16th June

2007

Spoke to Mog. I've been a little crazy this week: fine with Mum but not quite able to stifle or cover up my demons in the night. I can't lose it yet. I must keep going. And I will. I can do anything for Maisie. Mog - so helpful, so tolerant of me. She is instrumental in my self-preservation. She has a plan for me, a list of things I must try and do. They are all to help myself. How difficult it is to look after oneself. It takes time and energy which should, exclusively, be for Maisie. My head doesn't seem to accept that, in order to look after Mum, I must care for myself.

The usual Saturday row between Dad and Ethan. Voices shouting obscenities, all too clearly heard by Mum lying in bed. I try and talk to her so she doesn't listen to what is happening but my attempts of distraction are, as always, in vain. The arguing upsets Mum greatly.

Having not felt well all day, by the evening Mum is struggling. It takes all her energy to prop herself up. She hunches over the plastic bowl, nauseated, but unknowing whether she will actually be sick. Her tiny frame groans with the effort. I draw up an additional vial of nozinan. I tell her, step by step, what I am doing. Mum likes me explaining. Even if she isn't fully understanding, it comforts her.

Injecting the drug though, is painful to her. She calls out as I push the syringe through. It stings terribly. My voice is calm, controlled. I speak to her softly, slowly offering reassurance. She thinks something must be wrong. This is not the case, nozinan is just a particularly prickly drug. I inject it so slowly, I wonder if I'm squeezing any in at all. I give Mum little breaks. Short term pain for long term gain. I know this will benefit Mum but I find it incredibly difficult to continue to hurt her. She bravely perseveres. My Mum, the bravest, strongest person I know. I then give her temazepam and the combination of drugs sends her into a deep sleep.

I retreat to my room and cannot sleep. Being with Mum is safe. I am so calm that, afterwards, I surprise myself. How do I keep so unpanicked, unswayed by situations, so sane? Because afterwards, once Mum is calm, our emotions are reversed. I sit shaking on my bed. Physically, I would be unable to handle a needle. My head is confounded by frantic and fraught thoughts, at the horror of seeing Maisie in such distress and then of me, adding to her pain.

2008

Morning brought a trip to hospital to have my bloods done for lithium levels. This is such a frequent occurrence – I even recognised the phlebotomist!

Afternoon: I get the train to London to see Mog. Initially I wanted to see her before I kill myself but I decide that is rather drastic. I need her advice. Even with all the help I am getting, there are still desperate times. I don't know what to do or how to change.

We walk along the river, over the bridge with its vast expanse of murky water beneath, then settle in a coffee bar. It is lovely to see Mog and talk to her; I feel safer, not just when the noise and crowds and sights pain my head, but inside as well, a more content feeling.

I don't want to say goodbye, I want to remain in that hug, suspended in time, a bubble of protection. But we depart and I sit on the train, looking out of the window, trees and pylons and platforms jumping past, a stuttering view of the world.

Walking home, I realise I have a host of missed calls from Francis and ISS. Dr. Floyd had apparently asked Francis to see me today and, unable to find me, had got ISS on the case! I always worry with the flurry of activity from psych services. I think they are about to section me as soon as I reappear. It was gone 9pm so I phoned ISS and said I was fine. Francis is to see me tomorrow.

17th June

2007

Mum wakes feeling ill. This is the hardest. She is drowsy - feels dreadful – but it is so non-specific I find it incredibly hard to know how to help. I am the one who makes the decisions. Mum trusts me to do what is right. In these situations, she is just too poorly to enter into a rational discussion over what *we* think will help. She purely wants me to take over, relieve her of responsibility. I am her sole decision maker. This job, although honouring and privileged, is also scary. The responsibility weighs heavy in my jam-packed mind.

Mum feels dizzy, has aches over her shoulders, back and tummy, stabbing pains grip her in varying locations and nausea is nagging in the background. She is hot and clammy. I am confronted by this range of symptoms and I wish I knew that what I was doing was right. I give her diamorphine, hoping that, if the pain subsides, the sickness will as well, as has happened in the past, but also knowing that morphine can make you feel sick – I don't want to make her nausea worse. The difficulty of decisions.

I press cold flannels on Mum's forehead and open the windows wider but, this isn't medicine. I always feel I should be doing more but I never know what. I am a wannabe doctor but, in reality, I am a flawed carer, desperately wanting to do my best but always feeling let down with myself. Why is everything I have learnt deserting me now?

Lily comes, changes drugs, is wonderful with Mum. We are so blessed to have her. I watch and try and learn her brilliance with people. But is that a learned ability or is it something that only the chosen possess? I want to do better. I want the knowledge of a doctor. Knowledge is required for reassurance. Lily is partly so good because she can offer explanations in such depth. She can actually answer why. Why? My favourite question. I wish I knew the answers.

2008

A good day for me, starting with a run which perhaps set the tone. I enjoyed my solitary exercise, tunnel vision, music in ears. I am getting stronger, running wasn't an exhausting struggle but actually enjoyable. I think it really does siphon off some of my overflowing nervous energy.

Francis (my social worker) saw me in the afternoon. We sat at the kitchen table and drank tea. Francis likes running too and was going this evening with a jogging group from work. She says she is going to Finland for three weeks, the time when it will be Mum's anniversary and her birthday. I won't tell them any specific dates (although I'm sure if they tried, they could find out) because I'm concerned they'll put me back in hospital. Anyway, Francis says Carrie (whom I liked very much from ISS) has changed teams and, as I know her, will come and see me instead. I'm enthusiastic about this idea. I still find it hard with different people, all strangers to me but they have read my notes so I am not a stranger to them. It will be good to see Carrie again and, in all honesty, I know I'll need her support. Inside, I can feel the anticipation brewing.

Bit worried about Ethan. He says he is depressed and having panic attacks. He's got a GP appointment which is good but I'm not sure if I'm helping as best I can. Ethan's not sleeping that well so tonight I sat in the front room with him, late into the evening, just talking. I get on with Ethan fabulously. He has been my saviour at home. I hope I can be his too.

18th June

2007

Mum full of morphine; it addles her brain. She drifts in and out of consciousness: it doesn't look like sleep. Sometimes she is unrousable, too tired to open her eyes and acknowledge I'm there. She isn't agitated but is certainly restless.

I watch her. She flails her arms, slowly, not in distress but reaching out for some unknown object in her mind. She grasps at her cheek and gently scratches the back of her hand. She vaguely tugs at her syringe driver line, not aggressively as to dislodge it, but in a disoriented way, unsure as to why she has a needle in her arm. She opens and closes her mouth, emitting a quiet pop. She draws her legs up towards her chest then straightens them again. She'll push the duvet away, only to clasp another section and pull it high up to her chin, then, using thumb and forefinger, pluck at the sheet. Mummy, what are you doing?

Mum in bed all day. I have a couple of successful attempts in giving her a drink. Her mouth is terribly dry. I give her the glass. She can remember the action she is supposed to do but it's all slightly uncoordinated. I hold my hand over hers so she doesn't drop the cup and guide the straw to her mouth. Her teeth and lips root around, like a suckling baby, until she has enough purchase on the straw to be able to drink. She takes a little water into her mouth, holds it there, then slowly swallows. I hear her gulp and gurgling in her tummy follows. She burps a lot but always says sorry immediately. Impeccable manners as always.

Mum wakes and announces she needs the toilet. She holds my forearm and, with me supporting her around the waist, she sits up. She tries to stand immediately, but I make her stay. She forgets that standing too quickly makes her dizzy. She pauses and leans her head against my shoulder. We sit there together, holding hands.

Mum half pulls the pad off her pants and the stuffing falls to the floor. Mum then tries to wipe herself with the torn bit of pad. I hastily grab it off her. She protests but I give her toilet paper as a replacement and she relents. I peel the rest of the pad off her pants and stick down a fresh one.

Mum has always said to me that, if she gets old and develops dementia and is confused, then I know what she would want if she was well. Mum was concerned over hygiene. She is fastidious but feared that this may slip. She told me that, whatever she said in altered mind to ignore and ensure I kept her clean. She said that, therefore I know what to do now.

Mum staggers back to bed and is unconscious almost before she lies down. I have to lift her legs into the bed as she has no energy left. I don't know whether she hears me or knows but I get a soapy flannel and carefully wash her hands, towelling them dry. I then go back to the commode. It is a bright reddish brown, a stark visible sign of Mum's illness. I shouldn't be shocked but, initially, am slightly alarmed at the colour. I wash the bowl, willing it to go away.

When Dad gets home from work, I give him a letter. I wrote that I was sorry. I have been so mean and horrid to him this weekend. I told him how hard I found everything even if I seemed calm. I said how frightening it was to be responsible for Mum's drugs. I said I didn't want to let him down. I said I wanted him to be proud of me and not disappointed as I get upset and cross.

Dad finds me later and tells me I shouldn't be sorry to him. He says everything at the moment is really hard. He says Mum would be in the Hospice without me. He tells me not to be scared and then hugs me. Dad hugs me. Tears come rushing down my face. All I can say is, "Sorry, Dad. I'm so sorry". At that moment I am filled with such an overwhelming feeling of love from my Father, one that has never happened before. He has never hugged me. I know right then his love. And me, within his arms, crying profusely, know

I'm safe. My Dad has me protected. I feel how much he cares for me.

At 11pm I leave Mum. Dad is lying in bed but I'm not sure if he's asleep. I try and wake Mum to see if she needs the toilet but her eyes open and are unfocused. She does look at me but there is nothing there. This is what people must mean when they describe an empty expression. I can't see my Maisie.

I stroke her hair and hold her hand. I whisper how brave she is, tell her how well she is doing, how much I love her. She says, "I love you lots too", perhaps a learned, automatic response but, for me, such a wonderful, meaningful sentence to hear.

At 1am Mum is awake and trying to talk but weakness and lethargy reduce it to a mumble. I can't understand what she is saying. I ask her simple questions but she latches on to words and repeats them back to me. I give her a drink, bobbles of white cling to her lips, a protest of how dry her mouth is. Mum says, "Temazepam" and starts slowly jerking her hand towards the table. I get the spoon and the bottle but then it seems as if Ma has forgotten. I gently ease her head more upright and bring the spoon to her lips. She remembers what to do but takes care to lick the spoon several times, trying to get the last dregs of an already empty container.

At 2am, I hear Dad walking around. I go downstairs to check. He has had a nose bleed and blood is over the sheets and pillows. The washing machine goes on. We then sit in the front room whilst Dad pinches his nose to stem the bleeding. He doesn't say much but I am there. I tell him not to tilt his head back. I tell him don't swallow the blood. And then we sit in silence. He is tired. He doesn't want to talk. But that is OK. He knows I'm there. He knows I can help if he wants.

2008

Ethan was prescribed fluoxetine (an antidepressant) by his GP – follow up in two weeks. He doesn't want to take it but trusts this doctor with whom he has built up a respectful relationship. Ethan doesn't think tablets will help. He is starting to sound like me at the very beginning, battling against one drug. I, however, am now on hundreds!

Lindsey needed help today to move a shed in her new garden (of which she bought the house). Before we start, we sit on the decking, drinking fresh coffee. Warm up over, the shed is tackled – huge and far too heavy. We decide to remove the roof – mallets, hammers, planks as levers – and finally prise off the steadfast nails. We push the roof, unceremoniously, off the shed, over the fence and into scratchy bushes from the wasteland adjacent. How we shall retrieve it once again seems to have been neglected. The shed is still too heavy to shift. Ethan and I can lift it but, because of its size, it tilts. Four people are definitely required. We resign. Not much more we can do about that now.

Lindsey shows me the cannabis plants she is nurturing. We laugh at how, when Holly had her break down, it was the cannabis harvesting season so whenever a doctor or nurse came, the entire house reeked of that distinctive aroma! Honestly, our family. Ethan will end up in the psych unit next and then they really will know us all.

In the evening, I played hockey. I got more and more frustrated. I couldn't do things I had learnt and knew so well. Skills deserted me. My arms were shaking – I hadn't taken diazepam beforehand. I was straining to haul my concentration into what I was doing, make myself move how I know.

Towards the end of the game, someone's stick smacked me in the eye. I kneeled on the floor, head in hands. When I pulled back my fingers, my glove was covered in blood. I could feel it rolling then dripping down my face. They sat me down on the side line. I had a cut just below my eyebrow and another on my cheek bone. I felt like crying. Not from the pain, it didn't hurt bar a pressure sensation as the swelling grew, but from my own pathetic self. I cannot play hockey like this, I am fractionally delayed in my movements and my brain is struggling to absorb and analyse the ever changing, racing game. Maybe I am mentally too slow.

Everyone tells me it is good to be doing things but, as soon as I try, things go wrong. How is hockey helpful when the entire time is a physical and extreme mental struggle? It makes me feel crap and proves that I can no longer do things I once enjoyed. That was another life. That was another me. I am now a creature seeking solitude.

19th June

2007

Mum just sleeps. She has noisy nasal breathing which I find a comfort: it tells me she's still alive. She dribbles and every so often I wipe the spittle that has collected on the side of her cheek where she leans against the pillow. Her mouth must be so dry. Her lips and teeth are covered in a film of whitish, opaque mucus that accumulates into sticky blobs.

Mum can't lift her head. She is too weak. I get the pink sponge on a stick and soak it in cool water. I dab it over Mum's lips, twirling it within my fingers so the strings of mucus attach. I then do the same over her teeth, as best I can because it's like white sticky glue and if I pull it off, the string thins until it snaps and leaps back into Mum's mouth, recoiling from the sponge. Mum, aware of what I am doing, tries to mould her mouth into the most helpful shape. She protrudes her tongue. It looks like cracked clay. White plaques hide the usual plump pink. My trusty sponge has an attempt at removal but also provides the moisture that is longed for. The sponge is sapped dry.

Mum needs extra drugs but, being no longer able to take them orally, the diclofenac comes in a suppository. I insert it. This is incredibly hard. It highlights how frail Ma is, how vulnerable, how weak, how incapacitated. My darling poorly Maisie, a curled body of protruding bones, all angular. When I lift your arms or legs, the skin hangs off, limp, flaccid. You are jelly, no form.

I wet a flannel and drape it across your forehead, feeling the heat. You are so hot Mummy. Little beads of sweat sit dotted above your top lip. The windows are open and there is a breeze. I stroke the back of your hand with my middle finger only, like you did to me. It is ever so gentle. Can you feel me Mummy? I am here with you. You look so peaceful, the calmest I have seen you. You are tired and you need your rest but I will watch. I won't disturb, just look and love.

2008

I awoke half an hour before I got up but I still felt asleep, my body and mind ached with such lethargy. For the past three nights, I have been unable to get to sleep, even my meds don't knock me out. I lie there and hopping through my head are images of Mum, when she was well, when she was ill, when she was dead, no order, but interspersed with snapshots of how I am going to die, overdose, slashed artery, drowning, hypothermia. My head is calculating.

If I can't sleep, I have been getting up and going for a walk in the deserted streets then making myself a cup of tea once home, activity to escape from the trap of insomnia. Last night, I finally fell to sleep in front of the television, not watching but listening. This intruded upon the thoughts.

Seeing Rachel (clinical psych) was a effort. I felt so tired as if I could have laid back my head and slipped into sleep immediately. Talking to her became an almost physical strain with such a muggy, heavy head. Lots of stares from strangers on my way home: the girl with two black eyes.

Dad being nice to me. He was talking about finding me a second hand car as Mum's is a nippy run-around but too impractical for me. Dad was asking what I wanted to drive and said we could go to the auction house together. This is very generous of him and, with a task in hand, it will be good. I will need Dad's advice too! I am being spoilt. Dad is going to buy me a car. Thank you, Dad. I know this is your way of showing you care.

20th June

2007

Ethan has stopped going to work. He stays and spends time with me in Mum's room. He is ever so sweet. He finds it really hard with Mum this ill. He is lovely. I do get on with Ethan extremely well. We talk quietly or sit in silence. It matters not. His presence in the house is so welcoming. I thank him. My isolation is suddenly apparent. Up until today, I didn't realise how lonely I was.

Ethan calls Mum "my baby". He says for me, Mum has become my child. She is so vulnerable, so helpless. He knows I get up throughout the night. He sees the maternal instinct within me. Where has it come from? I don't have my own children. But then I realise, Mum has taught me everything. Mum has already shown me how to look after her in the best possible way. Knowing her so well has installed that within.

2008

Appointment with Dr. Floyd. Whilst waiting, Joanne, from ISS, sees me and gives me a hug. It is so lovely to see her. She sits down and speaks to me for almost half an hour, the dear thing. I find it easy to talk to her and she is so generous to spend the time with me, especially as I no longer see the ISS. She is great; she knows I am struggling. They read me like an open book, I can no longer conceal. Joanne urges me to be honest with Dr. Floyd although I am terribly anxious I'll be back in hospital, a place I do not wish to return. They all know Mum's anniversary is approaching; they know this will be a hard time. I feel encouraged talking to Joanne, she puts me at ease. I find words that I say become more comprehensible.

Dr. Floyd calls me in, black and scarred eyes in tow. She doesn't like the sound of my suicidal thoughts; she isn't happy that, increasingly, I don't want to leave the house, activities are an effort. I am given temazepam to help me get to sleep. Dr. Floyd is concerned over the seeming lack of improvement. It could be circumstantial for, the next few weeks, in remembrance of Mum, will be tough but, conversely, I may be getting worse.

Dr. Floyd wants me to come into hospital. She says it is too dangerous to change my medications if I'm not closely monitored. I refuse. Dr. Floyd needs assurances that I will be safe. I have to see Francis and clinical psychologist next week, appointment with Dr. Floyd in a couple of weeks time. Everyone is becoming anxious over me. I just want to be able to go to the crematorium on Mum's anniversary, see her name in the remembrance book, and then do something with Ethan. We need to be together. This is all I want.

All week I have been phoning patients for some follow up work I am doing for Lily. This has been cathartic. I feel safer, that distance a phone call creates. I have enjoyed chatting to this select cross section of society and the data was interesting because I could talk at length. Patients are ever so compliant. I do like medicine. I do like people. Diseases and treatment are fascinating, so why can't I cope with a whole day in the surgery? Why am I flagging after only a few hours? Why does my mind slowly skate away so I am no longer listening or processing what is being said, what I am being told? I don't understand and the questions are mounting and forming steps in my mind, a never ending, ever growing staircase. What is the matter with me? I can't go on at this unrelenting, spinning pace.

21ˢᵗ June

2007

You are weary my Mummy but you are my superstar. You wake in the morning and say, in that whispery voice of yours, that you need the toilet. I cannot imagine the courage needed for this great feat. You can no longer even prop yourself onto one elbow. I wiggle my arms beneath your armpits and, ever so slowly, we rise together: you, edging your sore, stiff legs to the side of the bed; me, desperately trying not to cause you any additional pain. Once sitting, you cannot hold your body upright. I sit next to you, hips pressed together and wrap my arm across your back. You lean against me and I feel so strong, so protective. You are anxious. You know you can't prevent yourself from slipping. You feel rather helpless but do not worry; do not be afraid, I am not going to let you fall.

Our next step in this clumsy dance is the swivel. I give you a great bear hug, my arms beneath yours, and I spin you on your feet, the ninety degrees to the commode, wedged beside the bed. The commode is uncomfortable - you barely have the energy to stop yourself leaning forward - but I am in front of you Mummy. You can see me. I am here. I am not going to let you slip.

Getting back into the bed is always more ambitious. The bed, now with your pressure mattress, is much higher than the commode chair. Embraced in our bear hug, I scoop you up and we stand as one. I hold you tight. I straighten your pants and nightie. You tilt your head against mine. We are ear to ear. You nuzzle and give me such a delicate kiss on my neck that it is barely perceptible but I do feel it, that tender offering. You whisper that you love me. I love you too Mummy. You are the most precious person to me. I feel so protective over you. I can guard you from all the bad. In my arms Ma, you are safe and sound.

I gently lower you to the bed then, with my arms still wrapped around you tight, I lie down and you follow, strapped to me like a splint. We sink into your special soft pillow and are still. You are exhausted by such an expedition that you cannot lift your legs. I slide them beneath the bed sheets but I don't know if you realise. Mum, you are already asleep. Well done Mummy, my superstar. How you amaze me with everything you manage to do, even now. I see the strain on your face, the sheer exhaustion in your limbs and yet you still do these things. Do you realise what an astounding achievement that is?

Nevertheless, I can understand what you say Ma, even if I may ask you to repeat things occasionally, but sometimes, your mouth so dry it is hard for you to speak. You will always be an actress though Ma, because your hand gestures are so lovely: they are so gentle. You spell "A" and "W" and "M" with your index finger, curly in the air for "apple juice", "water" and "Movecol" respectively. You point to where people have been standing earlier in the day if you want me to say their name because you have a question about them. You draw a little box with buttons for "radio" and, using your right hand, scribble on your left, demonstrating your notebook. You point a finger to your lips to indicate a "straw".

I don't want to forget our little forms of communication because I find them endearing, that is why I must write them down.

Will incidents like this go away? Will time and pain scratch away at my memories, chipping off the edges until whole days are erased? I don't want to forget a single moment I've had with you.

You are hot, Mum. The roots of your hair are damp so, when I stroke your head, I inadvertently style a swooped back quiff. I like it. It keeps the hair off your face. Stray locks do not escape and tickle at your forehead or irritate your eyes.

Ethan and I sit on the bed with you. We talk and you open your eyes. Your mouth is dry. I offer you orange juice through a straw. Looking at me, you defiantly announce that you are hungry. Ethan and I exchange glances before Ethan replies that he'd be starving if he hadn't eaten for a day, let alone a week. We want to giggle but are not sure whether it's laughter or anguish. Mum, I'm not going to give you any food. You can no longer keep solids down. It makes you terribly uncomfortable and you are almost immediately sick. You told me food was to be no more. I don't think you can remember properly.

On consideration and in response to your repeated peckish comments, I suggest the perfect solution: ice lolly! I made them for you a few days ago, a small luxury I can offer. I take your hand and curl it around the plastic stick. You bring it towards your mouth but miss, and the cold sensation on your top lip gently startles you. Your lips root around and your parched mouth sucks the ice, a welcome relief. You look like an eager, contented child, guzzling at your treat.

I didn't pause to contemplate the logistics of eating an ice lolly, supine in bed and the inevitable mess evolves. I have towels as a bib and squeeze a wad of tissues between your hand so the melted juice doesn't run down your arm. I wipe your face with baby wipes as, every time you put the ice lolly to your mouth, it touches your cheek first. Your proprioception has been lost slightly but you manage, all in good spirits. You result in a great blackcurrant clown mouth, as if painted on. We laugh and joke and, typically, my cleaning efforts are not terribly good and there are a few purple stains on the clean nightie I put you in this morning. Not to matter. It was fun. You fall asleep before you finish the lolly and I grab the stick, slipping from your now limp hand.

You wake at 2.30am and need the toilet. We engage in the dance of the commode. For you, it is painful to move and, for me, agonizingly slow as I see your discomfort. Once back in bed, you fancy a hot chocolate. I put the milk in the cup you gave me as a child, rabbits skip around the handle. I heat the milk and test it with my little finger, how you said you did when we were babies. I kneel beside you and guide the straw to your lips. You take tentative, tired sips and have to hold the drink in your mouth before thinking about the coordination in order to swallow.

I sit and whisper to you as Dad is asleep. I stroke your forehead with my middle finger, that comfort you taught me. I tell you that you are a star. You reply in a croaky whisper that you are my starfish and explain: strewn across the bed, unable to move yourself, relying on me to lift you. I smile and a wave of warmth envelops me. Maisie, my darling Mummy, you can be my starfish always.

I stay with you until you fall asleep, then quietly pad out of your room, leaving the door ajar.

23rd June

2007

You wake at 4am and I sit you on the commode. You need the toilet but can't go. You find it too exhausting to sit for long and end up in pain, your bony bottom lacking sufficient padding to keep you supported.

At 7am you say you need the toilet again and we try the slipper pan. Lying down to go to the toilet must feel so unnatural. We are trained from so young not to. You can't relieve yourself and the pan boars into your coccyx and you begin flinching in pain. Going to the toilet, the one thing I can't do for you. I can wash you, clean you, change your nightie, lift you, turn you, inject your drugs but I can't go to the toilet for you. Oh, but how I wish I could and take away the extreme effort that it takes you.

Within your indistinguishable days and nights full of sleep, you still do utter a few words. You are now more confused and when I gave you pen and paper on your request, you slowly scrawled a stream of illegible words. Your writing was small and sloped down before tapering off at the end of a sentence I could not read.

But, Maisie, you are such a delight. In response to one of my many monologues (I talk to you to offer comfort so you know you are not alone, mostly I am unsure as to whether you hear or not), you made me so happy. I say that I love you and you reply that you love me too. And then, with wobbly arm, you outstretch your index finger and bring it towards my face. You try to stroke me on the forehead, how you've done so many times, but, uncoordinated, you miss and brush the side of my face. You emit a little laugh and tenderly roll your eyes at your own blameless mistake. Having found your bearings of the contours of my face, you place your finger centrally, at the right spot - a final movement, because your arm succumbs to weakness and folds back onto your chest. Mum, this gesture fills me with such warmth. I will never know of the strength required to generate that symbol of love. Thank you. I will cherish these moments for ever.

24th June

2007

In the afternoon you are restless. You lie on your side and stretch your arms out, reaching for something: I know not what. Your hands make fists as if to grab hold of an object only you can see. Your legs move, sliding off the pillow I have put there to stop you getting pressure sores. I talk to you. I ask you what's wrong but you cannot answer. You make grimaces with your face, screwing your eyes up tight. I go through my list of questions, willing you to nod or say yes or give me any indication of what I can do. I am so desperate to help you Mummy. Seeing you in distress is absolute agony.

I stroke your hair and whisper to you. You mumble incoherently and then move your mouth silently. You rub your tummy. I wish I could sit you on the commode but is this what you want? I tell you that I have put a pad on you so it doesn't matter if you wet the bed. Do you hear this though? I don't know. My complete helplessness is consuming and I am filled with such frustration, self-hatred and uselessness. I can't bear myself for not being able to help you.

Dad and Ethan come in your room, they don't know what you want either, and they feel that I probably know best - I've cared for you for so long - but I don't. The tears, that had threatened all day, come tumbling down my face and I hold your fist in my hands and kneel over you, my body shaking with sobs. I say, and then keep repeating, "I don't know what to do, I just don't know" and rock back and forth on my knees, probably unconsciously attempting to rid my body of all this pent up anxious energy. And then Dad grabs my shoulder to stop me moving and says that it's OK, I don't have to always know what to do, it is not my fault. I feel myself melt into his firm hand. It feels strong and safe.

At that moment, Dad seems to realise the load I am carrying. The weighty burden of responsibility is getting heavier and I am getting tired. I want to thank Dad so much for that simple gesture. I want to tell him how much it means. Will he appreciate the enormity of that one sentence? It is so rare of him to say such things, that I think he does, to an extent. Thank you Dad, those words shall keep me going, keep me strong for a little longer. Thank you.

2008

Sarah was down visiting her sister (who lives a few miles away from here) so she picked me up and took me to lunch. We went to a nice little restaurant in town, and sat outside, the weather pleasantly warm. As ever, lovely to see Sarah and listen and talk to her.

We came back home and sat on the sofa, Sarah cradling my little body which is losing weight outside of hospital. I lay in her arms and was enveloped in that motherly protection. I wanted to see Sarah for lots of different reasons but the bad in my head alters my perception so I no longer know what is right. The conclusion I am given: gradually I am crossing off the list of people I must see before I die. Family are too hard, I could not go and see Aunty Beth for that reason, but I have seen Mog, had lunch with Sarah, spent an hour with Lily yesterday, who returned at the weekend. Lily gave me lots of hugs too and took me for a walk once it got dark so I wasn't on my own. It was such a warmth to have Lily back.

I have constant input from these amazing people and yet the gaping hole of death is still dragging me in. How do I escape from the suffocating chains? And do I, honestly, want to? I don't know. Sometimes thoughts are not my own. I need to decipher then comprehend which are mine and which are the impostors, hammering their way in.

Dad is spoiling me. When he got home from work tonight, he took me to the garage and showed the car he wants to buy me: twelve years old, Ford Fiesta, CD player, sunroof, high spec, low mileage, five door, exactly, in fact, what I need but all these motoring words spun by me and my fixed smile made me dizzy. I thanked Dad; I said it was perfect, which was true.

Dad likes pleasing me with physical things, a car, a hockey stick, a bike. If only this was what I needed to make me want life. I should be excited but this I have to feign. But, thank you Dad, I know you are trying. As Mum said, you like to be able to fix things and perhaps my problem just doesn't have that quick answer you strive for.

25th June

2007

I lift you onto the commode. You try to help but your weak little legs betray you and start to buckle. You slump there, body almost defeated, and can't even hold yourself up. I'm up on my knees in front of you, my arms wrapped round, supporting your back. Your arms limply grip me and, ear to ear, you rest your chin on my shoulder: a jigsaw, a perfect fit. Your breathing is laboured, no energy to open your eyes. I tell you that I'm strong, that I've got you, that you are safe with me because, Mum, I'm never going to let you go.

We remain there, in that embrace, and neither of us want to move. But, you cannot sustain this for long. You slightly relax, regain a morsel of that deepest effort you are reaching for, and I lift you back to bed. You cry out in pain then lie there unmoving, my starfish once again.

2008

Dreadful night, awoke twice and was sick. Got up at 8am but could barely make it down the stairs so I returned back to bed until 10.30am. I felt a tremendous lethargy all day, even sitting I could feel my bones aching. Coffee didn't inject a short lived burst of energy. I felt withered, a shrivelled mess.

In the evening, I was supposed to be playing hockey. I debated all afternoon to send that guilty text and say I wasn't going to come. But no, my resolve to leave the house for at least one thing every day won. I got ready, I went, I played, we won the match. I ran around and was animated afterwards. My friends called me "hyper". Where this zest came from, I have no idea. In itself, it is confusing and troublesome to cope with. I feel I am on a pendulum, swinging from inertia to euphoria with no warning and no discernable pattern. I am in a mixed state: manic and depressed. A decidedly odd combination.

Arriving home, I laughed with Ethan, drank tea with Ethan, talked with Ethan and then had a bath. I needed some "essence of tranquillity" (written on the bubble bath bottle) to calm me down before sleep could even be attempted.

26th June

2007

You are agitated Mum. Your breathing is irregular and has a sighing quality. Your arm wanders, groping for something. I ask you all the usual questions: drink? toilet? cold flannel? pain? drugs? You slowly answer, "hug". I put my arms around you and your weak hand cradles my neck. As you get sicker, your need for physical contact increases. I relish the closeness and don't want to part from that exquisite embrace. My body melts into your touch.

I sit you on the commode and we remain bear hugged. All your weight leans forward onto my shoulders; your arms hang limp around my neck. You cannot support this disintegrating body of yours.

Exhausted, and back into bed, I clean you, legs so small I easily manoeuvre them with one arm. You seem fretful Mummy. You open your eyes with sudden alarm and grip my hand, "Don't leave me", you say, "I don't want you to go". I hold your hand in both of mine and curl down beside you on the bed. I'm always here, Mum. You have my unwavering attention. I stroke you, that rhythmical movement hoping to induce calm, but you do not rest. Although you are quiet, your body occasionally writhes an arm or leg and your breathing is all wrong. Breathing is a secret device. I know when you are sleeping just by listening but this time, you do not slip into that post-exertion unconsciousness. I lie there for hours.

I get you a sponge to moisten your mouth as you cannot seem to negotiate the straw to drink. I Vaseline your lips. I'm there beside you. Please draw comfort from my presence. I'm always here Mum. I won't leave you alone. Slowly, your anxiety dissipates and sleep creeps upon you, wrapping you up in a blanket of calm.

2008

It took a while but eventually I succeeded in getting to sleep last night. Once engaged in my unconsciousness, I had the most exquisite dream. I was driving home from Newcastle. I reached the house, opened the door and many of Mum's friends were there, chatting. I had to weave my way through, all of them smiling, eyes on me, as if they knew this would be a poignant moment. And there she was, Mum walking down the stairs, everything in slow motion, and then her and I had arms entwined, a full bear hug, contours mirroring, fitting together like a genetic jigsaw puzzle. I tucked my chin into Mum's shoulder and squeezed tight. My darling Mummy.

I didn't know Mum was dead in the dream, every day seeing her was special because of how dear she was to me. When I woke, I tried to force myself back to sleep, back into that dream where Mum was alive, where I could see her, touch her, hug her. My attempts were in vain. That dream was not to be revisited.

27th June

2008

The pull of specific dates thwarting my every waking moment and disturbing my sleep with alarming clarity. I have seen my death and the timing is heaving at my mind, tugging me behind, following is no longer a choice, it is the only option. The hideous, mounting pressure, a furnace ready to blow. Have these things been decided or can I resist? Strength, an attribute I need now. For no one, but myself, can stand up to this frightening onslaught. The bad within may overtake. Do I have any substance in this shell?

28th June

2007

I write the date but it is now meaningless. Days are no longer distinguishable. Mum, you have not slept for ages. You occasionally slip into a few minutes of rest but then you are awake once more. The drugs do not sedate you for any length. You slept two hours last night. You must be too tired to even sleep. One night, I had Lily round at 2am. You were in such pain and distress, Mum, I didn't know what to do. I wanted to be able to knock you out but none of the drugs I have seem to produce this effect on you any more. I phoned Lily. Dad slept throughout; he didn't even know Lily was here.

Now, you are in continual discomfort - a word that the medical profession appear to favour - but it is a spectacular understatement. Discomfort: what does that mean to you, Mum? Not agony but pain. You have a continuous, unrelenting nausea. You are thirsty and want a drink but a tiny sip from the straw causes you to retch and burp and hiccup. You are agitated. Calmness only seems apparent in your brief episodes of sleep. You tell me that you just feel poorly, descriptions now escape you. You say you are scared. You want me to hold your hand always, just so you know I am near. I stroke your hair; I rub your back. Hours of night and day pass. You want hugs. I cuddle you tight. When you need the commode, I lift you. You are too weak to sit so your body slumps against mine. I can scoop you up, one arm across your back, the other beneath your knees. You are dreadfully thin. Your skin hangs unceremoniously off your all too visible skeleton.

This is not you winding down, calmly slipping away. This is you getting more and more ill and increasingly awake and feeling the dreadful symptoms of this cruel cancer. It gets you, then kills you slowly, destroying everything except life. This is torture and the end can't be seen. How long can this be sustained? No more suffering for my darling Maisie, no more. Please God, no more pain.

Severed string puppet
Stranded sea-less starfish
Amalgamation of metaphors
Because nothing can describe
This hideous disintegration of the human body

I look into your eyes, desperately seeking a way through, but that window has closed. There is no door; I cannot break in. Mummy, where have you gone?

30th June

2007

Saturday: the worst week of my life (and I should imagine yours as well, Mum) has almost come to an end. I watch you breathing: deep breaths that get slower, shallower, then stop. Those seconds without breath seem to lengthen each time. Your breathing then resumes: a sharp gasp of longed for air and the cycle repeats once again. Interminable suffering that seems never ending for, when will it end? When will that day come? The date that will be indelibly etched in my mind forever? Is it close? Is it now?

I'm nearing the end of this notebook – daft coincidences that can manifest great meaning if too carefully considered. But this book is no longer an innocent object. I have tainted its pages with my evil scrawl. Perhaps I'll have to destroy it. But physical destruction is only temporary, a short-lived cover for what will eventually surface, weaving its way up like a worm wiggling from the soil, bringing the darkness into the light. For, in this world, there is no escape from the haunting badness. I can hide; I can run. But they are always in pursuit. You cannot outwit the devil within. It knows you better than you know yourself: it can see inside.

1st July

2007

You haven't moved all night. You still lie, curled on your side. Sticky mucus has stained the pillow, threads hanging from your half open mouth.

The nurse comes in the morning to help me wash you. You have wet yourself. Brown urine has stained your pants, the pad, the sheets. We manoeuvre you to slide a clean sheet beneath and I see your pained face as we try, ever so gently, to roll you. I daren't move you again to remove your nightie – there has been too much tugging and pulling already. The scissors are out and I cut the soiled clothing off. I wash you and the clean pads and waterproof sheets are carefully placed.

We lie you on your back, plump the pillows to support your lolling head. Your eyes aren't properly closed, your cheek bones stand prominently, as if raised. I see your emaciated naked body and softly drape the duvet over you. My poorly, tiny Mummy. I feel I am laying you out to die.

I lie beside you in bed. I stroke your forehead. I stroke your cheek. I stroke your shoulders. I use only two fingers – you are too delicate for my whole hand. I pray over you Maisie. I pray and pray.

7.15pm You are dead. No more breath. Goodbye my darling Mother. The end is now. Does the time matter? For time is quick, time is slow or time stops altogether. All there is to know, is that you are gone.

2008

One year, an anniversary in time. How to surmise? I know I was living in an exchanged life, somehow there was a swap. My nightmares became my real world, my reality was a hoax. Being well and without fear, was a concept I could not obtain. But then the coin flipped and thrust me back into a world I once inhabited.

I was released into real life, free from all the hospital restraints that were imposed. I was able to wear articles with any similarity to rope: shoes with laces; dressing gown cords, no more will they flap open resembling cloaks; hoodies, with ties actually in the hood.

I was able to linger in the shower without having to ask staff to open the bathroom door with a key, and use a razor on my hairy legs. I was able to dry my hair without needing to ask for a hairdryer, of which use was monitored. My coffee was boiling hot, steam curling from the cup, instead of spooning a heap of decaf into a half sized mug and filling it with barely hot water from the machine with a limited temperature gauge.

I was able to eat what I wanted, when I wanted. No more hospital grub at 8am, 12.15pm and 5.30pm only. I was able to sleep in the dark with no window in the door, allowing light to stream in. I didn't have a torch beam aimed at my face throughout the night, as staff carried out their checks.

Despite those small luxuries that were missed, I don't regret my time in the psychiatric unit. Those twelve and a half weeks have taught me an awful lot. I was dubious about my diagnosis and perhaps there are two outcomes: I am either in denial about everything, Mum dying, self-harm, depression, episodes of psychosis; or, I am right and this was just a natural reaction to my life circumstances. Either way, it seems to no longer matter.

Maybe I'll look back on the stint in hospital as a beneficial blip in my life and, now I'm home, hopefully it will curb this incessant writing.

Reading this, I don't want you to think I have a cavalier attitude towards abuse, violence, self-harm, suicide, only, in order to cope, you have to make light of dire situations, it has to be amusing some of the time, otherwise the depression and darkness will consume you.

I have no idea how you, or anyone else, would cope under similar circumstances. Each to their own it very much is. Madness is a private affair. Other people's advice may appear demoralising, patronising, inappropriate or just down right outrageous and would probably send you further into the bleak underworld of mental anguish. So, go it alone, with help, but decide for yourself.

Not to leave you completely without aid, here are some parting words of wisdom: don't smoke; don't drink to excess to disguise feelings or numb the pain, however briefly; tell psychiatrists your exact symptoms and emotions, how can the help otherwise?; don't pretend...and always, always take your medication. This is Dr. Alice speaking. Do as I say, not as I do. Don't become the doctor's menace – an uncompliant patient – which is the norm in psychiatry.

But what of me? The glass half full, half empty conundrum. Each has their own half measure, only God possesses the full glass. I focused on the emptiness of my cup, I thought I'd given all to Mum, but that was a desire that is unachievable. Our glass remains half whatever we do, spill it or fill it. Life's lesson is to learn when the glass needs turning over and being able to see just how full half means. But now I'm looking at my cup and I don't know which way the water falls. Has my naïve optimism been replaced by a life-experiencing cynicism?

The choice is there: medical school or suicide. Either or. I have to decide. For, my mother was the essence of my life. Now that is lost, can I scramble together the pieces that Mum was the epicentre of? Can I grasp my players and induce an order which vaguely resembles life? That is the question.

9th July

2007 - Mum's Funeral

If I speak in the tongues of men
And of angels, but have not love,
I am only a resounding gong or clanging cymbal.
If I have the gift of prophecy
And can fathom all mysteries and all knowledge,
And if I have a faith that can move mountains,
But have not love, I am nothing.
If I give all I possess to the poor
And surrender my body to the flames,
But have not love, I gain nothing.
Love is patient, love is kind.
It does not envy, it does not boast,
It is not proud. It is not rude,
It is not self-seeking, it is not easily angered,
It keeps no record of wrongs.
Love does not delight in evil
But rejoices with the truth.
It always protects, always trusts,
Always hopes, always perseveres.
Love never fails.

1 Corinthians 13v1-8

Mum was the epitome of love. She had such unrelenting, overwhelming fondness for all her family and friends. She always sacrificed herself. Her needs, her own preoccupations were neglected as she lavished care on others. Her love, which was so instinctive, was in abundance in everything she did.

I appreciate that everyone here knows what an extraordinary person my Mum was, her dazzling personality always shining through. Some of you have known Mum even longer than me, but I had the ultimate privilege of spending every day by Mum's side since she was diagnosed in February. I realise what a tremendous honour my position was, one which many of you longed to have, but Mum was too poorly too quickly. She did not want to be remembered as ill, she wanted each person to keep their own memories of all the wonderful times you have had with her.

Mum disliked the term "fighting" with her cancer. For her, this was not a battle. She was not at war. She knew the inevitability of death. This was an endurance. Mum suffered greatly but, confronted with horrific adversity, her perseverance was carried out with exemplary politeness, kindness and tenderness, just as she had lived. Mum has taught me that you do not have to be fighting to be strong. The last five months reinforced, all too apparently, that my mother *is* the strongest person I know.

My fantastic Mum, to whom I owe everything. I depend on her in so many ways. She was and always will be my best friend. A daughter's partiality aside, she truly was the greatest.

My darling, darling Mother, thank you.

2008

In the end
I had to choose life.
I had to struggle to cross
The bridge between
The dead and the living.
I had to rebuild
What had been destroyed.
I had to deny death.

Malka B

If only choosing life was a simple, immoveable stance. The ongoing lesson, a battle within, the taming of the deathly longing. It comes in waves, the pulling of my blackened mind, how to learn to tame the monster, keep it locked away. I am fighting for my life.

"Hello, my name is Alice; I am a student doctor. I have been raped, beaten up, verbally abused and recently bereaved. I was committed to a psychiatric unit for over three months. I have been diagnosed with depression, anxiety, dissociative identity disorder, psychosis. I was suicidal yesterday. Now, would you mind if I examined you?"

Training resumed. My life as a medical student: Part Two.

Starfish

Lightning Source UK Ltd.
Milton Keynes UK
UKOW04f1152170615

253660UK00001B/1/P